Illustrated Record of German Army Equipment 1939–1945

ARTILLERY
PART ONE

Published by
The Naval & Military Press Ltd
Unit 10, Ridgewood Industrial Park,
Uckfield, East Sussex,
TN22 5QE England
Tel: +44 (0) 1825 749494
Fax: +44 (0) 1825 765701

www.naval-military-press.com

© The Naval & Military Press Ltd 2004

Reproduced by kind permission of the Central Library,
Royal Military Academy, Sandhurst

ILLUSTRATED RECORD
OF
GERMAN ARMY EQUIPMENT
1939-1945

FOREWORD

1. The issue of this publication, three years after the end of the war in Europe, is designed to put on record essential information on the armament of the German Land Forces during the war. It includes some of the more interesting equipments which were developed, but which, due to the conclusion of hostilities, or to production difficulties, did not come into general service.

The publication is primarily a photographic record, supported by a brief specification, and in some instances a short description. The material has been drawn from the large collection of matter compiled by the Technical Intelligence Services during and subsequent to the war. Much of it has appeared in the various Technical Intelligence Summaries and Bulletins issued by the War Office, and by G.H.Qs. overseas, supplemented by photographs and details added from German sources after the collapse.

2. Handbooks have already been published on some of the more important equipments. The volume of material and the scope of the present publication, have precluded detailed descriptions. For any recipient officially requiring fuller information on any particular subject, the records available can be consulted through M.I.10, The War Office, up to 30 May 1949. Thereafter they will be disposed of.

3. This publication is laid out in the form of a reference album showing a photograph of each equipment, together with the specification or brief description. It has been divided into five separate volumes under the following subject headings:-

Vol.I	Infantry Weapons		
Vol.II	Artillery	Part I	Anti-Tank, Field, Medium, Heavy and super Heavy Weapons.
		Part II	Anti-Aircraft, Coast Defence and Railway Weapons.
Vol.III	Armoured Fighting Vehicles		
Vol.IV	Vehicles (other than A.F.Vs.)		
Vol.V	Mines, Mine Detectors, and Demolition Equipment		

4. It will be noted that the sections dealing with mines, mine detectors, and demolition Equipment have been written up rather more fully, but in no case do these sections claim to be exhaustive.

5. It should be noted that all figures quoted are taken from German sources. It is appreciated that in many instances these differ from the figures quoted in official British and American reports.

6. In conclusion it is hoped that this publication will serve a purpose as a brief permanent record of the major German Army weapons and equipments developed and used during the 1939-1945 war.

Director of Military Intelligence

The War Office

508/24/3/48.

ILLUSTRATED RECORD OF GERMAN ARMY EQUIPMENT

1939-1945

VOLUME II

ARTILLERY

PART 1

CONTENTS

		Page
	Explanation of terms	(i)
Chap. I.	The Development of German Artillery	1
Chap. II.	Development of German Anti-Tank Artillery	5
	2.8 cm. S. Pz.B. 41	7
	2.8 cm. S. Pz.B. 41 (Airborne)	7
	3.7 cm. Pak 35/36	12
	4.2 cm. le. Pak 41	16
	5 cm. Pak 38	17
	7.5 cm. Pak 40	20
	7.5 cm. Pak 41	25
	Utilisation of captured guns in an Anti-Tank Role	31
	75 mm. Pak 97/38	31
	7.62 cm. Pak 36	32
	7.5 cm. Pak 44	32
	7.5 cm. Pak 50	37
	8 cm. PAW 600 (PWK. 8 H. 63)	40
	8.8 cm. Pak weapons	41
	8.8 cm. Pak 43	46
	8.8 cm. Pak 43/41	47
	Sights for German 8.8 cm. model 43 Anti-Tank guns	48
	Ammunition for 8.8 cm. model 43 Anti-Tank guns	50
	12.8 cm. Pak Artillery Development	50
	12.8 cm. Pak K. 44 - Krupp Model	56
	12.8 cm. Pak K. 44 - Rheinmetall Model	56
Chap. III.	Development of German Infantry Guns	62
	7.5 cm. le I.G. 18	62
	7.5 cm. le Geb. I.G. 18	66
	7.5 cm. I.G. L/13	68
	7.5 cm. I.G. 37	70
	7.5 cm. I.G. 42	72
	7.5 cm. I.G. 42 (Smooth bore)	73
	15 cm. s. I.G. 33	79
Chap. IV.	Development of German Recoilless Guns	81
	7.5 cm. L.G. 40	82
	7.5 cm. Rf. K. 43	87
	8cm. Rf. W. 43	91
	10.5 cm. Recoilless weapons	92
	10.5 cm. L.G. 40	92
	10.5 cm. L.G. 42	100
	10.5 cm. L.G. 43	105
	Comparative data for equipments actually introduced or accepted for service use	109
	Recoilless Gun development by Krupp	110
	Recoilless Gun development by Rheinmetall Borsig	111

		Page
Chap. V.	Development of German Mountain guns	112
	7.5 cm. Geb. G. 36	112
	7.5 cm. Geb. K. 15	115
	7.5 cm. Geb. G. 43	117
	10.5 cm. Geb. H. 40	121
Chap. VI.	Development of German Field Artillery	127
	7.5 cm. F.K. 16. n. A	129
	7.5 cm. le F.K. 18	131
	7.5 cm. F.K. 38	135
	7.5 cm. F.K. 7M 85	138
	10.5 cm. le F.H. 16	138
	10.5 cm. le F.H. 18	140
	10.5 cm. le F.H. 18 (M)	146
	10.5 cm. le F.H. 18/39	148
	10.5 cm. le F.H. 18/40	148
	10.5 cm. le F.H. 18/42	155
	10.5 cm. le F.H. 42	155
	10.5 cm. le F.H. 43	157
	10 cm. K. 17	162
	10 cm. le K. 41	164
Chap. VII.	Development of German Medium Artillery	165
	10.5 cm. s.K. 18	168
	15. cm. s.F.H. 18	168
	10.5 cm. s.K. 18/40	176
	15. cm. s.F.H. 18/40	176
	10.5 cm. s.K. 18/40 (42)	176
	15. cm. s.F.H. 13	182
	15. cm. s.F.H. 36	182
	15. cm s.F.H. 40	185
	15. cm. s.F.H. 43	188
	15. cm. s.F.H. 18/43	188
	12.8 cm. Krupp K. 43	190
	12.8 cm. K. 44	190
	12.8 cm. K. 81)	
	12.8 cm. K. 81/1)	191
	12.8 cm. K. 81/2)	
Chap. VIII.	Development of German Heavy and Super-Heavy Artillery	197
	15. cm. K. 16	199
	15. cm. K. 18	199
	15. cm. K. 39	201
	15. cm. SK. C/28	207
	Development of a mobile heavy coastal gun	212
	15. cm. SK. C/28 in Mrs Laf	214
	17. cm. K. 18 in Mrs Laf	215
	21. cm. Langer Mörser	218
	21. cm. Mrs 18	219
	21. cm. Krupp L/50 Gun	226
	21. cm. K. 38	227
	21. cm. K. 39	232
	24. cm. H. 39	234
	24. cm. K. L/46	235
	24. cm. K. 3.	241
	24. cm. K. 4.	247
	28. cm. H. L/12	247
	28. cm. Kust Haubitze	247
	35.5 cm. H. M.I.	250
	42. cm. "Gamma" Mörser	251

Appendices.

"A"	Anti-Tank Guns.	253
"B"	Infantry Guns.	255
"C"	Recoilless Guns.	257
"D"	Mountain Guns.	258
"E"	Field Guns.	259
"F"	Medium Guns.	260
"G"	Heavy and Super-Heavy Guns.	261

LIST OF PLATES

		Page				Page
1.)		(8	36.)			(63
2.)	2.8cm. S. Pz. B. 41	(9	37.)	7.5cm. le. I.G.18.		(64
3.)		(10	38.)			(65
4.	2.8cm. S. Pz. B. 41 (Airborne)	11	39.	7.5cm. le. Geb.I.G.18		67
5.)	3.7cm. Pak. 35/36	(14	40.	7.5cm. I.G. L/13.		69
6.)		(15	41.	7.5cm. I.G. 37		71
7.)	4.2cm. le. Pak. 41	(18	42.)	7.5cm. I.G. 42.		(74
8.)		(19	43.)			(75
9.)		(21	44.	7.5cm. I.G. 42.a.A.		76
10.)	5.cm. Pak 38	(22	45.)	7.5cm. I.G. 42(Smooth bore)		(77
11.)		(23	46.)			(78
12.)		(24				
13.	7.5cm. Pak. 40	26	47.	15cm. s.I.G. 33		80
14.)		(28	48.)			(84
15.)	7.5cm. Pak. 41	(29	49.)	7.5cm. L.G. 40		(85
16.)		(30	50.)			(86
17.)	75mm. Pak. 97/38.	(33	51.)	7.5cm. Rf. K. 43		(88
18.)		(34	52.)			(89
			53.)			(90
19.)	76.2mm. Pak. 36.	(35	54.)	8cm. Rf. W. 43.		(93
20.)		(36	55.)			(94
21.)	7.5cm. Pak. 50	(38	56.)			(96
22.)		(39	57.)	10.5cm. L.G. 40		(97
			58.)			(98
23.)		(42	59.)			(99
24.)	8cm. PAW. 600	(43	60.)	10.5cm. L.G. 42.		(103
25.)	(PWK. 8H. 63)	(44	61.)			(104
26.)		(45				
27.)		(51	62.)	10.5cm. I.G. 43		(107
28.)	8.8cm. Pak. 43	(52	63.)			(108
29.)		(53				
30.)	8.8cm. Pak. 43/41.	(54	64.	7.5cm. Geb. G. 36.		114
31.)		(55	65.	7.5cm. Geb. K. 15.		116
32.	12.8cm. K. 81/1.	58	66.)	7.5cm. Geb. G. 43.		(119
33.	12.8cm. K. 81/2.	59	67.)			(120
34.	12.8cm. Pak. K.44(Krupp)	60	68.)	10.5cm. Geb. H. 40.		(125
35.	12.8cm. Pak. K. 44. (Rheinmetall)	61	69.)			(126

		Page			Page
70.	7.5cm. F.K.16.n.A.	130	100.) 101.) 102.)	15cm. K. 39	204 205 206
71.	7.5cm. le.F.K. 18.	134	103.) 104.) 105.)	15cm. S.K. C/28	209 210 211
72.) 73.)	7.5cm. F.K.38.	136 137	106.) 107.)	17cm. K. 18 in Mrs Laf	216 217
74.	7.5cm. F.K. 7M. 85	139	108.	21cm. Langer Mörser.	220
75.) 76.)	10.5cm. le F.H. 18	144 145	109.) 110.) 111.)	21cm. Mrs. 18.	223 224 225
77.	10.5cm. le F.H. 18(M)	147	112.) 113.) 114.)	21cm. K. 38.	229 230 231
78.	10.5cm. le F.H. 18/40	154	115.	21cm. K. 39.	233
79.	10.5cm. le F.H. 18/42	156	116.) 117.) 118.) 119.)	24cm. H.39.	236 237 238 239
80.	10.5cm. le F.H. 42	158			
81.) 82.) 83.)	10.5cm. le F.H. 43	159 160 161	120.	24cm. K. 3.	246
84.	10cm. K. 17	163	121.	28cm H.L/12.	248
85.	10cm. le. K. 41.	166	122.	28cm. Kust Haubitze.	249
86.) 87.)	10.5cm. s.K. 18	172 173	123.	42cm. "Gamma" Mörser.	252
88.) 89.)	15cm. s. F.H. 18.	174 175			
90.	15cm. s.F.H. 18/40.(42)	180			
91.	15cm. s.F.H. 13	181			
92.	15cm. s. F.H. 36	184			
93.	15cm. s. F.H. 40.	186			
94.	15cm. s. F.H. 43.	187			
95.	12.8cm. K.43(Krupp)	189			
96.) 97.)	12.8cm. K.44	195 196			
98.	15cm. K. 16.	200			
99.	15cm. K. 18.	202			

Explanation of Terms

A short explanation of terms is given to insure proper interpretation of data in this history.

a. Length of Gun in Calibers

This refers to the length of the gun from the muzzle to the rear face of the breech ring.

b. Maximum Range

Maximum range, where known, is given for each type of ammunition. Maximum effective range will be less than this figure, due to limits of observation, penetration, and accuracy.

c. Penetration of Homogeneous Armour

Information on penetration qualities has been obtained from various sources, and in many cases has not been checked by firing. Figures on penetration should be used as a general guide only.

d. German Artillery Terms

Abbreviation	Signification	British Equivalent
A	Artillerie	Artillery
a/A	alter Artillerie	of old pattern
abg	abgeändert	converted
(b)	belgisch	Belgian
Bett. Gesch.	Bettungs Geschütz	Gun on platform mounting
(E), Eis.	Eisenbahn	Railway mounting
(f)	französisch	French
Fest	Festung	Fortress
F.H.	Feld Haubitze	Field Howitzer
F.K.	Feld Kanone	Field Gun
Flak	Flugzeug Abwehr Kanone	Anti-aircraft Gun
Flzg	Flugzeug	Aircraft
Geb.	Gerbirgs	Mountain (gun)
Gesch.	Geschütz	Gun
gez.	gezogen	rifled
gl.	glatt	smooth bore
Gr.	gross	Large
H.	Haubitze	Howitzer
H.T.	Haubitze Turm	Turret mounted howitzer
i.H.	in Haubitzen Lafette	On howitzer carriage
Inf. Gesch. or I.G.	Infanterie Geschütz	Infantry Gun or Howitzer
i.Kas.L.	in Kasematten Lafette	On casemate mounting
i.Kst.L.	in Küsten Lafette	On coast defence mounting
i.P.L.	in Panzer Lafette	On shielded mounting
i.R.L.	in Rad Lafette	On wheeled carriage
(i)	italianisch	Italian
(j)	jugoslavisch	Jugoslavian
K	Kanone	Gun
K.H.	Kanone Haubitze	Gun-Howitzer
K.K.	Kanone Kasematte	Casemate Gun
kl.	klein	Small
KwK	Kampfwagen Kanone	Tank Gun
k, kz.	kurz	short
Kg.	Kilogramm	kilogram (2.2 lb.)
Kst. H.	Küsten Haubitze	Coast Defence Howitzer
Kst. K.	Küsten Kanone	Coast Defence Gun
Kst. Mrs.	Küsten Mörser	Coast Defence Heavy Howitzer or Mortar.
K.T.	Kanone Turm	Turret-mounted Gun

Abbreviation	Signification	British Equivalent
L/	Lang/	Length of gun in calibers (length follows diagonal line)
L. or Laf.	Lafette	Gun or Howitzer Carriage
l. or le	leicht	light
l.F.H.	leichte Feld Haubitze	Light Field Howitzer
lg.	lang	long
L.G.	Leichtes Geschütz	Light Recoilless Gun
l.I.G.	leichtes Infanterie Geschütz	Light Infantry Howitzer
M	Marine	Naval
m	mit	with
Mrs.	Mörser	Heavy Howitzer or Mortar
n/A., or n.A.	neuer Artillerie	New Model
Nr.	Nummer	Number
(ö)	österreichisch	Austrian
(p)	polnisch	Polish
Pak	Panzer Abwehr Kanone	Antitank Gun
(r)	russisch	Russian
Rf.K.	Rückstossfreie Kanone	Recoilless Gun
R.L.	Rad Lafette	Wheeled Carriage
R.W.	Raketen Werfer	Rocket Projector
s.	schwer	medium, heavy.
Sch.Grab.K.	Schützen Graben Kanone	Trench Gun
St	Schusstafel	Firing Table
Sf. or Sfl.	Selbstfahrlafette	Self-propelled mounting
s.Pz.B.	Schwere Panzerbüchse	Heavy antitank Rifle
Stu.G.	Sturm Geschütz	S.P. Assault equipment
Stu.H.	Sturm Haubitze	Assault Howitzer
Stu.K.	Sturm Kanone	Assault Gun
(t)	tschechisch	Czechoslavakian
u	und	and
umg	umgeändert	modified
Vers	Versuchs	experimental

CHAPTER I

THE DEVELOPMENT OF GERMAN ARTILLERY

A. Introduction

In general, the chief standard equipments of the German Field Army were in service by the beginning of the War or were introduced soon afterwards and with a few exceptions remained in production throughout the war. In most cases, improvement in performance was demanded by the Army and their requirements were invariably met by the German designers and Ordnance engineers, although in most cases the improved models did not, owing to production difficulties, reach service scale production.

Particular attention was paid to the use of guns up to and including Medium equipments in the anti-tank role, though problems of stability at low angles of elevation were not overcome in all cases. To this end hollow charge projectiles were introduced for all low and medium velocity equipments.

Further considerable experimental work was carried out to develop sub-calibre projectiles and a short account outlining the German attitude to this is given later, entitled "Increased Performance of Artillery Pieces".

B. General Trends in Development

1. The general trend was towards larger calibre and longer range guns. The requirements of the German High Command were invariably for all types of artillery, increased ballistic performance, greater mobility and versatility. Further, for field medium artillery all round traverse and ability to fire in the upper register were considered almost essential. In most cases, the ordnance designers and engineers met their demands though usually at the expense of simplicity of design and cheapness of production.

2. Gun and Barrel Design

Muzzle brakes were developed for most equipments, in some cases giving up to 60/70% efficiency. The use of low temperature propellants was found to reduce barrel wear considerably, this meant increasing the size of chamber but this presented no serious obstacle in design. In this connection, the German designers tended to prefer a long narrow chamber since they claimed that cartridge case manufacture was simpler, that less erosion in the forcing cone was experienced with long chambers, and that by using tubular propellant powders they had no trouble with ignition and a high density of loading could be achieved.

Sintered iron and soft iron almost exclusively replaced copper for driving bands and was entirely satisfactory and this it was claimed tended further to simplify the design of bands and grooves in the rifling. Three heavy long range guns, the 21 cm K12 and 28 cm K5 Railway guns, also the 24 cm K3 were designed to give splined or pre-engraved shell which it was considered reduced barrel wear for high muzzle velocities of about 1200 met/secs and over. This practice was discontinued largely owing to difficulties of manufacture of these projectiles. The Germans favoured QF obturation with sliding breech block action, claiming that sealing was satisfactory, that the use of cartridge cases with the igniter in position was safer than loose charges and that manufacturing processes were simpler.

However, in the later stages of the war, serious shortages of metals for cartridge cases led to the adoption of BL (screw breech) obturation for several new designs and "Ring" obturation was introduced as a modification to a number of 15 cm Howitzers (S.F.H.18) in service.

3. Carriage Design

To meet increased demands for mobility, designs tended to become more complicated. For field and medium artillery, the split trail field carriage of welded construction with torsion bar suspension, prefabricated metal wheels with solid rubber tyres, became a standard type of design. The carriage articulation was locked in the firing position.

Recoil systems were of orthodox designs, the Germans tending to favour a hydraulic buffer below and a H.P. recuperator above the piece, this simplified cooling and the even distribution of weight. Rear trunnions with pneumatic equilibrators to balance muzzle **prep**onderance were usually adopted.

Light metal alloys were extensively used in carriage construction to reduce weight though latterly these were in short supply and the Luftwaffe had overriding priorities for such materials. In order to provide 360° traverse & high angle fire for all degrees of traverse, the cruciform platform with folding outriggers and travelling bogies fore and aft seemed to offer the best solution.

For the heavier equipments a firing platform, integral with the lower carriage, and a dual recoil system were favoured.

4. The German High Command expressed itself reasonably satisfied with the ballistic performance of their super-heavy equipments, including railway guns but demanded greater mobility, simplified assembly and fewer travelling loads. This led to the development of the so-called R (Raupen) Gerät, i.e. tracked equipments, of which there were many designs and projects. The 54 cm 60 cm heavy mobile seige howitzers designed by Rheinmetall Borsig were introduced into service and were used with some success on the Russian front.

The basic idea was to use railway transport for long distances coupled with the ability to fire from the track if necessary and to use one or more tracked vehicles, based on the heavier (i.e. Tiger) tank chassis, but unarmoured, for cross country or to approach a selected firing position independent of the railways. Usually designs provided for a heavy howitzer and a long range gun as alternative ordnance on a common carriage.

It may be noted that the German Navy was interested in this development for coast defence and "Colonial warfare". An appreciation by Krupp dated December, 1944, lists however only three major projects, the K4 motorised, K5 motorised and the R2.

C. Increased Performance of Artillery Pieces (based on a German appreciation).

1. With a gun of orthodox design this is almost exclusively a matter of increasing muzzle velocity. This may be achieved by:-

    (a) Increase in barrel length.

    (b) Increase in propellant used.

    (c) Increase in chamber pressure.

    (d) Reduction in projectile weight.

    (e) Rocket assistance.

    In practice, (a) and (b) must go together.

In round figures, given a fixed chamber pressure of 3000 kg. per sqr. cm., to increase MV from 900 to 1500 metres/secs, an increase in barrel length from 60 to 200 calibres would be necessary and four times the weight of propellant charge, or by increasing the chamber pressure to 4500 kg. per sqr. cm., a barrel length 130 cals would be required. Using the same barrel and propellant, a reduction in projectile weight by one half will increase MV from 1000 to 1400 m/sec, but deceleration is relatively rapid. Barrel

/life

life increases rapidly in inverse proportion to MV and, for a normal high velocity gun, 1200 m/sec is technically about the limit.

2. Use of Sub-calibre Projectiles presented an important method of increasing muzzle velocity and, throughout the war, research and development was carried out on the design of sub-calibre projectiles and firing from standard and specially constructed barrels.

Although latterly the development of sub-calibre projectiles was more concerned with the increased performance of Anti-Tank and AA Guns, "Sabot" (Both HE and AP) shell were introduced in limited quantities for service with the 10.5 cm, the FH 18 and 15 cm s.FH.18 series. The advantage of using a standard gun capable of firing normal projectiles and Sabot from the same barrel is obvious, but difficulties arose from the design point of view in connection with suitable rifling to stabilise the projectiles. Also muzzle brakes interfered with the discarding parts. Three main types of sub-calibre projectiles were developed:-

(a) Discarding "Sabot" in which both bourrelet and base elements are discarded after leaving the muzzle.

(b) Flanged or skirted projectiles fired from coned bore barrels or barrels with a muzzle squeeze attachment. Although the only squeeze bore guns to be introduced into service were the A/Tk guns of the 2.8 cm, 4.2 cm and 7.5 cm 41 series, the possibility of using a standard barrel with interchangeable muzzle attachments (cylindrical for use with normal full bore projectiles, and tapered bore for use with skirted projectiles) was explored. In this way a suitable design of rifling for each type of projectile could be provided to ensure correct stabilisation.

(c) Long sub-calibre, fin stabilised projectiles. Shells with a much larger length to calibre ratio than that normally used were developed in a number of calibres. In practice such projectiles must be stabilised by fins. Two important types were developed:-

(i) Roechling Shell. These were super-long shells designed in 3.7 cm, 5 cm, 10 cm, 15 cm, 17 cm, 21 cm and 34 cm calibres. Both full bore and sub-calibre projectiles were designed, mostly experimentally, but in the case of the 21 cm Roechling Anti-Concrete Shell for the 21 cm Mrs 18, extensive production was planned early in 1942 although there is some evidence that it was not used operationally. Here the intention was not to increase the range of the 21 cm Mrs., but to increase the effectiveness of this standard equipment in the specific task of attacking concrete or other permanent fortifications.

The 21 cm RO br was claimed to have a penetration in concrete two and a half times as great as that attained by the standard projectile. Fin stabilisation was achieved by spirally wrapped fins contained in a cylindrical sleeve fitting over the base of the shell and also serving to support a driving band - on firing, the sleeve is discarded after leaving the muzzle and the fins spring out to stabilise the shell in flight.

(ii) PPG (Peenemunder Pfeil Geschoss) - "Dart shell" named after the experimental station at Peenemunde on the Baltic. Tests in the supersonic wind tunnel showed that the fin assembly as designed for the Roechling shell had many disadvantages aerodynamically. The PPG is a long sub-calibre projectile with a fixed fin assembly and is fired from a smooth bore barrel. Extensive research was carried out over a number of years to achieve optimum design for the fin assembly and to reconcile the opposed requirements of design from the aerodynamic and internal ballistic point of view.

In 1941, firing trials at HILLERSLEBEN with 7.5 cm PPG from an FK 16 n.a. gave a good average maximum range of 13120 metres (14,350 yards), an increase of 30% on the performance with

/standard

(ii) Contd.

standard HE shell.

A provisional design for PFG for the 28 cm K5(E) - the 11 inch Railway gun, was made in November 1940, and from the wind tunnel measurements an increase in maximum range of some 65% was anticipated. Further development, however, resulted in even greater ranges obtained with this equipment.

The PFG did not reach operational use, but the official Ordnance list of development projects in hand during 1943 names four separate firms engaged in work on different types of such projectiles.

Manufacture of such specialised projectiles in quantity and the scarcity of raw materials necessary for the high grade steels required, undoubtedly presented problems for large scale use, which were never overcome and latterly development of PFG was almost exclusively confined to AA equipments.

The question of increased performance in this connection can also be approached from the opposite direction; that is to increase the performance of the gun barrel. But it is likely to be more economical to provide it with sub-calibre attachments in order to fire it from a larger calibre barrel of standard proportions, than to provide an equal calibre high performance barrel of great weight and length and the extra heavy mounting and recoil gear necessary.

3. Shell with pre-engraved rifling were used in several high velocity long range guns, notably the 21 cm K 12, the 28 cm K5 Railway Gun and the 24 cm K3. This resulted, it was claimed, in less barrel wear than with normal banded projectile at M/Vs of over 1200 met/secs, but such projectiles were expensive to manufacture and their use was discontinued.

4. Rocket Assisted Shells were used operationally for the 15 cm FH 18 and the 28 cm K5, but dispersions at extreme range were very irregular.

Considering further the manufacture of the various types of projectiles, the normal type of shell is by far the simplest and cheapest to produce. Flanged and sabot projectiles require more workmanship, but are rather similar in the processes involved. The PFG requires 35 to 50% more steel for the same pay load of HE and demands specially high grade material, while the fin assembly needs skilful welding. A rocket assisted shell takes three times the steel used in the normal shell and the manufacture of numerous specialised components.

In terms of high performance, the standard gun firing full bore projectiles will have a relatively short life. Rocket assisted projectiles will not produce undue wear. The smooth bore barrel for PFG will have a longer life than either barrels for Sabot or Flanged projectiles; in the latter case 3 to 4 replacements of the muzzle squeeze must be reckoned for the life of one barrel.

5. To summarise, the conclusion arrived at by the Germans, in 1942, is that where greatly increased performance is necessary:-

(a) the normal type of projectile is out of the question.

(b) rocket assisted shell on grounds of expense can only be used in special cases where the rifling of an existing gun allows no other solution.

(c) for anti-tank work Sabot or Flanged projectiles give the best performance.

(d) the PFG is the most satisfactory solution for long ranges, if the cost of the projectiles is acceptable in terms of the advantage gained.

CHAPTER II

THE DEVELOPMENT OF GERMAN ANTI-TANK ARTILLERY

A. General

1. Introduction

At the close of the 1914-18 war no purely anti-tank weapon had been produced by either Germany or the Western Allies. It was fully appreciated, however, that the tank had come to stay as a major weapon of war and that appropriate counter-measures would need to be taken, in order to neutralise the initial success which it had enjoyed. It was also evident that the further development of the tank in regard to its mobility, armour and armament would be given high priority by foreign armies when making specifications for further armament requirements.

The fundamental requirement for an anti-tank gun was that it should fire a projectile capable of penetrating the protective armour of the tank before exploding. This demanded the construction of a gun with a high muzzle velocity to give a high striking velocity, and of a projectile sufficiently robust to penetrate the armour without breaking up. As a result of the essentially high velocity, the time of flight of the projectile was reduced and its trajectory became almost flat. Both of these features were an advantage for an anti-tank gun, since it was to be employed against a moving target and also because, in its early conception, the anti-tank gun was essentially a light and comparatively close quarter weapon.

German anti-tank gun development was governed from the outset, very naturally, by the assumed strength of armour to be penetrated. As this was always increasing the performance of each new gun developed was correspondingly higher than its predecessor. To achieve this progressive increase in armour penetrating performance, development fell roughly in the following categories:-

    (a) Increase in gun calibre.

    (b) Internal barrel construction.

    (c) Ammunition design.

Generally speaking, the development and design of anti-tank guns ran concurrently with that of tank guns and self propelled anti-tank guns. That is to say, a 7.5 cm anti-tank gun on a field carriage would have its counterpart as an SP anti-tank gun and/or tank gun. Apart from the calibre, the ordnance may differ either in length, type of breech mechanism or chamber capacity and often in all three.

Common to all, however, were the projectiles used, although the design of cartridge case would vary according to the dimensions of the chamber of the particular piece.

2. Increase of Gun Calibre

The German first line anti-tank gun at the outbreak of war in 1939 was the 3.7 cm weapon. Increase of calibre was progressive throughout the war, except in one or two special projects, the 5 cm appeared during the closing months of 1940, the French 75 mm on a 5 cm carriage during the summer of 1941. Towards the end of 1941 the Germans brought their 7.5 cm Models 40 and 41 into operational use. The model 41 was of a new type having a muzzle squeeze bore or cone bore attachment in an effort to increase the muzzle velocity with a new type of projectile. This led to the introduction about this time of two equipments with cone bore barrel construction, which were retrograde

/equipments

equipments as regards size or calibre. These were the 2.8/2.0 cm (i.e. 2.8 cm at the commencement of rifling and 2 cm at the muzzle) and the 4.2 cm anti-tank weapon. (The latter being 4.0 cm at the commencement of the rifling and 3.0 cm at the muzzle.)

The 7.5 cm Model 40, like its predecessor the 5 cm Model 38, proved to be a good weapon and capable of defeating the armour then in use; but thickness of armour increased, therefore the size and performance of the anti-tank gun had to increase. The year 1943 saw the appearance of the celebrated 8.8 cm anti-tank and tank guns. These were a development from the much talked of 8.8 cm Flak (A.A.) guns. There was no finality in size and the latter stages of the war saw the introduction of the 12.8 cm tank and assault guns and with them the 12.8 cm anti-tank gun Model 44.

December 1944 saw the introduction into the service of the 8 cm P.W.K 8.H.63, a smooth bore infantry gun firing a fin stabilized projectile of 9.59 lbs and having a very satisfactory anti-tank performance when using the hollow charge projectile.

3. Internal Barrel Construction

The ceaseless endeavour to improve velocity and thus penetration, led to the development of the cone bore weapons, referred to in the previous paragraphs. It was found that a higher velocity could be obtained by using a special type of skirted projectile in conjunction with a cone bore barrel, i.e. a larger diameter at the commencement of rifling that at the muzzle. In some cases an ordinary parallel barrel was used in conjunction with a cone bore length, which screwed on to the muzzle.

Smooth bore barrels were also developed for use with special fin stabilized hollow charge projectiles. This type of weapon did not require a high velocity, indeed a higher velocity decreased the efficiency of the weapon when firing hollow charge projectiles.

4. Ammunition Design

In addition to the ordinary armour piercing projectiles three new types of projectiles were developed for anti-tank work in an additional effort to increase velocity and thereby penetration. The fourth gave increased lethality without increased velocity. This type burned through the armour.

(a) Skirted projectile for use with cone bore barrels.

(b) Discarding Sabot projectiles.

(c) Composite Rigid and

(d) Hollow charge projectile.

The projectiles (a), (b) and (c) worked to the principle that for a given weight the greater the area within reason, at the base of the projectile, for the chamber gases to exert their pressure on, the greater would be the resultant muzzle velocities. The hollow charge projectile which burns through the armour has a more efficient lethality at lower velocity. This gives time for the fuze to initiate the explosive and so produce the burning jet to impinge on the armour before the rear end of the projectile reaches the armour.

5. (a) The skirted projectiles increase the area at the base of the shell by the use of an extended skirt at the base and another one at the shoulder to ensure correct centring in the bore and thus stability or steadiness. During the passage of the projectile through the cone bore the skirts are squeezed inwards into the annular recesses in the main body of the projectile. The effect of this is that when the projectile reaches the muzzle the skirts are conforming to the general outline of the main body of the projectile, having been reduced to the diameter of the bore at the muzzle

/(b)

(b) Projectiles of the discarding sabot type use the normal parallel bore barrel but after leaving the muzzle discard rings or one of many different type of jacket, the result being a smaller and streamlined projectile of high velocity.

(c) The composite rigid projectiles, as their name implies, are of composite material construction to give large area and relatively light weight. It carries an inner pointed core of specially hardened steel, or some such like material, to give high penetration performance. The whole of the projectile travels to the target. The cap of the composite material jacket is normally made of some light metal, which will add some measure of protection and lubrication to the pointed core during penetration.

All these projectile types have the disadvantage that the effective fighting range is very limited, approximately up to about 2000 yards, above this range the velocity and effectiveness falls away fairly rapidly, owing to the relatively light weight of the projectile.

(d) The hollow charge projectile is much more effective when it is fin stabilised i.e. not spin stabilised as when ejected from a rifled gun; the spin of the projectile degrades the performance.

In the following pages each equipment will be covered in fair detail. Equipments will not be taken in their chronological order of appearance but in sequence according to size, although as stated before, with one or two exceptions the sequence is the same under both headings.

B. 2.8 cm. S.Pz B.41.(1.1 inch/.787 inch A.Tk.Gun Model 41) See Figs.:- 1, 2 and 3.

1. This light quick firing anti-tank gun was an exceptionally good weapon judged by the standards existing at the time of its introduction into the German Service. It was described by some as the first really "secret" weapon brought into service during the war. Be that as it may, it saw the introduction by the Germans of a new principle in artillery weapons- the use of the tapered or cone bore. It fired a special skirted type of projectile at an extremely high muzzle velocity. The first indication of its high velocity was given in a captured German note book which gave the muzzle velocity as 6250 ft secs. This was subsequently proved to be inaccurately high, the correct velocity being around about 4,600 ft sec.

The barrel which tapers from a diameter of 28 mm (1.1 ins) at the commencement of the rifling to 20 mm (.79 ins) at the muzzle, becomes unserviceable after about 500 rounds have been fired.

The equipment is exceptionally light and is essentially an infantry anti-tank weapon mounted on a carriage which has free elevation and traverse, i.e. the gun can be elevated and traversed by pressure of movement applied to handgrips instead of having to turn the normal type of handwheels.

2. 2.8 cm S Pz B. 41 (Airborne Version) See Fig:4

The main differences between the airborne model and the older ground equipment are:-

(a) The whole of the carriage is of light tubular metal, with small wheels having pneumatic tyres.

(b) There is no protective armour for the crew.

(c) The total weight of the airborne is 260 lbs as against 501 lbs of the ground equipment. The outstanding fact is that, though the barrel and cradle remained unchanged, there was almost a 50% saving in total weight. Both equipments used the same ammunition consisting of A.P. and H.E. The A.P. projectile was constructed in five parts viz:-

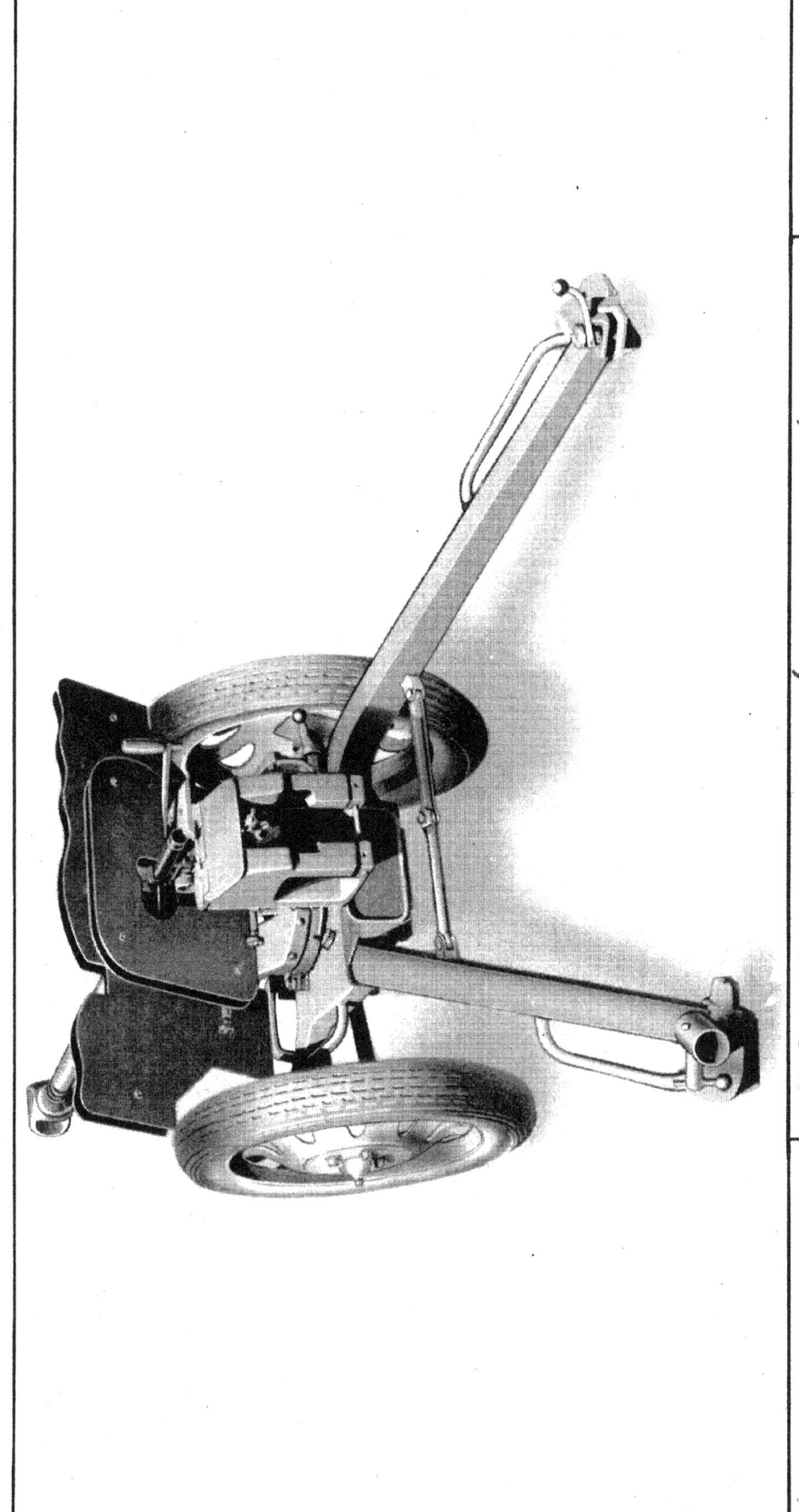

FIG.1. 2·8 cm. Pz. B41. (CONE BORE 2·8/2·0 cm.)
[1·1 in. ANTI-TANK GUN MODEL 41]
CONE BORE 1·1/·8 ins.

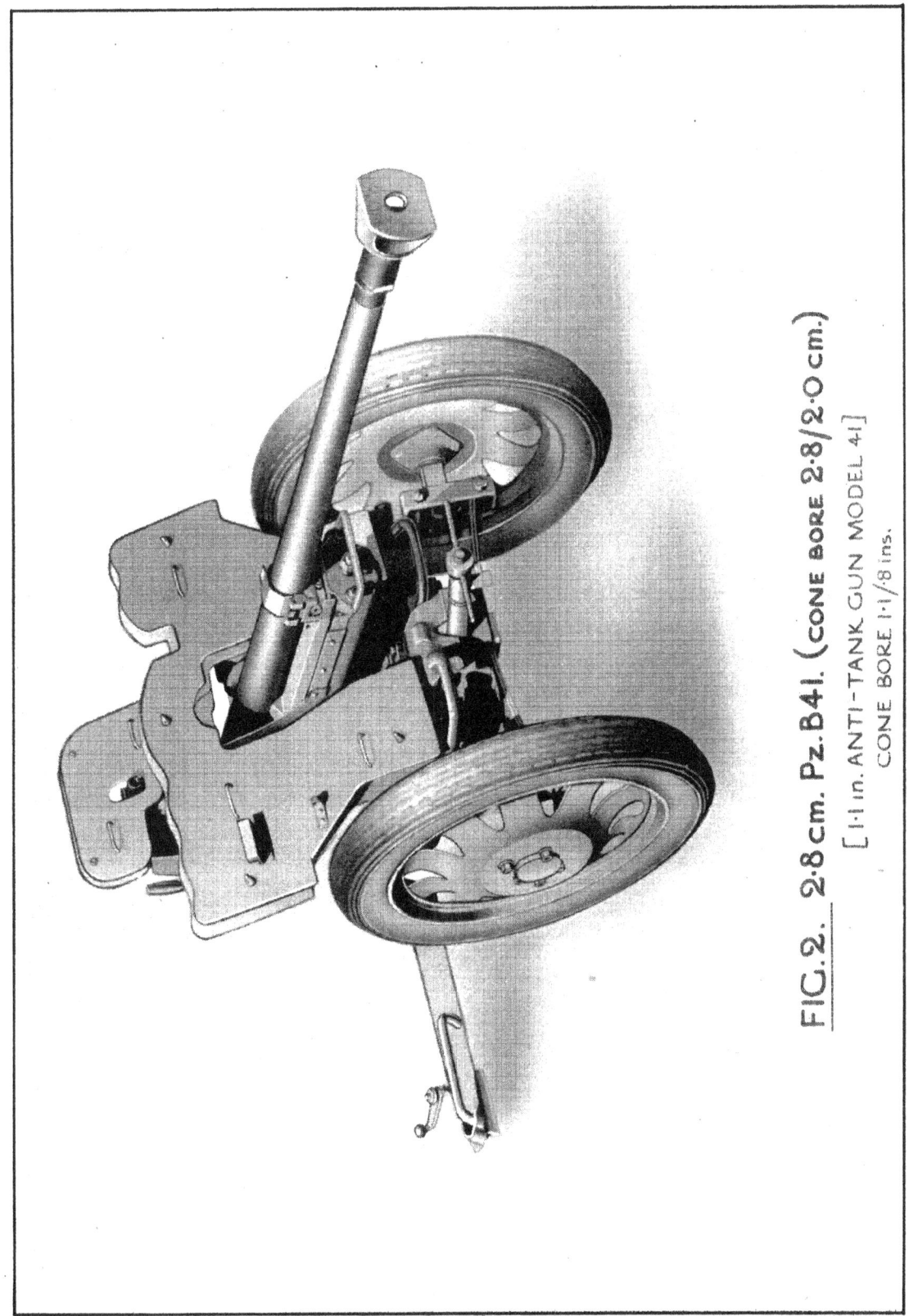

FIG. 2. 2·8 cm. Pz.B41. (CONE BORE 2·8/2·0 cm.)
[1·1 in. ANTI-TANK GUN MODEL 41]
CONE BORE 1·1/·8 ins.

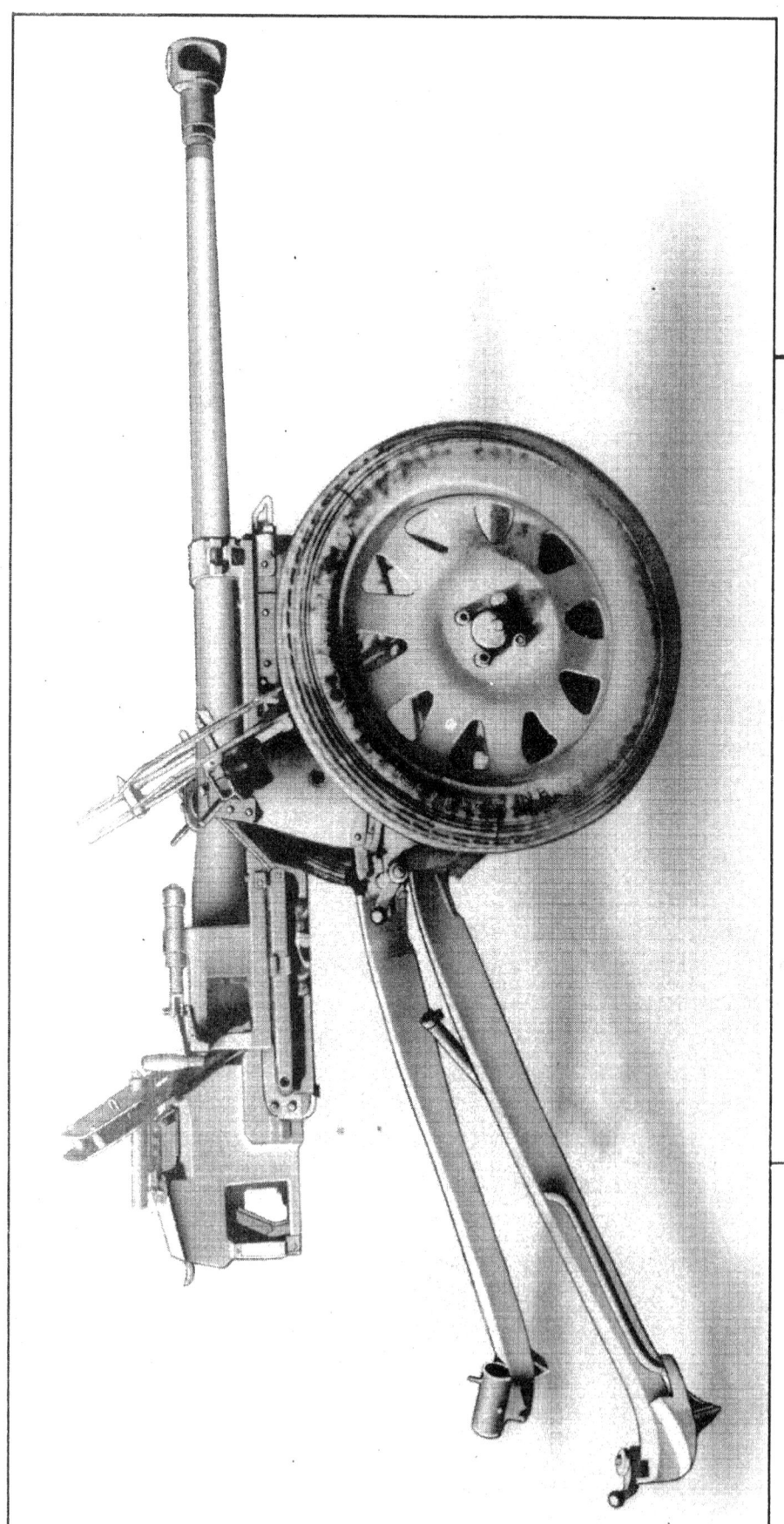

FIG. 3. 2·8 cm. Pz. B41. (CONE BORE 2·8/2·0 cm.)
[1·1in. ANTI-TANK GUN MODEL 41]
CONE BORE 1·1/·8 ins.

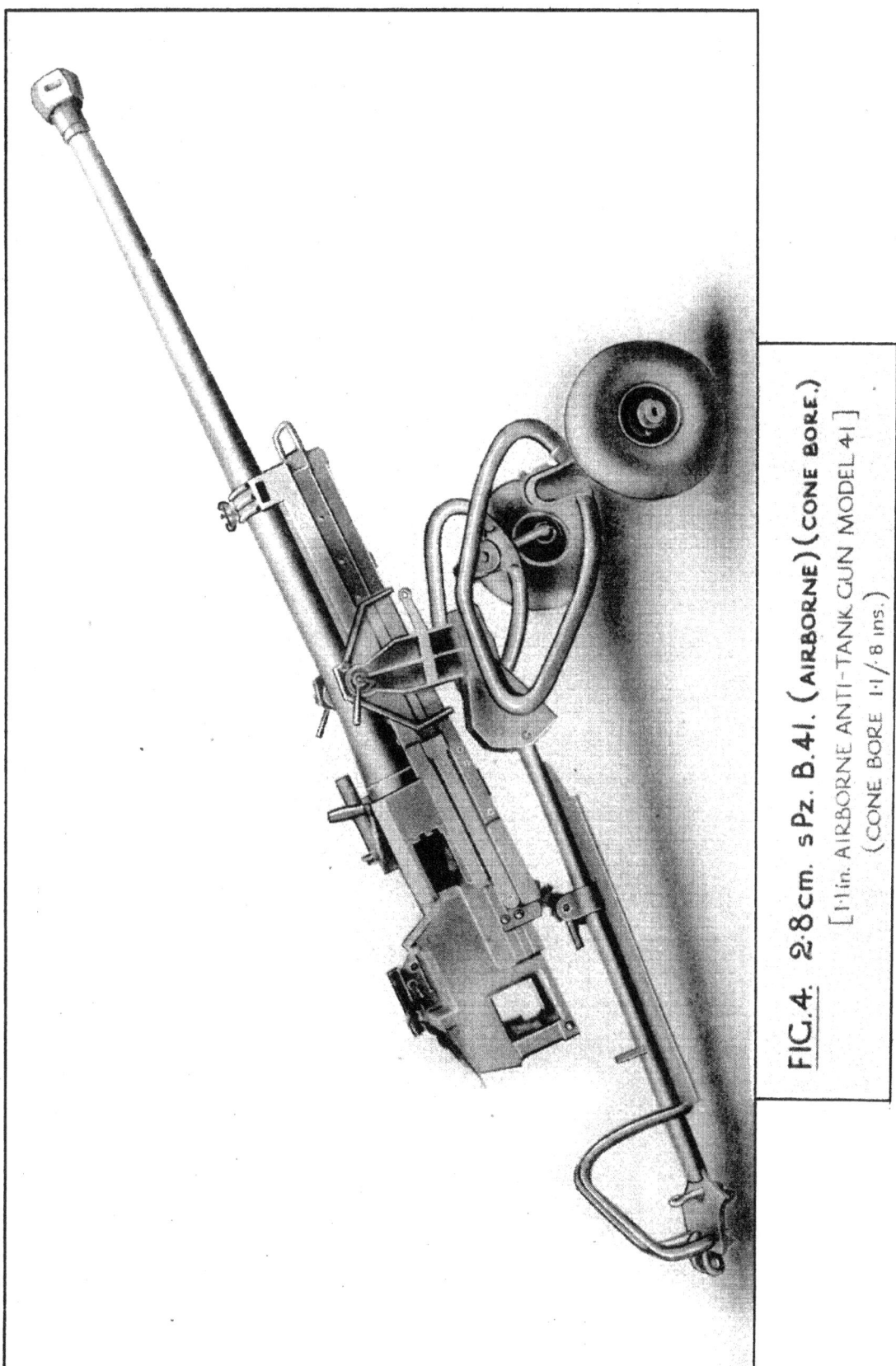

FIG. 4. 2·8 cm. s Pz. B. 41. (AIRBORNE) (CONE BORE.)
[1·1 in. AIRBORNE ANTI-TANK GUN MODEL 41]
(CONE BORE 1·1/·8 ins.)

(i) Magnesium alloy ballistic cap.

(ii) Front steel skirt.

(iii) Rear steel skirt.

(iv) Cemented carbide A.P. core.

(v) Lead sleeve.

The propellant used was graphited tubular nitrocellulose powder moderated with ethylcentralite.

3. Data 2.8 cm S.Pz B. 41

(a) Calibre   1.1/.787 ins. (28/20 mm)
Length of ordnance   67.51 ins. (1714 mm)
Rifling   Right Hand increasing

    "   length   50 ins. (1270 mm)
No. of grooves   12
Traverse at full
          elevation   30°
     "   horizontal   90°
Elevation   -5° to +45°
Recoil Normal   9.49 ins. (241 mm)
    "   Max   11.02 ins. (280 mm)
Overall length of
          equipment   8 Ft. 10 ins. (2690 mm)
    "   height   2 Ft. 9 ins. (838 mm)
    "   width   3 Ft. 2 ins. (965 mm)
Wt. of equipment complete   505 lbs (229 Kg.)

(b) Ammunition

Nomenclature	M.V.	Wt. of Proj.
2.8 cm Pzgr Patr 41	4599 f/s (1402 m.s.)	4½ ozs. (.1305 Kg.)
2.8 cm Sprgr Patr 41	4593 f/s (1400 m.s.)≠	3 ozs. (.085 Kg.)

≠ Estimated M.V.

(c) Armour Penetration

Firing 2.8 cm. Pzgr Patr 41

Range yds.	Penetration Normal	in mm. 30°
100	94	69
200	86	65
300	79	60
400	72	56
500	66	52
600	60	48
700	54	44
800	49	41

C. **3.7 cm Pak 35/36** (1.46 inch Anti-Tank Gun Model 35/36) See Figs: 5 and 6.

1. This was Germany's first line anti-tank gun at the outbreak of world war II. The weapon is thought to have been developed about 1933/4 and it is probable that it was used operationally by the German forces who took part in the Spanish civil war. This undoubtedly gave the Germans a considerable amount of operational experience in the use of the equipment, and in 1939 it was undoubtedly as good an anti-tank gun as any in use by the armies of the major powers.

It was used with considerable success in the campaign against Poland, although it must be said that the Polish equipment was too limited to withstand the new German Blitzkreig technique then, and later in France, demonstrated to an astonished world.

Consideration of the fact that this equipment was developed as early as 1933/4 shows that the weapon was of sound basic design to remain the front line weapon until the latter months of 1940, although it was considered by some experts to have been a comparative failure against the French tanks.

Two factors contributed to the lengthly retention of this equipment; they were:-

(a) The introduction of improved A.P. ammunition, A.P. 40, which increased the penetration performance of the weapon by about 30%.

(b) The inability of the Germans to produce a better and heavier weapon, until the latter months of 1940 when the 5 cm Pak 38 was introduced into service.

The 3.7 cm Pak 35/36 was not an outstanding weapon and indeed, the penetration performance of the gun, at angles of attack other than normal, was considered disappointing.

The efficiency of the equipment rested very much on its good mobility. It was normally towed on its two wheeled carriage but could be transported in a light motor vehicle.

The equipment was near ideal for airborne use as its total weight was only approximately 8 cwts.

The ammunition used consisted of the standard types of H.E. and A.P. and a combination of the two, with and without tracers.

2. Data: 3.7 Pak 35/36

(a)
Calibre	1.46 in.	(37 mm)
Length of ordnance	65.5 in.	(1665 mm)
Rifling r.h. Uniform		
" Length	51.19 in.	(1301 mm)
No. of grooves		16
Chamber capacity		380 c.c.
Traverse		60°
Elevation		25°
Recoil Normal	22.05 in.	(560 mm)
Overall length of equipment	11 Ft. 2 in.	(3400 mm)
" height	3 Ft. 10 in.	(1170 mm)
" width	5 Ft. 5 in.	(1650 mm)
Wt of equipment complete	952 lbs	(432 Kg.)

(b) <u>Ammunition</u>

Nomenclature	M.V.	Wt of Proj.
3.7 cm Pak Pzgr	2499 f/s (762 m.s.)	1 lb 8 ozs (.68 Kg.)
3.7 cm Pak Pzgr40	3378 f/s (1030 m.s.)	12½ ozs (.354 Kg.)
3.7 cm Spgr		1 lb 6½ ozs (.625 Kg.)
⌀ 3.7 cm Stiel Gr41	360 f/s (110 m.s.)	18 lb 14 ozs (8.5 Kg.)

(c) Armour Penetration

* Firing 3.7 cm Pak Pzgr   ∓ Firing 3.7 cm Pak Pzgr 40

Range yds.	Penetration Normal	in mm 30°	Range yds.	Penetration Normal	in mm 30°
200	56	42	100	79	68
400	51	38	200	72	61
500	48	36	300	65	55
600	46	34	400	58	49

∓ Estimated performance.
⌀ Fin stabilised hollow charge round of mortar bomb shape, fitted with short rod for firing from the muzzle.

/D.

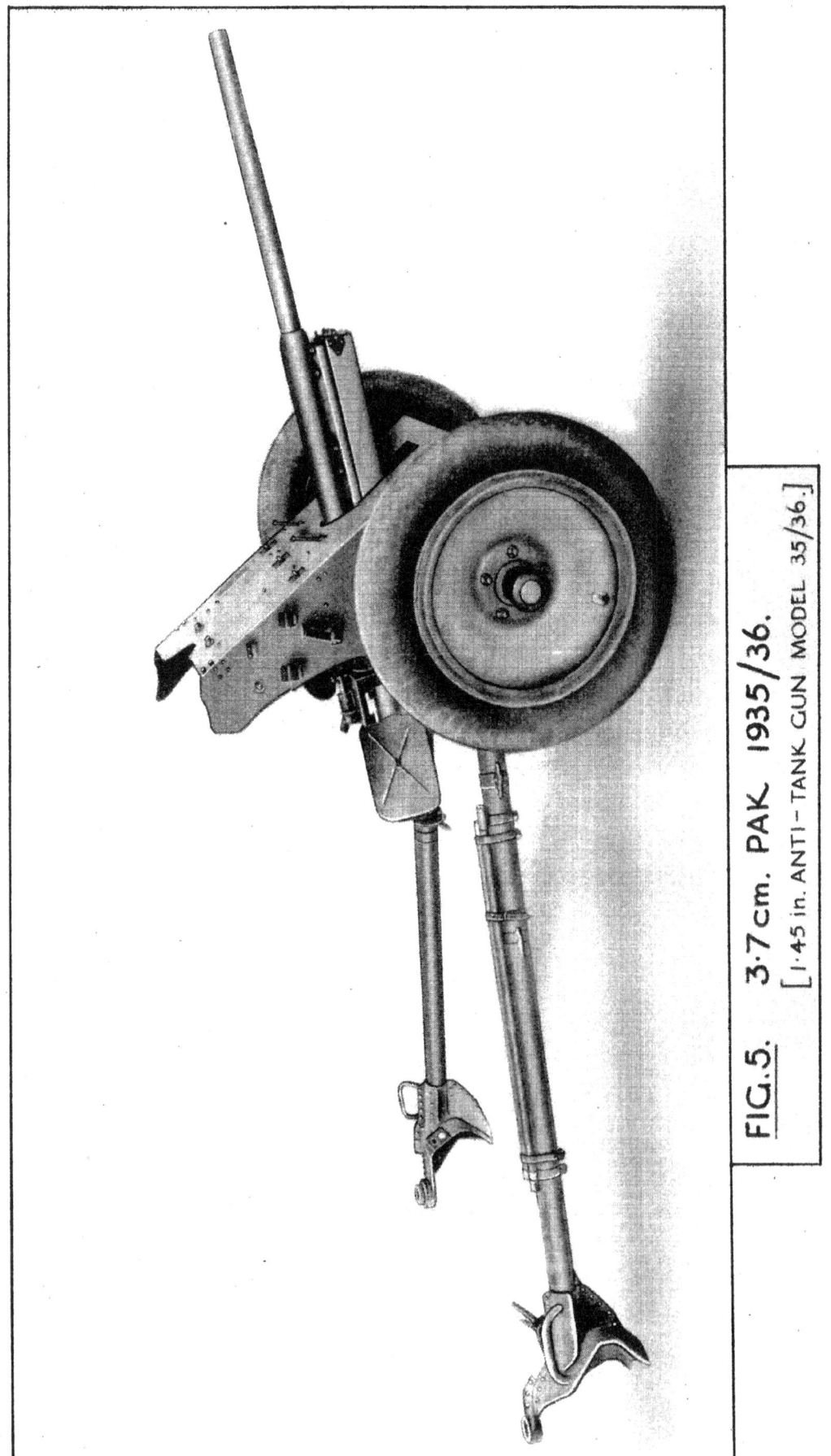

FIG. 5. 3·7 cm. PAK 1935/36.
[1·45 in. ANTI-TANK GUN MODEL 35/36.]

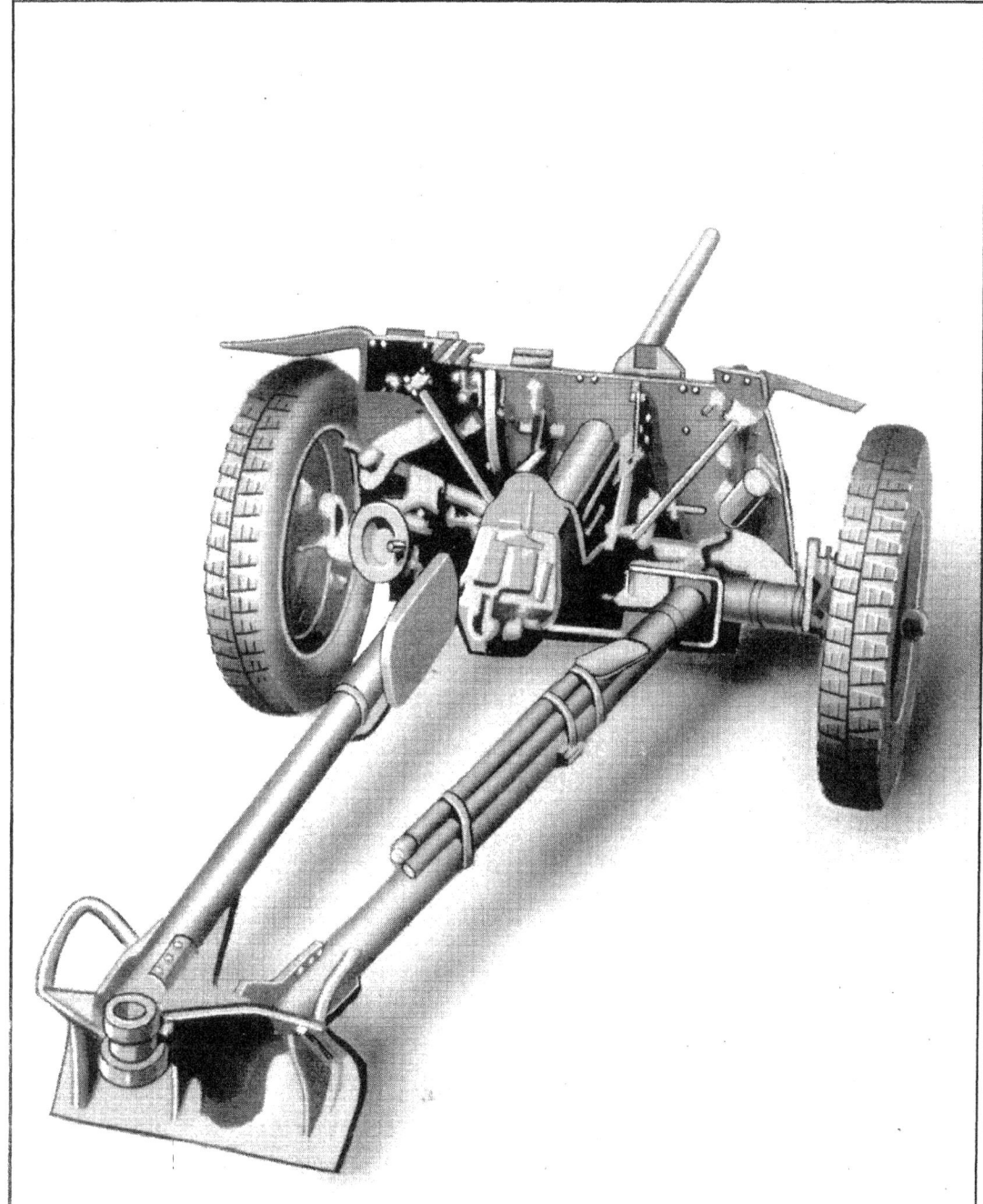

FIG. 6. 3·7cm. PAK 1935/36 (AIRBORNE)
[1·45 in. ANTI-TANK GUN MODEL 35/36] (AIRBORNE)

D. **4.2 cm le Pak 41 (1.65 inch light Anti-Tank Gun Model 41). See Figs:7 and 8.**

1. This cone bore weapon was introduced into service at about the same time as the other guns of similar type i.e. the 2.8 cm S Pz B 41, already referred to, and the 7.5 cm Pak 41.

This gun was mounted on a modified 3.7 cm Pak carriage, the principle of the cone bore being, as stated before, the development of higher velocity than that normally obtained from the orthodox parallel bore.

The nomenclature of 4.2 cm is not in accordance with the sizes of bores which have been measured and it is assumed that the calibre specification was changed from the 4.2 cm originally specified. As an example of the precise diameters of an almost new barrel the measurements were 4.061 cm (1.599 inches) at 1 inch from commencement of rifling and 29.41 cm (1.158 inches) at $\frac{1}{2}$ inch from muzzle.

This equipment was beautifully well balanced and incorporated several new features in gun and carriage construction, the most notable being in the springing of the carriage. This consisted of a laminated square section bar, $1\frac{1}{2}$ inches square formed by 6 layers of $\frac{1}{4}$ inch x $1\frac{1}{2}$ inch spring steel welded at one end. Only one other German artillery equipment, within the writer's knowledge, has this laminated type of torsion bar suspension, the equipment being the 8 cm smooth bore anti-tank weapon (8 cm PAW 600); indeed this latter equipment is unique in that its equilibrator also makes use of a laminated bar of similar assembly.

The equipment is designed for one man control of sighting, elevating, traversing and firing and unlike the 3.7 cm Pak equipment, is fitted with a double shield.

The big improvement in muzzle velocity, about 35 per cent over that of the 3.7 cm was somewhat offset by the smaller emergent projectile i.e. 2.9 cm as compared with 3.7 cm, and also of lighter weight.

The ammunition used is all, of course, of the type suitable for use in cone bore, i.e. skirted projectiles, similar in construction to that fired by the 2.8 cm S Pz B 41.

2. Data: 4.2 cm le Pak 41

(a) Calibre   1.65/1.18 ins. (42/30 mm)   Actual 40.5/29.4 mm
    Length of Ordnance   88.58 ins. (2250 mm)
    Rifling   Right Hand increasing

    "   length   66.93 ins. (1700 mm)
    No. of grooves   12
    Length of Chamber   16.69 ins. (424 mm)
    Traverse   41°
    Elevation   15°
    Overall length of
        equipment   13 Ft. (3690 mm)
    "   height   3 Ft. $11\frac{1}{2}$ ins. (1210 mm)
    "   width   5 Ft. $5\frac{1}{2}$ ins. (1660 mm)
    Wt of equipment complete 992 lbs (450 Kg.)

(b) Ammunition

Nomenclature	M.V.	Wt of Proj.
4.2 cm Pzgr 41	4149 f/s (1265 m.s.)	$11\frac{3}{4}$ ozs (.336 Kg.)
4.2 cm Spgr 41		10 ozs (.280 Kg.)

/(c)

(c) Armour Penetration

❋ Firing Pzgr 41

Range Yds.	Penetration Normal	in mm 30°
0	124	95
250	105	83
500	87	72
750	73	62
1000	60	53

❋ Estimated performance.

(d) Details of Ammunition

Type	Weight of Complete Round	Length of Complete Round	Weight of Projectile	Fuze Marking
AP Tracer Pzgr 41	3 lb 4 ozs (1.48 kg)	18.1 inches (46 cm)	11 ozs 336 gms	None. Cap painted olive green.
HE Spgr 41	3 lbs (1.36 kg)	17.9 inches (45.6 cm)	9 ozs 280 gms	Nose Percussion AZ 5073

E. **5 cm Pak 38** (1.97 inch Anti-Tank Gun Model 38) (See Figs: 9, 10, 11 and 12).

1. Design of the 5 cm Pak 38 had commenced in 1938 but production was not sufficiently advanced in the early part of 1940 to permit of introduction into service and employment in the campaign against France. This equipment finally replaced the 3.7 cm Pak during the latter months of 1940. Its design incorporated the use of a muzzle brake to restrict recoil and the employment of a torsion bar sprung carriage with solid rubber tyred wheels. These two features were employed in the design of all subsequent single axle field and anti-tank weapons and contributed considerably in keeping down the overall weight of an equipment, firstly in allowing the use of a smaller and therefore lighter recoil mechanism and a lighter carriage. This was assisted by the spring suspension since a lighter carriage could be used because a large part of the travelling stresses were absorbed by the said spring suspension. Introduced about the same time were two tank guns of differing lengths, all three guns used the same types of ammunition thereby effecting a standardization of ammunition production.

The 5 cm Pak 38 was decidedly a very good anti-tank weapon judged by the standards of 1941, indeed, the German Air Force thought highly of it, and, having had a ring semi-automatic feed fitted to it, mounted the gun and superstructure in aircraft such as the JU 88. During the latter months of the war the equipment came full circle and arrangements were made to mount the aircraft version on a Flak mounting and use it as a stop gap AA weapon, to replace the comparative failure - the 5 cm Flak 41.

The weapon fires AP shell, HE shell and AP 40 shot. The latter is a light shot with a ballistic cap, and incorporating a tungsten carbide core which has a good AP performance at ranges under 500 yards.

Good as this weapon was, it was soon to be supplanted, but never completely replaced, by the subsequently famous 7.5 cm Pak 40 and to a lesser extent by the 7.5 cm Pak 41 (a cone bore), but that is history later than that dealt with by this section.

/2. Data:

FIG.7. 4·2 cm. PAK 41 (CONE BORE 4·2/2·8 cms.)
[1·65 in. ANTI-TANK GUN MODEL 1941] (CONE BORE 1·65/1·1 ins.)

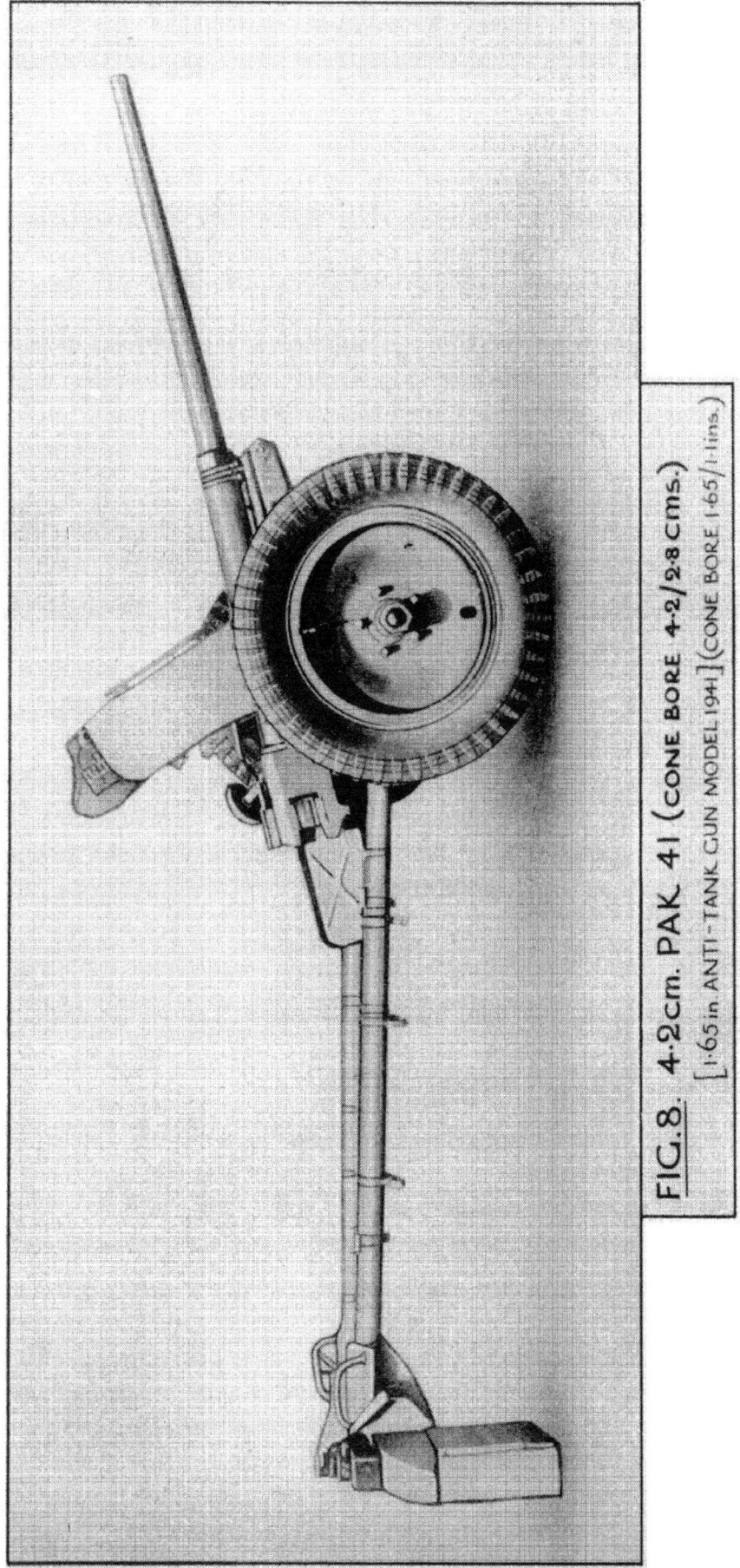

FIG. 8. 4.2 cm. PAK 41 (CONE BORE 4·2/2·8 CMS.)
[1·65 in ANTI-TANK GUN MODEL 1941] (CONE BORE 1·65/1·1 ins.)

2. Data: 5 cm Pak 38

(a) Calibre 1.97 ins. (50 mm)

Length of ordnance	124.96 in (3173 mm.)
Rifling R.H. increasing	
" length	93.75 ins. (2381 mm)
No. of grooves	20
Length of chamber	17.48 ins. (444 mm)
Traverse	65°
Elevation	-8° to +27°
Recoil normal	27.56 ins. (700 mm)
" max	28.74 ins. (730 mm)
Overall length of equipment	15 Ft. 7 ins. (4750 mm)
" height	3 Ft. 7½ ins. (1105 mm)
" width	6 Ft. 0½ ins. (1830 mm)
Wt of equipment complete	2174 lbs (986 Kg.)

(b) Ammunition

Nomenclature	M.V.	Wt. of Proj.
5 cm Pak 38 Pzgr	2700 f/s (823 m.s.)	4 lbs 15¼ ozs (2.25 Kg.)
5 cm Pak 38 Spgr	1800 f/s (549 m.s.)	4 lbs 5 ozs (1.96 Kg.)
5 cm Pak 38 Pzgr 40	3930 f/s (1198 m.s.)	2 lbs 2¼ lbs (.975 Kg.)

(c) Armour Penetration

Firing 5 cm Pak 38 Pzgr			Firing 5 cm Pak 38 Pzgr 40		
Range yds.	Penetration Normal	in mm 30°	Range yds	Penetration Normal	in mm 30°
0	99	73	0	165	143
250	88	67	250	141	109
500	78	61	500	120	86
750	69	56	750	101	69
1000	61	50	1000	84	55
1250	53	45	1250	70	44
1500	47	40			

(d) Rate of Fire   12 rpm.

F. 7.5 cm Pak 40 (2.95 inch Anti-Tank Gun Model 40)   See Figs: 13.

1. As soon as the Russian campaign started it became apparent that the 5 cm guns did not have a sufficiently high performance to deal effectively with the Russian armour encountered.

Contracts had been placed in 1939 with Krupp and Rheinmetall Borsig for the design and production of a 7.5 cm anti-tank gun. Neither equipment was ready for full scale production in time for the first Russian campaign and in order to reduce the heavy handicap under which the German anti-tank artillery found itself, when confronted with the heavy Russian Armour, it was decided to use or modify such captured enemy artillery weapons as could be used in an anti-tank role. These equipments will be dealt with according to size in subsequent sections; meanwhile the design of the 7.5 cm Pak 40 and the 7.5 cm Pak 41 designed respectively by Rheinmetall Borsig and Krupp, was being hurried along on top priority. Both equipments came into service towards the end of 1941.

Although the two 7.5 cm equipments were built to approximately the same specifications, the two firms employed different methods of approach in order to attain the required performance. Rheinmetall Borsig produced a standard parallel bore gun similar in design to the 5 cm Pak 38, while the Krupp gun barrel was made in two sections, the rear portion being a standard parallel bore, and the front section, screwed to the muzzle end of the rear section,

/being

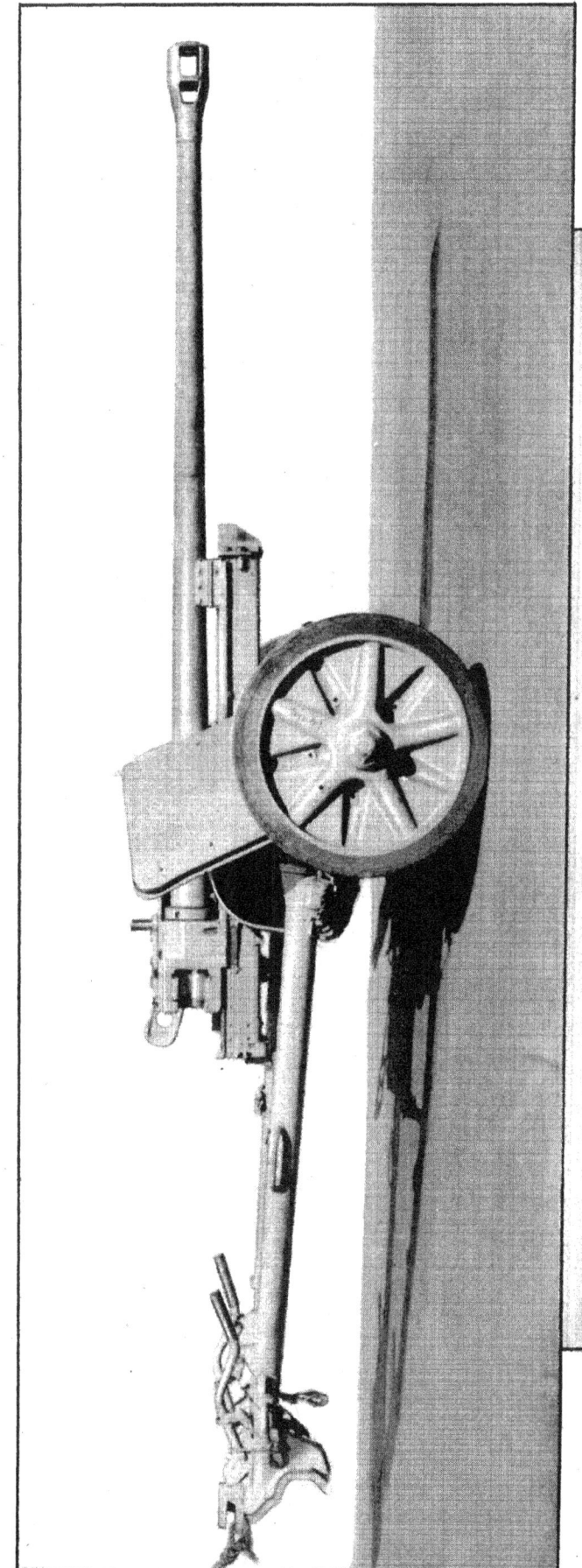

FIG. 9. 5 cm. PAK 38. [1·97 in. ANTI-TANK GUN MODEL 1938]

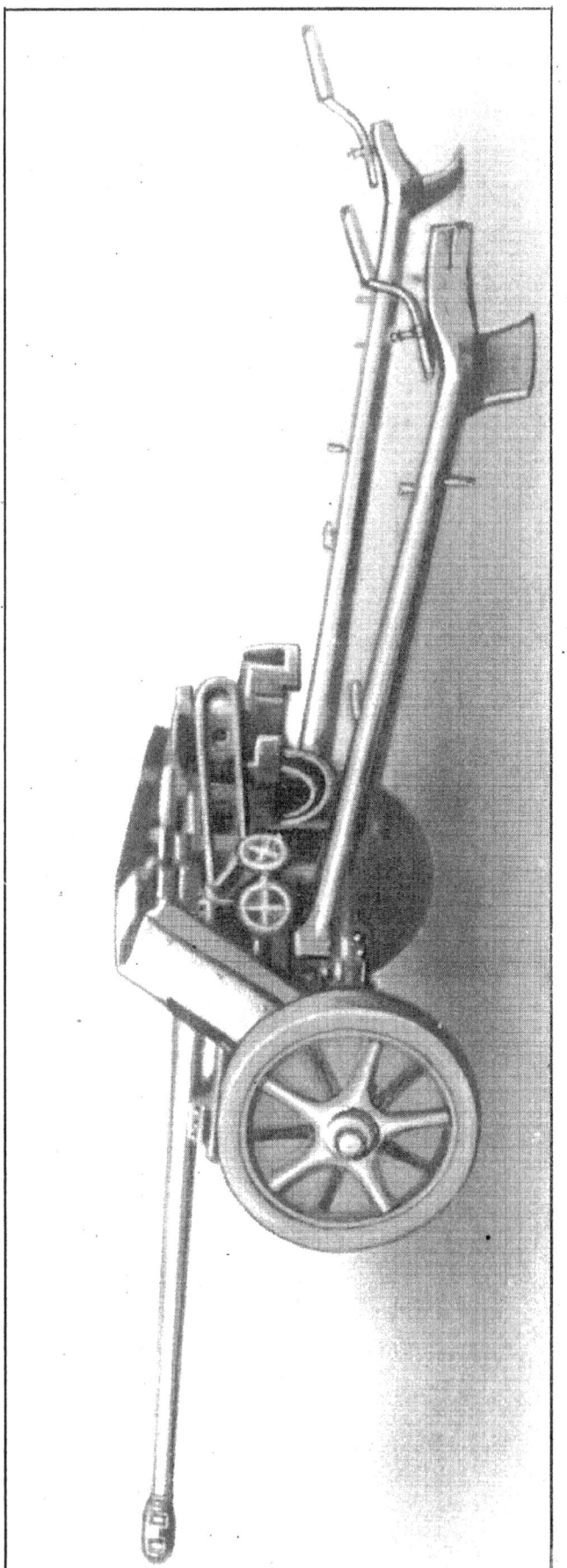

FIG. 10. 5 cm. PAK 38. [1·97 in. ANTI-TANK GUN 1938.]

FIG.11. 5cm. PAK 38. [1·97in. ANTI-TANK GUN 1938.]

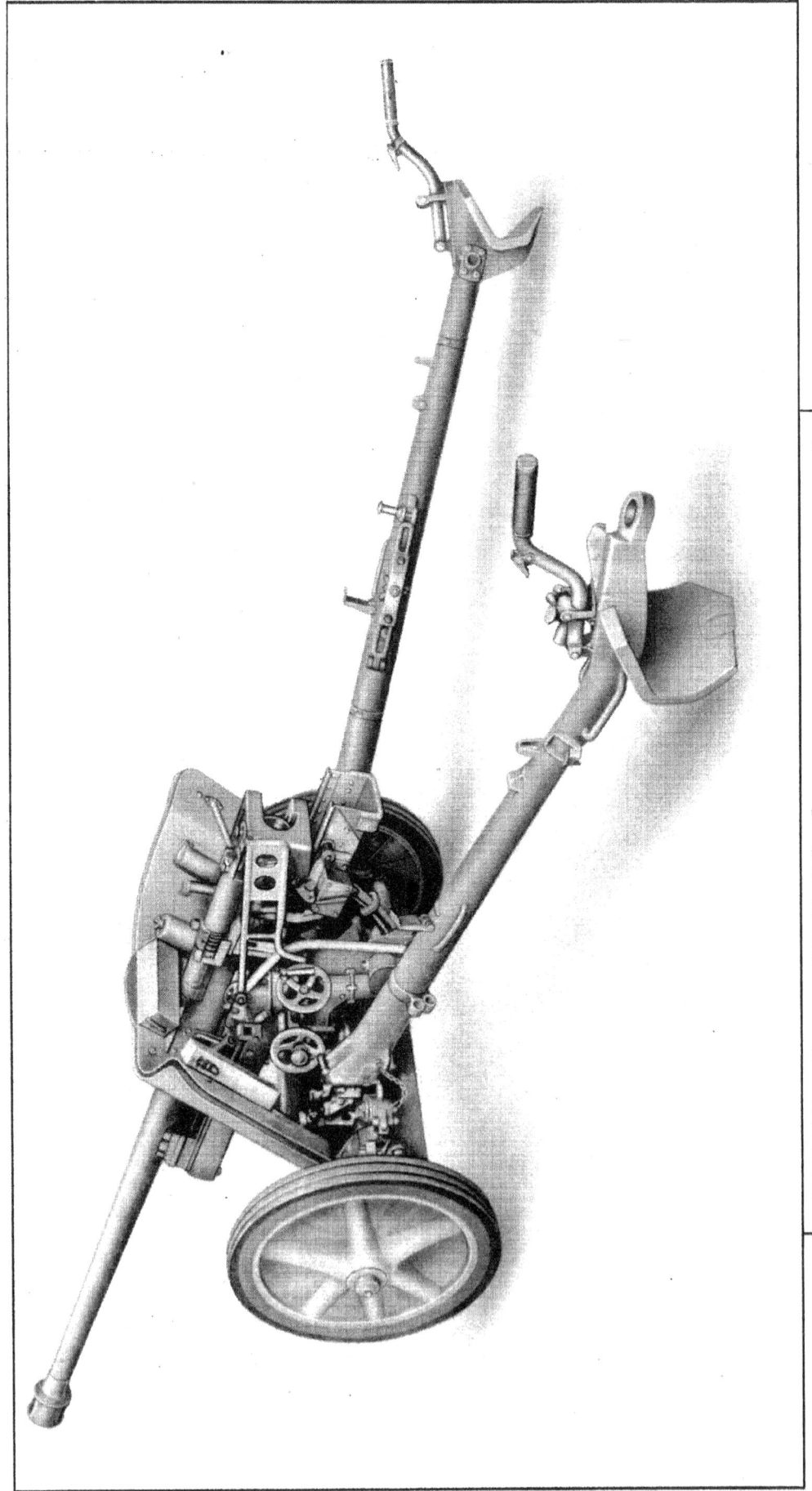

FIG.12. 5 cm. PAK 38. [1·97in. ANTI-TANK GUN 1938.]

being a smooth bore muzzle squeeze, the emergent calibre of which was 5.5 cm. Of the two guns the 7.5 cm Pak 40 was adopted as the standard anti-tank weapon and was used consistently and with success throughout the rest of the war. Its penetration performance of 94 mm/30° attack/1000 metres was considered very satisfactory at the time and both designers and users were pleased with the results obtained. This opinion was modified later on when the overall weight of the equipment (1 ton 8 cwts) was thought to be excessive. It was made particularly apparent when, during the months of winter and spring retreat which followed in Russia, large numbers of serviceable guns had to be abandoned, owing to the inability of the gun crews to man-handle them over the heavy terrain.

2. Data: 7.5 cm Pak 40

(a) Calibre   2.95 ins. (75 mm)
    Length of ordnance
    (incl muzzle brake)   145.67 ins. (3700 mm)
    Rifling R.H. increasing
    "   length   96.85 ins. (2461 mm)
    No. of grooves   32
    Length of chamber   28.19 ins. (716 mm)
    Chamber capacity   213.6 c.ins. (3500 c.c.)
    Traverse   65°
    Elevation   -5° to +22°
    Recoil normal   34.06 ins. (865 mm)
    "   max.   35.43 ins. (900 mm)
    Overall length of
        equipment   20 Ft. 3½ ins. (6185 mm)
    "   height   4 Ft. 1 in. (1245 mm)
    "   width   6 Ft. 10 ins. (2080 mm)
    Wt of equipment complete   3306 lbs (1500 Kg.)

(b) Ammunition

Nomenclature	M.V.	Wt. of Proj.
7.5 cm Sprgr Patr 34	1803 f/s (550 m.s.)	12 lbs 10½ ozs (5.74 Kg.)
7.5 cm Pzgr Patr 39	2598 f/s (792 m.s.)	15 lbs (6.8 Kg.)
7.5 cm Pzgr Patr 40	3060 f/s (933 m.s.)	7 lbs (3.2 Kg.)

(c) Armour Penetration

Firing 7.5 cm Pzgr Patr 39			Firing 7.5 cm Pzgr Patr 40		
Range yds.	Penetration Normal	in mm 30°	Range yds.	Penetration Normal	in mm 30°
0	149	121	0	176	137
500	135	106	500	154	115
1000	121	94	1000	133	96
1500	109	83	1500	115	80
2000	98	73	2000	98	66
			2500	83	53

A limited number of hollow charge projectiles was used in this weapon at a lower velocity than that used for AP and HE. (Not considered a standard projectile.)

7.5 Pak 41 (2.95 inch Anti-Tank Gun Model 41). See Figs: 14, 15 and 16.

1. The 7.5 cm Pak 41 also went into production at the same time as the Pak 40, but only a limited number were ordered and some 150 equipments were made in all, after which it was decided to discontinue production altogether. The reason for this was that the design of the gun barrel, a cone muzzle squeeze, necessitated the use of a skirted tungsten cored AP shot and because the supply of Wolfram, used for the production of tungsten steel, was severely restricted by the end of 1941; development and production of tungsten cored ammunition and equipments, requiring its exclusive use, were dropped. Otherwise the Pak 41 was considered to be a

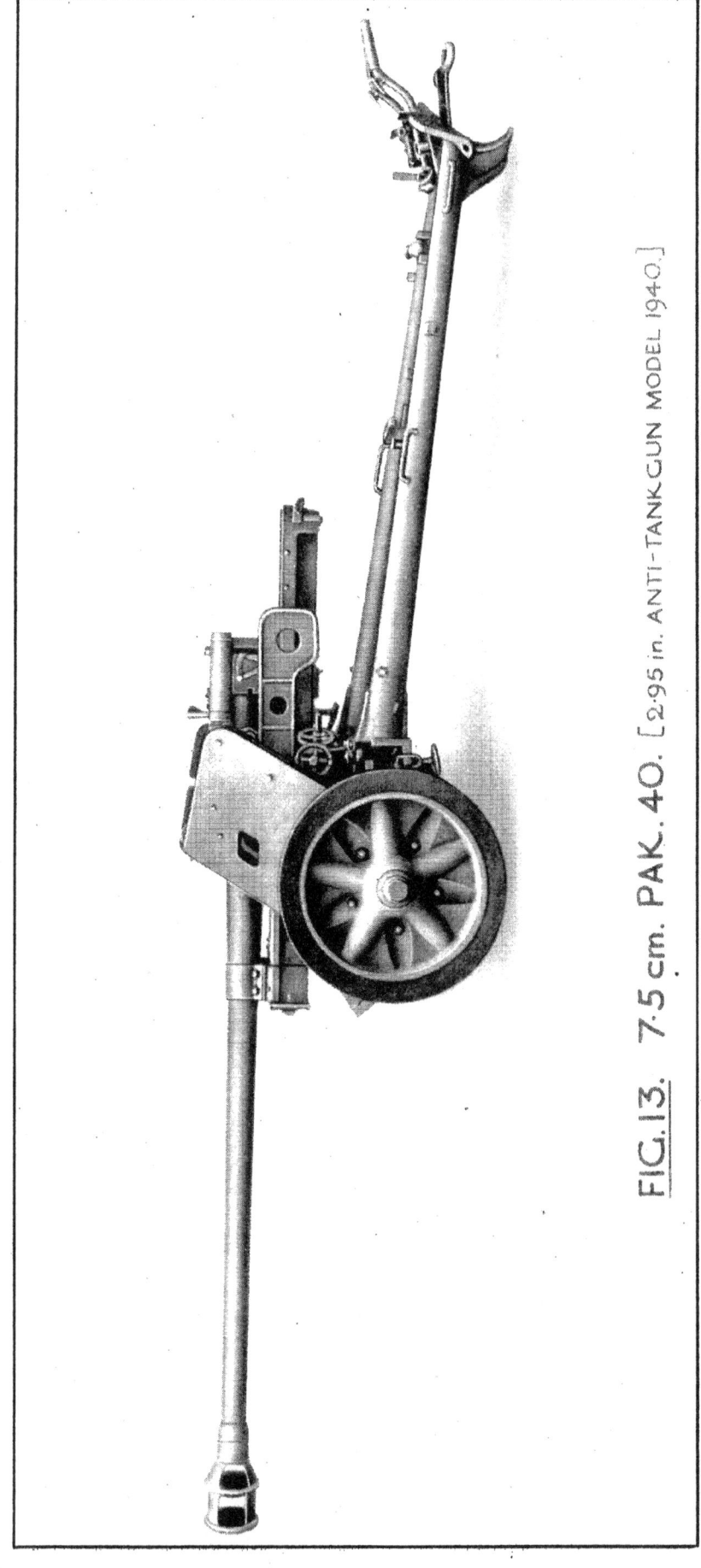

FIG. 13. 7.5 cm. PAK. 40. [2.95 in. ANTI-TANK GUN MODEL 1940.]

well designed and practical equipment and it was the opinion of many technicians at the time that, had it not been for the difficult Wolfram position, this gun would have taken precedence over the 7.5 cm Pak 40 as the main front line anti-tank weapon at that time. It had the advantage of having a higher penetrative performance at ranges up to 1000 metres but at greater ranges its performance fell off steeply, due to the lightweight of shot, and did not equal that of the Pak 40. The life of the muzzle squeeze attachment was approximately 500 rounds, but it could be readily changed in the field although the extra time and expense required in manufacture were not in its favour. The few guns that were produced were issued to special duty regiments and employed until available stocks of ammunition were used up.

The carriage, like that of the 7.5 cm Pak 40, was very well designed. It was low in silhouette, sturdy of construction and, for the calibre of the gun, a lightweight. It was during this period of 1940/41 that the Germans produced several sturdy low and lightweight carriages for other equipments; quite a "vintage" period for carriages.

The ammunition was, of course, the standard skirted type; the AP kind consisted of the usual pointed core variety with sleeve jacket, forward and rear skirts, and screwed head covered by a ballistic cap.

Hollow charge projectiles, although used with the Pak 40, were not used with this weapon.

2. Data: 7.5 cm Pak 41

   (a) Calibre   2.95/2.17 ins. (75/55 mm)
        Length of ordnance   170.08 ins. (4320 mm)
        Rifling R.H. - increasing twist

        "   length   94.88 ins. (2410 mm)
        No. of grooves   28
        Length of chamber   21.26 ins. (540 mm)
        Traverse   60°
        Elevation   16° 45'
        Recoil Normal   26.61 ins. (676 mm)
        "   Max   32.99 ins. (838 mm)
        Overall length of
            equipment   24 Ft. 7 ins. (7490 mm)
        "   height   5 Ft. 11 ins. (1800 mm)
        "   width   6 Ft. 3 ins. (1900 mm)
        Wt of equipment
            complete   2988 lbs (1356 Kg.)

   (b) Ammunition

Nomenclature	M.V.	Wt. of Proj.
7.5 cm Pzgr 41 (HK) Pak 41	3690 f/s (1124 m.s.)	5 lbs 11¼ ozs (2.59 Kg.)
7.5 cm Pzgr 41(n) Pak 41 (practice)	3969 f/s (1210 m.s.)	5 lbs 7¼ ozs (2.48 Kg.)

   (c) Armour Penetration

        Firing 7.5 cm Pak 41 Pzgr 41

Range	Normal	30°
0	245	200
250	226	185
500	209	171
750	192	157
1000	177	145
1250	162	133
1500	149	122
1750	136	111
2000	124	102

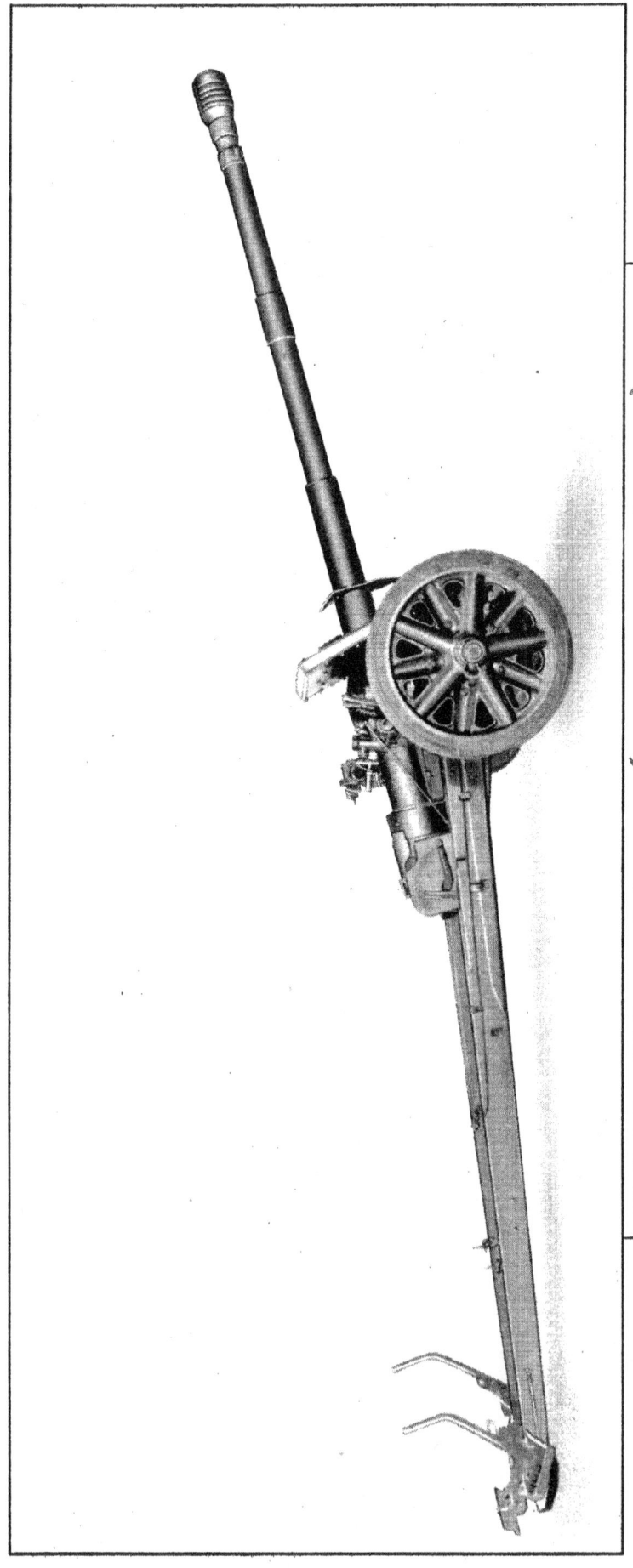

FIG.14. 7.5.cm. PAK 41. (CONE BORE 7.5/5.5 cm.)
[2·95 in. ANTI-TANK GUN MODEL 41.] (CONE BORE 2·95/2·16 ins.)

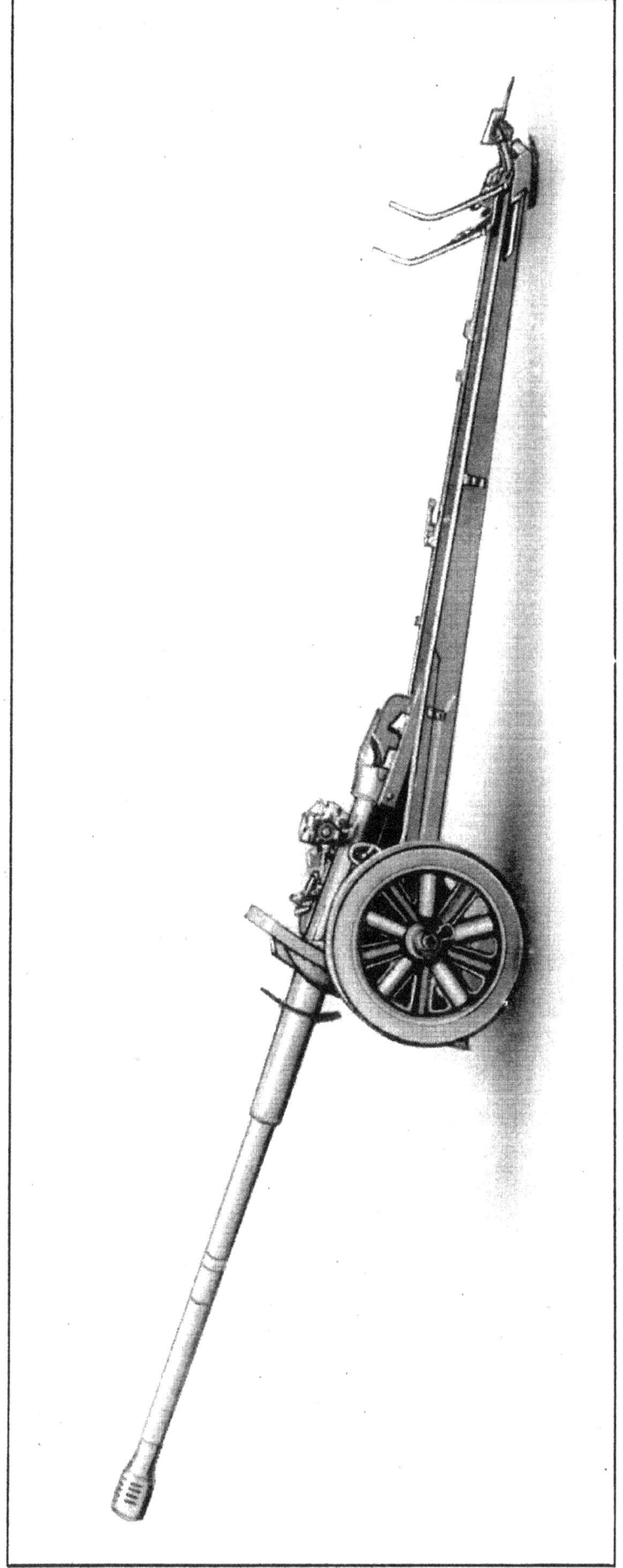

FIG.15. 7.5 cm. PAK 41. (CONE BORE 7.5/5.5 cm.)
[2.95 in. ANTI-TANK GUN MODEL 41.] (CONE BORE 2.95/2.16 ins.)

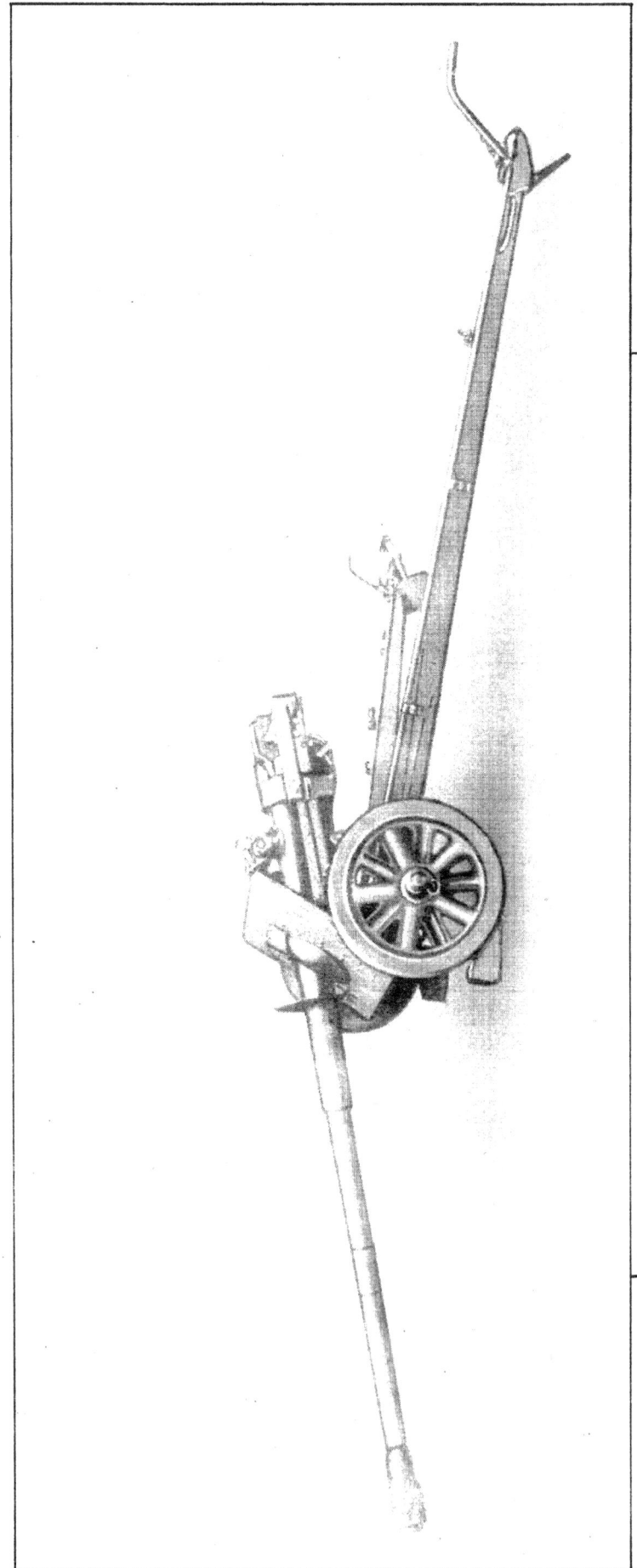

FIG. 16. 7·5 cm. PAK 41. (CONE BORE 7·5/5·5 cm.)
[2·95 in. ANTI-TANK GUN MODEL 41.] (CONE BORE 2·95/2·16 ins.)

H. Utilisation of Captured Guns in an Anti-Tank Role

The Germans quickly realised that, in both quality and quantity, their anti-tank artillery was inadequate to cope with the situation that arose during the summer of 1941 when it was brought up against the heavy Russian Armour. It was soon decided that every use must be made of such captured weapons as were available. The types are too numerous to cover in adequate detail, therefore it is proposed to describe only the two weapons of which most use was made, viz: the Russian 76.2 mm Model 36 and the French 75 mm Model 97, both of which were given a German nomenclature.

1. **75 mm Pak 97/38 (2.95 inch Anti-Tank Gun Model 97/38).** See Figs: 17 and 18.

   This equipment consisted of the French 75 mm Field Gun Model 97 mounted on the German 5 cm Pak 38 carriage. Hollow charge ammunition was used for anti-tank work but the gun never achieved great success and was not liked by the troops owing to its instability in action.

2. **76.2 mm Pak 36 (3 inch Anti-Tank Gun Model 36).** See Figs: 19 and 20.

   As a result of their earlier successes in the War against Russia, the Germans captured considerable quantities of a standard Russian field gun - the 76.2 mm Field Gun Model 36 - which they took direct and modified into use in their own army under the nomenclature 76.2 mm FK 296 (r), (Field Gun 296 (Russian)). Later, by increasing the chamber capacity, adding a muzzle brake and providing German ammunition they produced a gun much more useful for anti-tank work. The elevating handwheel was brought across to the left-hand side of the gun by means of a transverse shaft, enabling one man to control both elevation and traverse. The Germans gave the anti-tank version the nomenclature 76.2 mm Pak 36 and took it into service as a standard equipment.

   The maximum horizontal range is about 10,000 metres (11,000 yards).

3. **The Russian 76.2 mm Model 39 Field Gun** was also used in more limited numbers in the anti-tank role being given the nomenclature of Pak 39.

   The acquisition of the three above-mentioned anti-tank equipments certainly helped the Germans over a sticky patch during 1941 and 1942.

4. **Data: 75 mm Pak 97/38**

		British	Metric
(a)	Calibre	2.95 ins.	7.5 cm
	Length of ordnance without muzzle brake	8 ft. 11 ins.	2721 mm
	Rifling Uniform RH twist		
	" length		
	No. of grooves	24	
	Length of chamber		
	Chamber capacity		
	Traverse	60°	
	Elevation	-8° +25°	
	Recoil normal		
	Recoil maximum		
	Overall length of equipment	15 Ft. 3 ins.	4650 mm
	" height	3 Ft. 5½ ins.	1050 mm
	" width	6 Ft. 1 in.	1850 mm
	Weight of equipment in draught	1.3 tons	1246 Kg.
	Weight in action	1.25 tons	1190 Kg.
	Maximum Range (Hollow Charge)	2070 yds.	1900 metres
	" (anti-tank) (HE)	3270 yds.	3000 metres
	" " " (AP)	1417 yds.	1300 metres

Sights and Carriage of 5 cm Pak 38.

The sights are graduated in metres as follows :-

        Gr 38 HL/B (Hollow Charge)   -1900
        Sprgr   -3000
        K.Gr.Pz.   -1300

(b) Ammunition used:

H.E.
    7.5 cm Sprenggranat patrone   233/1 (f)
    7.5 cm Sprenggranat patrone   230/1 (f)
    7.5 cm Sprenggranat patrone   231/1 (f)
    7.5 cm Sprenggranat patrone   236/1 (f)

A.P. (Hollow Charge)
    7.5 cm Granat patrone   38/97 H L/B (f)
    7.5 cm Granat patrone   15/38 HL/B (f)

A.P. (Armour Piercing)
    7.5 cm Kanonengranat patrone Panzer (P)

(c) Muzzle Velocity

H.E.	577 m/s	1788-1892 f.s.
Hollow Charge	450 m/s	1476 f.s.
A.P.	570 m/s	1870 f.s.

5. Data: 7.62 cm Pak 36

(a)
Calibre	3 ins. (76.2 mm)
Length of ordnance (incl muzzle brake)	164.56 ins. (4179 mm)
Rifling Uniform R.H. twist	
" length	115.32 ins. (2930 mm)
No. of grooves	32
Length of chamber	28.27 ins. (718 mm)
Chamber capacity	212.6 c.ins (3485 c.c.)
Traverse	60°
Elevation	-6° to +25°
Recoil normal	35.43 ins. (900 mm)
" max	39.37 ins (1000 mm)
Overall length of equipment	24 Ft 0¼ ins. (7320 mm)
" height	4 Ft 7 ins. (1400 mm)
" width	6 Ft 6¾ ins. (2000 mm)
Wt of equipment complete	3770 lbs (1730 Kg.)

(b) Ammunition

Nomenclature	M.V.	Wt. of Proj.
7.62 cm Pzgr 39	2427 f/s (740 m.s.)	16 lbs 9½ ozs (7.54 Kg.)
7.62 cm Pzgr 40	3249 f/s (990 m.s.)	8 lbs 14½ ozs (4.05 Kg.)
7.62 cm Sprgr 39	1803 f/s (550 m.s.)	13 lbs 11 ozs (6.2 Kg.)

(c) Armour Penetration

Firing 7.62 cm pzgr 39   Firing 7.62 cm Pzgr 40

Range yds.	Penetration Normal	in mm 30°	Range yds.	Penetration Normal	in mm 30°
0	133	108	0	190	152
500	120	98	500	158	118
1000	108	88	1000	130	92
1500	97	79	1500	106	71
2000	87	71	2000	84	55
2500	78	64	2500	65	43

J. 7.5 cm Pak 44. (2.95 ins. (2.95 ins./2.16 ins.) Anti-Tank Gun Model 44)

This experimental equipment was under development from 1942 until the advent of the 8 cm Smooth Bore Anti-Tank Gun during 1945. It was a coned bore barrel weapon of rather peculiar construction for this type of barrel, consisting of the chamber, then a conical smooth bore portion, followed by the rifled forward

/portion

FIG. 17. 7.5 cm. PAK 97/38. [2.95 in. ANTI-TANK GUN MODEL 97/38.]

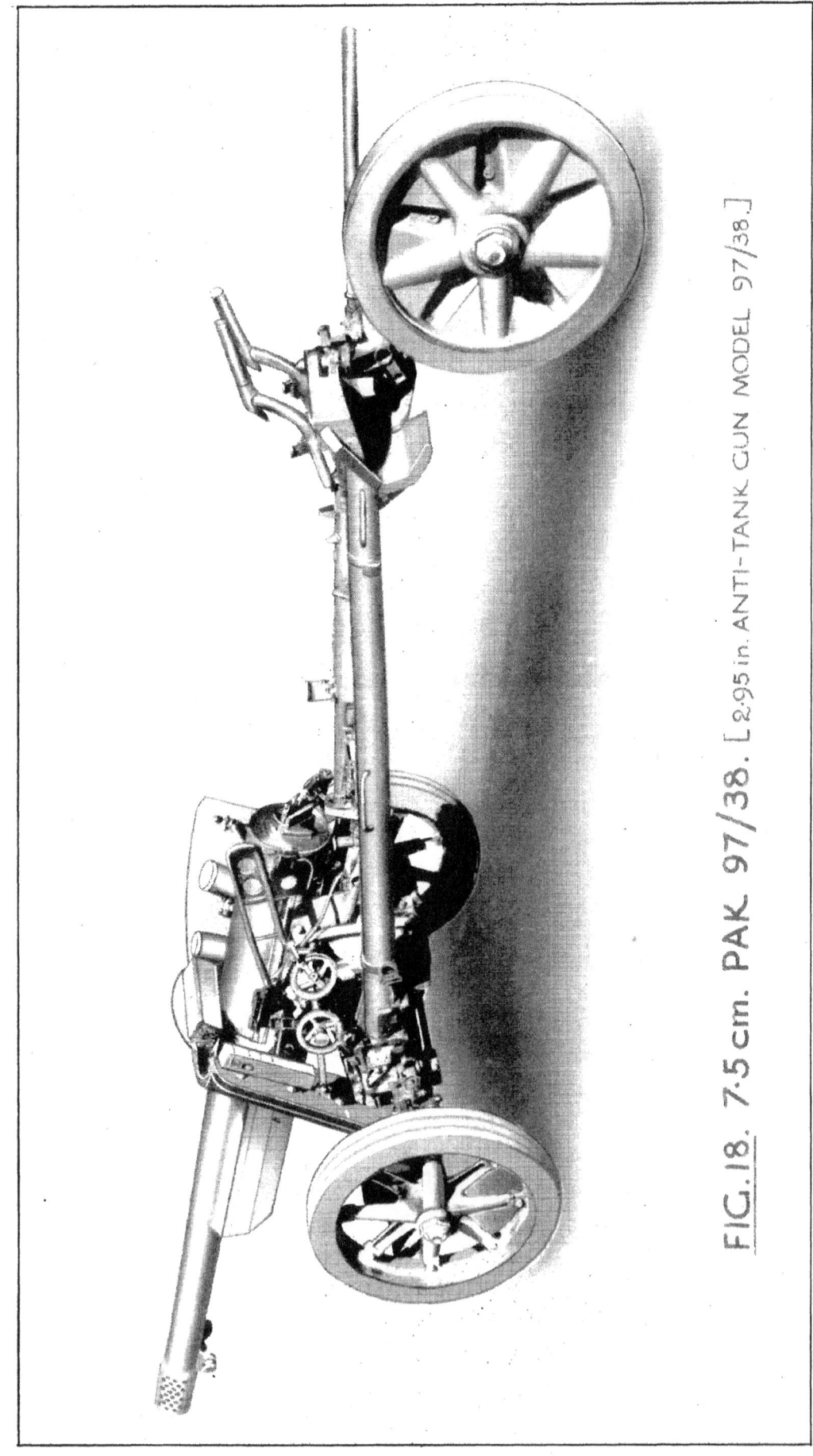

FIG. 18. 7.5 cm. PAK 97/38. [2.95 in. ANTI-TANK GUN MODEL 97/38.]

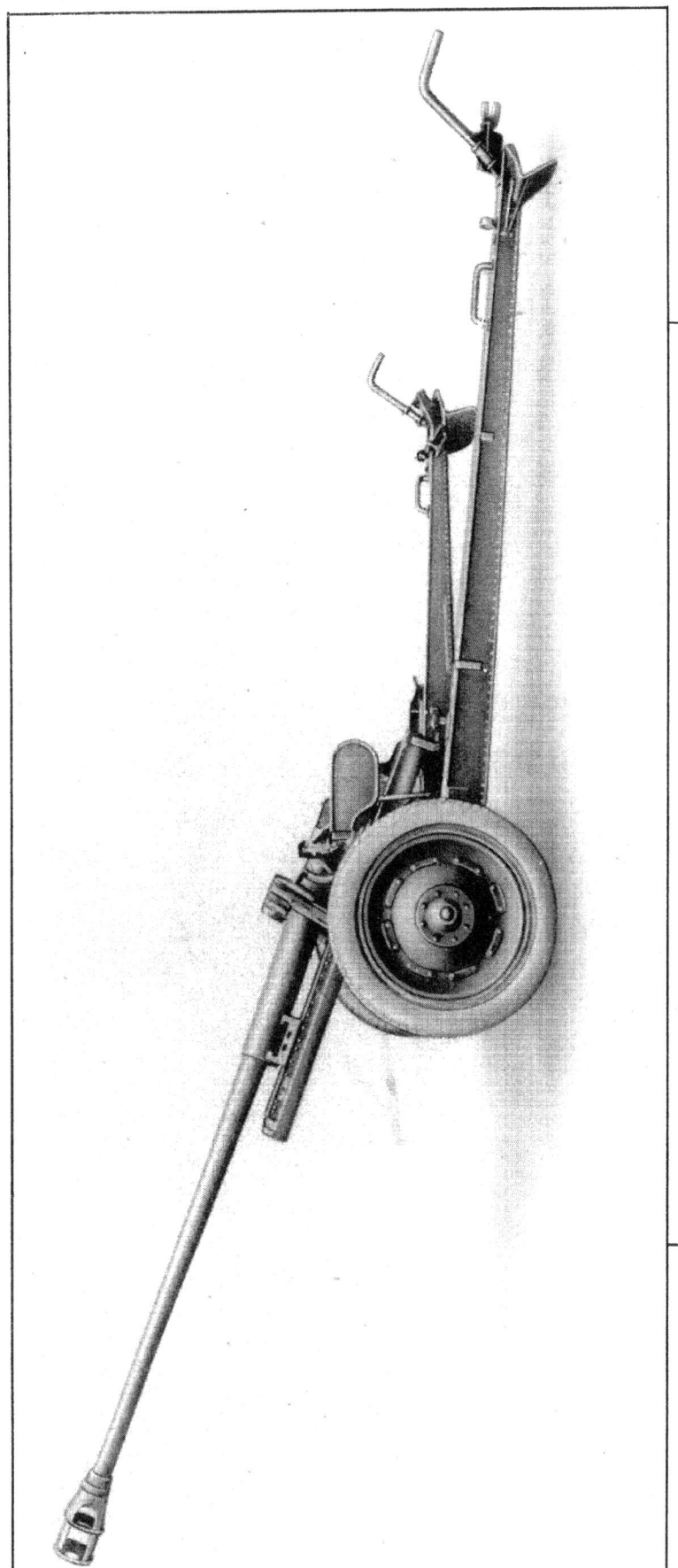

FIG.19. 7.62 PAK 36 (r) [3 in. ANTI-TANK GUN MODEL 36 (r) (RUSSIAN 7.62 cm. GUN MODEL 36 (r) MODIFIED.)]

FIG. 20. 7.62 PAK 36(r) [3 in. ANTI-TANK GUN MODEL 36(r) (RUSSIAN 7.62 cm. GUN MODEL 36(r) MODIFIED.)]

portion. The wear of the chamber and conical part was not abnormal but the wear of the rifled portion was so excessive (about 200 rounds life) that this was made detachable for easy changing. Scoring and stripping of lands occurred and various types of rifling were tried, including one at 0° to 5° increasing.

The following barrel performance, attained experimentally, was claimed by Dr. GROTSCH the designer:-

Calibre	7.5/5.5 cm	2.95 ins./2.16 ins.
Muzzle Velocity with hard core AP	1300 m/s	4265 f.s.
Penetration (Range not stated)	120 mm	4.7 inches
Charge Weight	2 Kg.	4.4 lbs
Muzzle Velocity with soft iron AP	1500 m/s	4920 f.s.
Penetration at 60° (Range not stated)	120 mm	4.7 inches
Charge Weight	2.5 Kg.	5.5 lbs
Shell Weight	2.5 Kg.	5.5 lbs
Length of piece	1070 mm	3 Ft. 6 ins.
Chamber pressure	3000 At	19.7 tons sq. ins.
Barrel life, rifled part	200 rds	

The carriage was of the split trail type, the forward ends of the trail legs being connected to the axle assembly, or supporting bracket, by longitudinal horizontal bearings. To change from the firing position to the travelling position and vice versa, the trail legs are rotated. The axes of the bearings being at an angle, rotation of the legs caused the axle-tree to be raised or lowered.

On closing the trails, the C of G of the whole gun is pushed forward over the wheel stub axles, in consequence of which the weight of the trail tow bar is reduced by about 20-30 Kg.

By raising the trails, a point is reached where the weight at the trail tow bar is in effect zero. At the same time the ground clearance is increased, permitting rotation of trail legs.

On opening the trails the adjustable tie bar connecting the trails at their forward ends must be locked with a pin thereby making the trail legs rigid with each other.

To close the trails it is only necessary to remove the pin locking the tie bar and to elevate the rear part of the cradle. A downward pull forward at the muzzle causes the trails to close of their own accord.

In explanation, it is to be noted that the trails rotate clockwise, and anti-clockwise left and right respectively. A tongue on the outside of each trail rises within a vertical groove as the trails are opened.

This system permits the ready manhandling of the equipment to an alternative site.

The gun travelled at approximately 30° elevation.

The design was said to have been commended by the O K H, Ministry of Supply, but was "too late" to make it standard design for other weapons.

K. 7.5 cm Pak 50 (2.95 inch Anti-Tank Gun Model 50) See Figs: 21 and 22.

1. This short barreled anti-tank gun consisted of a shortened version of the 7.5 cm Pak 40 barrel mounted on a slightly modified carriage of the 5 cm Pak 38. Both the muzzle brake and the breech mechanism are of somewhat different types to those used with the 7.5 cm Pak 40. Two types of muzzle brake were found, both of square box shape, one having 3 baffles and the other 5 baffles. A heavy collar is secured to the barrel directly behind the muzzle brake.

The sighting consisted of a 3 x 8° telescope for direct fire and the auxiliary sight Aushilfsrichmittel for indirect fire.

/2.

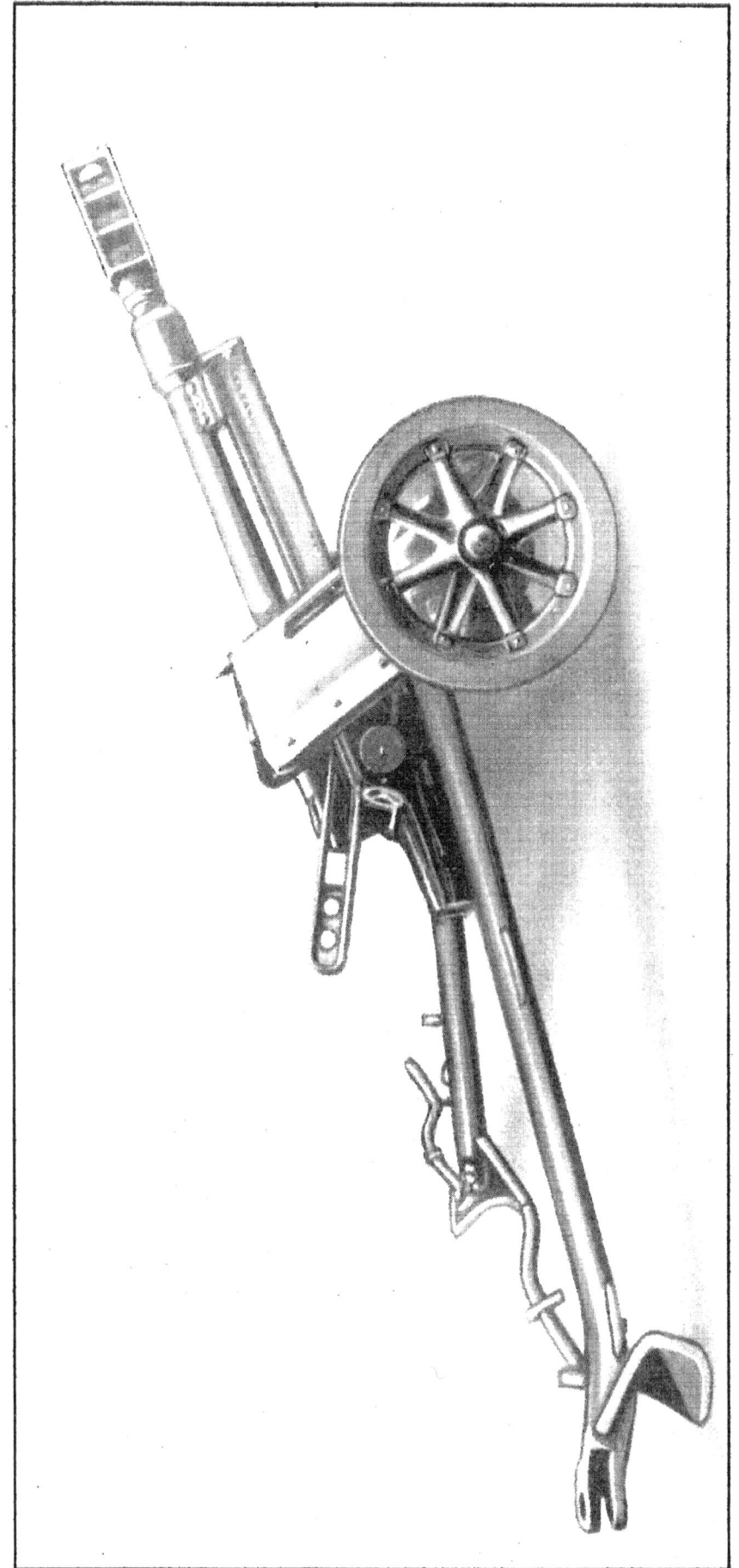

FIG. 21. 7.5 cm. PAK 50. [2.95 in. ANTI-TANK GUN MODEL 50.]

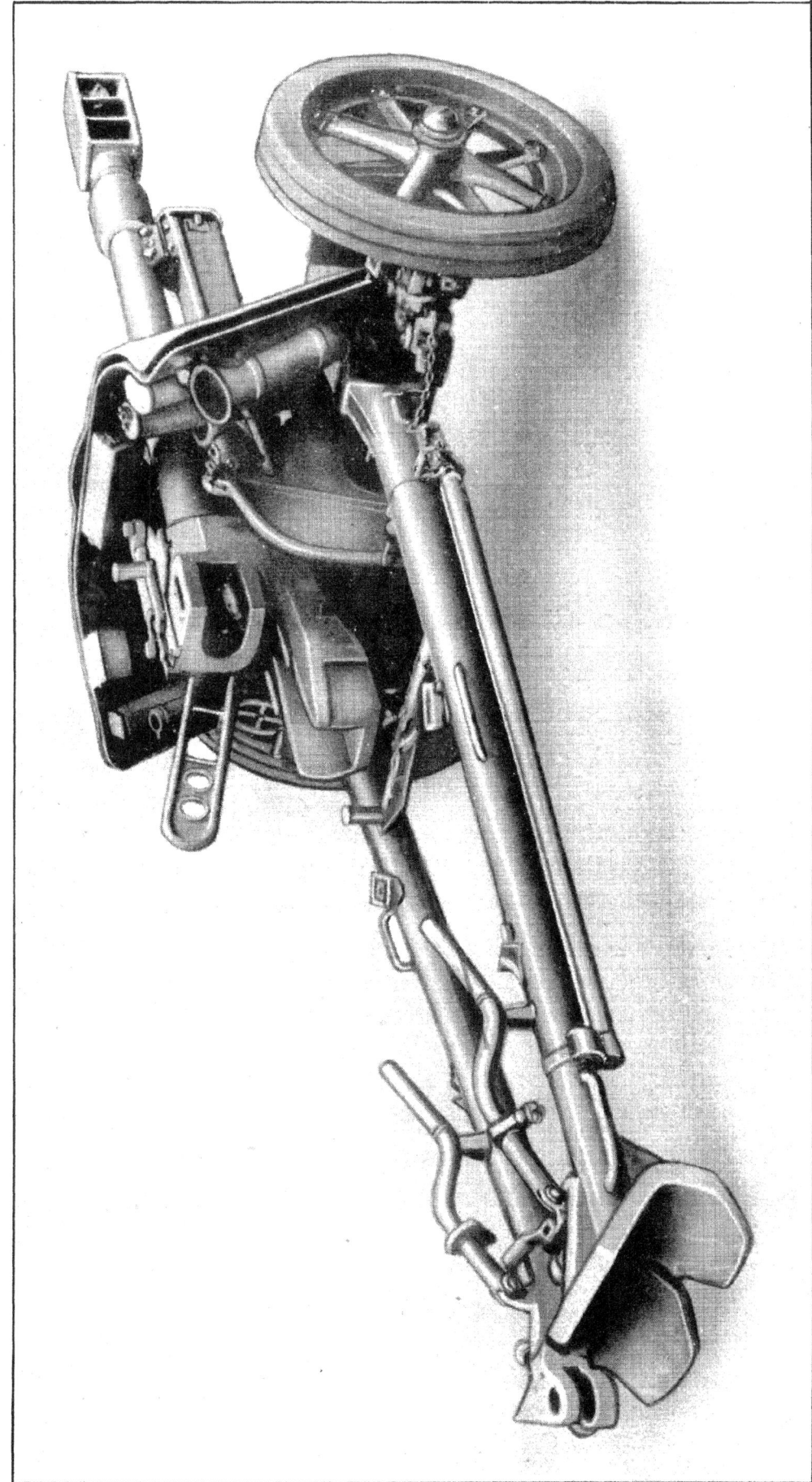

FIG. 22. 7.5 cm. PAK 50. [2.95 in. ANTI-TANK GUN MODEL 50.]

2. Data: **7.5 cm Pak 50**

Calibre	7.5 cm	2.95 ins.
Length of gun including muzzle brake	2245 mm	7 Ft. 4 3/8 ins.
Length of chamber	259 mm	10 3/16 ins.
Length of rifling	1435 mm	56 7/16 ins.
Overall length (travelling position)	4016 mm	13 Ft 2 ins.
Overall width	1855 mm	6 Ft 0 7/8 ins.
Overall height	1054 mm	3 Ft 5½ ins.
Elevation	-8° +27°	
Traverse	65°	

J. **8 cm PAW 600 or PWK 8 H 63 (3.2 inch Smooth Bore Anti-tank Gun 8 H 63)**
See Figs: 23, 24, 25 and 26.

1. This outstandingly modern equipment was intended to be a standard infantry anti-tank gun. Production of it commenced during December 1944 with a completion of 40 equipments during the first month and an additional 220 weapons during the following three months. The production target aimed at was considerably higher than the achieved output.

Two different carriages were produced both mounting the same type gun. The first carriage was extremely light, and it is believed that it was found to be too frail for the job of work it had to do. This possibly experimental carriage had several unique features, indeed the construction of the cradle and equilibrator was a complete departure from orthodox design. The equilibrator, or elevating balancing spring, consisted of a laminated iron torsion bar in a tubular housing about which the rear of the cradle pivotted as about a trunnion. The cradle is of cage construction and houses the recoil system. Another laminated iron torsion bar, housed in the axle assembly, provides the carriage suspension.

The later carriage is of more robust and orthodox construction, but it's aggregate weight is very little more than that of the first carriage.

The smooth bore barrel has a chamber the construction of which is worthy of note. There is a distinct step in the chamber, formed by the end of the barrel within an extension piece chamber. The latter appears to be shrunk on to the barrel. This type of chamber is used with a special type of ammunition having a fin stabilised mortar bomb shaped projectile with a special construction cartridge case assembly.

The cartridge case has a perforated disc fitted and crimped into its front end. This disc has a central external spigot which fits into the hollow tail unit of the projectile.

The ammunition is breech loaded. The projectile fits in the barrel, while the disc in the top of the cartridge case bears against the shoulder step in the chamber.

On firing, the propellant gases pass through the eight perforations in the disc and the projectile is forced forward in the same way as a mortar bomb, i.e. the guide band on the body of the projectile acts as the gas seal. The cartridge case and perforated disc remain unseparated in the breech.

On firing, the venturi plate delays the build up of pressure in the bore, thus making the bore pressure during shot travel appreciably more constant than in the orthodox gun. For a specified muzzle performance the maximum bore pressure is reduced, thus allowing lighter barrel construction. The high/low pressure system combined with a very efficient muzzle brake allows the use of a lighter than normal carriage in this equipment, the total weight of the 8 cm P.W.K. 8H63 is 11¾ cwt.

2. Data: **8 cm PWK 8 H 63**

(a) Calibre	8 cm	3.2 ins.
Length of Ordnance (less muzzle brake)	2951 mm	116.2 ins.

/Chamber

2. Contd.

   (a) Contd.

Chamber length	165.1 mm	6.5 ins.
Traverse		55°
Elevation		-6° +32°
Recoil normal	782 mm	31 ins.
Overall length of equipment		
Firing position	5175 mm	16 Ft 11 ins.
" height " "	1130 mm	3 Ft 8½ ins.
" width " "	3166 mm	10 Ft 3½ ins.
Weight in action	600 Kg.	11¾ cwts.

   (b) Performance

      (i) <u>Ammunition - 8 cm Hollow Charge Shell</u> (8 cm W:Hl Gr Patr 4462)

Weight of Projectile	2.7 Kg.	5.94 lbs
Muzzle Velocity	520 m/s	1704 f.s.
Penetration	140 mm	5.5 inches
Maximum Battle Range	750 metres	820 yards
Fighting Range	600 metres	660 yards
50% zone at 820 yds	1 metre x 1 metre	1.09 yds x 1.09 yds

      (ii) <u>Ammunition - 8 cm HE Shell</u> (8 cm W.Gr Patr 5071)

Weight of Projectile	4.46 Kg.	9.59 lbs
Muzzle Velocity - Low Charge	220 m/s	720 f.s.
Maximum Range - Low Charge	3400 metres	3720 yds
Muzzle Velocity - Medium Charge	320 m/s	1050 f.s.
Maximum Range - Medium Charge	5600 metres	6124 yds
Muzzle Velocity - Super Charge	420 m/s	1380 f.s.
Maximum Range - Super Charge	6200 metres	6780 yds
Nose Percussion Fuze	AZ 5075 St	

M.   <u>8.8 cm Pak Weapons</u> (3.46 inch Anti-Tank Artillery)

In 1940, the firms of Rheinmetall Borsig and Krupp had been ordered to develop an anti-aircraft gun, of 8.8 cm calibre, capable of ground as well as high angle employment to supercede the standard 8.8 cm Flak 36. The Rheinmetall gun was completed first and accepted for production as the 8.8 cm Flak 41. It was then decided that the Krupp version should continue to be developed as an anti-tank gun as well as for mounting in tanks. It appeared in service as an anti-tank gun in 1943. The standard field carriage was of the cruciform platform type and was transported on two single axle limbers or transporters similar to the normal AA mounting. This had all round traverse and was designed:-

1.   <u>8.8 cm Pak 43</u> (3.46 inch Anti-Tank Gun Model 43) See Figs: 27, 28 and 29.

   This equipment is an exceptionally good weapon, has a very low silhouette and extremely efficient traversing gear incorporating a pedal operated release to give free traverse.

   Swing over jack pads at the extremities of the side members of the cruciform platform enabled the weapon to be brought into action very rapidly without lowering the platform and taking the transporter limbers from the equipment. The gun was fired by electric firing operated by the layer at the elevating handwheel. The firing circuit embodied both elevation and traverse circuit breaking switches which prevented the gun from being fired if it was at an elevation above 28 degrees and at the same time had the breech of the gun over a leg of the cruciform platform.

   The semi-automatic gear is very efficient and positive and this weapon was one of the very few German equipments which employed a vertical sliding block.

/An

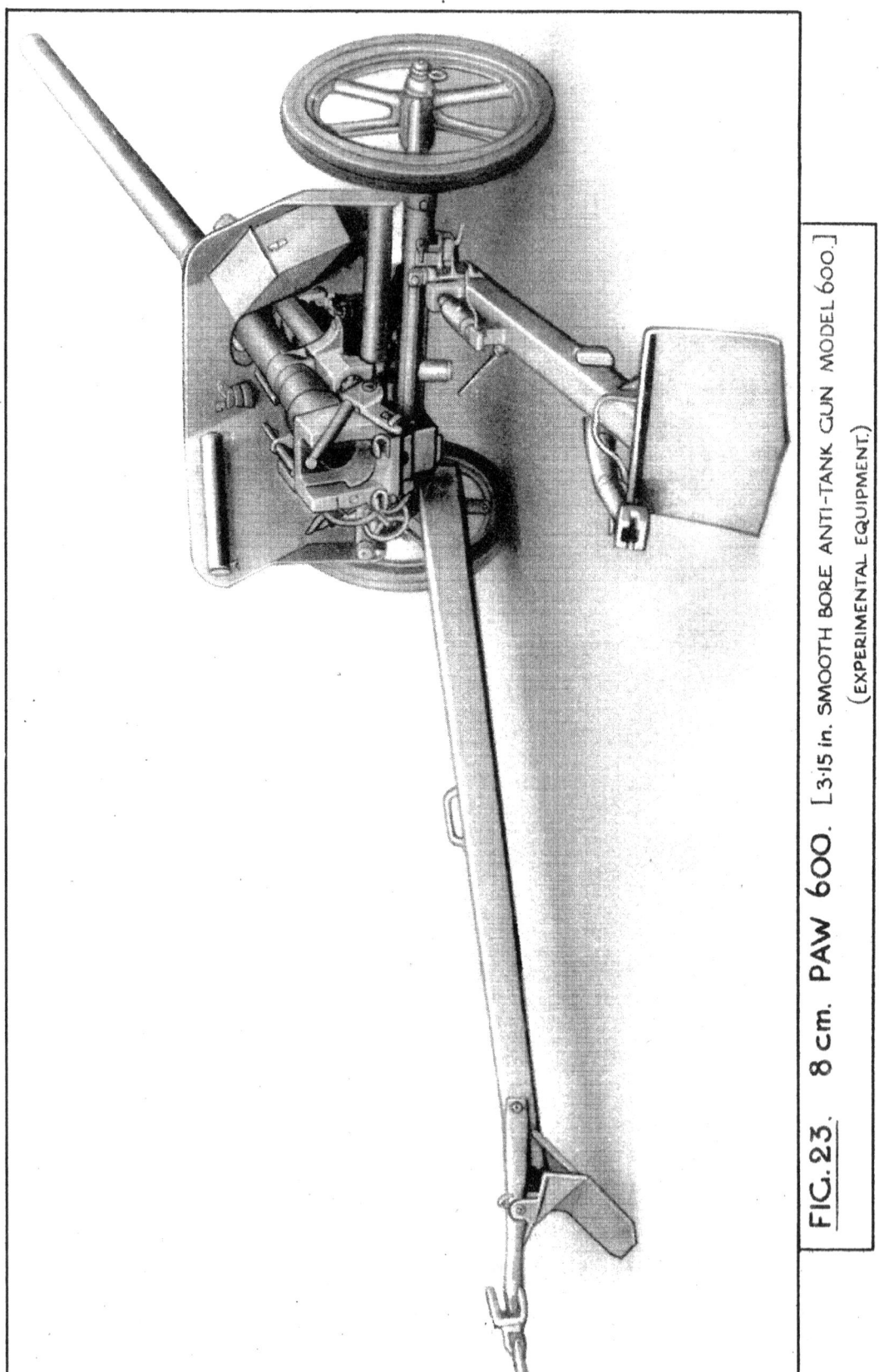

FIG. 23. 8 cm. PAW 600. [3·15 in. SMOOTH BORE ANTI-TANK GUN MODEL 600.] (EXPERIMENTAL EQUIPMENT.)

FIG. 24. 8 cm. PAW 600. [3.15 in. SMOOTH BORE ANTI-TANK GUN MODEL 600.] (EXPERIMENTAL EQUIPMENT.)

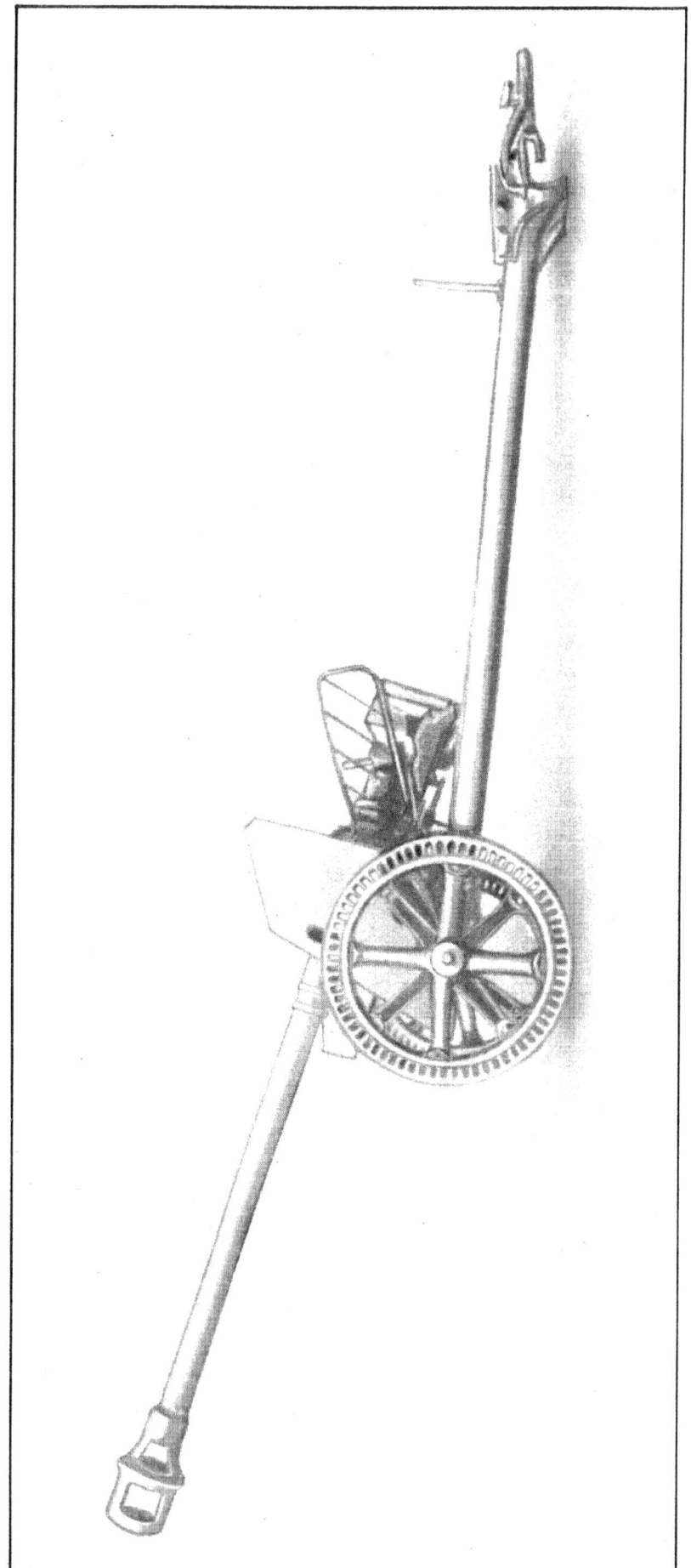

FIG.25. 8cm. PWK. 8.H.63. [3·15 SMOOTH BORE ANTI-TANK GUN MODEL 8.H.63.] (DEVELOPED FROM 8cm. PAW. 600.)

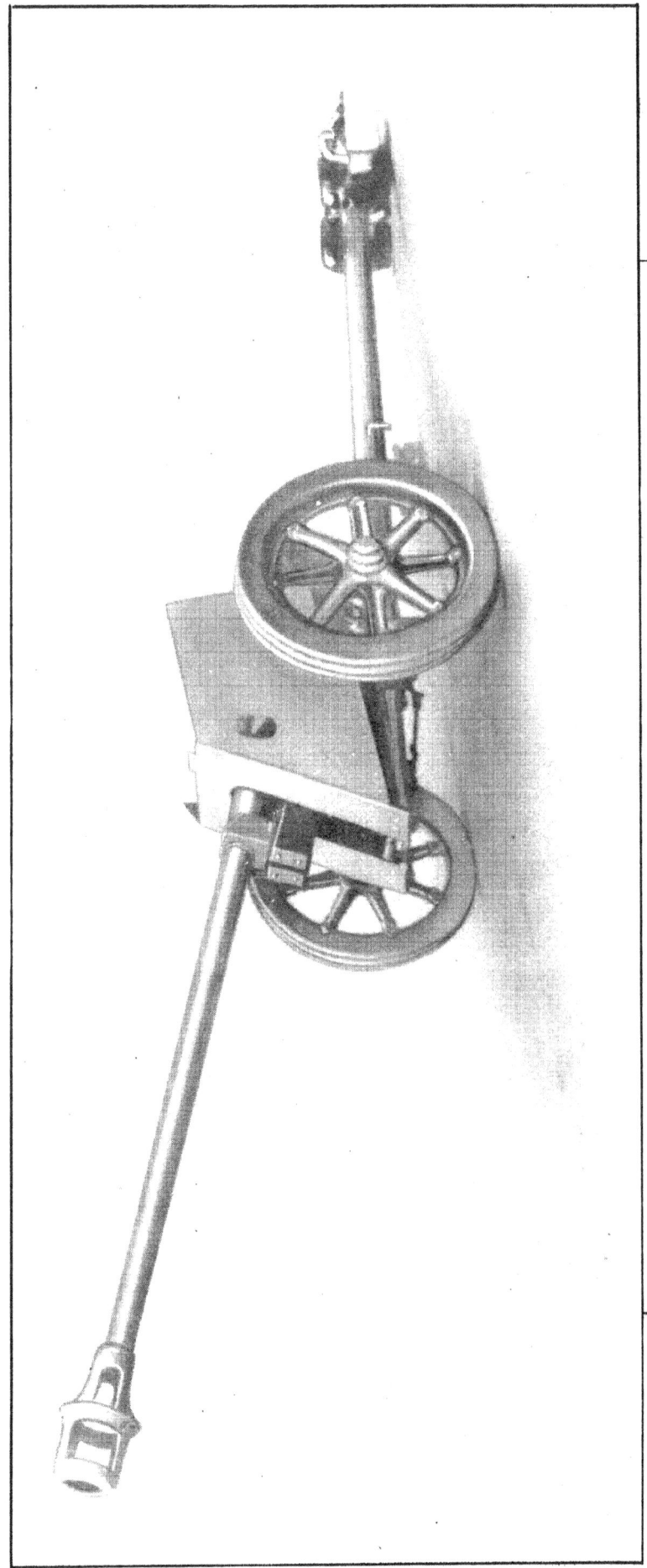

FIG. 26. 8 cm. PWK. 8.H.63. [3·15 SMOOTH BORE ANTI-TANK GUN MODEL 8.H.63.] (DEVELOPED FROM 8 cm. PAW. 600.)

An ingenious bracket on the saddle operates the graduated control of the recoil by a push-pull action.

The barrel is of the two section type and recoils through a sleeve type cradle.

In action the top of the well sloped shield is about 5 ft 8 ins from the ground.

2. Data: 8.8 cm Pak 43

(a)
Calibre	3.46 ins. (88 mm)
Length of ordnance (incl muzzle brake)	260.23 ins. (6610 mm)
Rifling: Uniform r.h. twist	
" length	201.75 ins. (5125 mm)
No. of grooves	32
Chamber length	33.88 ins. (859 mm)
Chamber capacity	549 cu.ins. (9000 c.c.)
Traverse	360°
Elevation	-8° to + 40°
Recoil normal	29.5 ins (750 mm)
" Max	47.25 ins. (1200 mm)
Overall length of equipment	30 Ft. 2 ins. (9200 mm)
" height " "	6 Ft 9 ins. (2050 mm)
" width " "	7 Ft 2½ ins. (2200 mm)
Wt of equipment complete	11,025 lbs (5000 Kg.)

(b) Ammunition

Nomenclature	M.V.	Wt of proj.
8.8 cm Sprgr Patr KwK 43	2298 f/s (700 m.s.)	20 lb 5½ ozs (9.4 Kg.)
8.8 cm Sprgr Patr 43 KwK 43	2460 f/s (750 m.s.)	20 lb 5½ ozs (9.4 Kg.)
8.8 cm Pzgr Patr 39-1 KwK 43	3282 f/s (1000 m.s.)	22 lb 14½ ozs (10.4 Kg.)
8.8 cm Pzgr Patr 39/43 KwK 43	3282 f/s (1000 m.s.)	22 lb 9 ozs (10.16 Kg.)
8.8 cm Pzgr Patr 40/43 KwK 43	3708 f/s (1130 m.s.)	16 lb 1½ ozs (7.3 Kg.)
8.8 cm Gr Patr 39 Hl KwK 43	1968 f/s (600 m.s.)	16 lb 14 ozs (7.65 Kg.)
8.8 cm Gr Patr 39/43 Hl KwK 43	1968 f/s (600 m.s.)	16 lb 14 ozs (7.65 Kg.)

(c) Armour Penetration

Firing 8.8 cm Pzgr 39/43			⁺ Firing 8.8 cm Pzgr 40/43		
Range yds	Penetration Normal	in mm 30°	Range yds	Penetration Normal	in mm 30°
0	225	198	0	311	265
500	207	182	500	274	226
1000	190	167	1000	241	192
1500	174	153	1500	211	162
2000	159	139	2000	184	136
2500	145	127	2500	159	114

⁺ Estimated performance

3. **8.8 cm Pak 43/41.** (3.46 inch Anti-Tank Gun Model 43/41) See Figs:30 & 31.

Either, owing to the slow production of the cruciform platform of the Pak 43, or, more likely, due to the urgency of the war situation, which demanded the rapid employment of as many of the finished guns as could be put into the field, the gun was also mounted on a single axle field carriage and the equipment designated the 8.8 cm Pak 43/41.

The carriage was of the split trail type, the trail legs were similar to those of the 10.5 cm light Field Howitzer Model 18 (a standard weapon). There is no doubt but that the construction of the carriage was a stop gap emergency measure, and was a composite one made up of components from various standard equipments including the wheels used with the 15 cm medium Field Howitzer.

Compared with the low silhouette of the Pak 43, the Pak 43/41 equipment looked high and clumsy, which indeed it was.

The breech mechanism was of the normal horizontal sliding block type and used a semi-automatic gear much inferior to that of the Pak 43.

The tank and assault guns in this 8.8 cm series have approximately the same performance and fire the same ammunition as the field versions Pak 43 and 43/41. Some of the barrels are of monoblock one piece construction, others of the divided monobloc barrel type. The third model was also of divided monobloc barrel construction but the length of rifling was increased and this model formed the armament of the Tiger B Tank (KwK 43), the Elephant SP equipment (Pak 43/2) and the Jagd Panther SP weapon (Pak 43/3).

4. Data: 8.8 cm Pak 43/41

(a)
Calibre	3.46 ins. (88 mm)
Length of ordnance (incl muzzle brake)	260.23 ins. (6616 mm)
Rifling increasing r.h. twist	
" length	201.75 ins. (5125 mm)
No. of grooves	32
Chamber length	33.88 ins. (859 mm)
" capacity	549 cu.ins. (9000 c.c.)
Traverse	56°
Elevation	-5° to +38°
Recoil normal	26.77 ins. (680 mm)
" max	28.35 ins. (720 mm)
Overall length of equipment	30 Ft. 1 in. (9144 mm)
" height " "	5 Ft. 8 ins. (1981 mm)
" width " "	8 Ft. 3½ ins. (2527 mm)
Wt of equipment complete	9656 lbs (4380 Kg.)

(b) Ammunition

Nomenclature	M.V.	Wt of proj.
8.8 cm Sprgr Patr KwK 43	2298 f/s (700 m.s.)	20 lb 5½ ozs (9.4 Kg.)
8.8 cm Sprgr Patr 43 KwK 43	2460 f/s (750 m.s.)	20 lb 5½ ozs (9.4 Kg.)
8.8 cm Pzgr Patr 39-1 KwK 43	3282 f/s (1000 m.s.)	22 lb 14½ ozs (10.4 Kg.)
8.8 cm Pzgr Patr 39/43 KwK 43	3282 f/s (1000 m.s.)	22 lb 9 ozs (10.16 Kg.)
8.8 cm Pzgr Patr 40/43 KwK 43	3708 f/s (1130 m.s.)	16 lb 1½ ozs. (7.65 Kg.)

(c) Armour Penetration

Firing 8.8 cm Pzgr 39/43   * Firing 8.8 Pzgr 40/43

Range yds	Penetration Normal	in mm 30°	Range yds	Penetration Normal	in mm 30°
0	225	198	0	311	265

(c) Contd.

Range yds	Penetration Normal	in mm 30°	Range yds	Penetration Normal	in mm 30°
500	207	182	500	274	226
1000	190	167	1000	241	192
1500	174	153	1500	211	162
2000	159	139	2000	184	136
2500	145	127	2500	159	114

* Estimated performance

5. **Sights for German 8.8 cm 43 Series Atk Guns**

   (a) The following information, received from France, is extracted from an official German document dated July 1944. Sighting gears used with the two models of 8.8 cm A-Tk Gun are as follows:

Equipment	Sight
8.8 cm Pak 43 (Cruciform mounting)	(i) Zieleinrichtung 43 S Vo with telescope 3 x 8° or 3 x 8°/11. Open sights, Auxiliary sight 38 (Aushilfsrichtmittel 38)
	or
	(ii) Winkelzielfernrohr ¼ (periscope sight) Open sights. Auxiliary sight 38.
8.8 cm Pak 43/41 (Splitrail field carriage mounting)	For direct laying only (iii) Zieleinrichtung 43 SVo with telescope 3 x 8° or 3 x 8°/11. Open sights.
	and
	For direct or indirect laying
	(iv) Zieleinrichtung 34 with panoramic sight 32 or 36. (Rbl 32 or 36).

   (b) **Zieleinrichtung 43 S Vo (for 8.8 cm Pak 43)**

   This sight has four range scales graduated as follows:-

   Pzgr 39/43 - APHE.   0-4000 m. Red figures.   In 200 m. intervals
   Pzgr 40/43 - AP40   0-2400 m. Green figures   "   "   "
   Sprgr 43   - HE   0-3500 m. Black figures   "   100 m "
   Gr 39 Hl   - H C   0-2500 m. Yellow figures "   "   "

   The HE Scale is graduated for the later type ammunition (M.V.750 m.s.)

   If the old type ammunition (M.V.700) is used, range settings will be adjusted in the following manner :-

Range	Add to range setting
0-1000 m	Nil
1000-2000 m	100 m
2000-3000 m	200 m
3000-4000 m	300 m
4000-5000 m	400 m

(c) <u>Zieleinrichtung 43 S Vo</u> (for 8.8 Pa 43/41)

There are several differences between range scale graduation on this sight, of which two models are in service, and those on the Z.E. 43 S Vo as used with the 8.8 cm Pak 43.

(i) <u>Old type with two scales</u>

Pzgr 39 - APCBC   0-4000 m.   Black figures   in 200 m intervals

Pzgr 40 - AP40   0-4000 m.   Red figures   "   "   "

(ii) <u>New type with four scales</u>

Pzgr 39 - APCBC   0-4000 m.   Red figures   in 200 m intervals

Pzgr 40 - AP40   0-4000 m.   Green figures   "   "   "

Sprgr   - HE   0-3400 m.   Black figures   " 100 m   "

Gr 39Hl - H C   0-2500 m.   Yellow figures "   "   "

The range graduations are for ammunition with M.V. + 750 m.s. When using ammunition with M.V. 700 m.s., the same adjustment to range setting will be made as described above.

(d) <u>Telescopes 3 x 8° and 3 x 8°/11</u>

Both telescopes have a field of view of 8° and magnification 3.

The chief difference between them is in the design of the graticules. The 3 x 8° telescope has a central conical graticule with one smaller graduation on either side. The distance from the point of the central graticule to the small graticules is equal to ± 10 mils aim off.

The 3 x 8°/11 telescope has a central conical graticule with three smaller conical graduations on either side. In between each of the smaller graticules is a vertical mark. From conical to vertical graticule, aim off is equal to ± 4 mils. Maximum aim off is ± 24 mils.

(e) <u>Winkelzielfernrohr 1/4</u>

This sight consists of a range drum and a 7 x 10° telescope.

Range scales for AP, HE, AP40 and Hollow charge ammunition are as on ZE 43 S Vo except that all graduations are in 100 m intervals. The same adjustment to range settings will be made as on ZE 43 S Vo when firing old type ammunition (M.V. 700 m.s.)

The graticule of the 7 x 10° telescope is of similar design to that of the 3 x 8°/11 telescope.

(f) <u>Zieleinrichtung 34 and dial sight</u>

The range scales on this sight are graduated for ammunition with M.V. 700 m.s.

Graduations are as follows:-

(i) in mils from 0-800 (45°)

(ii) in metres for HE from 0-5500 in 200 m intervals up to 2000 m. then in intervals of 100 m. in metric for H C from 0-3000 in 100 m intervals.

(g) <u>Aushilfsrichtmittel 38</u>

This sight may be used for indirect fire with HE up to 15500 m. (M.V., 750 m.) or 14500 m (M.V. 700 m.s.)

6. Ammunition for the 8.8 cm Kw K 43, Stu K 43, Stu K 43/1 Pak 43 and Pak 43/41

The ammunition is QF fixed.

(a) H.E.

(i) 8.8 cm Sprgr Patr KwK 43

(ii) 8.8 cm Sprgr Patr 43 KwK 43

Weight of projectile	9.40 Kg (20.5 lbs)
Nose fuze percussion	A.Z.23/28 v.
T and P	Dopp Z.s/60 Fl
Propellant charge	3.4 Kg. Gu R.P.-GO-$\left(\frac{700.8/6}{650}\right)$

+ igniter = 100 gm. Ngl.Bl.P.-12,5 - (4.4.1)
+ flash reducer = 10 gm potassium sulphate.

(b) APCBC

(i) 8.8 cm Pzgr Patr 39/1 KwK 43

(ii) 8.8 cm Pzgr Patr 39/43 KwK 43

Weight of projectile	10.20 Kg. (22.4 lbs)
Base fuze	Bd Z 5127
Propellant charge	6.8 Kg.Gu R.P.-G1,5$\left(\frac{725\ 5,\frac{1}{2}}{650}\right)$

+ igniter - 100 gm Ngl.Bl.P - 12,5 - (4.4.1)

(c) Hollow Charge

(i) 8.8 cm Gr Patr 39 Hl KwK 43

(ii) 8.8 cm Gr Patr 39/43 Hl KwK 43

Weight of projectile	7.65 Kg. (16.8 lbs)
Nose percussion fuze	A.Z. 38
Propellant	1.7 Kg. Gu R.P. - GO -$\left(\frac{700.7/6}{650}\right)$

+ igniter = 100 gm Ngl.Bl.P. - 12,5 - (4.4.1)
+ flash reducer = 7 gm potassium sulphate

(d) AP 40

(i) 8.8 cm Pzgr Patr 40/43 KwK 43

Weight of projectile 7.30 Kg. (16 lbs)

Note: Projectiles listed under (i) appear to be similar to those used in the 8.8 cm Flak 41. Those listed under (ii) have been specially designed for the above equipments.

It appears that those projectiles listed under (i) are not suitable for firing from worn guns. The Germans have issued a warning that they are not to be used in guns that have fired more than 500 rounds.

An electric primer, C/22 is fitted to the cartridge case.

N. 12.8 cm Pak Artillery Development (5 inch Anti-tank Gun Development)

The final stage of development of anti-tank armament which came into operational use, was reached with the introduction into service in the latter stages of the war of the 12.8 cm tank and assault gun. This gun was known variously as the Pjk 44, Pak 44 and finally as Pak 80.

/At

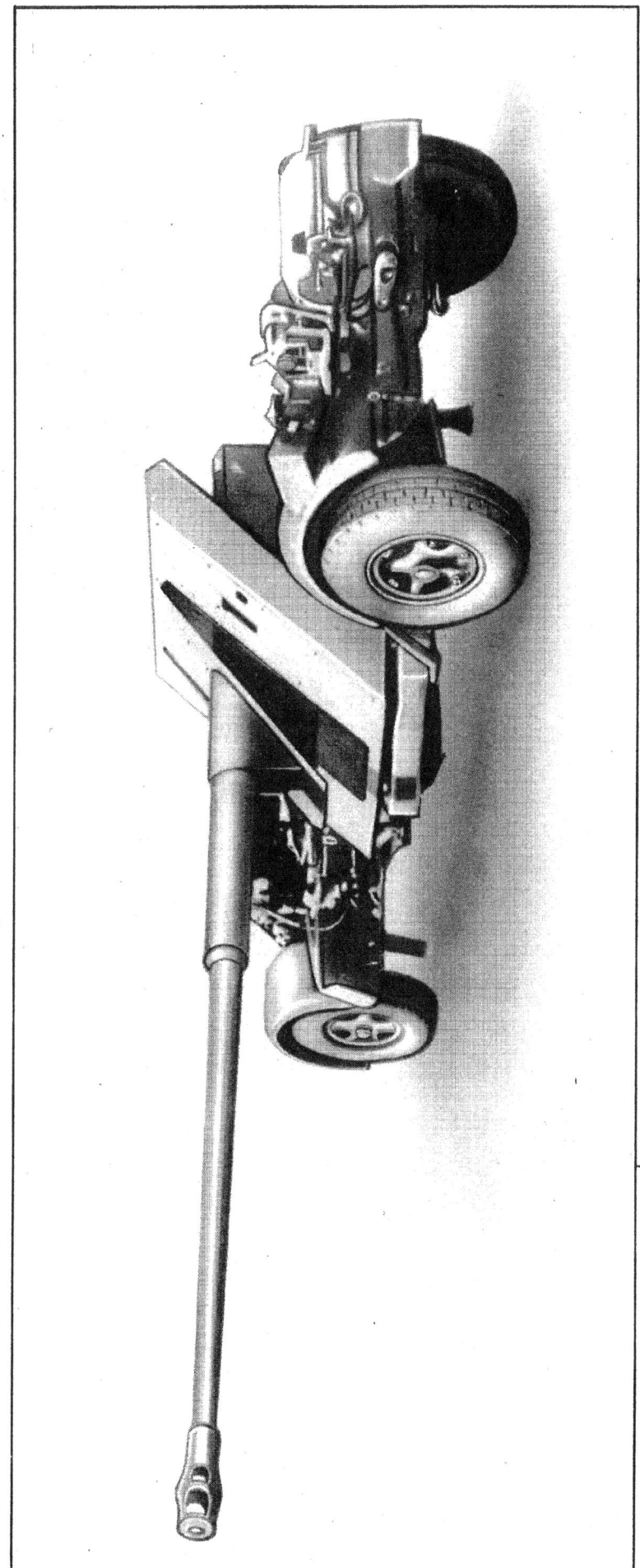

FIG. 27. 8·8 cm. PAK 43. [3·46 in. ANTI-TANK GUN MODEL 43.]

FIG. 28. 8·8 cm. PAK 43. [3·46 in. ANTI-TANK GUN MODEL 43.]

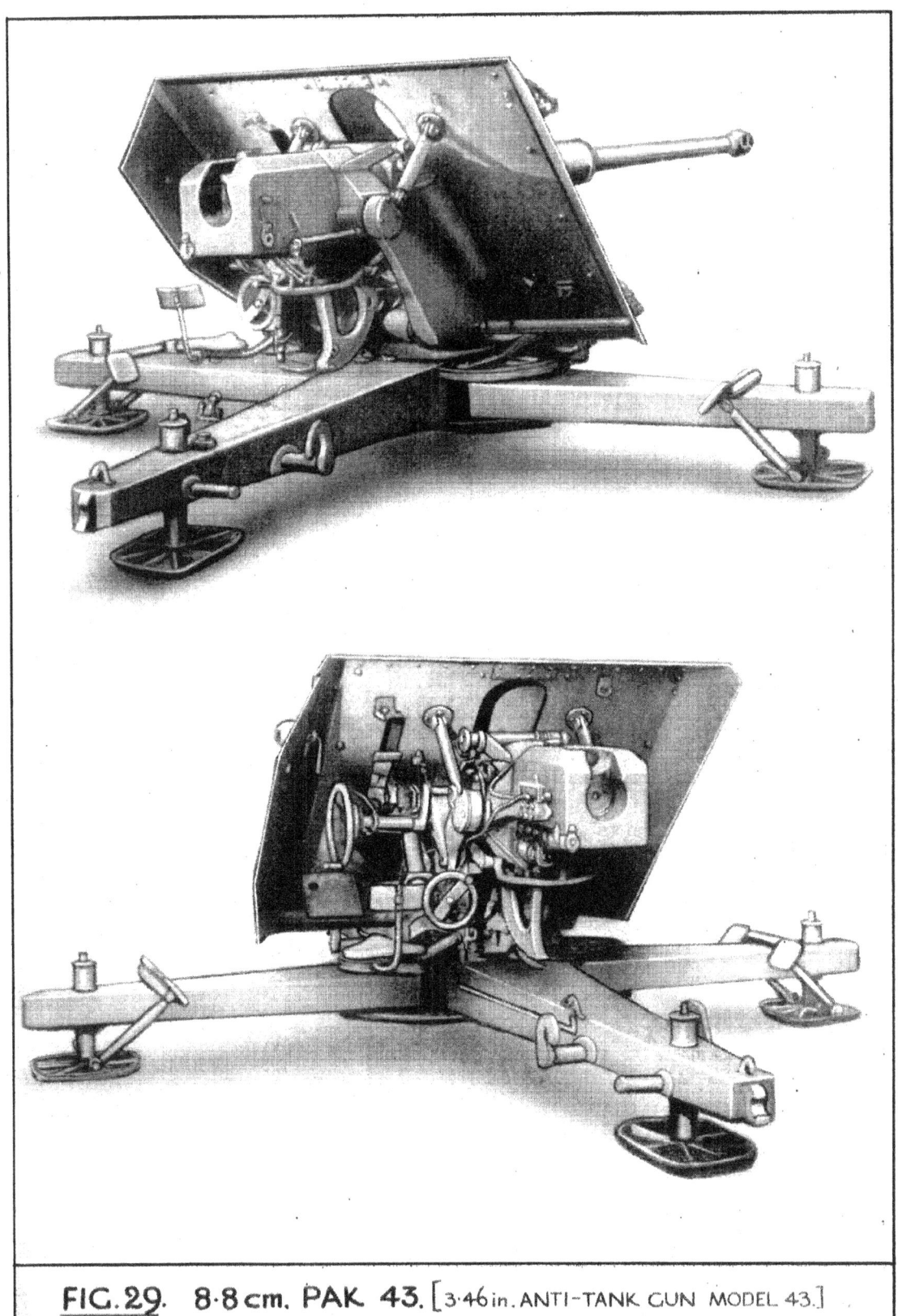

FIG. 29. 8·8 cm. PAK 43. [3·46 in. ANTI-TANK GUN MODEL 43.]

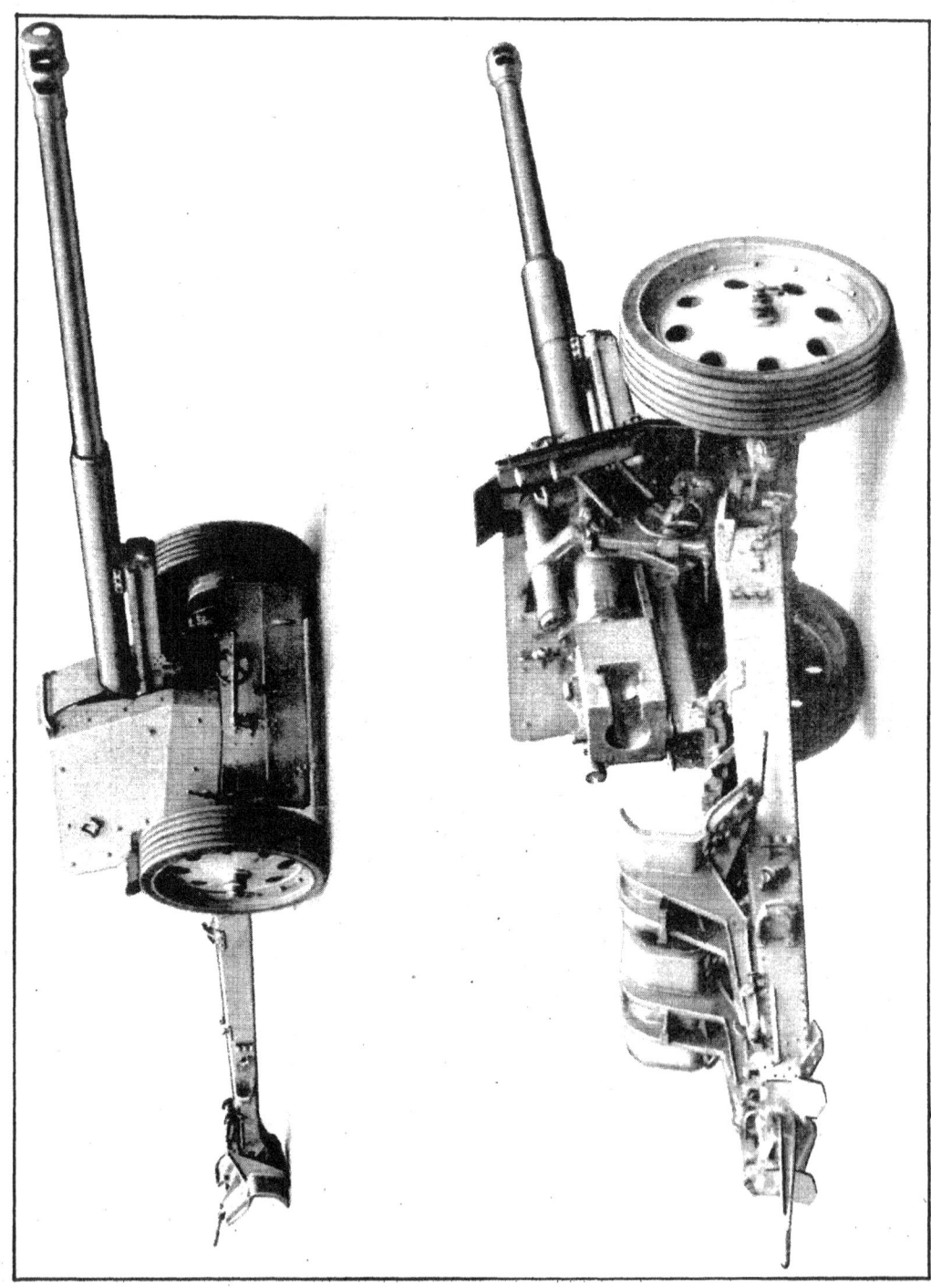

FIG. 30. 8·8 cm. PAK 43/41 [3·46 in. ANTI-TANK GUN MODEL 43.]

FIG. 31. 8·8 cm. PAK 43/41 [3·46 in. ANTI-TANK GUN MODEL 43]

N. Contd.

At one stage of development, in order to gain experience in the field, the gun was mounted on improvised carriages using the carriages of captured foreign equipments. These carriages were the French 155 mm GPF-T and the Russian 152 mm Gun Hotitzer Model 37, the hybrid equipments being known as the 12.8 cm K 81/1 and K 81/2 respectively; 51 of the latter type were issued to the troops. (See Figs:- 32 and 33).

As a result of the satisfactory performance of the 8.8 cm Pak 43 in action it was decided that the 12.8 cm gun should be mounted on a cruciform platform with front and rear travelling bogies or axle assemblies.

Both Krupp and Rheinmetall prototypes were produced and the final decision of the Ordnance Directorate is not recorded. The first Krupp prototype restricted maximum elevation and appears to have considered almost exclusively the Anti-Tank role. The later model allowed elevation from -5° to +45° and therefore could be classified as a dual purpose Field/Anti-Tank weapon.

The 12.8 cm gun on the cruciform carriage was known as the 12.8 cm K 43, 12.8 cm K 44, and 12.8 cm K 81 at various stages of development, the nomenclature is extremely confusing in the various documents recovered from the files of the designers and the official German ordnance publication.

1. <u>12.8 cm Pak K 44 Krupp Model (5 inch Anti-Tank Gun 44 Krupp Model) See Fig: 34.</u>

This equipment has the clean cut outline and low construction of a very business like weapon, dual purpose field and anti-tank.

The barrel is of monobloc construction with a breech and electric firing mechanism of simple design.

The carriage body is quite low and has rear trunnions. It has four rollers in its underface to assist in traversing the superstructure.

The shield sweeps back at a large angle to the vertical.

An interesting new feature is the use of vertical spades on the cruciform platform to assist in preventing ground recoil.

The wheels are raised clear of the ground when in the firing position, the axle assemblies being moved vertically by pinion gear and twin arc racks operated by winch crank type handles.

2. <u>12.8 cm Pak K 44 Rheinmetall Model (5 inch Anti-Tank Gun 44 Rheinmetall Model) See Fig: 35.</u>

This equipment has several very interesting features which differ from those of the 12.8 cm Pak K 44 Krupp Model.

The most striking feature is the employment of a four wheeled bogie assembly fitted to the carriage body which acts as the rear transporter. This is retained in action in a raised position, and, traversing with the superstructure, adds front weight and therefore stability to the equipment when in action.

A portion of the rear member of the platform is folded up for travelling.

The equipment is very low in action.

The mobility and speed into action of this equipment does not appear to be so good as the Krupp equipment.

The ball race which is interposed between the platform and superstructure of this equipment to facilitate traversing is much superior to the short pivot and four rollers with roller pathway of the Krupp Model. Pronounced indentations on the roller pathway indicated roller hammering during travel. This appeared to be the principle weakness of the Krupp model, plus signs of

2. Contd.

rushed design in the axle assembly shifting gear. Elimination of these two faults would have increased the superiority of the Krupp model over that of the Rheinmetall Borsig effort; indeed, it would have made the Krupp weapon almost their most outstanding weapon of the war.

The carriage springing of both models was of the torsion bar type, that of the Krupp model being more efficient.

There are slight dimensional and weight differences between the Krupp and Rheinmetall models and a data sheet for the Krupp model only is shown.

3. <u>Data: 12.8 cm Pak K 44 Krupp Model</u>

		Metric	British
(a)	Calibre	12.8 cm	5.047 ins.
	Length of barrel	6623 mm	260.7 ins.
	Rifling - System PPS increasing right hand twist 1 in 27 to 1 in 24.76		
	Length of rifling	5538 mm	217.95 ins.
	Grooves - number		40
	depth	1.52 mm	.06 ins.
	width	6.4 mm	.25 ins.
	Lands - width	3.8 mm	.15 ins.
	Maximum Traverse		360°
	Rates of Traverse, 1 turn of handwheel. High =		1° 36'
	Low =		48'
	Maximum Elevation		45° 27'
	Rates of Elevation. 1 Turn of Handwheel. High =		1° 07'
	Low =		20'
	Maximum Depression		7° 51'
	Maximum recoil	1300 mm	51.5 ins.
	Minimum recoil	700 mm	27.5 ins.
	Firing position - Length overall	10,900 mm	35'9"
	Height overall	1830 mm	6'0"
	Width overall	6125 mm	20' 1"
	Travelling Position - Length overall	10,900 mm	35' 9"
	Height overall	2160 mm	7' 1"
	Width overall	2480 mm	8' 1½"
	Weight - Gun complete	3353 Kg.	3.3 tons
	Gun and carriage complete	10,160 Kg.	10 tons

(b) <u>Ammunition</u> (Separate Loading)

			M.V.	Range
(i)	H.E.	12.8 cm Sprgr L/4.5 Projectile Wt 26.3 Kg. (57.3 lbs)	920 m/s (3018 f.s.)	21,000 metres (23,000 yards)
(ii)	H.E.	12.8 cm Sprgr L/5 Projectile Wt 28 Kg. (61.7 lbs)	920 m/s (3018 f.s.)	24,400 metres (26,700 yards)
(iii)	APCBC/HE	12.8 cm Pzgr 43 Projectile Wt 28.3 Kg. (62.4 lbs)	920 m/s (3018 f.s.)	Penetration 202 mm/1000m/30° (8 ins./1094 yds/30°)

This penetration fulfilled the specification for armour penetration laid down by the German General Staff in 1944, which was that the minimum penetration to be attained in the future anti-tank equipments was 200 mm at 1000 metres at 30°.

FIG. 32. 12·8 cm. K 81/1.
[5·05 in. ANTI-TANK GUN MODEL 80 on FRENCH 155 mm. GPF-T CARRIAGE.]

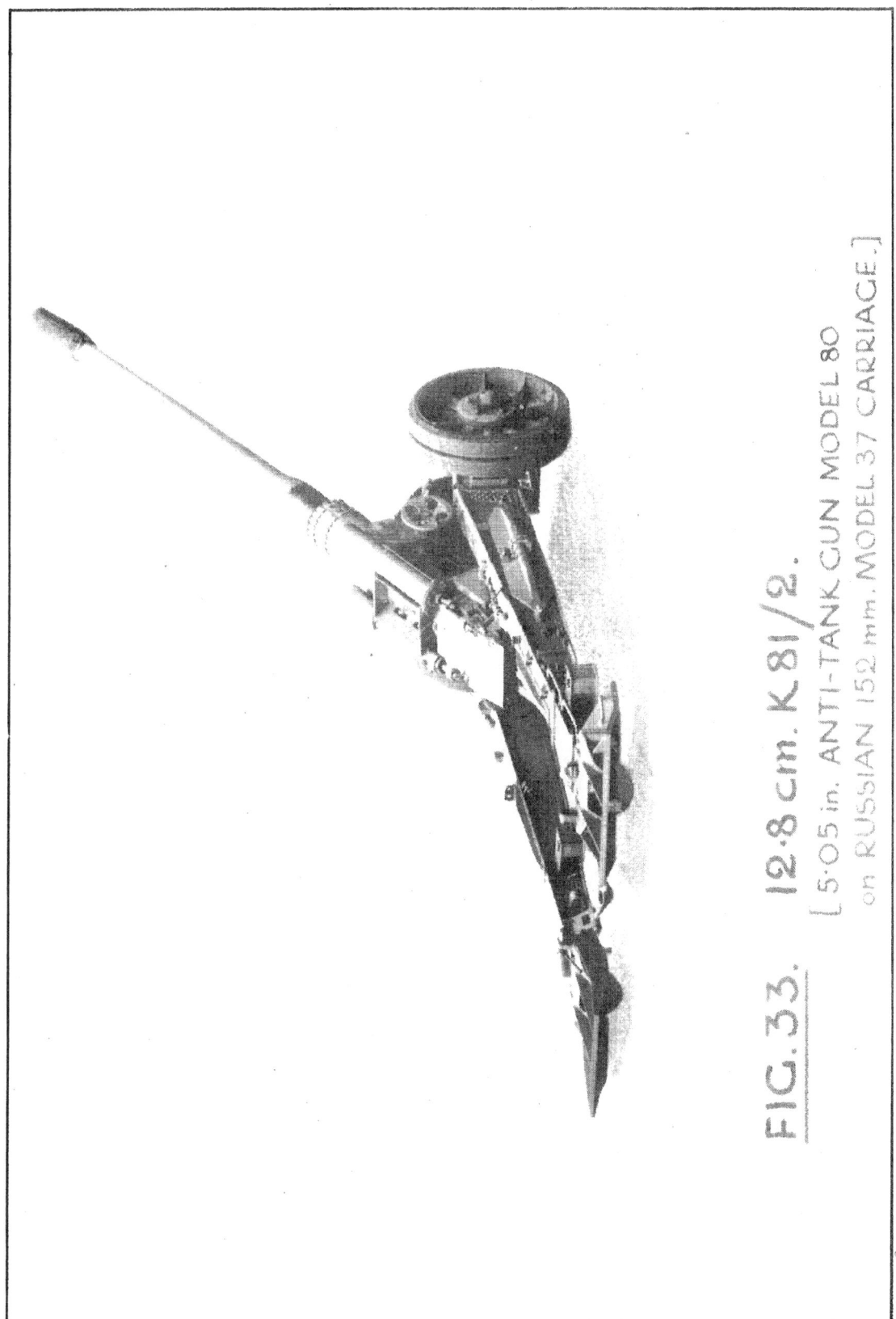

FIG. 33. 12·8 cm. K 81/2.
[5·05 in. ANTI-TANK GUN MODEL 80 on RUSSIAN 152 mm. MODEL 37 CARRIAGE.]

FIG. 34. 12cm. PAK. K44. – KRUPP MODEL –
(5·04-in. ANTI-TANK GUN MODEL K44 KRUPP MODEL.)

FIG. 35. 12·8 cm. PAK. K 44. — RHEINMETALL MODEL —
(5·04 in. ANTI-TANK GUN MODEL K 44, RHEINMETALL MODEL)

CHAPTER III

THE DEVELOPMENT OF GERMAN INFANTRY GUNS

A. General

The year 1927 saw the commencement of the development of the modern German infantry gun, and it is interesting to note that, about this same period, the other major powers were turning their attentions to weapons of this type also. Previously it had been the policy of the major powers to link the mortar weapon with the infantry and to keep the artillery weapon proper something apart, to be handled solely by the artillery arm of the service. It was considered that modern conditions demanded that the infantry should have light rapid firing guns with a calibre about 3 inches.

The first modern German Infantry gun was the 7.5 cm le I.G. 18 (2.95 inch Light Infantry Gun Model 18) developed by Rhinemetall and introduced in 1927. This weapon was of rather novel design, the barrel being totally enclosed in a square slipper and having a fixed breech block. To load the weapon, the rear end of the barrel was canted up clear of the breech block by the operation of a lever.

In 1944, a demand arose for an infantry weapon with an increased performance and robustness. As an emergency, a new barrel was developed fitted with a muzzle brake and mounted on the light modified carriage of the then obsolete 3.7 cm Pak 36. The equipment was first known as the 3.7 cm Pak 37, but later became known as the 3.7 cm le I.G. 37.

Later in the year, it was decided that a lighter carriage than that used with the I.G. 37 was required; therefore a much lighter tubular split trail carriage was produced, on which was mounted the gun barrel of the I.G. 37. This equipment became known as the 7.5 cm I.G. 42.

A smooth bore equipment marked I.G. 42 was captured at the end of the war, the carriage of which was much wider than the standard rifled I.G. 42 weapon.

Parallel with the development of the 7.5 cm I.G. 18 equipment in 1927, Rhinemetall produced the 15 cm I.G. 33, which became the standard close support howitzer weapon used by the Infantry Gun Companies during World War II.

B. 7.5 cm le I.G.18 (2.95 inch Light Infantry Gun Model 18). See Figs: 36, 37 and 38.

This weapon was developed by Rheinmetall Borsig in 1927. This gun possesses the unusual feature that the barrel is wholly enclosed in a slipper with a top cover plate, thus appearing to be square. At the rear end of the slipper is a solid block containing the percussion firing mechanism. Operation of the Lever, Breech Mechanism, causes the rear end of the barrel to rise clear of the breech block to permit loading. The gun is mounted on a light box trail carriage and is fitted with spoked artillery wheels or disc wheels and pneumatic tyres. The equipment is suitable for horse drawn or motorised transport. The recoil mechanism comprises hydraulic buffer and hydro-pneumatic recuperator housed in the cradle below the barrel. The total weight in action is some 800 lbs and the maximum range about 3550 metres using a standard high explosive projectile weighing 5.45 Kg.

/C.

FIG. 36. 7.5 cm. le. I.C. 18.
(2·95 in LIGHT INFANTRY GUN MODEL 18.)

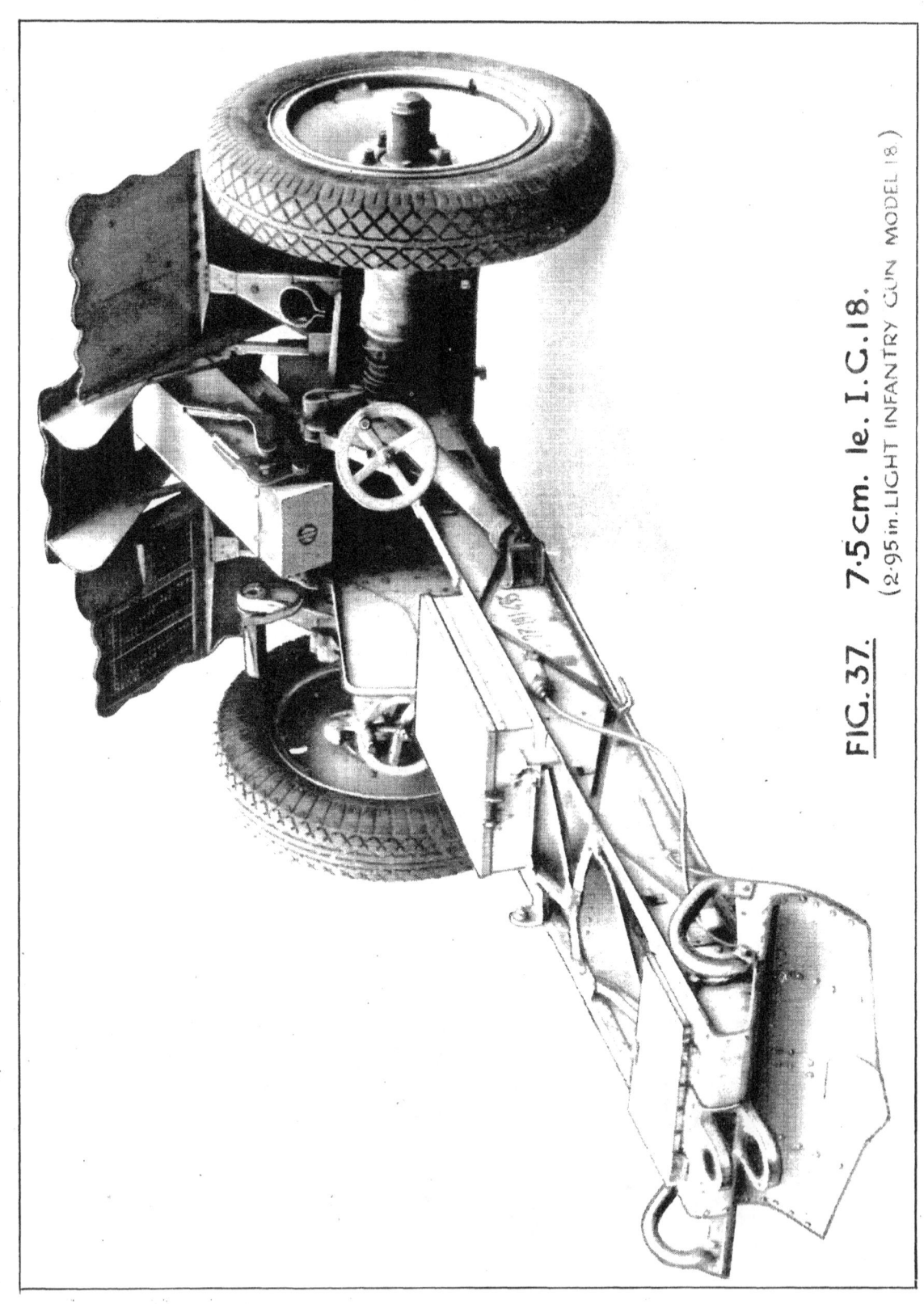

FIG. 37. 7.5 cm. le. I.G.18.
(2·95 in. LIGHT INFANTRY GUN MODEL 18.)

FIG. 38. 7.5 cm. le. I.G. 18.
(2·95 in LIGHT INFANTRY GUN MODEL 18.)

C. **7.5 cm le Geb: I G.18 (2.95 inch Light Mountain Infantry Gun Model 18)**
See Fig: 39.

1. A companion piece designed by Rheinmetall Borsig was introduced into the service for mountain troops in 1937 as the 7.5 cm le Geb I G 18. The gun is the same as for the standard model, but a split trail carriage is used, the trail legs being jointed to allow either "short" or "long" trail legs to be used, having detachable spades. This equipment breaks down into 6 pack or 10 manloads.

Both the standard and mountain versions were extremely light and compact equipments and it is understood that they were quite stable when firing, except that the mountain version did not fire charge V at ranges less than 2080 yards when using the lower register.

HE, Hollow Charge and Smoke shells are fired from both equipments; Charges I to V are used with the HE and Smoke, and Charge V and a special charge with the Hollow Charge shell.

In 1939 designs were prepared for a parachute model, known as the le I G 18 F, suitable for dropping in 4 containers each being approximately 140 Kg. (308 lbs). The equipment was generally similar to the mountain version, but was not fitted with a shield and had small diameter disc wheels — only 6 models in all are believed to have been made.

2. Data: I.G. 18

	Metric	British
(a) Calibre	7.5 cm	2.95 ins.
Length of Gun	900 mm	35.43 ins.
Length of barrel	884 mm	34.8 ins.
Length of rifling	674 mm	26.5 ins.
Rifling - Number of grooves		24
Type of Rifling - RH Polygroove Plain Section Constant Twist 1 in 25.		
Electric or Percussion Firing		Percussion
Maximum Recoil	480 mm	
Type of Sights		Rbl F 16
Traverse		12°
Elevation		-10° + 73°
Rate of fire		5-10 rpm
Weight in action		880 lbs

(b) Performance

(i) Firing 13.2 HE Shell

Charge	Muzzle Velocity	Range (yds)
I	302	875
II	359	1200
III	431	1640
IV	548	2560
V	690	3780

(ii) Firing 12 lbs HE Shell

I	310	930
II	368	1260
III	440	1750
IV	565	2680
V	730	3880

(iii) Firing 6.5 lbs Hollow Charge Shell

| V | 850 | 4150 |

(iv) Firing 6.6 lb Hollow Charge Shell

| Special Charge | 1130 | - |

/(c) Ammunition

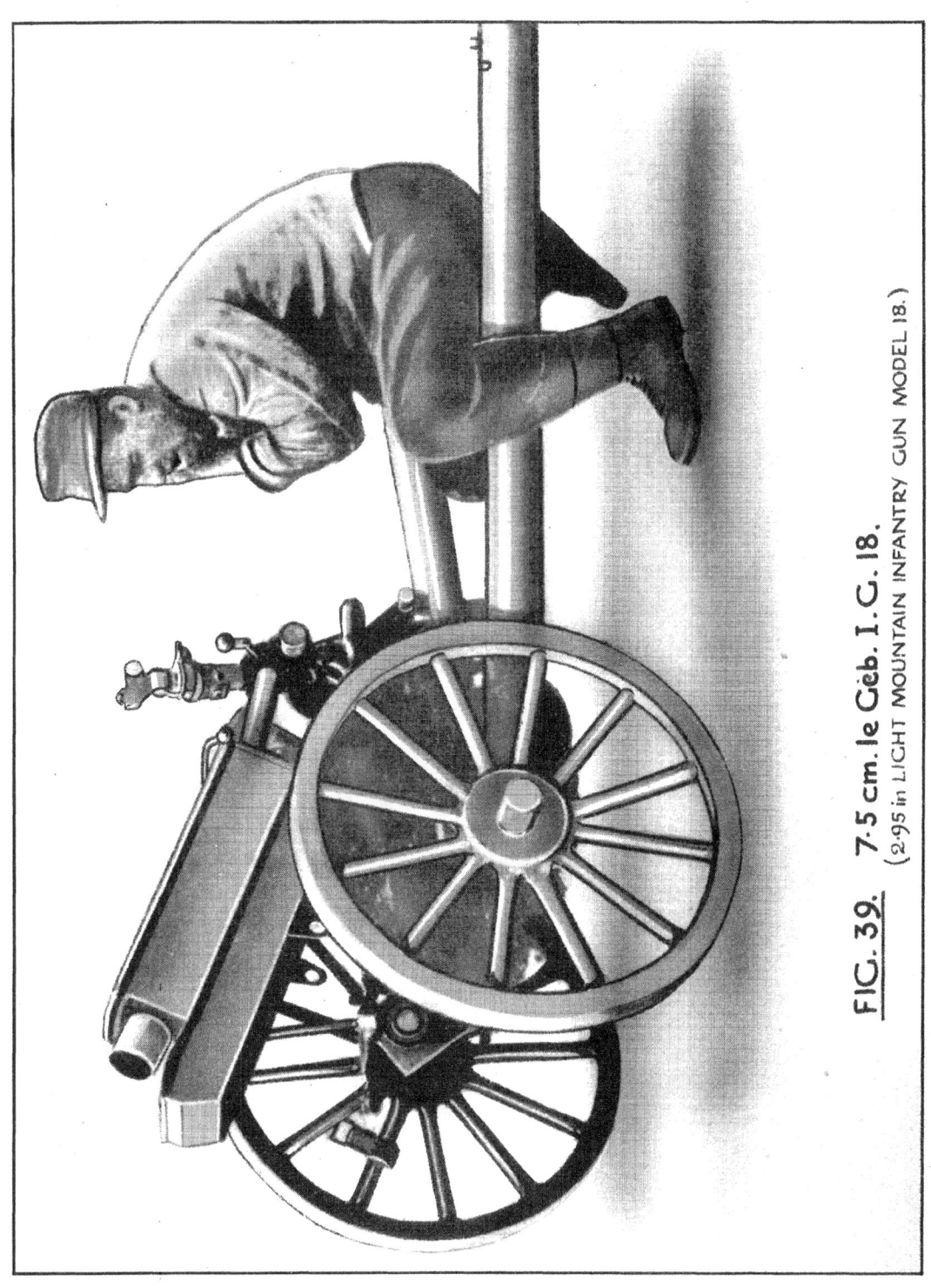

FIG. 39. 7·5 cm. le Geb. I.G. 18.
(2·95 in LIGHT MOUNTAIN INFANTRY GUN MODEL 18.)

(c) **Ammunition (Selection)**

7.5 Igr 18	HE	@ 13.2 lbs
7.5 Igr 18 A1.	HE	@ 12 lbs
7.5 Igr 38 Hl/A	Hollow Charge	@ 6.6 lbs
7.5 Igr 38	Hollow Charge	@ 6.5 lbs
7.5 Igr Deub	Smoke	@ 13 lbs

D. **7.5 cm I G L/13** (2.95 inch Infantry Gun L/13) See Fig: 40.

1. This equipment designed by Rheinmetall Borsig was produced in limited numbers only.

The monobloc barrel was 13 calibres in length, hence the nomenclature of L/13.

A horizontal sliding breech mechanism with firing gear operative from both sides is fitted.

The split trail carriage with trails of tubular construction is of the rear trunnion type and has spring equilibrators. The recoil system consists of a hydraulic buffer and spring recuperator. Disc type wheels are fitted.

The equipment is designed for both horse drawn and motor transport and can also be broken down into 4 or 6 pack loads.

Both HE and HE/AP projectiles were used.

2. **Data: I.G. L/13**

		Metric	British
(a) Calibre		75 mm	2.95 ins.
Length of piece		975 mm	38.37 ins.
Muzzle velocity	HE 6.5 Kg. shell	225 m/s	738 f.s.
	HE 4.5 Kg. shell	305 m/s	1000 f.s.
Muzzle energy	HE 6.5 Kg. shell	14.85 metric tons	
	HE 4.5 Kg. shell	21.1 metric tons	
Maximum range	HE 6.5 Kg. shell	3800 metres	4200 yds
	HE 4.5 Kg. shell	5100 metres	5600 yds
Traverse			50°
Elevation			-5° + 43°
Weight in action		375 Kg.	830 lbs
Rate of fire			20 rpm

(b) **Ammunition**

5 charges are used
Supercharge used with 4.5 Kg. projectile only.

HE	6.5 Kg.	14 lbs
HE	4.5 Kg.	10 lbs

(c) **Fuzes.** Two types are used viz: 1 Igr Z 23 nA Percussion
1 Igr Z 23.

E. **7.5 cm I G 37** (2.95 inch Infantry Gun 37) See Fig: 41.

1. As an emergency production, in 1944, a number of guns were mounted on a modified carriage of the obsolete 3.7 cm anti-tank gun. This was known at first as the 7.5 cm Pak 37 and later re-named cm I G 37. Ballistically the I G 37 and 42 are identical.

The gun is short barrelled and has a high efficiency four baffle box shaped muzzle brake. The breech mechanism has a vertical sliding block and incorporates a semi-automatic closing spring.

In a specimen of the I G 37 examined, the carriage suspension has an interesting feature. The springing of the carriage is effected by the action of cranked stub axles, the splines of which key into toe pieces, the

/latter

FIG. 40. 7.5 cm. I.G. L/13. (2·95 in. INFANTRY GUN MODEL L/13.)

latter bearing against a compressor cap on a horizontal spiral spring. The springs are housed in brackets keyed to the main axle. The thrust due to the weight of the main carriage is taken on the springs owing to the action of the cranked stub axles. During firing, the carriage springing is eliminated by locking the spring housing bracket, and thus the main axle to the cranked stub axles.

An interesting feature of the name plate on the lower shield of the equipment examined, is that it contains a Soviet Star showing that it had been captured from the Russians. The Russians purchased some 3.7 cm Pak equipments from the Germans before the war and also produced some in Russia.

A very comprehensive range of charges is fired with this equipment, charges 1 to 6 with HE shell in addition to two special charges for use with Hollw Charge projectiles. This gives a range of muzzle velocities from 350 to 1165 f.s.

The standard HE projectile of the old le I G 18 is fired as a semi-fixed round to a maximum range of 5150 metres (5630 yards). Against AFVs a 3.5 kg (7.7 lbs) hollow charge shell is fired with a super charge to give 350 m/s (1150 f.s.). It should be noted however that these guns cannot be fired in the upper register.

The total weight of the equipment in action is 510 kg (½ ton).

2. Data: I.G. 37

		Metric	British
(a)	Calibre	75 mm	2.95 ins
	Length of piece including muzzle brake	1815 mm	71.5 ins
	Length of rifling	1340 mm	52.75 ins
	Rifling:		
	Number of grooves	24	
	Width of grooves	6.1 mm	.24 ins
	Depth of grooves	1.00 mm	.04 ins
	Right hand twist		
	Percussion firing		
	Maximum recoil	432 mm	17 ins
	Sights: (i) Holder for direct sighting telescope		
	(ii) Drum graduated HE Charge V up to 1700 metres		
	HE Charge VI up to 2300 metres		
	HC up to 2500 metres		
	Elevation	-10° + 40°	
	Traverse	58°	
	Maximum Range HE I Gr 18 Charge VI	5150 metres	5630 yds
	Hollow Charge IGr 38 H1/A	4950 metres	5410 yds
	Overall length of equipment		11ft 7½ ins
	Weight in action	510 kg	1124 lbs
(b)	Muzzle Velocities: HE Charge 1	100 m/s	350 f.s.
	" " 2	120 m/s	395 f.s.
	" " 3	150 m/s	490 f.s.
	" " 4	190 m/s	625 f.s.
	" " 5	235 m/s	770 f.s.
	" " 6	280 m/s	920 f.s.
	Hollow Charge Special A	355 m/s	1165 f.s.
	Hollow Charge Special B	350 m/s	1150 f.s.

(c) Ammunition
Brass and steel cartridge cases are used.
Percussion primers of brass bodies. Type C/12nA
"   "   "   "   "   Type C/12nA St
Penetration of armour with Hollow Charge shell at 30° = 75 mm i.e. 2.95 inches.

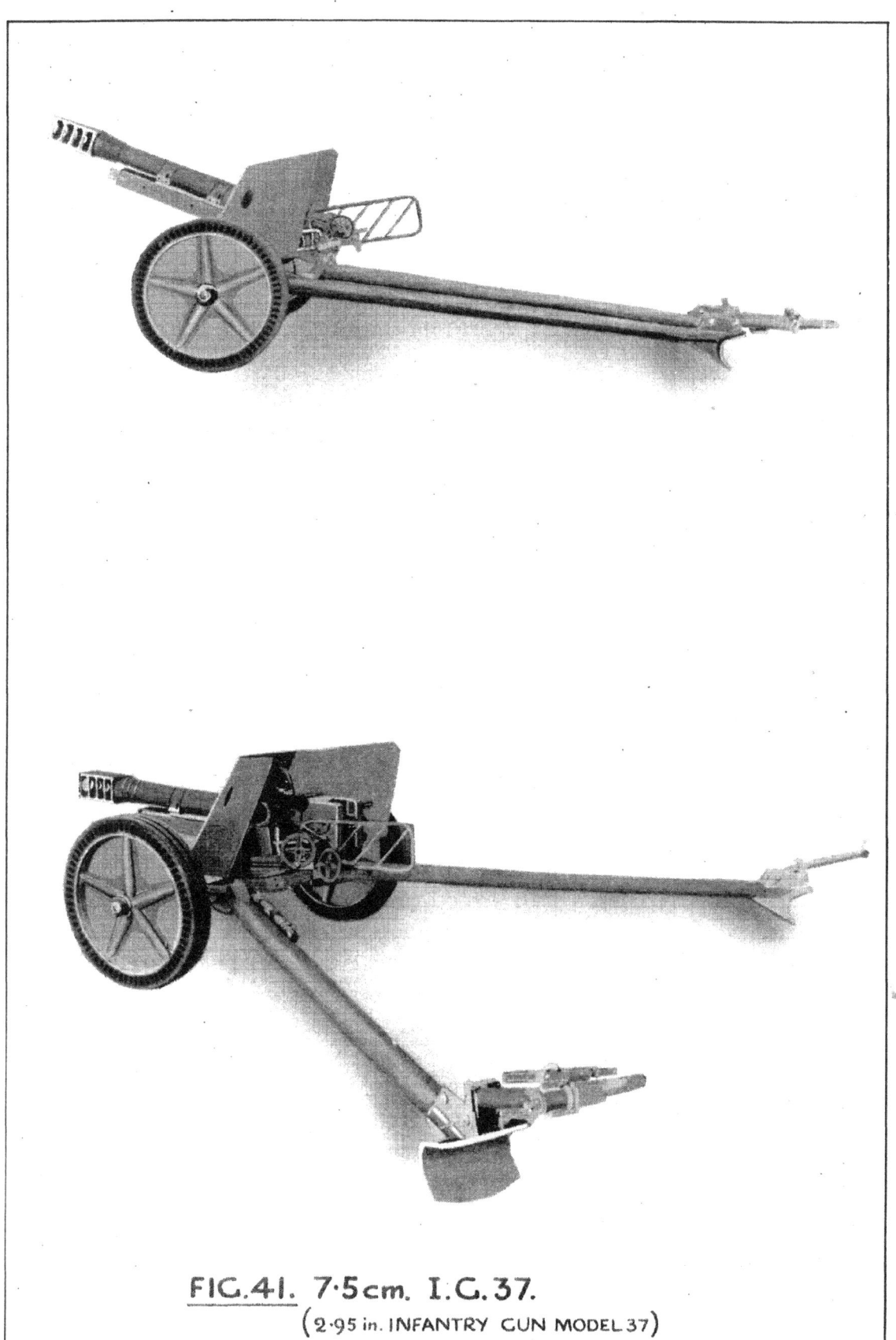

FIG. 41. 7·5 cm. I.G. 37.
(2·95 in. INFANTRY GUN MODEL 37)

Q.F. Separate ammunition (except for some hollow charge) is fired:

Nomenclature	Type	Fuzes used	Weight
7.5 cm I Gr 18	HE unstreamlined, nose fuze	le I Gr Z 23 nA	5.45kg(12 lb)
7.5 cm I Gr 18 Al.	HE streamlined, nose fuzed, aluminium powder incorporated in filling	le I G r Z 23 nA	5.45kg(12 lb)
7.5 cm I Gr 38.	Hollow charge, anti-tank (obsolete)	A Z 23	2.85kg(6.3 lb)
7.5 cm I Gr 38 H1/A	Hollow charge, anti-tank (sometimes QF fixed) (obsolescent)	A Z 38 or A Z 38 St.	3.0kg(6.6 lb)
7.5 cm I Gr Patr 38 H1/B	Hollow charge anti-tank (all QF fixed)	A.Z.38 St	3.5kg(7.7 lb)
7.5 cm I Gr Deut.	Bursting blue smoke indicator shell	—	5.98kg(13.2 lb)

(d) **Propelling charge**

Six charges are fired with the I Gr 18, 18 Al and 38. I Gr 38 H1/A and B have a special charge. The charge consists of the part charge of that number and all the lower numbered part charges, except in the case of charge 6 which consists of part charge 6 alone and is believed complete in a cartridge case.

Name of part charge	Weight	Propellant
Teilkart 1	15.5 g.	Ngl Pl P -12.5 -(50 mm x 0.2 mm) (circular disc of cordite)
Teilkart 2	6.5 g.	Ngl Pl P -12.5 -(73.5 mm x 0.8 mm)
Teilkart 3	9.0 g	"
Teilkart 4	16.5 g	"
Teilkart 5	24.0 g	"
Sonderhulsenkart 6	100 g	"
Charge for 7.5 cm I Gr 38 H1/B	110 g	Ngl Pl P -12.5 -(73.5 mm x 0.8 mm)
Charge for 7.5 cm I Gr 38 H1/A	10 g	Nz Nan N P 1.5 x 1.5 mm (igniter
	+ 7 g	Digl Pl P 10.5(50 mm x 0.15 mm)
	+ 150 g.	Digl. Pl P 10.5(73.5 x 0.6 mm) OR
	15.5 g	Ngl Pl P -12.5(50 mm x 0.2 mm)
	+ 90 g.	Ngl Pl P -12.5(73.5 mm x 0.8 mm)

7.5 cm I G 42 (2.95 inch Infantry Gun Model 42) See Figs. 42 and 43

1. In 1940 the Infantry decided that increased range and an improved performance against AFVs (Armoured Fighting Vehciles) was needed and Krupp designed the 7.5 cm I G 42 aA (A = Alter Art ike. old type) which was not accepted owing to technical difficulties in production. (See fig. 44).

Later the requirement was revived and the standard model I G 42 was designed in 1944 and produced in limited numbers using a light split trail field carriage which was also intended for the 8 cm P A W 600 (smooth bore Infantry A/Tank gun).

The I G 42 consists of the piece of the 7.5 cm I G 37 mounted on a tubular split trail carriage. The ballistics are identical with those of the I G 37.

The carriage is much lighter in weight than the one used with the I G 37. The elevating and traversing hand weels are on the left-hand side of the carriage, the elevating gear being of the nut and screw type, whilst the traversing gear is of the pinion and arc kind. An angular shield is fitted for the protection of the gun crew. Both direct and indirect sights are fitted, the direct sight is the 3 x 8° telescope and the sight for indirect laying is the auxiliary sight 38 (Aushilforichtmittel 38). The same range scale as that for the I G 37 is used

2. **7.5 cm Smooth Bore I G 42.** See figs. 45 and 46

A smooth bore weapon with the nomenclature "I G 42" marked on its shield was captured at a German Proving Ground at the end of the war. The diameter of the bore is 7.5 cm and the weapon appears to be an experimental model which has not been produced in any quantity. The piece, except for a new type muzzle brake and a counterweight which is located on the top of the breech ring is similar as is the breech mechanism, to that of the standard I G 42 rifled equipment. The muzzle brake is flat on the top and bottom and rounded at the sides. Four baffles on each side, with wide wings, deflect the propellant gases to the rear.

The carriage is of the split trail type, the trails being of tubular construction. The carriage is much wider than the standard I G 42.

3. Data: I.G. 42

	Metric	British
(a) Calibre	75 mm	2.95 ins
Length of piece including muzzle brake	1815 mm	71.5 ins
Length of rifling	1340 mm	52.75 ins
Rifling -		
Number of grooves	24	
Width of grooves	6.1 mm	.24 ins
Depth of grooves	1.00 mm	.04 ins
Right hand twist		
Length of chamber	111 mm	4 3/8 ins
Percussion firing		
Maximum recoil	520 mm	20.5 ins
Normal recoil	500 mm	19.5 ins
Elevation	-6° +32°	
Traverse	60°	
Maximum Range: HE I Gr 18 Charge VI	5150 metres	5630 yds
Hollow Charge I Gr 38 H1/A	4950 metres	5410 yds
Travelling Position -		
Overall length	4775 mm	187 ins
Overall width	1805 mm	71 ins
Overall height	1074 mm	42¼ ins
Weight in travelling position	595 kg	1311 lbs
Weight in firing position	590 kg	1300 lbs
Muzzle velocities: HE Charge 1	100 m/s	350 f.s.
" " 2	120 m/s	395 f.s.
" " 3	150 m/s	490 f.s.
" " 4	190 m/s	625 f.s.
" " 5	235 m/s	770 f.s.
" " 6	280 m/s	920 f.s.
Hollow Charge:		
Special Charge A	355 m/s	1165 f.s.
Special Charge B	350 m/s	1150 f.s.

(b) **Ammunition** (as for I G 37)
  Brass and steel cartridge cases are used.
  Percussion primers of brass bodies.   Type C/12 nA
  "   "   " steel   "   Type C/12 nA St.
  Penetration of armour with Hollow Charge shell at 30° = 75 mm
  i.e. 2.95 inches.

Q.F. Separate ammunition (except for some hollow charge) is fired:

Nomenclature	Type	Fuzes used	Weight
7.5 cm I Gr 18	HE unstreamlined, nose fuze	le I Gr Z 23 nA	5.45kg(12 lb)
7.5 cm I Gr 18 Al	HE streamlined, nose fuzed, aluminium powder incorporated in filling	le I Gr Z 23 nA	5.45kg(12 lb)
7.5 cm I Gr 38	Hollow charge, anti-tank (obsolete)	A Z 23	2.85kg(6.3 lb)
7.5 cm I Gr 38 H1/A	Hollow charge, anti-tank (sometimes QF fixed) (obsolescent)	A Z 38 or A Z 38 St	3.0kg(6.6 lb)
7.5 cm I Gr Patr.38 H1/B	Hollow charge anti-tank (all QF fixed)	A Z 38 St	3.5kg(7.7 lb)
7.5 cm I Gr Deut	Bursting blue smoke indicator shell		5.98kg(13.2lb)

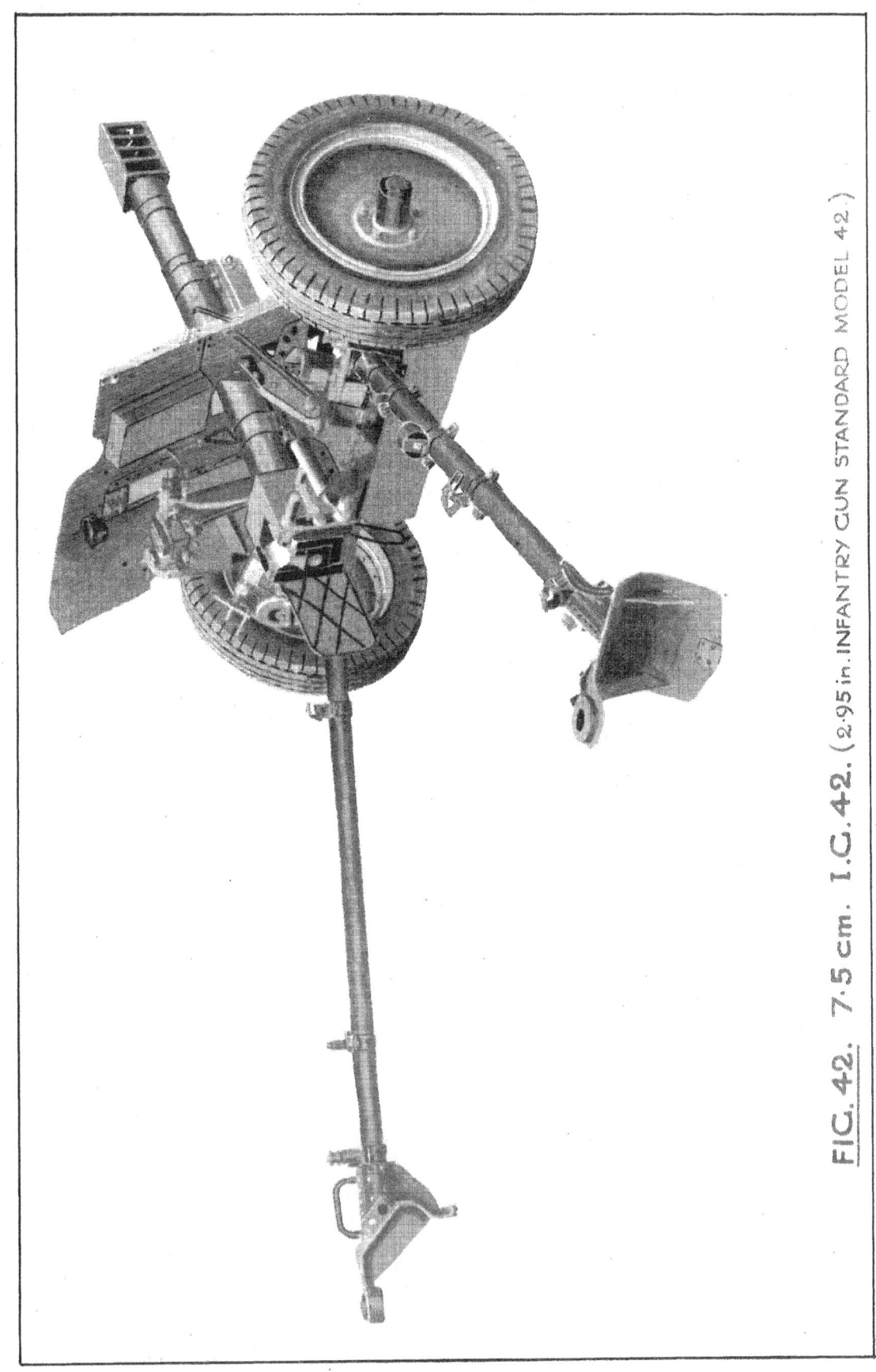

FIG. 42. I.G. 42. (2·95 in. INFANTRY GUN STANDARD MODEL 42.) 7·5 cm.

FIG. 43. 7.5 cm. I.G. 42. (2·95 in INFANTRY GUN STANDARD MODEL 42.)

FIG.44. 7·5cm. I.G.42.aA.
(2·95in. INFANTRY GUN MODEL 42, OLD TYPE — KRUPP PROTOTYPE.)

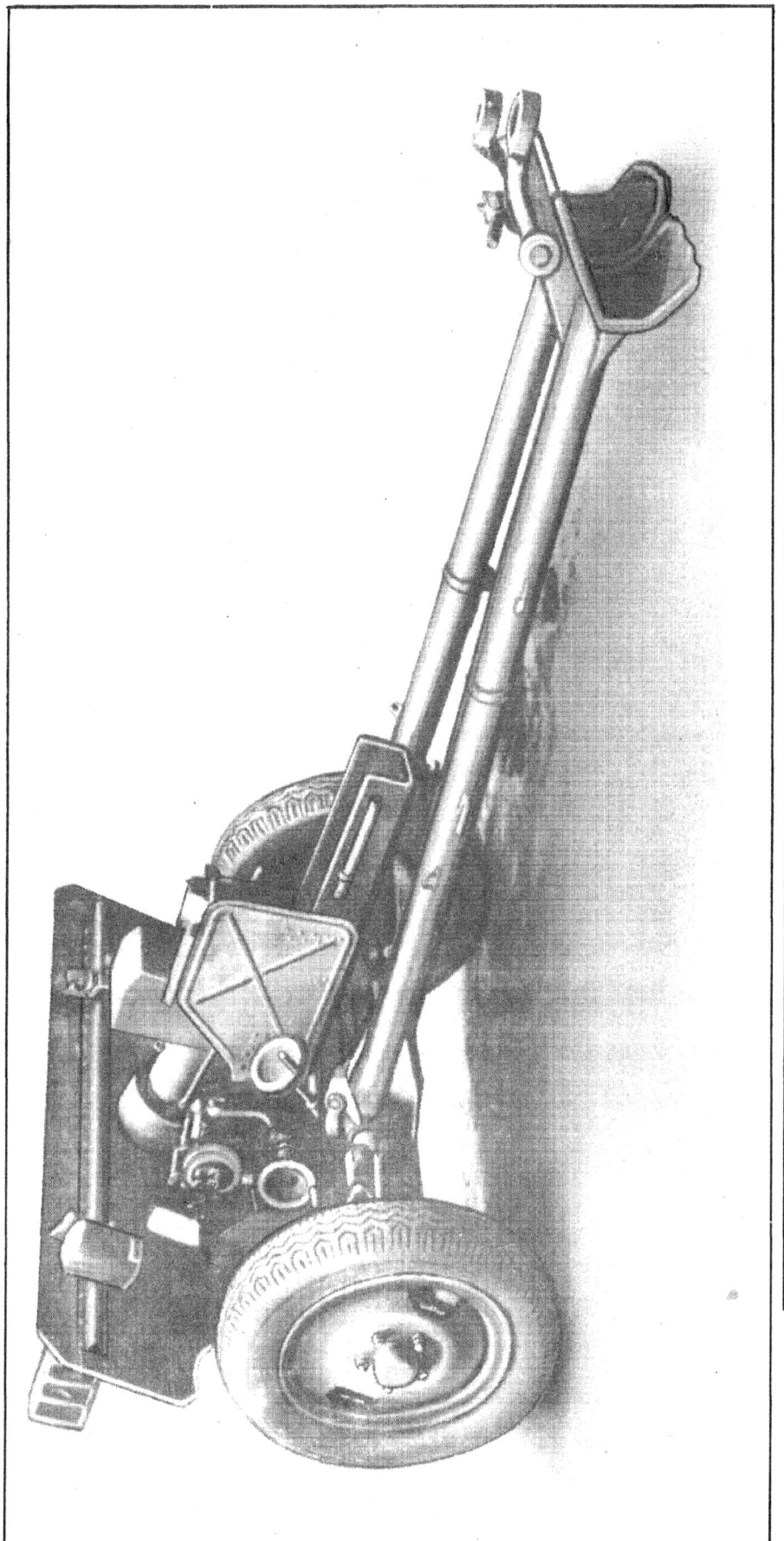

FIG. 45. 7.5 cm. I.C. 42.
(2.95 in. SMOOTH BORE INFANTRY GUN MODEL 42.)

FIG. 46. 7.5 cm. I.G. 42.
(2.95 in. SMOOTH BORE INFANTRY GUN MODEL 42.)

(c) **Propelling charge**

Six charges are fired with the I Gr 18, 18 A1, and 38. I Gr 38 H1/A and B have a special charge. The charge consists of the part charge of that number and all the lower numbered part charges except in the case of charge 6 which consists of part charge 6 alone and is believed complete in a cartridge case.

Name of part charge	Weight	Propellant
Teilkart 1	15.5 g.	Ngl Pl P -12.5-(50mm x 0.2 mm) (circular disc of cordite)
Teilkart 2	6.5 g.	Ngl Pl P -12.5-(73.5 mm x 0.8 mm)
Teilkart 3	9.0 g.	"
Teilkart 4	16.5 g	"
Teilkart 5	24.0 g	"
Sonderhulsenkart 6	100 g	"
Charge for 7.5 cm IGr 38 Hl/B	110 g	"
Charge for 7.5 cm I Gr 38 Hl/A	10 g + 7 g +150 g OR 15.5 g + 90 g	Nz Nan N P 1.5 x 1.5 mm (igniter) Digl Pl P 10.5 (50 mm x 0.15 mm) Digl Pl P 10.5 (73.5 x 0.6 mm) Ngl Pl P -12.5 (50 mm x 0.2 mm) Ngl Pl P -12.5 (73.5 mm x 0.8 mm)

G. **15 cm s I G 33** (5.9 inch Medium Infantry Gun Model 33). See Fig. 47.

1. This is the standard close support howitzer used by the Infantry Gun Companies. It is a compact sturdy equipment of orthodox design which was developed by Rheinmetall Borsig in 1927.

The piece comprises a monobloc barrel with detachable track ring prepared for a manually operated horizontal sliding block. HP recoil mechanism is in the cradle below the piece. The gun is mounted on a box trail carriage with steel rimmed or solid rubber tyred wheels. Two spring equilibrators are fitted.

Between 1936 and 39 steel was replaced as far as possible in the carriage construction by metal alloys to reduce overall weight. This resulted in reductions from 1700 to 1550 kg. but the practive was later discontinued owing to shortage of light metals and the priorities given to the Luftwaffe for such materials.

The I.G.33 is normally either horse drawn or towed by a 3 ton semi-tracked vehicle. Maximum range if 4700 metres with a 38 kg HE shell. Smoke and hollow charge are also fired and an unusual projectile, a muzzle stick bomb, weight $89\frac{1}{2}$ kg, is fired at ranges up to 1025 metres and was intended for blowing gaps in wire defences.

2. Data: I.G. 33

	Metric	British
(a) Calibre	150 mm	5.9 ins
Length of barrel	1650 mm	64.9 ins
Rifling:		
Twist 8° constant		
Number of grooves	44	
Width of grooves	6.64 mm	.26 ins
Depth of grooves	1.5 mm	.06 ins
Rate of Fire	4 rpm	
Muzzle Velocity	240 m/s	790 f.s.
Maximum range	4700 metres	5140 yds
Traverse	11° 30'	
Elevation	-0° + 73°	
Weight in action	1500 kg	3300 lbs
(b) Ammunition		
HE 15 cm I Gr 33 and 38	38 kg	83.6 lbs
Smoke 15 cm IGGr 38 Nb	38.5 kg	85 lbs
Hollow Charge 15 cm I G H1/A		

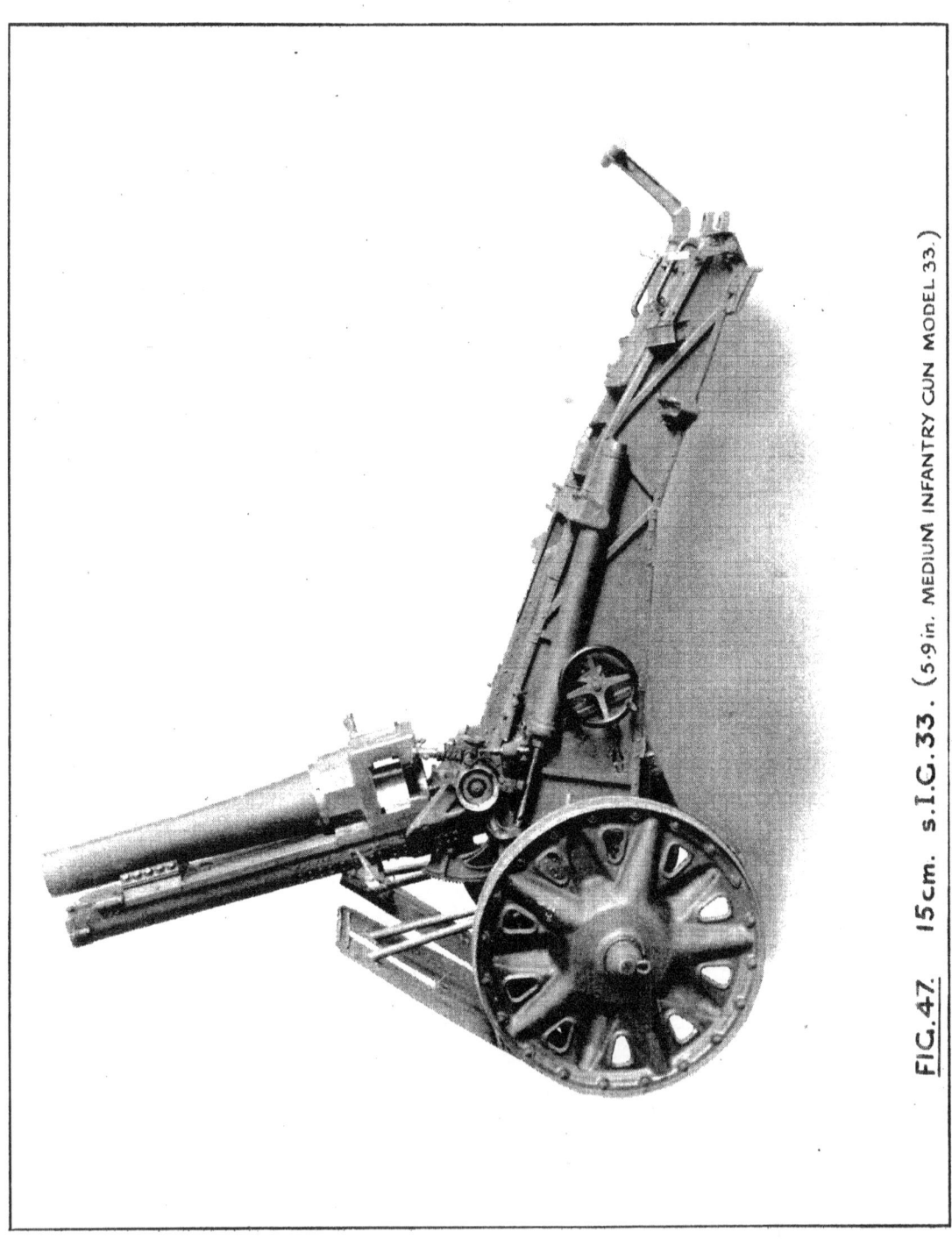

FIG. 47. 15 cm. s.I.G. 33. (5.9 in. MEDIUM INFANTRY GUN MODEL 33.)

CHAPTER IV

THE DEVELOPMENT OF GERMAN RECOILLESS GUNS

A. General

The weapons were developed and put into operational use, for special purposes, in the 7.5 cm and 10.5 cm calibres, while larger equipments were in process of development. The demand for a high muzzle performance, in terms of high muzzle energy to overall weight of equipment, encouraged this development.

The principle was not a new one and originates in the idea embodied in the Davis gun of firing projectiles in opposite directions with the same propellant charge. In the Leichtes Geschutz or Dusengeschütz (Nozzle Gun), the recoil forces are balanced by allowing a proportion of the propellant gases to escape to the rear through a venturi, attached to the breech.

Research and experiment showed that with suitable quantities of propellant and design of venturi, for all practical purposes recoilless firing could be achieved, even for a number of different charges. Standard projectiles were used, while cartridge cases were developed in which the walls of the case were made of plastic material, which would disintegrate on firing, but which was sufficiently robust to allow initial pressure to be built up in the bore for suitable shot propulsion.

In practice, therefore, with a recoilless gun the only requirements for the carriage were that it should be robust enough to permit the fitting of elevating and traversing gears and to withstand travelling stresses and manhandling. It is also necessary to ensure that no part of the carriage or components should be situated in the path of the rearward escaping jet. In addition the detachment must be located to the side of the gun, so as to avoid the danger zone to the rear of the venturi nozzle.

The first recoilless gun to be introduced operationally by the Germans was the L.G.1 later known as the 7.5 cm L.G.40 designed for use by paratroops.

Certain modifications in design were found necessary in the 10.5 cm recoilless guns. Owing to the powerful erosive effect of the escaping gases over the components of the firing mechanism, lateral ignition was adopted using a special cartridge case with the primer inserted at the side. This involved the positioning of the cartridge case in the chamber on loading, and alterations to the igniter, but otherwise it was satisfactory.

The early 10.5 cm equipments showed pronounced torque on barrels, resulting in deformation of the trunnions and damage to the sighting apparatus. This torque was eliminated by using three counter torque vanes welded inside the venturi cones.

Various models have been encountered indicating modifications in carriage design to make the recoilless gun suitable as a light infantry gun, for use by special units, parachute and mountain troops. For the last mentioned role, ability to fire in the upper register and to break down into suitable loads for transportation were of prime importance.

A 15 cm Recoilless gun was developed on similar lines to the 10.5 cm for use by airborne troops or to replace the s. I.G. 33 Infantry Howitzer. Introduction into service was however delayed and it was not used operationally, except in very limited numbers. Its maximum effective range was in the region of 16-18000 metres (17,500 - 19,700

/yards

yards). It was given the name of L.G.3 and it is understood that it was also mounted as a self-propelled weapon.

Recoilless development was taken up by the German Navy, who proposed to build 8.8 cm, 15 cm and 28 cm guns for use as mobile coast defence weapons; for the heavier equipments the development did not proceed beyond the initial designs, and the construction of an experimental 24 cm barrel for research purposes.

The great advantage of the recoilless gun is relatively high muzzle performance per unit of weight, and the numerous and tactical possibilities resulting from this have been noted.

The main disadvantages are:-

1. The back blast on firing which is dangerous to the gun detachment or restricts their activity and tends to make concealment difficult.

2. The disadvantage of the special cartridge case construction involved and the difficulty of producing a plastic for the cartridge case base, which could be relied upon to function consistently.

3. The relatively high powder consumption as compared with guns of orthodox design.

In spite of these disadvantages, the development of recoilless guns for special purposes was continued on a relatively high priority from 1940 until the middle of 1944.

The latest trend was the development of a high-low pressure gun to serve the same tactical purpose as the recoilless gun. The only equipment of this type actually in service was a light anti-tank weapon, the 8 cm PWK 8 H.63 (formerly the 8 cm PAW 600), but experiments were carried out for large calibres.

The high-low pressure principle is to burn the propellant powder in a relatively high pressure chamber and to allow the gases to escape through a drilled venturi plate, a component of the cartridge case, to a low pressure chamber i.e. the barrel in rear of the projectile. This gives uniform ignition burning and results in an unusually high ratio of mean to peak pressure and therefore a steady and relatively flat pressure curve. This does not produce the violent recoil stresses of the normal gun and it follows that, for a given muzzle velocity, a much lighter gun will suffice allowing a relatively light equipment. Further a light weight and less robust shell can be used, on account of the relatively low initial pressures involved on firing, thus permitting a high ratio of filling to projectile weight.

B. 7.5 cm L.G.40 (2.95 inch Recoilless Gun Model 40) See Figs. 48, 49 & 50

1. This equipment, originally known as the L.G.1, was the first German recoilless gun to be introduced into service. It was designed for use by paratroops, and fired both H.E. and Hollow Charge projectiles, the maximum range being 6800 metres (7500 yards). The total weight of the equipment was 145 kg (320 lbs i.e. less than 3 cwts).

It is understood that the first experimental weapons were first tried out in Crete. The equipments were dismantled into four parts, each part being dropped separately by parachute without being put into a container. So that it could be assembled quickly after landing each part was attached by a cord, some 30 metres long, to one of the members of the gun crew himself landing by parachute. Owing to the ease with which it could be transported, and the fact that it was very cheap to produce, the gun was later issued to army land units as well as to the parachutists. It was found to be particularly useful in Finland where it could be carried to positions where it was impossible to take the heavier normal type weapons.

A later method of dropping the equipment by parachute was to divide it into two loads contained in two wicker basket containers.

The gun piece consists of a barrel and breech ring which can be very rapidly separated or assembled.

The horizontal sliding breech block opens to the right. It is of very light weight construction and is so constructed that the venturi jet can be secured in the rear face. The venturi jet is easily recognisable by its shape which resembles a cone with the pointed portion cut away.

Owing to the absence of recoil stresses the carriage is of very light weight construction, indeed most of it is made of aluminium alloy. The carriage is designed so that when the equipment is in action it rests on a tripod. All three legs are pivotted in lugs of the base ring of the saddle body. In the travelling position one trail leg is secured to the barrel whilst the other two are linked together as with the normal split trail carriage.

The traversing rack is of the wormwheel type, an interrupted flange operating in conjunction with a traverse and elevating limiting stop, automatically limiting the traverse to 60 degrees when the elevation exceeds 20 degrees.

2. Special Safety Precautions

(The following paragraph is translated from a captured document).
The following safety precautions must be observed when firing the 7.5 cm. L.G.40.

(a) <u>In front of the muzzle</u> the same safety precautions apply as in the case of the other guns.

(b) <u>For practice and operational firing</u> respectively, the areas specified, to the side and rear of the mouth of the jet, must be avoided. The length of the danger area in rear of the jet is:-

    (i) for practice firing — 110 yds.
    (ii) for operational firing — 55 yds.
    (But see sub-paragraph (c) below).

(c) <u>The area in rear of the gun</u>, roughly in prolongation of the axis of the bore, may become dangerous for a distance of several hundred yards, owing to flying stones, etc. For this reason such an area should also be avoided if possible.

(d) <u>The blast from the jet</u> may endanger the ear drums of those in the immediate neighbourhood of the gun. The detachment must on principle, therefore, plug their ears with compressed clay or mud which must be rammed firmly into the ear. Commercial ear protectors (with the exception of "Akustike") can be used instead.

3. Data L.G.40

	Metric	British
(a) Calibre	75 m.m	2.95 ins.
Length of piece (10 Cals)	750 mm	29.5 ins.
Length of bore	458 mm	18.03 ins.
Length of rifling	252 mm	9.92 ins.
Length of chamber	206 mm	8.11 ins.
Rifling - Polygroove plain section, uniform twist 1 in. 52.		
– Number of grooves	28	
– Width of grooves	5.1 mm	0.2 ins.
– Depth of grooves	1.0 mm	0.03 ins.
Cubic capacity of chamber.		12.2 cu. ins.
Elevation: With traverse of 30° right and left	$-15° + 42°$	
: With traverse of 360°	$-15° + 20°$	
Traverse : With elevation $-15° + 42°$		30° right and left
: With elevation $-15° + 20°$		360°
Travelling Position -		
Overall Length	1970 mm	77.5 ins
Overall Height	970 mm	38.2 ins
Overall Breadth	1040 mm	40.9 ins
Weight in action	145 kg	321 lbs.
Standard Projectile Weight (HE)	5.83 kg	12 lbs 13 ozs
Muzzle Velocity - Standard Projectile	350 m/s	1150 f/s
Maximum Range - Standard Projectile	6800 metres	7435 yds

/Ammunition

FIG. 48. 7.5 cm. L.G.1. (KRUPP)
(2·95 in. RECOILLESS GUN MODEL I — KRUPP PROTOTYPE FOR AIRBORNE USE — LATER KNOWN AS THE L.G.40.)

FIG. 49. 7.5 cm. L.G. 40.
(2·95 in. RECOILLESS GUN MODEL 40.)

FIG. 50. 7·5 cm. L.G.40.
(2·95 in. RECOILLESS GUN MODEL 40)

(b) Ammunition

Three types are fired:

(i) H.E. Shell (7.5 cm. Gr 34): weight   12 lb 13 oz
                                           max. range   7436 yds
                                           M.V.   1150 f.s.
                                           Fuze A.Z. 38

(ii) A P C B C. Shell (7.5 cm Pz Gr rot.): weight 15 lb.

(iii) Hollow charge shell (7.5 cm Gr. 38 H1/B): This shell can not only be used against A. F.Vs but also against soft skinned targets owing to its considerable fragmentation effect.

Weight, filled and fuzed	10 lb. 2 ozs
Fuze	Nose Percussion fuze, without delay, AZ 38
Weight of propellant	2 lb. 10 oz.
Armour penetration performance	50 mm at 30° attack

A distinctive feature of all three types of ammunition is the base of the cartridge case. This consists of a plastic disc (pierced to receive the primer) which is blown out when the gun is fired, allowing part of the propellant gas to escape to the rear.

(c) Ballistic Characteristics

The particulars given below apply to the hollow charge round (Gr. 38 H1/B):-

Maximum Velocity   1197 f/s
Maximum Range   7437 yards

Range		T E		Drift	Time of flight	Length	50% Zone Breadth	Height
M	Yds	mils	degrees	degrees	seconds	yds	yds	yds
500	547	20	1° 8'	3'	1.4	25	0	1
1000	1094	42	2° 22'	3'	3.0	25	1	1
2000	2187	95	5° 21'	10'	6.6	27	2	3
3000	3281	161	9° 4'	17'	10.5	31	3	7
4000	4374	243	13° 41'	27'	15.1	36	5	12
5000	5468	343	19° 19'	40'	20.5	45	8	22
6000	6562	475	26° 45'	1° 1'	26.9	60	10	48
6800	7437	710	39° 58'	1° 35'	39.0	86	14	125

C. **7.5 cm Rf.K.43.** (2.95 ins Recoilless Gun Model 43) See Figs: 51, 52 and 53

1. This recoilless gun follows the design of earlier weapons of the same type, utilising a venturi tube to allow some of the propellant gases to escape to the rear.

The weapon was designed primarily as an infantry recoilless anti-tank weapon. BOHLER produced an experimental model, which was not accepted. The KRUPP equipment is of simple construction, weighs only 95-lbs and can be broken down into three loads consisting of the barrel, venturi and the tripod mounting.

In order to insert a round, the rear end of the rifled barrel is exposed. The equipment is fitted with a percussion firing mechanism, operated on the right side of the barrel.

The mounting consists of a small circular base supported on a tripod. A pintle extends up from the centre of the circular base to support the barrel in its trunnions. No traversing or elevating gear is provided. These operations are performed by pivoting the gun manually about the base in traverse and about the trunnions in elevation and depression. Float pads are welded to the extremities of the tripod legs.

Trials were carried out with a carboard cartridge case which proved

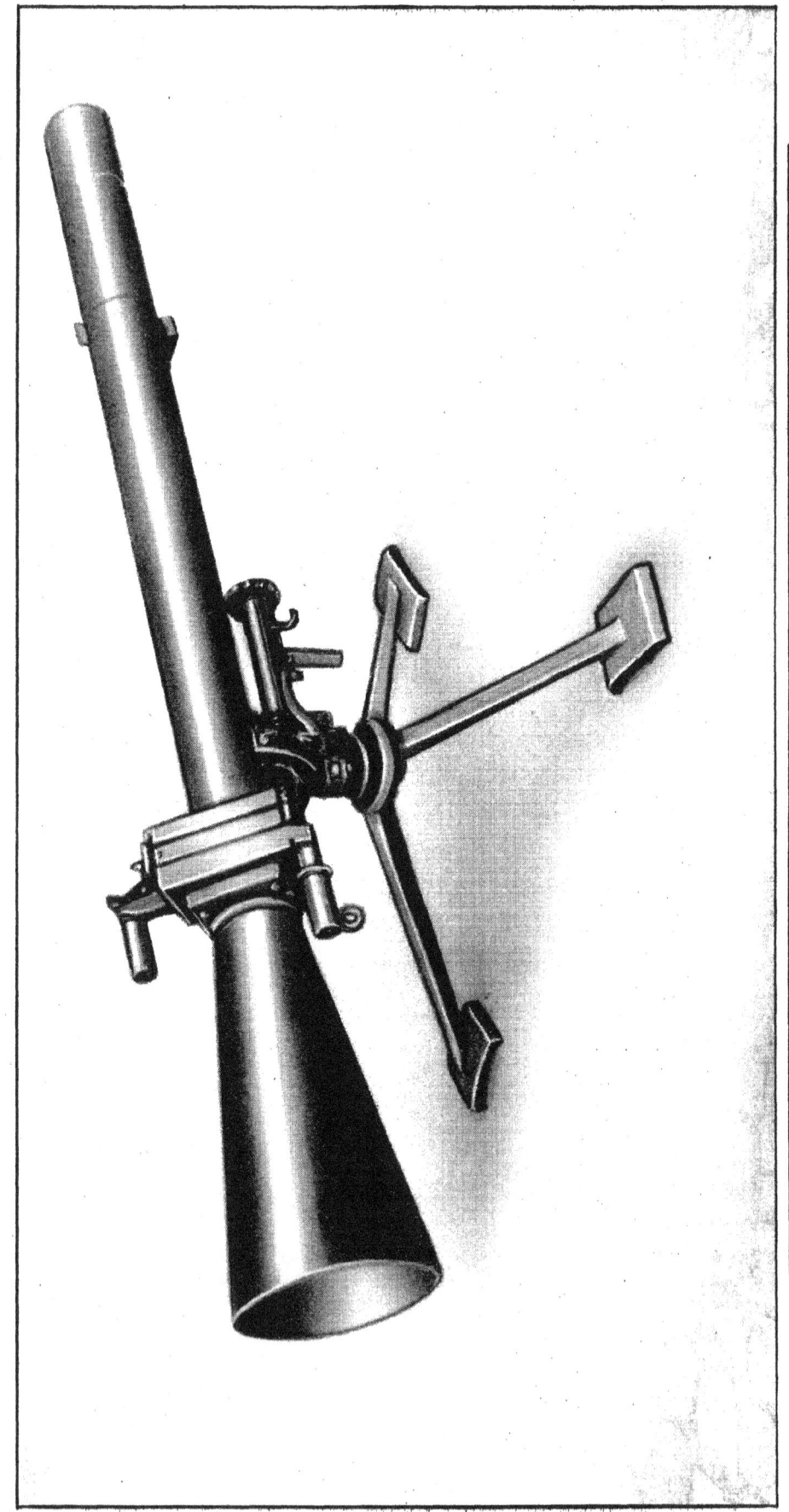

FIG. 51. 7.5cm. R.f.K. 43.
(2.95 in. RECOILLESS LIGHT GUN MODEL 43.)

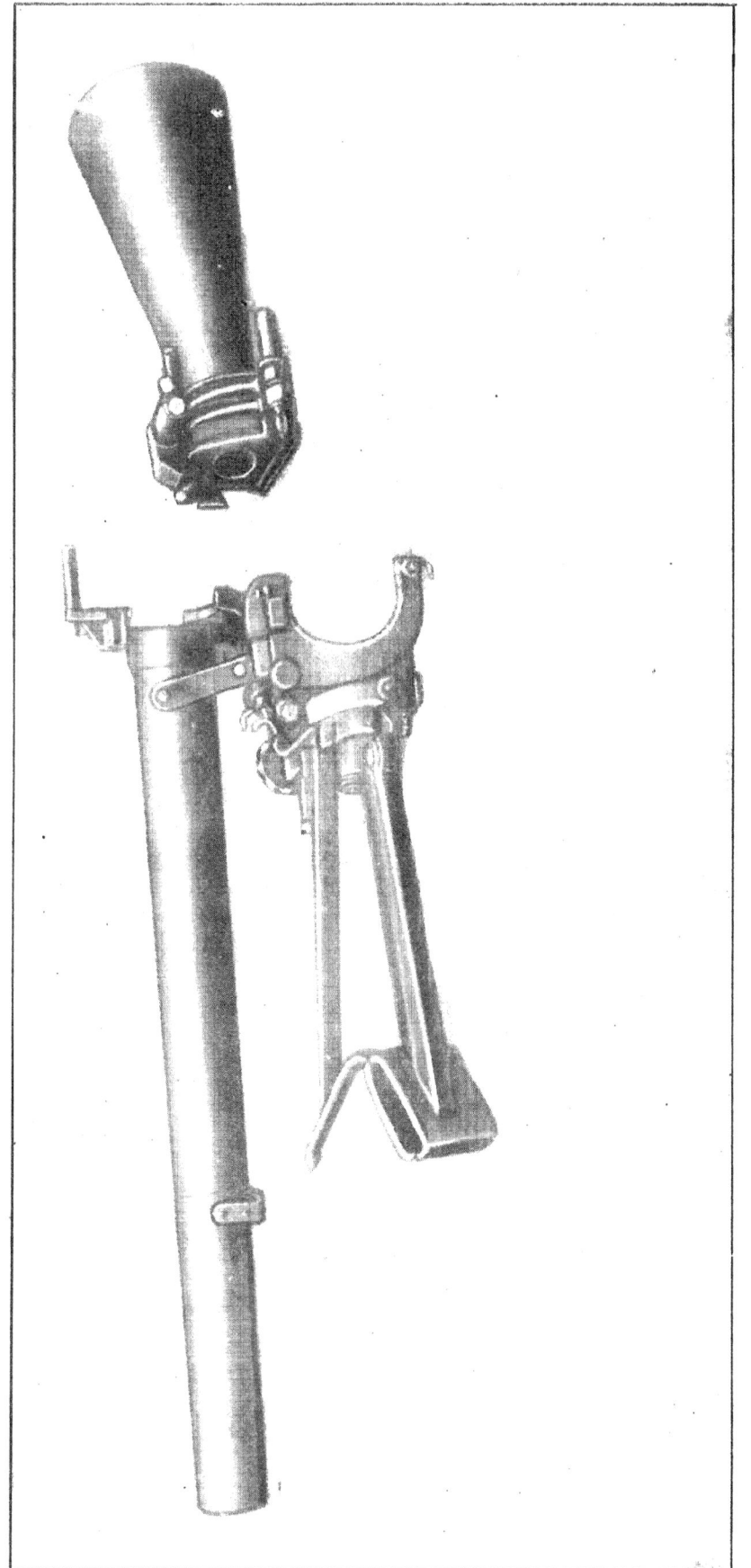

FIG. 52. 7.5 cm. R.f.K. 43.
(2·95 in. RECOILLESS LIGHT GUN MODEL 43.)

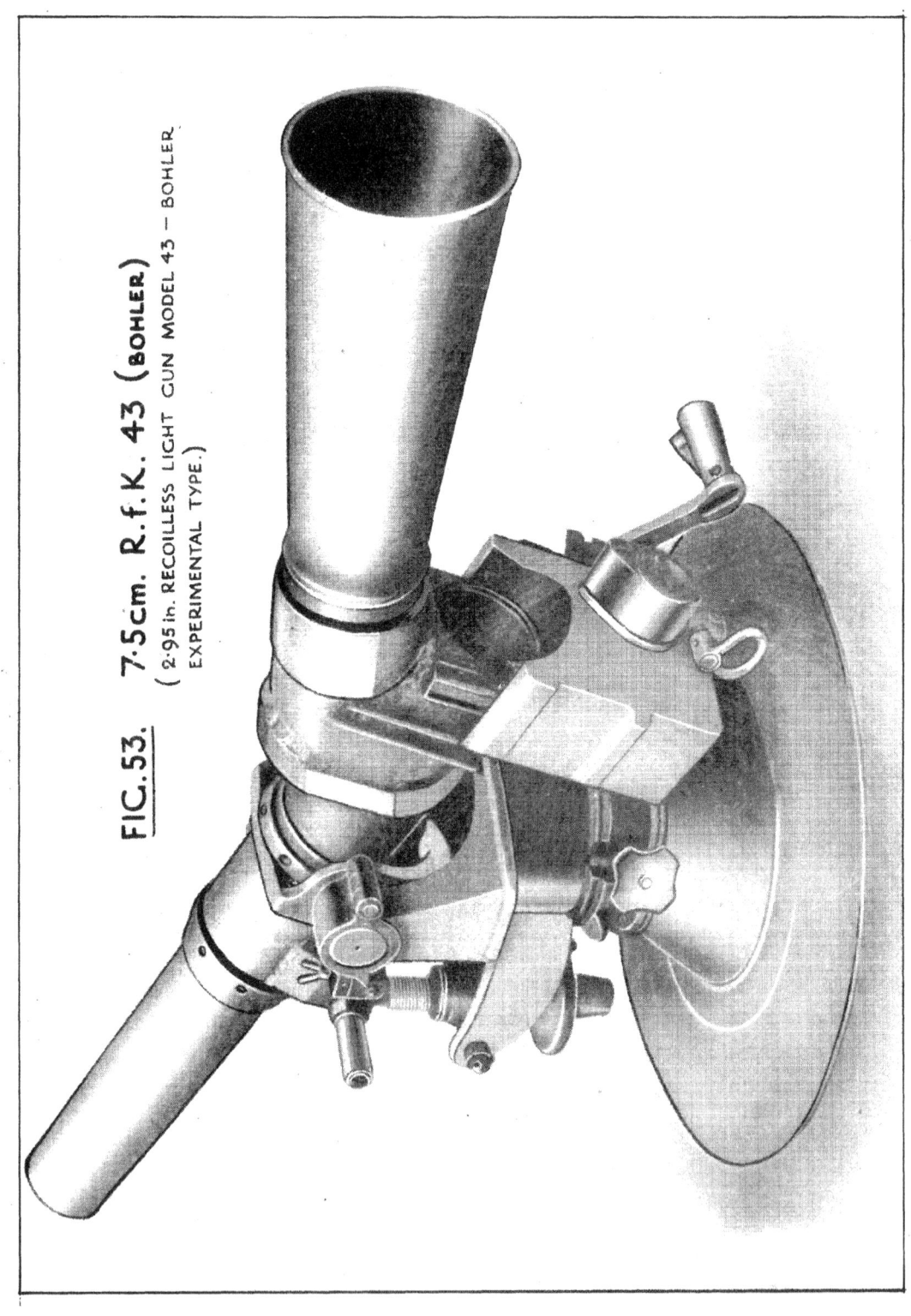

FIG. 53. 7·5 cm. R.f.K. 43 (BOHLER)
(2·95 in. RECOILLESS LIGHT GUN MODEL 43 – BOHLER EXPERIMENTAL TYPE.)

2. Data: Rf. K.43

	Metric	British
Calibre	75 mm	2.95 ins.
Fighting Range (Anti-Tank)	300 metres	327 yds
Maximum Range	2000 metres	2180 yds
Rate of Fire	20 r.p.m.	
Penetration at 60° attack	12 cm	4.72 ins
Shell of weight	4 kg	8.8 lbs
Weight of equipment	43.1 kg	95 lbs
Ammunition 7.5 cm Hl.Gr.Patr.43	(Anti-Tank Hollow Charge)	
Muzzle velocity	170 m/s	556 f.s.
Detachment	2	
Rear Blast Danger Zone – Width	30° Left and Right	
" " " " – Depth	20 metres	22 yds

D. 8 cm Rf.W.43 (3.2 ins Recoilless Mortar Model 43) See Figs. 54 and 55

1. General

This smooth bore recoilless weapon is most interesting in that it is fitted with a removeable bush, which enables the venturi throttle to be changed or varied in size.

It is presumed that the equipment was designated a mortar instead of a gun, as are the others, because of it being a smooth bore.

The precise method of attaching the barrel to the mounting is not known, as the equipment examined was deficient of cradle trunnions.

2. The Mortar

The removeable breech ring is attached to the barrel by a right hand screw thread. The venturi choke is fitted into the venturi tube from its front end. The venturi tube is then entered into the breech ring and is turned through a sixth of a circle, when the interrupted collars engage to secure the assembly. A stop stud and cut away portion indicate the locked and unlocked position.

3. The Firing Mechanism

This consists of a simple striker, spring and screwed bolt securing. The firing pin enters the chamber from the side and near the end of the barrel. There are two positions on the same circumferential line in which the striker assembly can be fitted. There does not appear to be any method of retracting the striker short of removing the assembly.

4. The Mounting

This consists of a simple wooden wheel type of base, the bottom of which is shod with a thin metal, resembling tin. The base is fitted with a spigot pivot with trunnion bearings.

5. Data: Rf.W.43

Calibre	3.2 inches
Length of barrel	57.9 inches
Length overall	79 inches
Length of venturi tube	21.3 inches
Interior diameter of venturi	2.75 inches
Weight of mortar	1 cwt 3 Qrs 11½ lbs

Weight of Base Mounting — 22 lbs

Total weight of equipment as examined — 2 cwts 0 qrs 5½ lbs

Details of performance and ammunition used are not known.

E. 10.5 cm Recoilless Weapons

The 10.5 cm L.G.40 series were of Krupp design, and the L.G.42 series were products of Rheinmetall Boesig.

The nomenclature of the 10.5 cm recoilless equipments has been obscured by changes made since their original introduction; therefore to clarify the position the correct listing is given:-

1. L.G.2 (350) kp (Manufactured by Krupp) subsequently known as 10.5 cm L.G.40

2. 10.5 cm L.G.40/2 a slight modification of (1) above.

3. L.G.2 Rh. (Manufactured by Rheinmetall) subsequently known as 10.5 cm L.G.42

4. 10.5 cm L.G.42/1 a slight modification of (3) above.

F. 10.5 cm L.G.40 (4.14 in Recoilless Airborne Gun) (See Figs. 56, 57, 58 and 59)

1. This equipment is somewhat similar in construction to the 7.5 cm L.G.40, except that instead of the striker mechanism being incorporated in the breech block as with the 7.5 cm., it is operated on the top of the breech ring with the striker passing through the breech ring into the chamber. The striker engages the primer in the side of the cartridge case. The venturi is of the hinged type.

2. Data: L.G.40

	Metric	British
(a) Calibre	105 mm	4.134 ins
Length of piece (including jet)	1902 mm	75 ins
Length of barrel (13 cals)	1380 mm	54.33 ins
Length of rifling	798 mm	31 ins
Length of chamber	481 mm	19 ins
Capacity of chamber	5.4 litres	329 cu. ins.
Twist of rifling	$10°19'$ to $15°$	
Rifling - Polygroove plain		
No. of grooves		32
Width of grooves	5.9 mm	.23 ins
Depth of grooves	1.27 mm	.05 ins
Elevation	-267 to + 719 mils	$-15° + 40° 30'$
Traverse	711 mils X 2	$40°$ X 2.
Weight in action	388 kg.	855 lbs
Muzzle velocity (H.E.)	335 m/sec.	1099 f.s.
Muzzle velocity (Hollow Charge)	373 m/sec.	1224 f.s.
Maximum Range (H.E.)	7950 metres	8694 yds
Maximum Range (H.C.) (A.Tk)	1500 metres	1640 yds

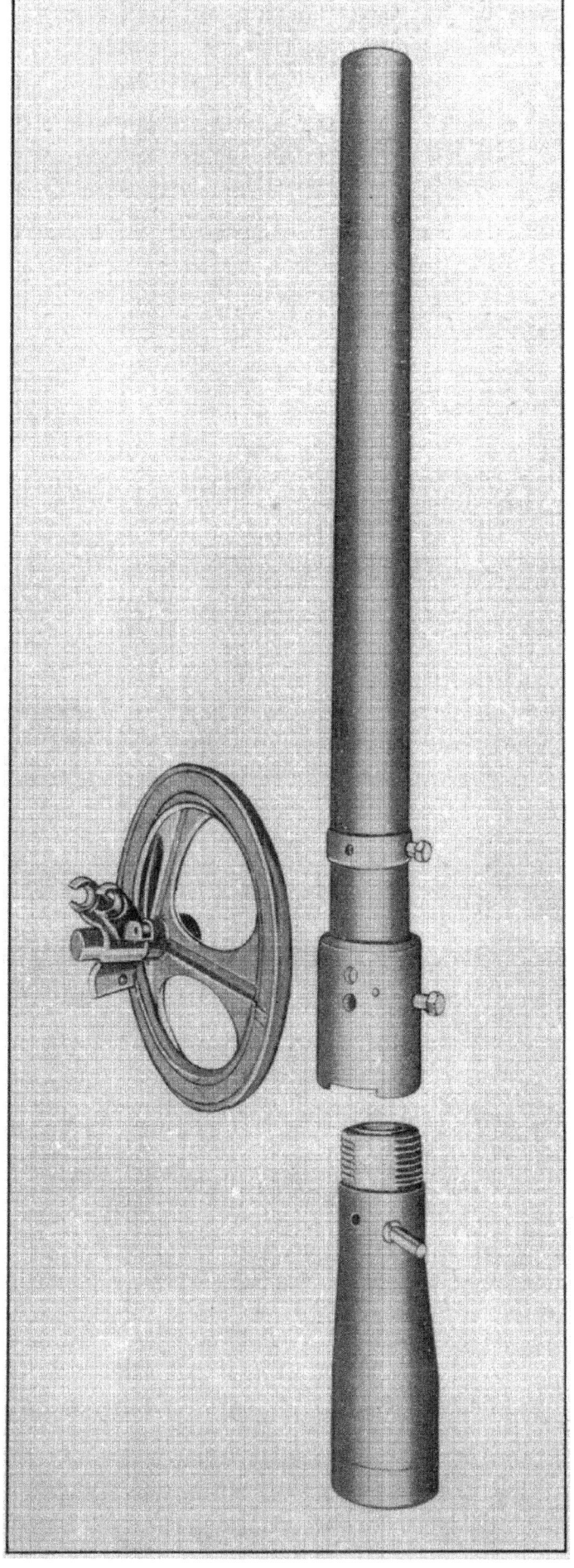

FIG. 54. 8 cm. R.f.W. 43.
(3·15 in. RECOILLESS LIGHT MORTAR MODEL 43.)

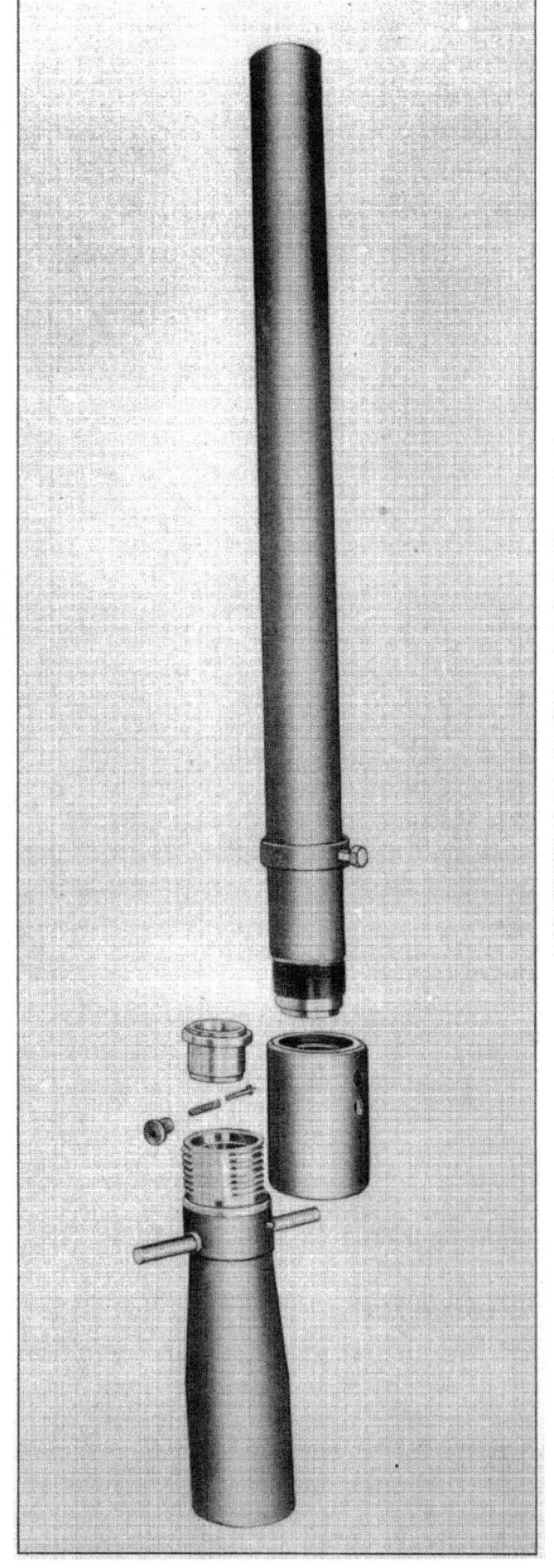

FIG. 55. 8 cm. R.f.W. 43.
(3·15 in. RECOILLESS LIGHT MORTAR MODEL 43.)

(b) Projectiles

Two types of projectiles are fired:-

(i) An H.E. shell (F.H.Gr.41) weighing 14.8 kg. (32 lb.10 oz.). It may be fitted with either a percussion fuze (AZ 23v0.15) or a T & P fuze (Dopp.Z.S/60 Fl*).

(ii) A hollow charge shell (10 cm. Gr.39) weighing 11.75 kg. (25 lb. 14 oz) fitted with the usual instantaneous percussion fuze AZ.38.

(c) Propellant

The same propellant is used for both types of ammunition and consists of a single charge in a separate brass-coated steel cartridge case.

The cartridge case has the following unusual features:-

(i) The base is composed of a circular bakelite disc which is destroyed when the gun fires, enabling a part of the propellant gas to escape to the rear.

(ii) The primer (C.13 A.St.) is fitted in the side of the cartridge case, near the base. It is fitted by means of an adaptor into a locating plate on the cartridge case, which ensures that the cartridge is loaded with the primer opposite the striker.

The charge consists of about 3 kg. (6 lb. 10 oz.) tubular Gudol contained in a white artificial silk bag. The usual igniter powder (Nz.Man.N.P.) is contained in twelve pockets round the base of the charge.

(d) Performance

(i) A range table for use with the H.E. shell (F.H.Gr.41) is given below.

(ii) The hollow charge shell (10 cm. Gr. 39) is used against armour at ranges up to 1500 metres (1640 yds.). Against other targets it may be used at ranges up to 6000 metres (6562 yds.).

3. Safety

The danger area in rear of the jet opening is 20 M (22 yds.) in width and 50 M (55 yds.) in length. This is the same as in the case of the 7.5 cm. (2.95 in.) L.G.40.

In the case of the present equipment, however, there is also a small danger area forward of the jet opening on both sides of the gun, 0.75 m (2.5 ft.) in length, and 5 - 8 m (5 . 9 yds.) in width.

4. Transport

The gun may be transported by air either:-

(a) in parachute containers. In this case the equipment is split up as follows:-

(i) the barrel in container 1. Weights - Container 54 kg. (119 lbs)
- barrel 135 kg.(298 lbs)

(ii) the breech ring and jet in container 2. Weight - container 52 kg. (115 lbs)
- contents 116 kg. (256 lbs)

(iii) the carriage body in container 3. Weights - container 51 kg. (112 lbs)
- contents 73 kg. (161 lbs)

(iv) the axle, shield and accessories in container 4. weights -
container 52 kg. (115 lbs)
- contents 83 kg. (183 lbs)

(v) the wheels (locked together and protected by wooden hub caps),

FIG. 56. 10.5 cm. LG. 40.
(4.14 in. RECOILLESS GUN MODEL 40.)

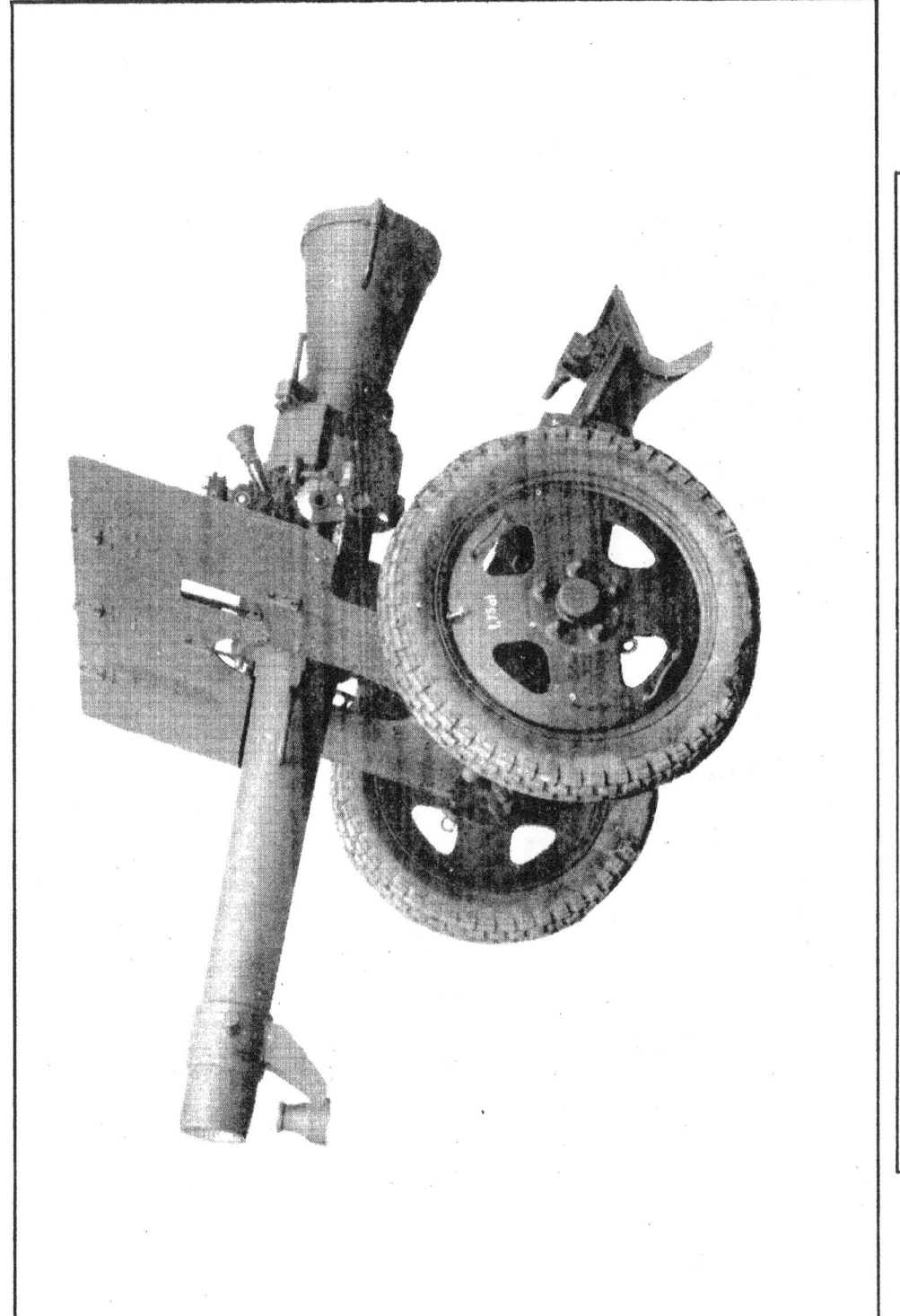

FIG. 57. 10·5 cm. L.G. 40.
(4·14 in. RECOILLESS GUN MODEL 40.)

FIG. 58. 10.5 cm. L.G. 40/2.
(4·14 in. RECOILLESS GUN MODEL 40/2.)

FIG. 59. 10.5 cm. L.G. 40/2.
(4.14 in. RECOILLESS GUN MODEL 40/2.)

not enclosed in a container.

Each container holds four complete rounds, a rifle, small arms ammunition and sundry other small stores, in addition to the loads shown in sub-paras. (i) to (iv).

(b) complete in a folding tubular metal frame. The frame is provided with buffers to absorb the force of impact. One of these operates a device for releasing the parachute on landing.

(c) complete by glider (Go-242). It is interesting to note in this connection that a tracked motor-cycle is included in the cargo, which may be used for towing the equipment when landed.

5. Range table for 10.5 cm. (4.14 in.)

Recoilless airborne gun (10.5 cm. L.G.40)

firing H.E. shell (F.H.Gr.41)

M.V. = 335 M.S. (1099 f.s.)

Range		T.E.		Time of flight. secs.	50% zone	
m.	yds.	mils.	degs.		width (yds)	length (yds.)
50	55	2	0° 7'	0.2	-	-
500	547	22	1° 14'	1.5	1	28
1000	1094	47	2° 39'	3.1	2	33
1500	1640	73	4° 7'	4.8	3	38
2000	2187	100	5° 38'	6.5	5	43
2500	2734	129	7° 16'	8.3	7	46
3000	3281	160	9° 0'	10.1	8	50
3500	3828	192	10° 49'	12.0	10	54
4000	4374	226	12° 43'	14.0	11	57
4500	4921	261	14° 42'	16.0	13	60
5000	5468	300	16° 53'	18.2	15	65
5500	6015	341	19° 12'	20.6	17	69
6000	6562	387	21° 47'	23.1	20	75
6500	7108	438	24° 40'	25.9	22	82
7000	7655	499	28° 6'	29.1	25	92
7500	8202	577	32° 29'	33.0	28	105
7950	8694	719	40° 29'	38.9	34	129

G. 10.5 cm. L.G.42 (4.14 in. Recoilless Airborne Gun) see Figs. 60 and 61

1. General:-

The following information is based on an official German range table and on reports of the examination of the gun.

The 10.5 cm. L.G.42 is a product of Rheinmetall and was originally known as the 10.5 cm. L.G.2 Rh. It was introduced into the German Army in 1943 concurrently with the 10.5 cm. L.G.40.

known as the 10.5 cm. L.G.42/1; this model differs slightly in weight from the L.G.42. Both models use the same range tables.

2. Description

The 10.5 cm. L.G.42 differs considerably in construction from the L.G.40. The salient features have been reported as follows:-

(a) The piece, of monobloc construction, incorporates a horizontal sliding breech block and rapid dismantling features similar to the 7.5 cm. L.G.40. The percussion firing mechanism is on top of the breech ring. The venturi tube also resembles that of the 7.5 cm. L.G.40, but has been fitted with three steel strips spirally welded to the inner surface in order to lessen the torque effect of the escaping propellant gases.

(b) Elevating and Traversing mechanisms Except that elevation is limited to approximately 20° by a fixed stop at positions outside the rear trail legs, the elevating and traversing mechanisms are similar to those of the 10.5 cm. L.G.40.

(c) The carriage differs considerably from that of the 10.5 cm. L.G.40. It is composed of a single tubular axle to which pivotted wheel spindles and the three folding trail legs are fitted. These members are made of fairly heavy steel tubing instead of the light alloys and aluminium formerly used on the carriage of airborne recoilless guns. Fittings for adaption to airborne use, which were on the 10.5 cm. L.G.40, have been eliminated, and the minimum number of fittings necessary to the manhandling of the gun have been retained.

The equipment has been designed for rapid dismantling and re-assembly. It is thought that it breaks down into five loads for use as pack or airborne artillery. The sight, of the dependent type, is mounted on the left trunnion; the range drum is graduated to 800 mils.

3. Data: L.G.42

	Metric	British
(a) Calibre	105 mm	4.14 ins
Length of piece (incl. breech ring and venturi)	1836 mm	72.28 ins.
Length of barrel	1374 mm	54.10 ins.
Length of rifling	798 mm	31.41 in.
Twist of rifling	10°	
No. of grooves	32	
Length of venturi tube	462 mm	18.18 in.
✕ Chamber - length	481 mm	18.93 in.
- capacity	5.4 litres	9.5 pints
Weight in action L.G.42	552 kg.	1217 lb.
" " " L.G.42/1	540 kg.	1191 lb.
Elevation	267 - 747 mils	15° to 42° 35'
Traverse: at elevations up to	6400 mils	360°
	355 mils	20°
at elevations over	335 mils	20°
	1244 mils	71° 15'

✕ These measurements are taken from the range tables and are based on the German method of measurement with a shot rammed.

/(b)

(b) **Ammunition**

(i) The 10.5 cm. L.G.42 fires the following projectiles:-

	Weight	Fuze	Type
F.H.Gr.FES		A.Z.23v(0.15)	H.E.
F.H.Gr.FES.	14.81 kg.	A.Z.23 (Pr)(0.15)	
F.H.Gr.38 Stg.FES	(32.58 lb.)	Dopp. Z.S/60Fl.	
F.H.Gr.41		Dopp. Z.S/60v.	
10 cm.Gr.39 rot.Hl/B	12.10 kg. (26.62 lb.)	A.Z.38 or	Hollow charge
10 cm.Gr.39 rot.Hl/C	12.35 kg. (27.17 lb.)	A.Z.38 St.	
F.H.Gr.38 Nb.FES	14.71 kg. (32.36 lb.)	Kl.A.Z.23 Kl.A.Z.23 Nb. Kl.A.Z.23 Nb. (Pr.) Kl.A.Z.40 Nb. (Pr.)	Smoke
F.H.Gr.Br.	15.24 kg. (33.52 lb.)	A.Z.23v (0.15) A.Z.23 (Pr) (0.15) A.Z.1. (0.15) A.Z.23 Zm. A.Z.23/42 (0.15)	H.E.Incendiary

(ii) There are two charges, known as small charge and large charge, contained in a cartridge case with C/13 n A primer. The composition of the charges is as follows:-

Small Charge

1400 grams Digl. R.P. - 9.5 - (310,3/2.2)
  30 grams Nz.Man.N.P. (1.5,1.5)
  20 grams Potassium sulphate.

Large Charge

2600 grams Gu.R.P. - Al - (330,2.6/1)
 300 grams Gu.R.P. - Al - (270,2.6/1)
 100 grams Gu.R.P. - Al - (270,2.6/1) (Adjusting charge bag)
  30 grams Nz.Man.N.P. (1.5, 1.5)

The "adjusting charge bag" is contained in the cartridge case as delivered but it to be extracted at charge temperatures of 30° C (86° F) and above. The normal range table charge temperature is 10° C. (50° F).

(c) **Ballistic Performance**

	Small Charge		Large Charge	
	M.V.	Max. Range	M.V.	Max. Range
(i) With F.H.Gr.FES F.H.Gr.38 FES F.H.Gr.38 Stg. FES. F.H.Gr.41	195 m.s (639 f.s)	3400 m. (3718 yds)	335 m.s (1099 f.s)	7950 m. (8694 yds)

/(ii)

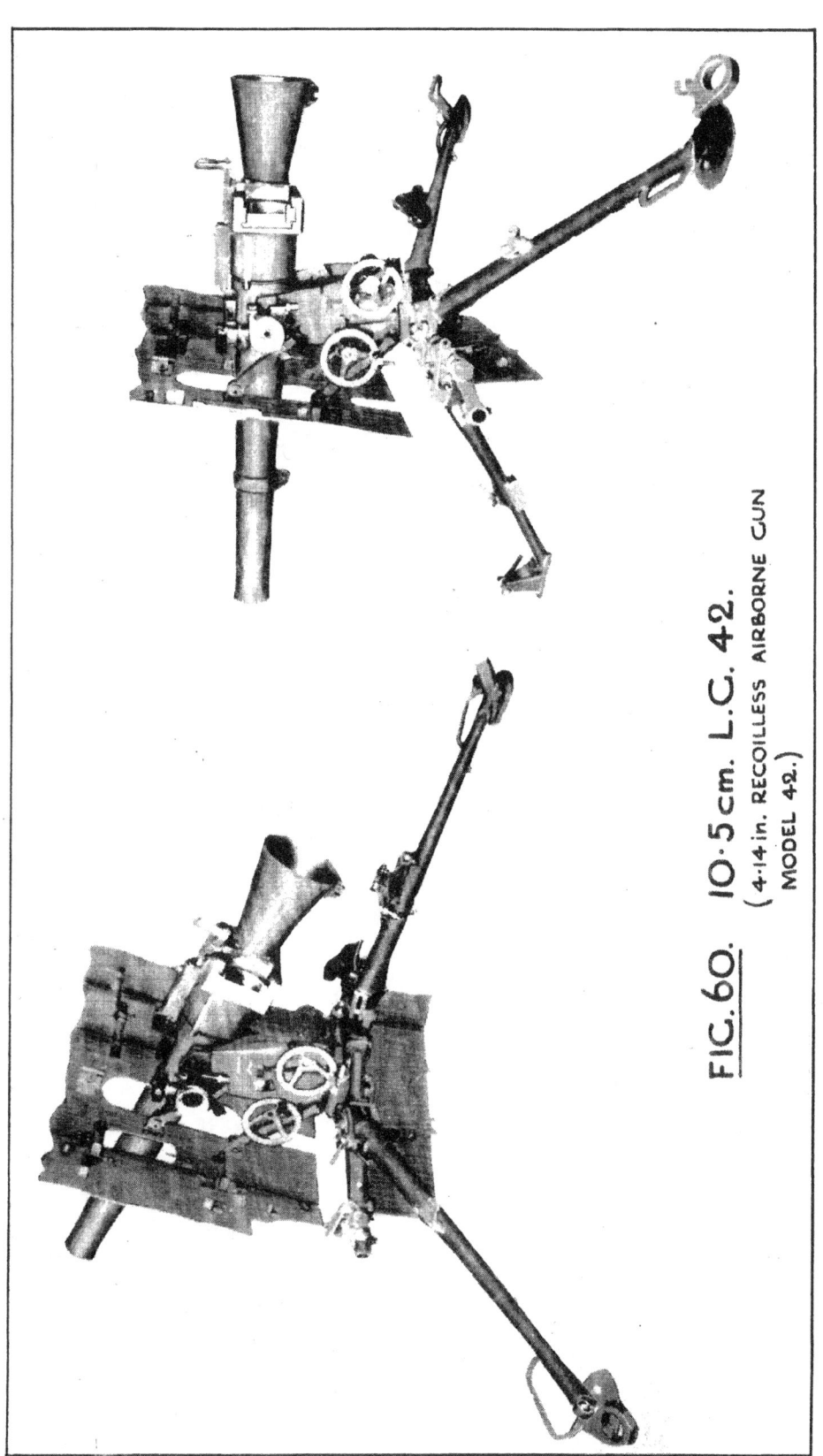

FIG. 60. 10.5 cm. L.G. 42.
(4·14 in. RECOILLESS AIRBORNE GUN MODEL 42.)

FIG. 61. 10·5 cm. L.C. 42/1
(4·14 in. RECOILLESS GUN MODEL 42/1)

	Small Charge		Large Charge	
(ii) With F.H.Gr.38 Nb. FES	185 m.s. (639 f.s.)	3400 m. (3718 yds)	335 m.s. (1099 f.s.)	780 m. (8530 yds)
(iii) With F.H.Gr.Br.	192 m.s. (630 f.s.)	3400 m. (3718 yds)	332 m.s. (1089 f.s.)	7800 (8530 yds)

h. **10.5 cm LG 43 (4.14 ins Recoilless Gun Model 43)** See Figs. 62 and 63

1. This equipment is generally similar to the 10.5 cm L.G.42 but there are several differences in carriage design, most noticeable in general appearance being the method of clamping the barrel in the travelling position.

The weapon is intended for use as a special purpose infantry gun and is suitable for use by airborne and mountain units.

The equipment can be rapidly dismantled into loads without use of tools other than the traversing and elevating handwheels. The latter are used to secure the trunnion clips and for the assembly of the traverse base with saddle to the axle assembly. The remainder of the components are locked to each other by quick release "D" barrel bolts.

In action the wheels are clear of the ground, the equipment being supported on a tripod formed by the trail legs. On coming into action the front trail leg is locked down in the firing position, and movement outwards of the rear trail legs has the effect of lifting the wheels clear of the ground. The ground bearing points of the three legs are each 2 feet 6 inches from the centre line of the axle produced. The equipment has all round traverse.

The single venturi tube, through which some of the chamber gases escape to the rear, is secured to the rear face of the sliding breech block. The inner face of the venturi tube has three swirl flares secured to it. These act as counter rotation vanes to prevent torque and twist being applied to the equipment.

The trunnions are fitted to the gun piece as is also the elevating arc.

The saddle is a light alloy casting.

Free traverse is obtained by the operation of a clutch controlled by a lever on the left saddle.

Elevation is limited to 13 degrees when the breech is outside the "segment" of 120 degrees formed by the rear trail legs.

Carriage suspension, or springing, is obtained by the use of "half axle" torsion rods with cranked stub axles.

2. It would appear that the equipment is divided into the following loads:-

	Metric	British
Barrel	135 kg	298 lbs.
Breech ring with breech mechanism	126 kg	178 lbs.
Upper shield	53.5 kg	118 lbs.
Lower shield with man handling bars	14.7 kg	33½ lbs.
Saddle and traverse base with tool boxes	72.3 kg	159½ lbs.
Rear trail legs	27.67 kg	61 lbs.
Front trail leg	13 kg	28½ lbs.
Axle assembly	71.4 kg	157½ lbs.

	Metric	British
Wheels (2)	47.6 kg	105 lbs.
Sight Bracket	7.5 kg	16½ lbs.

3. **Data: L.G.43**

	Metric	British
Calibre	105 mm	4.146 ins.
Length of barrel	1377 mm	54.26 ins.
Length of venturi tube	376 mm	14.8 ins.
Length of gun body including venturi tube	1845 mm	72.66 ins.
Length of gun body excluding Venturi tube	1479 mm	58.1 ins.
Length of rifling	789 mm	31.06 ins.

Rifling System – Polygroove Plain Section

   Increasing twist 1 in 18 to 1 in 16

Rifling Grooves – number		32
– Depth		.051 ins.
– Width		.25 ins.
Maximum traverse – at maximum elevation of 40°		70°
– at limited elevation of 13°		360°
Rate of traverse – 1 turn of handwheel		3°
Maximum elevation		40°
Rate of elevation – 1 turn of handwheel		2°2½′
Maximum depression		25°

	Metric	British
Wheels – diameter	675 mm	2 ft 2½ ins.
– tread	102 mm	4 ins.
– track	1420 mm	4 ft 8 ins.
Travelling position – length overall	2591 mm	8 ft 6 ins.
– height overall	1550 mm	5 ft 1 ins.
– width overall	1477 mm	4 ft 10 ins.
Firing position – length overall	1909 mm	6 ft 3 ins.
– height overall	1372 mm	4 ft 6 ins.
– width overall	2896 mm	9 ft 6 ins.
Weight gun complete	216 kg	476 lbs.
Weight of carriage complete	307.7 kg	678½ lbs.
Weight of gun and carriage	523.7 kg	1154½ lbs.

FIG. 62. 10·5cm. L.G. 43.
(4·14-in RECOILLESS GUN MODEL 43.)

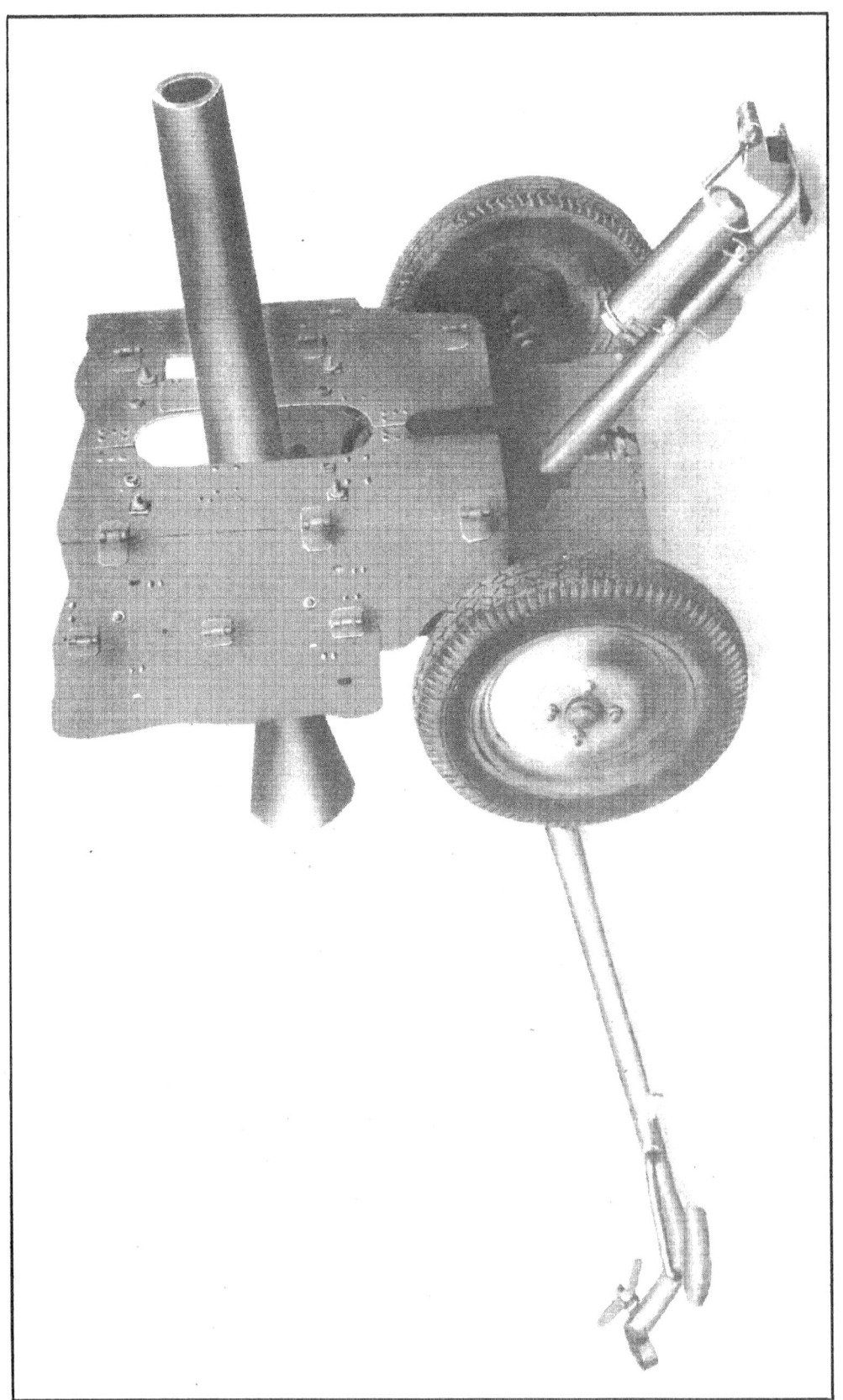

FIG. 63. 10.5 cm. L.C. 43.
(4.14 in. RECOILLESS GUN MODEL 43.)

3. Comparative Data for Equipments actually introduced or accepted for Service use.

Nomenclature Model (and designer) No.	7.5 cm L.G.40 (Rheinmetall)	10.5 cm L.G.42 (Rheinmetall)	15 cm L.G.42 (Rheinmetall)	15 cm L.G.240 (Rheinmetall)	15 cm L.G.290 (renamed L.G.42)
Calibre in mm	75 (2.95 ins)	105 (4.14 ins)	105 (4.14 ins)	150 (5.9 ins)	150 (5.9 ins)
Wt of standard HE shell (Kg.)	5.85 (12 lbs 13 ozs)	14.8 (32 lbs 10 ozs)	14.8 (32 lbs 10 ozs)	38 (83.6 lbs)	38 (83.6 lbs)
Muzzle Velocity (Metre/secs)	350 (1150 f.s.)	335 (1099 f.s.)	335 (1099 f.s.)	240 (787 f.s.)	290/300 (951 - 984 f.s.)
Wt of Propellant charge (kg.)	1.2 (2.64 lbs)	3 (6.6 lbs)	3 (6.6 lbs)	5.8 (12.76 lbs)	7.2 (15.84 lbs)
Barrel length including breech and venturi (mm)	1150 (45.3 ins)	1902 (75 ins)	1836 (72.2 ins)	1880 (74 ins)	2600 (102.4 ins)
Length of rifled part of barrel (mm)	458 (18 ins)	798 (31 ins)	798 (31 ins)		
No. of grooves Angle of Pitch	28 10° Constant	10°19' to 15°	32 10° Constant	44	
Elevation **	-15° to +20°	-15° to +40°	-15° to +42°		
Traverse *	360° 60°	80°	360° 70°	360°	360°
Max. Horiz Range (Metres)	6800 (7435 yard)	7950 (8700 yards)	7950 (8700 yards)	4700 (5740 yards)	6000 (6560 yards)
Weight in action (kg.)	145 (321 lbs)	388 (855 lbs)	552 (1214.4 lbs)	850 (1874 lbs)	850 (1874 lbs)
Remarks:-	Sliding breech block. Percussion firing	Percussion firing lateral ignition.	Percussion firing lateral ignition.	Electric firing lateral ignition.	Proposed to adopt. Bl Ring obturation

* At max elevation traverse is limited to 60° arc
** later models up to 70°

K. Recoilless Gun Development by KRUPP - Prototypes and Misc. Projects

	L.G. 1.300 75 (2.95 ins)	L.G. 1.500 105 (2.95 ins)	L.G. 2 Glatt* 105 (4.14 ins)	L.G. 2.350 105 (4.14 ins)	L.G. 2.550 P 105 (4.14 ins)	L.G. 2.550 105 (4.14 ins)	L.G. 3. Glatt 105 (Smooth Bore) (5.9 ins)
Nomenclature Calibre in mm							
MV (net/secs)	270/280 (885-918 f.s.)	490/505 (1609-1656 f.s)	240 (787 f.s.)	335/340 (1099-1115 f.s)	460/475 (1510-1558 f.s.)	550/565 (1804-1853 f.s)	260 (853 f.s.)
Wt of Projectile kg	5.75 (12.65 lbs)	5.75 (12.65 lbs)	35 kg Roechling** Shell (77 lbs)	14.81 (32.56 lbs)	14.81 Fixed Round (32.56 lbs)	14.81 (32.56 lbs)	90 kg Roechling Shell (198 lbs)
Length of barrel (mm) (in Calibres)	1114 L/15 (43.9 ins)	1925 L/25 (75.6 ins)		1905 L/18.3 (74.9 ins)	2320 L/22 (91.3 ins)	2860 L/27 (112.6 ins)	
Wt of Propellant (kg)	0.87 (1.91 lbs)	1.45 (3.19 lbs)		3.0 (6.6 lbs)	3.45 (7.6 lbs)	4.45 (9.8 lbs)	
Max. Long range (Meters)	5000 (5468 yds)	9500 (10390 yds)	5000 (5468 yds)	8000 (8750 yds)	7500 (8200 yds)	12000 (13125 yds)	6000 (6560 yds)
Weight in action (Kg)	120 (264 lbs)	450 (992 lbs)	450 (849 yds)	385 (849 yds)	-	900 (1984 lbs)	7/800 (1540-1760 lbs)
Elevation	-15° to +70°	-15° + 70°	+ 45°	-10° + 40°	-10° + 20°	-15° + 70°	+ 45°
Traverse	80°	80°		80°	360° Turret traverse	80°	
	Intended as a light Infantry gun for paratroops	For mountain Troops	* Smooth Bore ** Fin stabilised sub-calibre projectile	The production model was known as LG 40	Intended for SP Mounting	Div and Mountain Arty	Designs only

L. Recoilless Gun Development by RHEINMETAL BORSIG.- Prototypes and Misc. Projects

Nomenclature and Calibre in mm	L.G. 1.285 (Rh) 75 (2.95 ins)	L.G. 1.495 (Rh) 75 (2.95 ins)	L.G. 2.350 (Rh) 105 (4.14 ins)	L.G. 2.540 (Rh) 105 (4.14 ins)	L.G. 2.540 and VK 302 105 (4.14 ins)
MV (Met/secs)	285 (935 f.s.)	495 (1623 f.s.)	350 (1148 f.s.)	540 (1771 f.s.)	540 (1771 f.s.)
Wt of Projectile (kg)	5.75 (12.65 lbs)	5.75 (12.65 lbs)	14.81 (32.56 lbs)	14.81 (32.56 lbs)	14.81 (32.56 lbs) (fixed at 30 kg) (66 lbs)
Length of piece (in Calibres)	L/18.8 (1410 mm) (55.5 ins)	L/21.8 (1635 mm) (64.4 ins)	L/17 (1785 mm) (70 ins)	L/32 (3360 mm) (132.2ins)	L/32 (3360 mm) (132.2 ins)
Wt of Propellant (kg)	1.09 (2.4 lbs)	2.32 (5.1 lbs)	3.75 (8.25 lbs)	7.16 (15.75 lbs)	7.16 (15.75 lbs)
Max. Range (metres)	5000 (5468 yards)	9500 (10.389 yards)	7200 (7874 yards)	12000 (13.125 yards)	—
Wt in action (kg)	120 (264 lbs)	420 (926 lbs)	430 (948 lbs)	1050 (2315 lbs)	5000 (11025 lbs) (4.92 Tons)
Elevation *	-15° + 70°	-15° + 70°	-15° + 45°	-15° + 70°	-5° + 25°
Traverse *	360°	360°	360°	80°	80°
	* Restricted to 80° for elevations above 30°. Mountain Tps and Paratroops	Restricted to 80° for elevations above 15°. Mountain Troops	For Paratroops (suitable for break down)	Divl. and Mountain Arty.	SP Equipment S/A Breech Action. *Wt of gun 510 kg

CHAPTER V

THE DEVELOPMENT OF GERMAN MOUNTAIN GUNS

A. General

The two standard equipments used by the German mountain troops were the 7.5 cm Geb: G 36 and the 10.5 cm Geb: H 40 introduced into service in 1938 and 1936 respectively.

Pending adequate production of the Geb: G 36, the German Army used the le Geb: I.G.18, a modified version of the standard light infantry gun adapted for mountain warfare (see Chapter on infantry guns), also a number of 7.5 cm Skoda equipments known as Geb: K.15 (Mountain Gun M 15). This equipment was of orthodox if obsolescent design and fired a 5.47 kg (12 lbs) shell to a maximum range of 6650 metres (7275 yards). Weight in action was 630 kg (1390 lbs) with a breakdown into 7 pack loads from 78 to 156 kg (195 to 344 lbs) in weight.

B. 7.5 cm Geb: G 36 (2.95 inch Mountain Gun Model 36). See Fig 64

1. This equipment was designed by Rheinmetall Borsig and developed in the period 1935/1938. The barrel is 4 feet 9 inches long and is fitted with a cylindrical perforated muzzle brake. The recoil mechanism of variable control is housed in the cradle below the barrel. The gun is mounted on a split trail carriage and has rivetted box section trail legs, steel disc wheels and solid rubber tyres. There is no carriage springing and a single spring equilibrator to assist elevating is fitted. Weight in action is 750 kg (1654 lbs) and the equipment breaks down into six pack loads. Maximum range is 9150 metres (10,000 yards) with a 5.74 kg (12.6 lbs) HE shell and charge 5.

In October 1940 orders were given for a re-designed 7.5 cm mountain gun to replace the Geb: G 36, ballistically equal to the latter but with greater stability at low angles of elevation, with axle springing and having a better breakdown for transportation. Rheinmetall Borsig and Bohler were instructed to prepare designs for the new model, which was given the code number Gerät 99.

The Bohler design was accepted and four models in all were produced. The main features were, the use of a re-designed muzzle brake of 50% efficiency, torsion bar suspension as carriage springing, and a firing pedestal giving 3 point suspension in the firing position. The trails are perforated box section girders jointed at their centres by a quick release bolt - the equipment can be towed with trails extended or folded.

Weight was reduced from 750 kg (1654 lbs) to 650 kg (1433 lbs) with a breakdown into 7 loads varying from 105 to $117\frac{1}{2}$ kg (231 to $258\frac{1}{2}$ lbs).

The designers claimed that the equipment was stable firing charge 5 down to 5 degrees depression.

2. Data : Geb. G. 36

	Metric	British
(a) Calibre	75 mm	2.95 ins
Length of barrel	1450 mm	57.09 ins
Length of rifling	972 mm	38.27 ins
Rifling - Uniform Right-Hand Twist 1 in 24.		
No. of grooves	28	
Length of chamber	186 mm	7.32 ins
Capacity of chamber	0.9 litres	54.92 cu.ins
Maximum recoil	737 mm	29 ins
Minimum recoil	585 mm	23 ins
Maximum traverse	40°	
Rate of traverse 1 Turn of handwheel	40 minutes	

/Elevation

Data (cont.)   Metric   British

    Elevation   70°
    Rate of elevation 1 Turn of handwheel   1°
    Maximum depression   10°
    Rate of Fire   8 rpm
    Muzzle velocity   475 m/s   1558 f.s.
    Maximum range   9150 metres   10,000 yds
    Weight in action   750 kg   1654 lbs.

(b) Jump, firing 7.5 cm Ger: 34 Al. with new gun

    Charge 1 - 3   + 2 mils   +6 min 45 secs
    Charge 4 - 5   + 1 mil   +3 min 23 secs

       Firing K.Gr.rot.Al.and K.Gr rot Buntrauch
    Charge 1 - 3   + 2 mils   +6 min 45 secs
    Charge 4   + 1 mil   +3 min 23 secs
    Charge 5   + 0 mil   +0 min 0 secs

(c) Stability

    The gun is stable in action -
      0° Elevation to 15° with charge 1 to 4
    Over 15° with charge 5.

(d) The complement of ammunition carried is:-

	Mountains		Flat country	
HE 7.5 cm Gr Al (Fuze Percussion AZ 23)	175	70%	214	85%
HE K Gr rot Al (Time Percussion Dopp Z S/60)	39	15%	6	2.5%
HE K Gr rot Buntrauch (Time and Percussion Dopp Z S/60)	12	5%	6	2.5%
Hollow Charge 7.5 cm Gr 38 (Fuze Percussion AZ 38)	24	10%	24	10%

3. Ammunition

   (a) Projectiles

      (i) <u>HE Shell (Aluminium) (7.5 cm Gr 34 Al)</u>

        Weight filled and fuzed   5.74 kg (12 lb 10 oz)
        Fuze   Nose percussion, Kl AZ 23
        Bursting charge   TNT with 10% aluminium

      (ii) <u>HE Shell (Aluminium) (7.5 cm K Gr rot Al)</u>

        Weight filled and fuzed   5.83 kg (12 lb 13 oz)
        Fuze   T and P Dopp Z S/60s
        Bursting charge   TNT with 10% aluminium.

This shell is similar to that fired by the le F K 18. It differs from (i) above in that it is shorter in order to accommodate the T and P fuze, which is longer than the percussion fuze.

      (iii) <u>HE Shell (Multi-coloured smoke) (7.5 cm K Gr rot Buntrauch)</u>

        Weight filled and fuzed   5.83 kg (12 lb 13 oz)
        Fuze   T and P Dopp Z S/60s

This shell is extremely similar to (ii) above. (Both have a red band above the driving band). It appears, however, to be intended to produce multi-coloured smoke on detonation.

      (iv) <u>Hollow Charge Shell (7.5 cm Gr 38)</u>

        Weight filled and fuzed   4.40 kg (9 lb 12 oz)
        Fuze   Nose percussion A Z 38.

/ This

FIG. 64. 7·5 cm. Geb. G. 36.
(2·95 in MOUNTAIN GUN MODEL 36.)

This appears to be identical with that fired by the 7.5 cm KwK 38. It is used against armour, charge 4 being loaded. The muzzle velocity is 1280 f/secs, and the maximum range 1000 m (1094 yds) as shown on the sight drum.

(b) Propellant

(i) Composition

There are five charges composed as follows :

Charge	Nz Man N P (1.5,1.5)	Digl R P –10.5 – (2,2/1)	Digl R P–9.5 (130, 2.5/1)
1	–	123 gm (4 ozs 5 dr)	–
2	–	158 gm (5 oz 9 dr)	–
3	–	203 gm (7 oz 2 dr)	–
4	–	273 gm (9 oz 10 dr)	–
5	10 gm (6 dr)	–	530 gm (18 oz 11 dr)

(ii) Preparation for firing

The cartridge case is issued with charge 4 in position. If a smaller charge is required the top bag is removed revealing the figure 3 on the next bag, and 2 on the one after that, etc. For firing with charge 5 the cartridge case must be emptied and charge 5 inserted.

The primer used is the Percussion Type C/22.

C. **7.5 cm Geb: K 15 (2.95 ins Mountain Gun Model 15).** See Figs:- 65

1. Data

	Metric	British
Calibre	75 mm	2.95 ins
Length of Piece	1155 mm	45.4 ins
Length of barrel	802 mm	31.4 ins
Rifling – Details not recorded.		
Length of chamber	160.4 mm	6.31 ins
Volume of chamber	.67 litres	33.4 ins
Maximum recoil	850 mm	15.3 ins
Minimum recoil	390 mm	
Rate of Fire	8 rpm	
Traverse	7°	
Elevation	–9° + 50°	
Maximum Range	6,650 metres	7250 yds
Number of load = 7 Heaviest = 150 kg		
Weight in action	630 kg	1380 lbs

2. Propellant charges :-

	I	II	III	IV
Muzzle velocity, metres/secs	235 m/s	263 m/s	304 m/s	386 m/s
Muzzle energy in metric tons	15.4	19.3	25.8	41.5
Pressure in atmosphere	800	1000	1200	1700

Weight of shell Geb. Gr 15 with percussion fuze AZ Geb or T & P fuze Dopp Z S/60 Geb = 12 lbs.

	Max Range Yds	M.V. f.s.	R.V. f.s.	Weight charge oz.	Time of flight secs	50% Zone, yards Length	Breadth
Charge I	4270	770	554	5.2	29	113	5.45
II	5000	865	596	6.42	31.8	126	6.55
III	5900	1000	625	8.2	35	240	8.7
IV	7250	1270	692	11.6	37	196	13

Note: The splinter effect of the shell is about 20 yards laterally and 11 yards forward.

FIG. 65. 7.5 cm. Geb. K.15.
(2·95 in. MOUNTAIN GUN MODEL 15.)

3. Ammunition

   (a) Projectiles

   The following are known types :

   (i) **Geb Gr 15** This is a HE shell and is fitted with a nose fuze. Immediately below the fuze is a Zdlg c/98 Np type of gaine, which is set in a steel holder. The holder is screwed into an adapter, which is in turn screwed into the nose of the shell. The bursting charge consists of TNT which is contained in a cardboard wrapping. There is a smoke box situated beneath the gaine.

Weight of shell	5.47 kg (12 lbs)
Weight of bursting charge	500 gm
Fuze	AZ 23 Geb (nose percussion)
or	Dopp Z S/60 Geb (T and P)

   (ii) **Geb Gr 15 Al** This is similar to the Geb Gr 15 except that the bursting charge consists of TNT containing approximately 10% aluminium.

   (iii) **7.5 cm Gr 39.** This shell incorporates the hollow charge principle. Externally it resembles the standard German shell of this type.

Weight of shell	4.5 kg (9.9 lbs)
Fuze	A Z 38 (nose percussion)

   (iv) **7.5 cm Gr 15 Rot.** Little is known about this except that it is probably a HE shell. The following details are available :

Weight of shell	5.47 kg (12 lbs)
Fuze	Dopp Z S/60 Geb.

   So far samples of the Geb Gr 15 only have been recovered. The shells are very similar externally to those for the 7.5 cm le.I.G.18. The main difference is that the former has a wider driving band.

   (b) **Cartridge Case**   Design No.   6335
                           Primer   c/12nA (percussion type)

   (c) Propellant Charge

   This is divided into four parts, the first three constituting the normal charge and the latter, the supercharge. Each part is contained in a silk bag, the normal charge being packed in a cartridge case and the supercharge in a cardboard carton.

   The charge parts are made up as follows :

   Part 1. This is in two parts :
   (i) 60 gm of Ngl.Bl.P.-12,5 - (4 . 4 . 1)
   This is a double base propellant in the form of flakes 4 x 4 x 1 mm.
   (ii) 87 gm of Ng.bl.P. - 12,5 - (10. 10. 1,5)
   This is similar to (i) but is 10 x 10 x 1.5 mm.
   Part 2. 35 gm of Ngl.Bl.P.-12,5 - (10 . 10 . 1,5)
   Part 3. 50 gm of Ngl.Bl.P. -12,5 - (10 . 10 . 1,5)
   Part 4. This is in two parts:
   (i) 10 gm of Ngl.P.l.P. - 12,5 - (50 . 0,2)
   This is a double base propellant in the form of leaves of the following dimensions :

Diameter	50 mm
Thickness	0.2 mm

   (ii) 320 gm of Ngl.R.P. - 9,5 - (125 / 3/1,8)
   This is a double base propellant containing nitroglycerine in the form of tubes. It has the following dimensions :

Length	125 mm
External diameter	3 mm
Internal diameter	1.8 mm

/ Sub-sections

Sub-sections (i) of Parts 1 and 4 are igniters and are arranged nearest the primer.

(d) **Flash Reducers**

Flash reducers are supplied. These consist of 20 gm of a potassium salt. The package is labelled Kast. vorl. d. Geb.K 15 u 14 Kp.

(e) **Packing**

The following are packed in a wooden box :
- 6 shells
- 6 cartridge cases, each containing a normal charge
- 6 supercharge
- 9 flash reducers

The weight of the package is 56 kg.

D. **7.5 cm Geb: G.43 (2.95 ins Mountain Gun 43). See figs.- 66 and 67**

1. This mountain gun, of which only four were produced, shows considerable advance on the 7.5 cm Geb. 36.

The equipment can be readily broken down into seven loads. The heaviest component is the piece at 242 lbs.

The piece is monobloc and is integral with the breech ring.

The breech mechanism is of the horizontal sliding wedge type closing to the left.

Three types of muzzle brakes were under trial with the equipment all being of welded construction. The third one to be designed was devised by Bohlers and was accepted in 1943; it had an efficiency of 85%.

The recoil system was of the normal hydraulic buffer with hydro-pneumatic type recuperator.

Twin elevating arcs were fitted to the equipment.

Both saddle and undercarriage are of similar construction to the Geb. G.36.

Torsion bar suspension with crank stub axles is of normal design, having spring loaded plungers for locating the axle cranks of the wheels.

The wheels are of the press steel spoke plate type to the rims of which are fitted solid perforated rubber tyres.

A firing pedestal is used and is attached to the front of the undercarriage by three quick release pins. The firing pedestal is brought into contact with the ground on moving the wheels with their axle cranks from the travelling to the firing position, giving three point support. The ground clearance is about 8 inches.

The middle support of the firing pedestal has a second position allowing the undercarriage to be lowered to an alternative firing position. In this position all the wheels make contact with the ground. In this lower position the ground clearance is about $4\frac{1}{2}$ inches.

The trail legs are perforated box section girders jointed at their centre by quick release pins.

The equipment may be towed with the rear trail sections extended, as for the firing position, or folded forward. Provision is made for the alternative position for the tow bar. Alternative traction is the N.S.U. Kettenkrad or horse.

The equipment was also referred to as the "GEBHARD" or "Gerät 99".

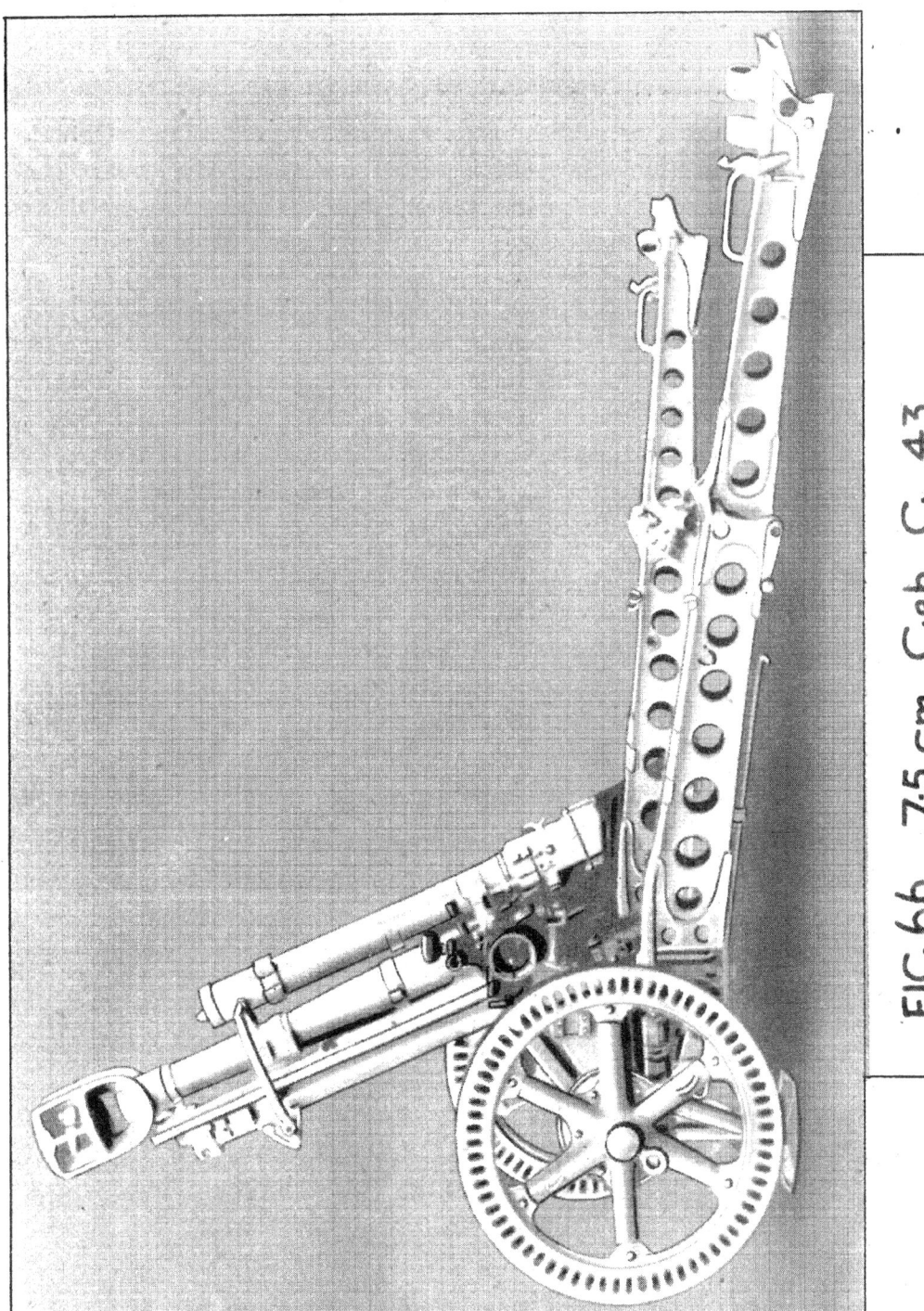

FIG. 66. 7.5 cm. Geb. G. 43.
(2.95 in. MOUNTAIN GUN MODEL 43.)

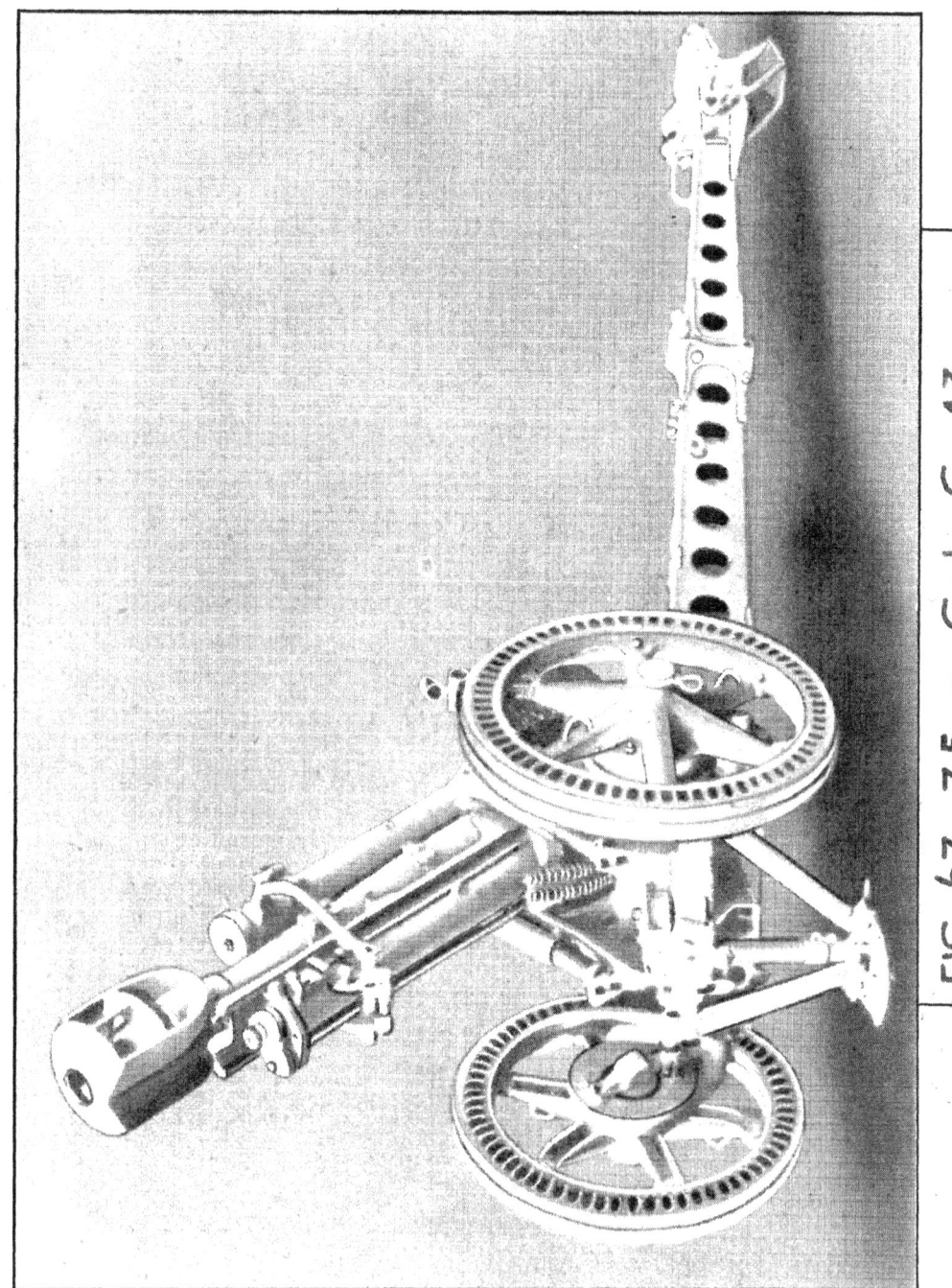

FIG. 67. 7.5 cm. Geb. G. 43.
(2.95 in. MOUNTAIN GUN MODEL 43.)

2. Data Geb. G.43   Metric   British

   (a) Calibre   7.5 cm   2.95 ins
       Length of piece with muzzle brake   163 cm   64.25 ins
       Length of piece without muzzle brake   139 cm   55 ins
       Length of calibres   18.5
       Length of muzzle brake detached   39.4 cm   15.5 ins
       Length of chamber   26.4 cm   10.4 ins
       Length of rifling   97.3 cm   38.3 ins
       Rifling system   P.P.S. RH constant 6°
       Twist   1 in 30
       Grooves - number   28
         "   width   4.5 mm   0.177 ins
         "   depth   1.2 mm   0.043 ins
       Ground clearance travelling pos. (ca)   270 mm   10.5 ins
       Diameter of wheels   800 mm   31.5 ins
       Width of tread   80 mm   3.15 ins
       Track width, centres   1000 mm   39.4 ins
         "   "   over axles   1220 mm   48 ins
       Overall length, firing position   3251 mm   128 ins
         "   width over open trails   2159 mm   85 ins
         "   length travelling
               position trails folded   2362 mm   93 ins
               forward
       Overall length, trails together   3353 mm   132 ins

   (b) Weights

       Piece   110 kg   242 lbs
       Muzzle Brake   16 kg   35 lbs
       Recuperator   65 kg   143 lbs
       Cradle with buffers   108 kg   238 lbs
       Lower carriage with brake and
         suspension   72 kg   158 lbs
       Firing Pedestal   11 kg   24 lbs
       Wheels   95 kg   209 lbs
       Trails   95 kg   209 lbs
       Sight   10 kg   22 lbs

   (c) Initial MV

       With normal HE   480 m/sec   1574 ft/sec
         " hollow charge   500 m/sec   1646 ft/sec
       Maximum range   9500 m   10,370 yds
       Charges, number   5
       Ammunition   As for Geb 36
       Firing detachment   4

   (d) Stability

       With normal HE   from 0° elevation upwards
         " hollow charge   " -5°   "   "
       Chamber capacity   As for Geb 36 (i.e. 54.92 cu ins)

       Recoiling mass   226 kg   497 lbs
       Recoil, Max.   800 mm   31.5 ins
         "   Min   400 mm   15.7 ins
       Braking pressure at 70°
         elevation   240 atm   3538 lbs sq in
       Recuperator pressure   43 atm   642 lbs sq in
         "   capacity   2.85 litres   5 pints
       Elevation   -5° to + 70°
       Traverse   40°
       Height in firing position   750 mm   29.5 ins
       Weight of saddle with sight   53 Kg   117 lbs

3. Pack loads (7)

   (a)   Piece   110 Kg
         Saddle frame   7.5 Kg
                                                              ―――――――
                                                              117.5 Kg   258 lbs

(b)	Cradle with buffer	108 Kg	
	Saddle frame	7.5 Kg	
		115.5 Kg	254 lbs
(c)	Recuperator	65 Kg	
	Saddle frame	7.5 kg	
	Collimator	13 kg	
	Accessories	30 kg	
		115.5 kg	254 lbs
(d)	Lower carriage	72 Kg	
	Saddle frame	7.5 kg	
	Front support	11 kg	
	Barrel mats	12 kg	
	accessories	6 kg	
		108.5 kg	239 lbs
(e)	Saddle	53 kg	
	Accessory box with muzzle brake and sight, etc	53 kg	
	Accessories, various	10 kg	
		116 kg	255 lbs
(f)	Wheels	95 kg	
	Accessories	10 kg	
		105 kg	231 lbs
(g)	Trails	95 kg	
	Spades	15 kg	
	Accessories	5 kg	
		115 kg	253 lbs

E. **10.5 cm Geb: H.40. (4.13 inch Mountain Howitzer Model 40). See Figs:- 68 and 69.**

1. The 10.5 cm Mtn Howitzer is the heaviest artillery equipment specially designed for mountain warfare. It was designed by Bohler, the Austrian firm, in competition with Rheinmetall, whose prototype 10.5 cm Geb: H L/80 was not accepted.

The equipment is of somewhat unorthodox design and constructed so as to facilitate quick assembly or dismantling. The carriage has several important features - it is of the split trail type but with massive trail legs which house the brake and shock absorbing gear for the wheels in the travelling position. The shock absorbing gear is so powerful that it has the appearance of having been designed with a view to possible use by airborne troops with the equipment having to be dropped by parachute; there are several minor features in this equipment to support this possibility. The position of the wheels in the break down into loads arrangement is at the centre of gravity of the trail assembly.

According to the gun drill, the normal method of transport is not "pack" but in four separate wheeled loads on single axle trailers towed by semi-tracked motor-cycle combinations, NSU Kettenvad. It is suggested that one of these loads is the trail assembly using the equipments' own wheels. The individual loads weigh 680, 685, 700 and 720 kgs respectively (1500, 1510, 1543 and 1588 lbs). The equipment also breaks down into five loads comprising breech ring and mechanism, barrel, cradle and recoil assembly, saddle and lastly trail assembly.

A bracket is provided for the support of the carriage body in the firing position.

The equipment in the firing position weighs 2660 kg (2.6 tons) and fires a 14.81 kg (32.6 lbs) projectile (as for the light Field Howitzer 18 series) to a maximum range of 12,625 metres (13,800 yards).

/ The

The ammunition listed for this weapon is most interesting and the standard HE shell has an addition of aluminium powder to the filling which gives a bright flash on burst - there is also a special HE round with a coloured (usually red) smoke indicator for ranging in snow covered terrain. Star shell and also hollow charge projectiles are also provided for this equipment, the latter weighing 12.3 kg (27 lbs) and fired with charge 6 at an MV of 460 m/s (1510 f.s.).

The use of recoilless weapons as mountain artillery was expected to be an unqualified success owing to the overall reduction in weight but did not prove to be so. This has been dealt with in detail in the chapter on recoilless weapons.

2. Data Geb. H.40

	Metric	British
(a) Calibre	105 mm	4.13 ins
Length of barrel	2870 mm	112.94 ins
Length of piece	3100 mm	122.05 ins
Length of rifling	2407	94.74 ins
Rifling - system. Polygroove - increasing RH twist 1 in 31.5 to 1 in 21.9		
Grooves - number		32
depth	1.22 mm	.048 ins
width	5.6 mm	.220 ins
Percussion firing		
Chamber capacity	3.1 litres	189.17 cu ins
Muzzle velocity HE	570 m/sec	1870 ft secs
Chamber pressure	2500 atmospheres	16.4 tons sq in
Muzzle energy	245.2 tons metric	241 tons
Traverse	51°	
Rate of traverse - one turn of handwheel	0°50'	
Elevation	-5°30' +71°	
Rate of elevation - one turn of handwheel	1°40'	
Overall length of equipment	5639 mm	18 ft 6 ins
Width overall	1371 mm	4 ft 6 ins
Height overall	1498 mm	4 ft 11 ins
Weight in action	1660 kg	3660 lbs (32 cwts)
Weight of standard projectile	14.81 kg	32.6 lbs
Maximum range	12.625 metres	13.800 yds

(b) Ammunition

Nomenclature	Type	Weight lbs	Fuzes used
F H Gr Al	HE Streamline. HE filling includes aluminium powder to give flash on burst	32.6	AZ 23/42(0.15) or AZ 1(0.15) or Dopp Z S/60 Flv or Dopp Z S/60 v
F H Gr Buntrauch	Streamline. Coloured Smoke. On bursting in the air, a smoke box falls to the ground and generates red smoke.	32.6	Dopp Z S/60 Flv or Dopp Z S/60 v
10 cm Gr 39 rot Hl/A or Hl/B or Hl/C	Hollow charge anti-tank shell	27.1 26.7 27.2	AZ 38 or AZ 38 St
10.5 cm Lt Gs	Star Shell	30.9	Dopp Z S/60 Flv or Dopp Z S/60 v

(c) Fuzes

AZ 23/42 (0.15 and AZ1(0.15) are percussion fuzes with

/an

an optional delay of 0.15 secs which will give a ricochet air burst with low angles of arrival.

AZ 38 and AZ 38 St are special percussion fuzes for use with hollow charge shell.

Dopp Z S/60 Flv and Dopp Z S/60 v are mechanical time and percussion fuzes.

(d) Cartridge case

Design No. 6327 - Brass.

(e) Primer

Percussion C/12 nA - Brass or
C/12 nA St - Steel.

(f) Propelling charge

Charge	Nz Man Granular 1.5 x 1.5 mm (igniter)	Potassium Sulphate Flash reducer	Digl. Flake 10.5 10x10x0.2 mm	Gudol Flake AO 4x4x0.6 mm	Digl Tubular G 1 180x2.9/1.5 mm
1	309 grains	154 grains	8.1 oz	–	–
2	"	192 "	9.4 oz	–	–
3	"	231 "	9.4 oz	1.9 oz	–
4	"	309 "	9.4 oz	5.5 oz	–
5	"	309 "	9.4 oz	10.8 oz	–
6	"	386 "	9.4 oz	21.5 oz	–
7	"	–	–	–	66½ oz

3. Ballistic performance

The howitzer fires in both lower and upper register.

	Charge	M.V f.s.	Max range-yds
F H Gr Al and F H Gr Buntrauch (HE and Smoke shell)	1	689	4210
	2	755	4890
	3	833	5800
	4	951	7160
	5	1115	8750
	6	1394	10580
	7	1870	12625
10 cm Gr 39 rot H1/A, or H1/B, or H1/C	6	1509	8750
10.5 cm Lt Gs	6	1575	7550 (with an ejection height of 1600 ft)

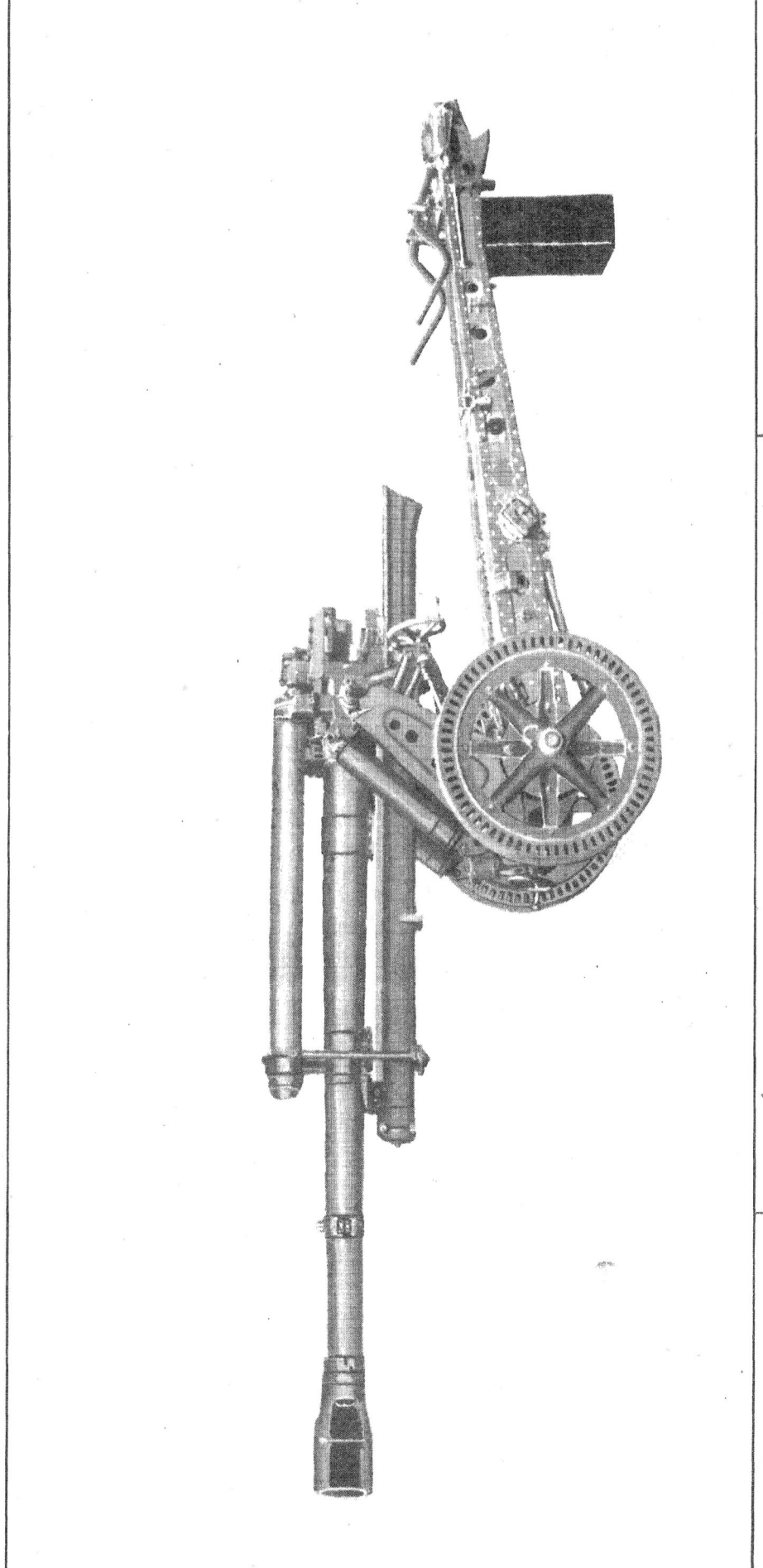

FIG. 68. 10·5 cm. Geb. H. 40.
(4·13 in. MOUNTAIN HOWITZER MODEL 40.)

FIG. 69.   10·5 cm. Geb. H. 40.
(4·13 in. MOUNTAIN HOWITZER MODEL 40.)

CHAPTER VI

THE DEVELOPMENT OF GERMAN FIELD ARTILLERY

A. General

The standard field gun and field howitzer of the German Artillery is of 75 mm (2.95 inch) and 105 mm (4.13 inch) calibre respectively.

1. The 7.5 cm Feldkanone (2.95 inch Field Guns) Models 16, 18 and 38 represent a series of light field guns of obsolete design intended basically for horse drawn transport in one load. They were used by units of the Light Artillery and in certain low grade formations.

2. The 7.5 cm Feldkanone 16 n.A (2.95 inch Field Gun Model 16 new type) is a modified version of the 77 mm field gun used in the 1914/18 war. Weight in action is 1524 kgs and max range is 12875 metres with a 6.6. kg H.E. shell. H.E. shell, AP/HE shell and latterly Hollow Charge shell were fired against A.F.V's.

3. The 7.5 cm leichte Feldkanone 18 (2.95 inch light Field Gun Model 18) was developed by Krupp and Rhienmetall in 1930/31, the production model being finally accepted in 1938. The equipment is of lighter construction than the FK 16 N.A. Weight in action is 1120 kg and max range 9425 metres with a 5.83 kg H.E. shell. Three charges only are fired as against four with the FK 16 N.A.

4. The 7.5 cm Feldkanone 38 (2.95 inch Field Gun Model 38) was originally designed by Krupp for a Brasilian order and 64 equipments were reported to have been delivered by 1940. A further 80 equipments were completed and taken into service in the German Army under the above nomenclature in 1942.

The Model 38 is a further development of the Model 18, a muzzle brake is fitted and the breech action is semi-automatic. Fixed type ammunition is fired and the max range is 11500 metres with the 5.83 kg H.E. projectile. Weight in action is 1366 kg.

As with the earlier models this equipment is designed for horse drawn transport.

5. The 10.5 cm leichte Feldhaubitze 18 (le FH 18) (4.13 inch Light Field Howitzer M. 18) was the standard field gun-howitzer of the Divisional Artillery in service at the commencement of the War - designs for this equipment to replace the earlier model 16 dated from 1928/29 and it was introduced into service in 1935.

The le FH 18 fires 6 charges and ranges up to 10675 metres with the standard 14.81 kg H.E. Weight in action is 1985 kg.

A wide range of ammunition was produced for the le FH series of equipments: H.E., Smoke, Coloured Smoke Indicator, Incendiary, HE/Incendiary, Star Shell, AP/HE Shell, AP/HE Subcalibre projectile, and a Propaganda Leaflet Shell. To meet the demand for increased performance the le FH 18 was soon modified by fitting a muzzle brake and adjusting the recoil mechanism in order to fire a long range shell with supercharge. The MV was increased from 470 Met/secs to 540 Met/secs and max range to 12325 metres.

This modified equipment was known as le FH 18 M.

A limited number of equipments, known as the le FH 18/39, was taken into service. This consisted of the le FH 18 M ordnance mounted on a Krupp carriage designed for export to Holland. This equipment is ballistically identical with the le FH 18 M and the later model 18/40 which, although a hybrid equipment, replaced earlier models in production.

/ In

In 1942 there was an urgent requirement for increased production of the le FH and especially for a lighter equipment than the standard model - speed of production was stressed in the specification. It was accordingly decided to use the tubular split trail carriage of the 7.5 PAK 40 (Anti-Tank 40) which was in large scale production and required a minimum of modification to take the piece of the le FH 18 M. This equipment was known as the le FH 18/40. New features were as follows:-

(a) The carriage incorporated torsion bar suspension which was locked in action.
(b) Both elevating and traversing hand wheels are on the left side of the carriage so that the layer can traverse, elevate and fire the gun.
(c) An increased efficiency muzzle brake is fitted. This is produced by welding projecting wings to the standard le FH 18 M brake.

The le FH 18/40 was to be regarded as a temporary solution of the problem of production and was certainly not intended as the final solution to the requirements of the German Army, indeed there is a good deal of evidence that the carriage did not prove robust enough for this equipment.

6. Meanwhile designs continued and Krupp completed prototype models of the le FH 42 which was originally intended to replace the le FH 18M. This new model was of orthodox design but considerably lighter in weight and had increased track width and a lower silhouette in action - the carriage incorporated torsion bar suspension and allowance was made for stability of the equipment in action on uneven terrain. Weight in action is reduced to 1630 kg. Total traverse is 70° and ballistically the le FH 42 is not inferior to the earlier models, and bears the standard projectiles of the le FH series.

The le FH 42 was not accepted for production because, by the time it was ready, the requirements of the Army had again been modified. Wartime experience had shown, especially in the Russian campaign, that artillery emplaced in forward zones of operation frequently found it necessary to deal with A.F.Vs at close range, also in well wooded country ability to fire in the upper register was indispensible.

7. Accordingly the German designers pressed forward with designs for the le FH 43 which had to satisfy these further requirements. Three different solutions were found.

(a) By Skoda

The gun is fitted with a muzzle brake similar to the le FH 18/40 but the ordnance is larger and chamber capacity is increased. Recoil mechanism is of the H.P. variable type with three stage variation and is located below the barrel. The carriage is unorthodox. A firing pedestal is integral with the lower carriage and an extra set of tracks are fitted which fold forward and in the travelling position are clamped to the barrel.

In the firing position the pedestal is pivoted downwards and locked in the firing position, both front and rear trails are spread and equally spaced at 90° around the pedestal and securing pickets driven into the ground.

Elevation is from - 5° to + 75° at all angles of traverse. Weight in action is 2200 kg and the gun ranges up to 13000 metres with the standard 14.81 kg H.E. shell.

(b) Krupp produced two solutions:-

(i) Working on somewhat similar lines to the Skoda design but using one forward trail leg only. Designs do not appear to have progressed beyond the wooden scale model stage.

(ii) Using a cruciform carriage with folding outriggers transported on travelling bogies for and aft. This type of carriage had proved most satisfactory with the 8.8 cm PAK 43 and it was intended to standardise this carriage and the recoil mechanism as far as possible to take the PAK 43 and le FH 43 ordnances.

/ Krupp

Krupp considered two types of barrel for the le FH 43, one being 28 calibres long the other which they appear to have favoured, 35 calibres long. The latter was provided with S/A sliding breech block action prepared for electric firing. Maximum range was estimated at 14200 metres with the standard 14.81 kg H.E. projectile and charge 7. In addition it was proposed to introduce a rocket assisted shell giving a maximum range of 16500 metres.

8. The leichte 10 cm Kanone 41 is not an important equipment. Experimental models were produced both by Krupp and Rheinmetall in 1941 but the equipment was not introduced into service. It was intended to meet the demand for increased performance of the le F.H. series. Maximum range was 15000 metres but at 2640 kg overall weight in action it was considered too heavy and the project was abandoned early in 1942.

9. The 10 cm Kanone 17 is an obsolete equipment designed by Krupp, for horse drawn transport in two loads, and introduced originally in 1917. A number of these equipments escaped destruction by the allies following the armistice in 1918 and the Treaty of Verseilles and were taken into service for low grade formations. This equipment weighs 3300 kg in action and has a maximum range of 15/16000 metres with a 15 kg shell.

B. **7.5 cm Feldkanone 16 n.A** (2.95 in Field Gun Model 16 new type) (See Fig: 70)

1. This light field gun was adopted in 1934 to replace the 77 mm FK Model 16, the carriage being retained and used to mount the 75 mm gun.

The weapon was intended for use with the cavalry and was, of course, horse drawn but may be towed by light motor vehicle. The breech mechanism is of the Q.F. horizontal sliding breech block type fitted with percussion firing gear. The piece is of monobloc or jacket and tube construction with detachable breech ring. The recoil system consisting of a hydraulic buffer and spring recuperator is housed in the cradle below the piece.

The box trail carriage is fitted with wooden spoked steel rimmed artillery wheels. The shield is in three portions the upper part having a pronounced curve to the rear.

The suffix N/A is attached to the model number to indicate new type.

2. Data: F.K. 16 n.A.

	Metric	British
Calibre	75 mm	2.95 ins
Length of piece (36 Cals)	2700 mm	106.3 ins
Length of rifling	2036 mm	80.15 ins
Type of rifling, Polygroove Plain Section		
Twist of rifling, Progressive Right Hand Twist		
Angle of pitch of rifling	5° to 7° 58' 5"	
Chamber capacity	1.84 litres	
Traverse	72 mils	4 Degs. approx.
Elevation	- 160 to + 782 mils	- 9° + 44°
Weight in action	1524 kg	1.5 Tons
Weight in travelling position	2415 kg	2.38 Tons
Maximum Muzzle Velocity	662 m/s	2172 fs
Chamber Pressure	2500 atmospheres	16.5 Tons sq. in.
Muzzle Energy	130 m/t	
Weight of Standard Projectile HE	6.62 kg	
Maximum Range	12.875 metres	

3. Ammunition

No. of charges - 4

Projectile	Fuzes	Weight of Projectile	Weight of HE
(a) HE - K. Gr Rot (Light Metal Fuzes)	A.Z.23V(0.15) Dopp Z.S/60S	5.83 kg (12.83 lbs)	0.515 kg (1.13 lbs)

/ (b)

FIG. 70. 7·5 cm. F.K.16. n.A.
(2·95 in. FIELD GUN MODEL 16 – NEW TYPE.)

Projectile	Fuzes	Weight of Projectile	Weight of HE
(b) HE - K. Gr Rot (Brass Fuzes)	A.Z.23.(0.15) Dopp Z.S/60	6.62 kg (14.56 lbs)	.37 kg (.814 lbs)
(c) HE - K. Gr Rot KPS	A.Z.23v(0.15) Dopp Z.S/60S	5.83 kg (12.83)	
(d) AP/HE - K. Gr Rot P3	Bd.Z. 75 mm Pzgr	6.80 kg (14.96 lbs)	
(e) Hollow Charge- 7.5 cm Gr 38 HL/B	A.Z.38 and A.Z.38 st.	4.57 kg (10.05 lbs)	
(f) Hollow Charge- 7.5 cm Gr 38 HL/C	A.Z.38 st	5.00 kg (11 lbs)	

	Charges	Muzzle Velocity	Max: Ranges
Projectile (a)	1	290 m/s (950 fs)	5,975 m (6535 yds)
	2	452 m/s (1486 fs)	9,350 m (10,225 yds)
	3	580 m/s (1902 fs)	11,300 m (12,360 yds)
	4	662 m/s (2172 fs)	12,300 m (13,450 yds)
Projectile (b)	1	275 m/s (902 fs)	5,650 m (6,180 yds)
	2	430 m/s (1410 fs)	9,225 m (10,090 yds)
	3	550 m/s (1804 fs)	11,500 m (12,575 yds)
	4	650 m/s (2132 fs)	12,875 m (14,080 yds)
Projectile (c)	1	290 m/s (950 fs)	5,925 m (6480 yds)
	2	453 m/s (1486 fs)	9,225 m (10,090 yds)
	3	580 m/s (1902 fs)	11,225 m (12,275 yds)
	4	662 m/s (2172 fs)	11,975 m (13,100 yds)
Projectile (d)	Full charge	630 m/s (2067 fs)	1500 m (1640 yds)
Projectile (e)	Full charge	450 m/s (1476 fs)	7100 m (7765 yds)
Projectile (f)	Full charge	440 m/s (1443 fs)	7500 m (8200 yds)

Projectiles (d) (e) and (f) Against A.F.Vs. up to 1500 m (1640 yds)

C. **7.5 cm leichte Feldkanone 18** (2.95 in Light Field Gun Model 18). See fig: 71

1. This equipment was developed during the period of 1930 - 1931 both Krupp and Rheinmetall producing prototype models. The Krupp equipment was finally adopted for production in 1938.

This light cavalry type artillery weapon is of lighter construction than the FK 16 N/A equipment. The carriage is of the split trail type with folding spades. Spring suspension is fitted and two spring equilibrators are used to balance the efforts required for elevating the gun. The carriage suspension is automatically locked when the trail legs are opened out to the firing position. Spoked artillery wheels are fitted.

The recoil system is of the hydraulic buffer and hydro-pneumatic recuperator type. The former is housed within the cradle below the gun, whilst the latter is supported above the piece.

2. **Data: le F.K.18**

	Metric	British
Calibre	75 mm	2.95 ins
Length of Gun	1940 mm	76.38 ins
Length of Barrel	1660 mm	65.2 ins
Length of rifling	1412 mm	55.6 ins
Length of chamber	248.3 mm	9.8 ins
Type of rifling	PPS Increasing Right Hand Twist Angle 5° to 7°	
Number of grooves	28	
Maximum Recoil	1150 mm	45¼ ins
Minimum Recoil	650 mm	25½ ins
Traverse	30°	
Elevation	-5° + 45°	
Type of Sights	Rbl. F.16	

/Travelling

-132-

Data (cont.)	Metric	British
Travelling Position -		
Overall length	5151 mm	203 ins
Overall width	1830 mm	72 ins
Overall height	1652 mm	65 ins
Travelling position weight	1324 kg	1.3 Tons
Weight in action	1120 kg	1.1 Tons
Maximum Range	9425 metres	10,300 yds
Maximum Muzzle Velocity	485 m/s	1590 fs
Chamber Pressure	2500 atmospheres	16.4 Tons sq.ins
Muzzle Energy	69.9 tm	

3. **Projectiles**

   (a) **K.Gr.rot K.P.S. (H.E. Shell with bi-metallic driving band)**

Distinguishing marks	- Projectile grey below fuze. Red band above single driving band, yellow band above red band. Black lettering.	
Fuze	Nose percussion fuze A.Z. 23v (0,15) (optional delay 0.15 secs.) or T. and P. fuze Dopp.Z.S/60 Fl*	
Driving band	Bi-metallic.	
Length of projectile (without fuze)	345 mm.	13.58 in.
Width of driving band	17 mm.	0.67 in.
Length of projectile below driving band	58 mm	2.28 in.
Weight of projectile (with fuze)	5.83 kg.	13 lbs.

   Note:(1) When engaging A.F.Vs with this ammunition, the fuze A.Z.23v (0,15) is used set at instantaneous.

   (2) With small charge M.V. = 180 m.s. (591 f.s.)
       Muzzle energy = 9.6 t/m
   With medium charge M.V.= 360 m.s. (1181 f.s.)
       Muzzle energy = 38.5 t/m
   With large charge M.V. = 485 m.s. (1591 f.s.)
       Muzzle energy = 69.9 t/m
       Gas pressure = 2500 at.

   (b) **7.5 cm Gr.38 (Hollow charge)**

Distinguishing marks	- Projectile grey. Single driving band. Black lettering.	
Fuze	Nose percussion fuze A.Z.38.	
Length of projectile (with fuze)	284 mm.	11.18 in.
Length of projectile (without fuze)	264 mm.	10.39 in.
Weight of projectile (with fuze)	4.83 kg.	11 lb.

   (c) **K.Gr.rot.Pz. (A.P.C.B.C. Tracer Shell)**

Distinguishing marks	- Projectile black, red band above single driving band, red lettering.	
Fuze	Base fuze Bd.Z.f 7.5 cm.Pzgr.	
Weight of projectile	6.8 kg.	15 lb.
Length of projectile (without fuze)	305 mm.	12 in.
Length of projectile (with fuze)	322 mm.	12.68 in.
Length of projectile (below driving band)	25 mm.	0.98 in.
Width of driving band	17 mm.	0.67 in.
Muzzle velocity (with large charge)	444 m.s.	1457 f.s.

/ (d)

(d) K.Gr.rot Nb. (Smoke Shell)

Distinguishing marks	Projectile grey, single driving band, large NB in white, other lettering in black.	
Fuze	Percussion nose fuze A.Z. 23 Nb	
Length of projectile (without fuze)	295 mm.	11.61 in.
Length of projectile (with fuze)	50 mm.	1.97 in.
Weight of projectile	6.2 kg.	13.64 lbs.
Width of driving band	17 mm.	0.67 ins.

4. **Propellant charge**

The propellant charge consists of three bags of propellant contained in a metal cartridge case.

The base of the cartridge case is occupied by bag 1. On top of bag 1 are bags 2 and 3 which are placed lengthwise side by side in the cartridge case.

Bag 1 = small charge.
Bag 1 + bag 2 = medium charge.
Bag 1 + bag 2 + bag 3 = large charge.

Length of cartridge case	260 mm.	10.24 in.
Width of cartridge case (rim)	91.7 mm.	3.61 in.
Width of cartridge case (front)	78.7 mm.	3.10 in.

Marking on cartridge case (stamped on base)

```
                                        0 BD    (no lead wire)
                                        (batch No)
           (initial of                              (year of
           manufacturer)                            manufacturer)
                            (case number
                            6316 or 6316 St)
                              1. F.K. 18
```

Primer	C/12 n.A. or C/12 St.
Markings on bags	All bags clearly numbered in black on top. Also marked to show weight and composition of filling, initial of manufacturer, year and batch number of powder, place and date of completion, and initial of person responsible.
Contents of bag 1	84 gr (3 oz.) Digl Pl.P plus 10gr (6 dr) Nz. Man.N.P.
Contents of bag 2	270 gr (9½ oz.) Digl. R.P.
Contents of bag 3	225 gr. (8 oz.) Digl. R.P.
Cartridge cover	The charge is covered by cartridge cover F.K. 16 n/A, which bears a label stating the nature of the contents.

5. **Performance (with K.Gr.rot K.P.S.)**

	Small charge	Medium charge	Large charge
Range			
Max.	2725 m. (2980 yds).	7375 m. (8065 yds).	9425 m. (10307 yds)
Min.	25 m. (27 yds).	25 m. (27 yds).	50 m. (54 yds).
Elevation			
Max.	736 mils. (41°30').	727 mils. (41°).	734 mils. (41°20').
Min.	4 mils. (0°13').	1 mil (0°3').	1 mil (0°3').
Drift			
Max.	+ 17 mils (57').	+ 21 mils (1°11').	+23 mils (1°17').
Min.	± 0	± 0	± 0

/ Time of flight

FIG. 71.   7·5 cm. le F.K.18.
(2·9 in. LIGHT FIELD GUN MODEL 18.)

Time of flight

Max. 22.9 sec.	38.9 sec.	45.1 sec.
Min. 0.1 sec.	0.1 sec.	0.1 sec.

M.V.

Max. 180 m.s. (591 f.s.)	360 m.s. (1181 f.s.).	485 m.s. (1591 f.s.).
Min. 180 m.s. (591 f.s.)	360 m.s. (1181 f.s.)	485 m.e. (1591 f.s.).

D. **7.5 cm Feldkanone 38** (2.95 in Field Gun Model 38) See Fig. No. 72 and 73

1. This weapon was designed by Krupp for a Brazilian order. Approximately 64 equipments were delivered and a remaining 80 were completed and over to O.K.H. in 1942. The equipment was introduced into service to replace the earlier model 18.

The gun is a further development of the cavalry gun. The piece is longer than that of the F.K.18. A muzzle brake is fitted, the overall weight is reduced and the performance increased. The breech action is semi-automatic with horizontal sliding breech block. The recoil system consists of a hydraulic buffer located in the cradle and a hydro-pneumatic recuperator above the piece.

Two vertical spring equilibrators are fitted to balance out muzzle preponderance.

The carriage is of the split trail type and is fitted with wooden spoked wheels with steel rims. Designed for horse transport.

Fixed ammunition, instead of the semi-fixed type as used with le F.K.18, is fired by the FK.38.

The sight is graduated in mils. from 0 to 800 mils. (0.45 degs). A red scale of metres is provided for firing with 7.5 cm K. Gr. Potr. rot FK.38 from 200 to 11,500 metres and a black scale of metres for firing with the 7.5 cm Gr/Hl/B (Hollow charge projectiles) from 100 to 5000 metres.

2. Data : F.K.38.

	Metric	British
(a) Calibre	75 mm	2.95 ins.
Length of piece	2550 mm	100.4 ins.
Length of barrel	2335 mm	92 ins.
Length of rifling	1914 mm	75.4 ins.
Length of chamber	421 mm	16.625 ins.
Chamber capacity	1.74 litres	106 cu. ins.
Rifling - Increasing right hand twist. 28 Grooves.		
Normal recoil	900 mm	35.4 ins.
Maximum recoil	1010 mm	39.8 ins.
Type of sights	R bl .F32, 36 or 37	
Traverse	50°	
Elevation	-5° + 45°	
Travelling Position -		
Overall Length	5613 mm	221 ins.
Overall Width	1880 mm	75 ins.
Overall Height	1575 mm	62 ins.
Travelling position weight	1860 kg.	1.83 Tons
Weight in action	1366 kg.	1.4 Tons.
Maximum Muzzle Velocity	605 m/s	1985 fs
Chamber Pressure	2600 atmosphere	17 Tons
Muzzle Energy	109 tm.	

(b) Ammunition

Nomenclature	Type	Weight	Fuzes used
7.5 cm K.Gr.Patr.rot F.K.38	H.E.	12.85 lb.	A.Z.23 v (0.15) or Dopp Z.S/60s
7.5 cm Gr.Patr.Hl/B F.K.38	Hollow Charge	10.07 lbs.	A.Z.38
7.5 cm Sprgr.L/4.8	H.E.	13.88 lb.	A.Z.23 v (0.15)

/ (c)

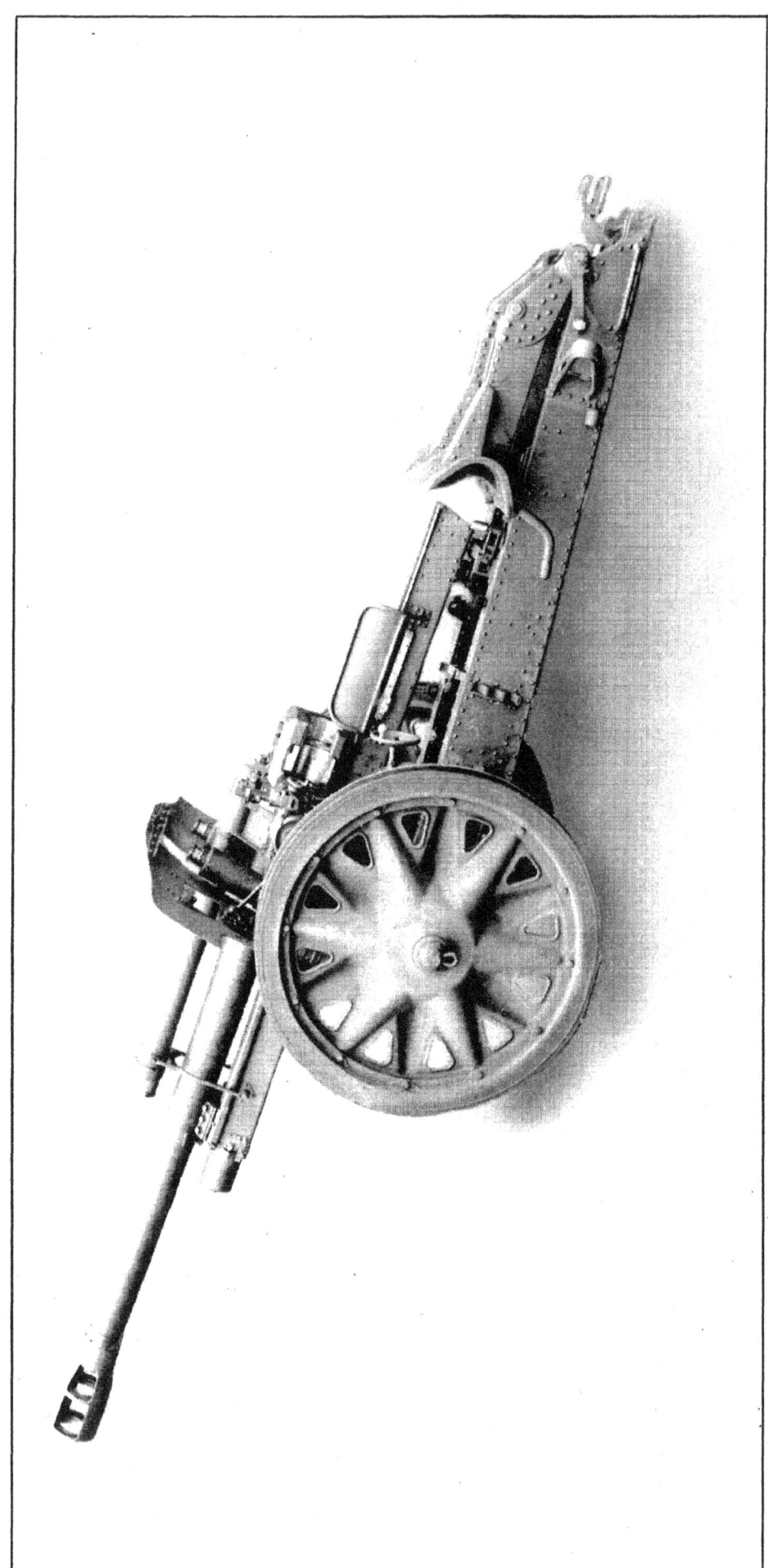

FIG. 72. 7.5 cm. F.K. 38.
(2.95 in. FIELD GUN MODEL 38.)

FIG. 73. 7.5 cm. F.K.38.
(2.95 in. FIELD GUN MODEL 38.)

(c) **Ballistic Performance**

With K.Gr.rot	Muzzle velocity:	1985 fs
	Max. range	12577 yards
With Gr.38 Hl/B	Muzzle velocity	1444 fs
	Max. range	8421 yards
With Sprgr.L/4.8	Muzzle velocity	1903 fs
	Max. range	12358 yards

Radius of burst of K.Gr.rot 20 m. sideways 10 m. forwards.

E. **7.5 Feldkanone (FK) 7M85** (2.95 in. Field Gun Model 7M85) (See Fig. 74)

1. This light Dual Purpose Field/A-Tank equipment consists of the 7.5 cm Pak 40 (2.95 in. Anti-Tank Gun Model 40) Gun, cradle and recoil system fitted on the carriage of the 10.5 cm le FH.18/40 (4.1 inch light Field Howitzer Model 18/40). A slight modification to the saddle appears to have been carried out to give effect to this arrangement.

It may be noted that the 10.5 cm le FH.18/40 had already incorporated the 7.5 cm Pak 40 carriage <u>with modifications.</u> In late 1944 this production was regarded as an emergency solution of the problem of reinforcing the field artillery with a number of dual purpose Field/Anti-Tank equipments, taking into account the existing manufacturing facilities then available.

The new mounting allowed an increase in the maximum elevation to 42 degrees (an increase of 22 degrees).

This new equipment considering its calibre and ballistic performance was regarded as being too heavy although entirely "battleworthy".

The last recorded stage in this development was to modify the 7.5 cm Pak 40 carriage to allow elevation up to 35°. The 7.5 cm Pak 40 (anti-tank) gun with increased elevation was known as the <u>7.5 cm K.7M59.</u> Total weight of the equipment is given as 3,200 lbs and maximum range firing full charge as 14,550 yards.

2. **Data:** F.K. Model 7M85

	Metric	British
(a) Calibre	75 mm	2.95 ins.
Length of Piece	3450 mm	11 feet $3\frac{1}{8}$ ins.
Length of Barrel	3201 mm	10 feet 6 ins.
Length of Rifling	2470.5 mm	8 feet $1\frac{1}{4}$ ins.
Length of Chamber	730 mm	2 feet $4\frac{3}{4}$ ins.
Rifling - Constant right hand twist		7 Degrees.
Traverse		30° 30'
Elevation		- 5° + 42°
Normal recoil	830 mm	32.7 ins.
Sighting ZE. 34/44 with R. bl .F 32 or 36		
ZE. 43/1 SVO with 3 X 8° telescope.		
Weight of standard projectile (HE)	5.74 kg	12.6 lbs.
Muzzle Velocity	550 m/sec.	1804 fs
Maximum Range	10,275 metres	11,200 yds.
Overall length travelling position	5850 mm	19 feet 2 ins.
" width " "	2110 mm	6 feet 11 ins.
" height " "	1830 mm	6 feet 0 ins.
Weight in action	1778 kg	1.75 Tons.
Chamber capacity	3.5 litres	6.25 pints.
Chamber pressure	1800 atmospheres	11.8 Tons sq.in.

(b) **Ammunition**

HE 7.5 cm Sprgr. Patr. 34 Pak 40 with Fuzes Kl .A.Z.23, 23/1, 23 Nb/Pr.

Smoke, A.P, APCBC/HE and Hollow Charge Shell also used.

F. **10.5 cm leichte Feldhaubitze 16** (le.F.H.16) (4.13 ins Light Field Howitzer Model 16)

1. This equipment was the standard light field howitzer of the German artillery until replaced by the le.F.H.18.

/ The

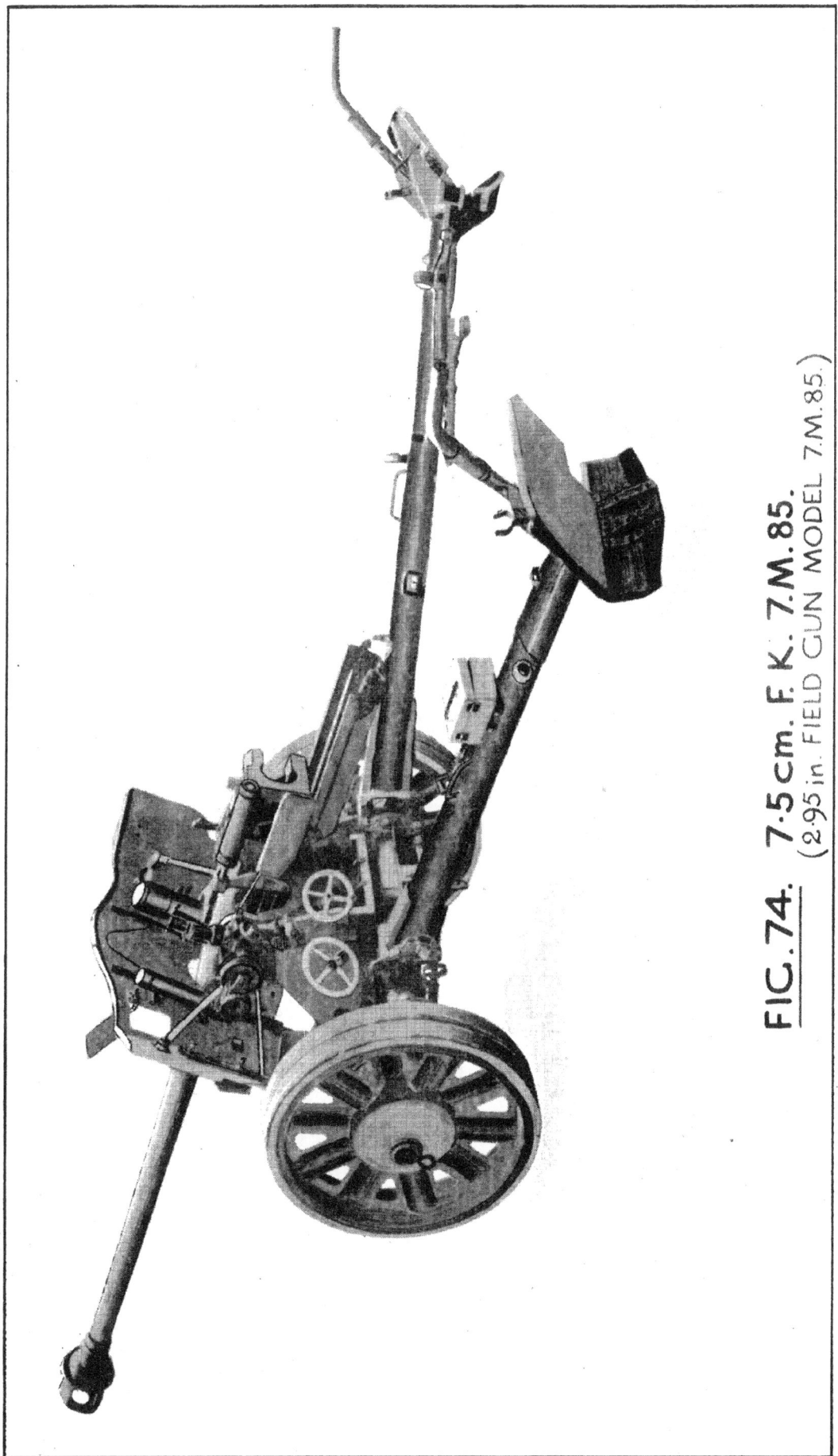

FIG. 74. 7.5 cm. F.K. 7.M.85. (2.95 in. FIELD GUN MODEL 7.M.85.)

The carriage is identical with those of the 7.7 cm Field Gun F.K.16.

The ordnance comprises a monobloc barrel 22 calibres long with a detachable breech block of the Krupp horzontal wedge type.

The recoil system is housed in the cradle below the piece and comprises a hydraulic buffer and a triple coil spring recuperator.

The gun is mounted on a box trail carriage of rivetted construction with a fixed spade and fitted with large artillery type spoked wheels.

Separate ammunition is used and 4 normal charges and supercharge are provided.

2. **Data : le F.H.16**

	Metric	British
(a) Calibre	105 mm	4.13 ins.
Length of piece (22 calibres)	2310 mm	90.95 ins.
Length of rifling	1878 mm	74 ins.
Capacity of chamber	1.17 litres	
Rifling Increasing right hand twist	$4°$ to $10°$	
No. of grooves	32	
Traverse	$4°$	
Elevation	$-10° + 40°$	
Rate of Fire	6 r.p.m.	
Weight in action	1450 kg	1.45 Tons
Weight in travelling position	2300 kg	2.3 Tons
Maximum Velocity HE	395 m/s	1295 fs
Maximum Range	9225 metres	10,000 yds
Chamber Pressure	2150 atmospheres	14.15 Tons sq. ins.
Muzzle Energy	118 t/m	

(b)

Ammunition	Fuze	Wt of projectile	Muzzle Velocity	Max Range
HE FH.Gr.	Percussion Fuze Optional delay.	14.81 kg (32.58 lbs)	199 m/s (656 fs)	3450 metres (3760 yards)
(Also uses other projectiles as for le F.H.18.).			233 m/s (755 fs)	4550 m (5000 yds)
			265 m/s (870 fs)	5700 m (6250 yds)
			320 m/s (1050 fs)	7425 m (8100 yds)
			395 m/s (1295 fs)	9225 m (10,000 yds)
Hollow Charge 10.5 G 39 Rot HL, HL/A, B and C.	Percussion A.Z.38.	11.76 to 12.35 kg (25.9 to 27.2 lbs)	405/410 m/s (13 25 fs) Against AFVs.	7600 m (8 310 yds) Max. 1500 m (1650 yds)

10.5 cm leichte Feldhaubitz 18 (le.F.H.18) (4.13 ins Field Howitzer Model 18)

(See Fig. 75 and 76).

1. This weapon was designed by Rheinmetall Borsig and introduced into the service in 1935. It became the standard field howitzer of the German divisional artillery and remained so, until replaced by the more recent models the le.F.H.18M and 18/40. The equipment, comparable to the British 25 Pdr, was found to be easy to handle both in and out of action, and the carriage is very steady. Laying is smooth and easy and definitely good against tanks or a moving target. The equipment was normally drawn by a half-tracked tractor, but may also be horse drawn.

A howitzer of orthodox German design, the barrel is a monobloc with detachable breech ring and horizontal breech block.

/The

The recoil mechanism comprises a hydraulic buffer with cooling jacket housed in a cradle, and a hydro-pneumatic recuperator, the latter located above the gun.

The gun is mounted on a split trail carriage with box section rivetted trail legs and folded spades. Wooden spoked artillery wheels or pressed alloy spoked wheels with solid rubber tyres are fitted to stub axles. The axle has transverse springing. A single hydro-pneumatic equilibrator is fitted between saddle and cradle.

The weapon fired HE, with either percussion or time and percussion fuzes, AP Shell, APCBC, Smoke Shell and also hollow charge projectiles.

2. Data : le F.H. 18.

	Metric	British
Calibre	105 mm	4.13 ins
Length of gun (26 Cals)	2941 mm	115.8 ins
Length of barrel	2612	102.8 ins
Length of rifling	2392 mm	94.4 ins
Length of chamber	213 mm	8.4 ins
Rifling - Increasing right hand twist		
	32 grooves	
Angle of pitch $6°$ to $12°$		
Normal recoil	1100 mm	43.2 ins
Maximum recoil	1170 mm	46.0 ins
Sights - ZE 34 with R.bl.F32, 36 or 37.		
Traverse	$56°$	
Rate of traverse - 1 Turn of handwheel 15 minutes		
Elevation	$- 6° 30' + 40° 30'$	
Rate of Elevation. 1 Turn of handwheel 45 minutes		
Rate of Fire	6 r.p.m.	
Travelling Position -		
Overall length	6100 mm	20 feet
Overall width	1977 mm	6 feet $5\frac{3}{4}$ ins
Overall height	1880 mm	6 feet 2 ins
Ground clearance	367 mm	14.5 ins
Weight	2535 kg	2.53 Tons
Weight in Action	1985 kg	1.98 Tons
Maximum Muzzle Velocity	470 m/secs	1540 fs
Chamber Pressure	2300 atmospheres	15 Tons sq in.
Muzzle Energy	167 t/m	
Maximum Range	10675 metres	11675 yards

3. Ammunition (6 Charges are used - Charge I to VI)

The 10.5 cm le.F.H.18 fires the following types of ammunition:-
(a) H.E. Shell (F.H. Gr and F.H. Gr.38 Stg)

    Length complete   49 cm.   19.29 in.
    Weight (fuzed)   14.81 kg   32. 6 lb.

This shell is filled with 3 lb T.N.T. and is fitted with either a percussion fuze A.Z.23.v. (optional delay 0.25 secs), or a time and percussion fuze Dopp.Z. S/60. The shell has a long streamline; it is painted dark green and has a single driving band.

(b) A.P. Tracer Shell (10 cm. Pzgr)

    Length complete   29.2 cm   11.5 in.
    Weight (fuzed)   14.25 kg   31.25 lb.

This A.P. shell is fitted with a base fuze (Bd.Z.f.10 cm.Pzgr), and is used to engage tanks up to 1600 yards: for this purpose charge 5 is used, muzzle velocity is 1295 ft. sec.

(c) A.P.C.B.C. Tracer Shell (10 cm Pzgr rot)

    Length complete   44 cm   17.32 in
    Weight (fuzed)   15.71 kg   34.6 lb

This shell, which has both a piercing cap and a ballistic cap, is replacing the 10 cm Pzgr shell for attack on tanks. It has a base fuze (Bd.Z.f.10 cm Pzgr) and is though to be fired with charge 5.

/The

The following figures for penetration of homogeneous armour with the A.P.C.B.C. shell are estimated:-

Range (yards)	Thickness of armour in mm	
	30°	Normal
500	56 (2.20 in)	67 (2.64 in)
1000	52 (2.05 in)	62.5 (2.46 in)
1500	49 (1.93 in)	59 (2.32 in)

(d) <u>Hollow Charge round</u> (10 cm Granate 39 rot)

Length complete	36.83 cm	14.5 ins
Weight (fuzed)	11.76 kg	25.9 lb

This A.P. shell, which embodies the hollow charge principle has a percussion (nose) fuze (A.Z.38), is fired with charge 5, and is used at ranges from 110 to 1650 yards. It is claimed that it will penetrate 70 mm (2.76 in) homogeneous "rolled steel" armour at 30° irrespective of range. The penetration at angles closer to normal is proportionately greater.

(e) Smoke Shell (F.H.Gr.Nb)

Length complete	48.9 cm	19.25 ins
Weight (fuzed)	14 kg	30.8 lb
Weight of charge (oleum and pumice)	1.87 kg	4.1 lb

The smoke cloud formed on burst has a diameter of 80 - 100 ft.

(f) <u>Smoke Shell</u> (F.H.Gr.38 Nb)

Weight (fuzed)	14.71 kg	32.4 lb

This shell is an improvement on F.H.Gr.Nb; the smoke cloud formed on burst has a diameter of 100 - 130 ft. The fuze used with both smoke shells is a D.A. and graze fuze, Kl.A.Z.23 Nb.

(g)
Type	Fuzes	Wt of Projectile	Muzzle Velocity
(i) H.E. Various types.	Percussion with optional delay of Time & Percussion		
FH.Gr.			I 200 m/s (656 fs)
FH.Gr. FES	A.Z.23.v (0.15) A.Z.23.v (0.25)		II 232 m/s (755 fs)
FH.Gr. 38	A.Z.23/42 (0.15) A.Z.23.Zn. A.Z.23 Pr. Dopp Z S/60^s	14.81 kg (32.6 lbs)	III 264 m/s (868 fs)
FH.Gr.38 FES	" " Fl. " " r.		IV 317 m/s (1050 fs)
FH.Gr.38 Stg			V 391 m/s (1230 fs)
FH.Gr.38 Stg FES			VI 470 m/s (1540 fs)

(Max. Ranges: Charge I 3575 metres (3910 yds).
Charge II 4625 m (5060 yds).
Charge III 5760 m (6300 yds).
Charge IV 7600 metres (8310 yds).
Charge V 9150 m (10,000 yds).
Charge VI 10,675 m (11,675 yds).

-143-

(ii) Smoke

F.H. Gr. Nb.	) Kl.AZ.23.Nb.	14.00 kg (30.8 lbs)	VI 480 m/s (1575 fs)
F.H. Gr. 38.Nb.	) Kl.AZ.23.Nb.P2	14.21 kg (31.26 lbs)	VI 478 m/s (1570 fs)
F.H. Gr. 40.Nb.	) Kl.AZ.40.Nb.P2) Dopp.Z.S/60 Fl.	15.25 kg (33.55 lbs)	VI 460 m/s (1510 fs)

(Max. Ranges for Smoke Projectiles: 10,200 to 10,600 metres (11,150 to 11,600 yds).

(iii) Colour Smoke Indicator

F.H. Gr. 40 Deut	Dopp.Z.S/60.Fl.	14.63 kg (32.2 lbs)	VI 470 m/s (1540 fs)

(Max. Range: 10,400 metres (11,370 yds).

(h)

Type	Fuzes	Wt of Projectile	Charge	Muzzle Velocity M/sec	Max. Range. Metres
HE/Incendiary					
FH.Gr. Spr. Br.	AZ 23 v (0,15)	15.75 kg (34.65 lbs	6	- 458 (1502 fs	
Misc. HE					
FH.Gr. 38 Kh.	Kl AZ 23	14.64 kg (32.2 lbs)	6	- 473 (1562 fs)	10450 (11,425 yds)
FH.Gr. 39	Kl AZ 23	13.48 (29.65 lbs)	6	- 487 (1600 fs)	10500 (11,480 yds)
Hollow Charge					
10 Gr 39 Hl	)	11.76 (25.87 lbs)	5 only	420 (1410 fs)	7200 (7,875 yds)
10 Gr 39 Hl/A	) A2 38) or) AZ 38 St	12.30 (27.06 lbs) 12.10 (26.62 lbs)	6	495 (1623 fs)	9400 (10,280 yds)
10 Gr 39 Hl/C	)	12.35 (27.17 lbs)	Against AFVs up to 1500 metres - battle ranges.		
Star Shell					
10.5 Leucht- -geschoss	)Dopp Z S/60)) FC))Dopp Z S/60)) v)	14.00 kg (30.8 lbs)	6 only	480 (1575 fs)	7800 (8530 yds)
Incendiary					
FH Gr Br	Nose percussion as for standard HE not T & P	15.24 kg (23.53 lbs)	6	462 (1513 fs)	107000 (11700 yds)

/Propaganda

FIG. 75. 10.5 cm. le F.H.18.
(4.13 in. LIGHT FIELD HOWITZER MODEL 18.)

FIG. 76. 10·5 cm. le F.H. 18.
(4.13 in. LIGHT FIELD HOWITZER MODEL 18.)

Propaganda Leaflet Shell					
Weiss-Rot-Geschoss	Z t Z M v3(t)	13.65 kg (30.03 lbs)	4 5 6	330 (1080 fs) 400 (1312 fs) 480 (1524 fs)	6000 (6560 yds) 6900 (7545 yds) 7700 (8420 yds)
"	Dopp.Z. S/60 FC	13.12 kg (28.86 lbs)	4 6	335 (1095 fs) 485 (1590 fs)	6500 (7110 yds) 9000 (9840 yds)
"	Brennzurder S/30 Lm	12.5 kg (27.5 lbs)	4 6	330 (1080 fs) 495 (1623 fs)	6300 (6890 yds) 7500 (8200 yds)
"	Brennzurder M.G.L.	13.65 (30.03 lbs)	4 6	330 (1080 fs) 480 (1574 fs)	5500 (6015 yds) 6800 (7435 yds)
HE (French Manufacture) FH Gr 35	French nose percussion fuzes	15.70 kg (34.54 lbs)	5	372 (1220 fs)	9000 (9840 yds)

H. **10.5 cm leichte Feldhaubitze 18. Mundungsbremse** (4.13 in light Field Howitzer Model 18 with Muzzle Brake)
(See Fig. 77)

1. This equipment consists of the standard field howitzer (le.F.H.18), modified by fitting a muzzle brake and adjusting the recoil mechanism in order to fire a long range shell with a special charge, i.e. to obtain increased performance.

The muzzle brake is of the single baffle type and has rather a low efficiency. It is interesting to note that no spare muzzle brake was carried with this equipment during the war. Firing can continue without the muzzle brake with all charges except the long range charge.

The buffer was slightly modified, alterations being effected in the control rod and piston sliding bush in addition to adjustment of a plug to avoid fouling the muzzle brake during recoil.

The air pressure of the recuperator is about 140 lbs more than the non-muzzle brake equipment and the equilibrator or balancing gear has also increased pressure.

It was found that it was not advisable to fire sabot discarding and vane or fin stabilised projectiles with the single baffle muzzle brake so a new cage type muzzle brake was developed for this equipment and the models 39/40 and 18/40.

2. Data: le F.H.18 M.
   (a) This the same as for the standard le.F.H.18 except for the following:-

	Metric	British
Length of piece with muzzle brake	3308 mm	13.23 ins
Maximum Velocity (HE long range with super charge)	540 m/s	1770 fs
Chamber Pressure	2400 atmospheres	15.8 Tons sq in.
Muzzle Energy	220 t/m	
Maximum Range	12325 m	13,500 yards

/ (b)

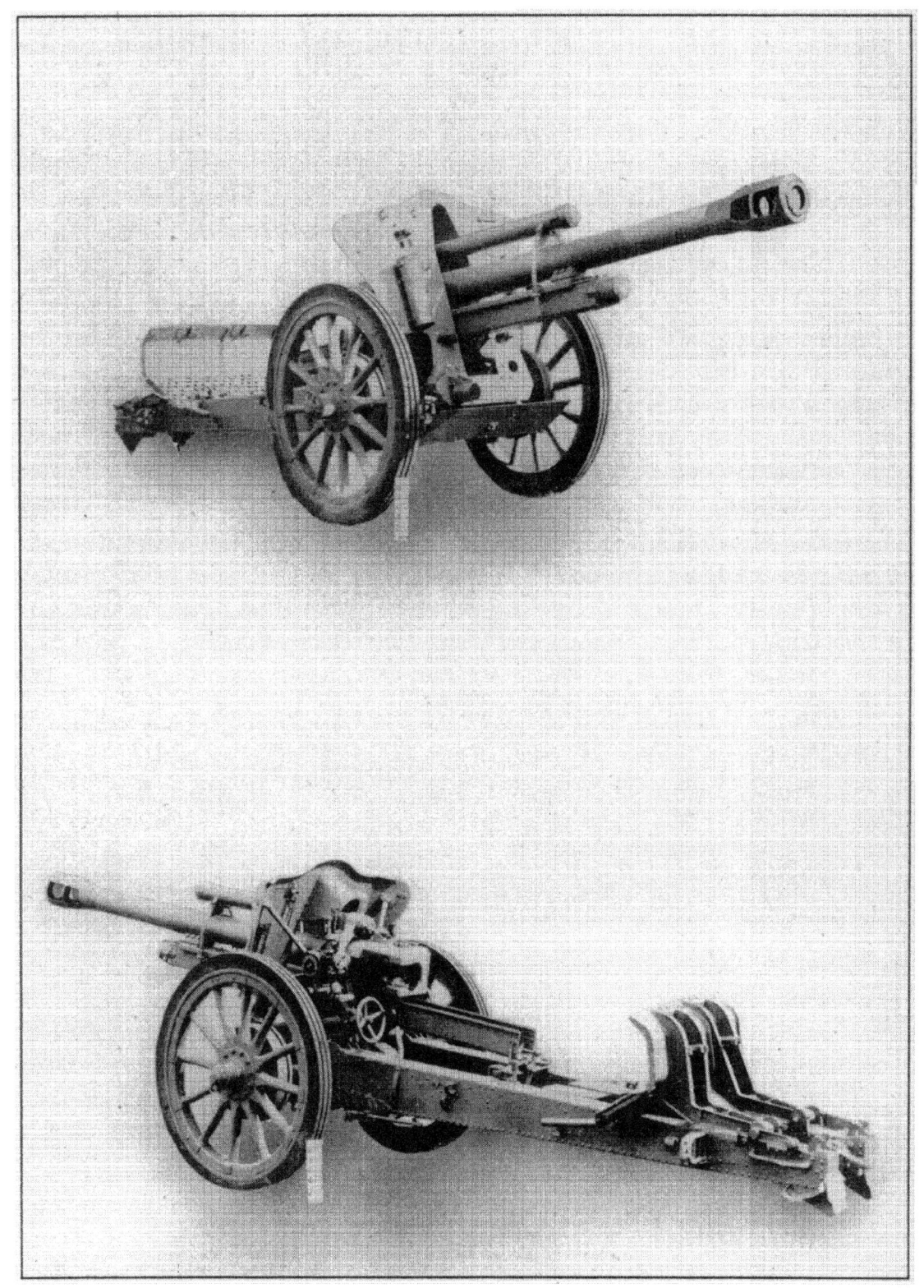

FIG. 77. 10·5 cm. le F.H.18.M.
(4·13 in. LIGHT FIELD HOWITZER MODEL 18 WITH MUZZLE BRAKE.)

(b) Ammunition

The standard ammunition of the le.F.H.18 is fired and in addition.-

	Fuzes	Wt. of Projectile	Muzzle Velocity	Max. Range
HE Long Range F.H. Gr. Fern.	AZ 23 v (0.15) Dopp Z.S/60 Fl Dopp Z.S/60.V	14.81 kg (32.6 lbs)	540 m/s (1770 fs)	12325 m (13,500 yards)

J. **10.5 cm leichte Feldhaubitze 18/39 (4.13 in light Field Howitzer Model 18/39)**

1. A limited number of these equipments were taken into the German service.

A number of 105 mm Field Howitzers were delivered to Holland by Krupp shortly before the outbreak of the war in 1939. About 80 of these were converted by mounting the piece of the le.F.H.18M on the carriage, designed by Krupp, and this equipment became known as the le.F.H.18/39.

Ballistically the le.F.H.18M and le F.H.18/39 are identical and have the same Range Tables as the le F.H.18/40.

2. Data : le F.H. 18/39.

	Metric	British
Calibre	105 mm	4.13 ins
Details of barrel rifling and chamber as for le F.H. 18 and 18 M.		
Traverse	60°	
Elevation	− 5° + 45°	
Minimum recoil	1030 mm	40.5 ins
Maximum recoil	1130 mm	44.5 ins
Height of trunnions	1180 mm	46.5 ins
Weight in action	1950 kg	1.9 Tons
Maximum Velocity	540 m/s	1770 fs
Chamber Pressure	2440 Atmospheres	15.8 Tons sq in
Muzzle Energy	220 t/m	
Maxmimu Range	12,325 m	13,500 yards

3. Ammunition

As used with the 10.5 cm le F.H.18 and 18M.

K. **10.5 cm leichte Feldhaubitze 18/40 (le.F.H.18/40) (4.13 ins light Field Howitzer Model 18/40)**

(See Fig. 78).

1. This equipment is an extensively modified version of the le.F.H.18 and 18M and was produced to meet the demand for an equipment lighter in weight than these, but not inferior ballistically. When the specification was issued (March 1942), speed of design and production were stressed and it was decided to use the tubular split trail carriage of the 7.5 cm Pak 40, which was in large scale production. This carriage required only a minimum of modification to enable the le F.H. 18M piece to be mounted in it.

Important new features in the equipment are as follows:-

(a) The carriage incorporates torsion bar suspension with the two torsion bars extending for the full width of the carriage body. The torsion bars are locked when the equipment is in action, the movement of the opening of the trail legs effecting the locking.

(b) Both elevating and traversing handwheels are on the left side of the carriage, so that the layer can both elevate and traverse the gun and fire it.

(c) An increased efficiency muzzle brake is fitted. This was effected by welding projecting wings to the le F.H.18M muzzle brake.

Ballistically the le F.H.18/40 is identical with the le F.H.18M and 18/39. The original wheels of the carriage were too small to permit recoil at high angles of elevation and also for man handling, so larger wheels were fitted.

/ 2.

2. **Data: le F.H. 18/40.**

   (a) Ballistic details

   Using HE Shell (32.7 lbs) with percussion fuze A.Z.23:

Charge	MV (fs)	Max. Range (yards)	Time of flight (Secs)	50% Zone Length (yards)	50% Zone Breadth (yards)	Drift (minutes)
I	656	3900	26.6	313	10	97
II	760	5050	30.2	112	7	97
III	865	6270	34.4	96	10	93
IV	1040	8275	39.8	55	15	93
V	1280	9975	43.8	46	14	93
VI	1540	11640	48.9	59	9	97

	Metric	British
(b) Calibre	105 mm	4.13 ins
Length of Gun	2940 mm	115.75 ins
Length of barrel	2710 mm	106.66 ins
Length of rifling	2364 mm	93.06 ins
Rifling –		
Number of grooves	32	
Depth of grooves	1 mm	.04 ins
Width of grooves	5.5 mm	.22 ins
Type of rifling	Poly groove Increasing Twist 1 in 12 to 1 in $17\frac{3}{4}$.	
Percussion or electric firing	Percussion.	
Maximum recoil	1170 mm	46 ins
Normal recoil	1150 mm	$45\frac{1}{4}$ ins
Type of Sights – ZE 34 with R.bl.F.32, 36 or 37.		
Traverse	56°	
Rate of traverse 1 Turn of Handwheel	1° 13'	
Elevation	– 6° + 40°	
Rate of elevation 1 Turn of Handwheel	46'	
Rate of fire	6 r.p.m.	
Travelling Position –		
Overall length	6150 mm	20' 2"
Overall width	2110 mm	6' 11"
Overall height	1830 mm	6' 0"
Method of Transport H.D. or 3 Ton Semi-tracked vehicle.		
Travelling Position Weight	1955 kg	1.9 Tons
Weight in action	1955 kg	1.9 Tons
HE Maximum Velocity	540 m/s	1771 fs
Chamber Pressure	2400 atmospheres	15.8 Tons sq in
Muzzle Energy		710.6 f/Tons
Maximum Range	12325 metres	13,479 yds

3. **Ammunition**

   (a) Projectiles

   It should be noted that in every case the weight of projectiles quoted is the range table figure.

   (i) H.E. shell

   A large variety of H.E. shell, which do not differ greatly among themselves, is fired. These are:—

F.H. Gr.		(A.Z.23 v (0.15))
		(A.Z.23 v (0.25))
		(A.Z.1.) Per-
F.H. Gr. FES		(A.Z.1.) cussion
	Fuzed	(A.Z.23 Zn.)
F.H. Gr. 38		(A.Z.23 Pr.)

   / (i) Contd.

(i) contd)

F.H. Gr. 38 FES　　　　　(Dopp.Z.s/60 s^2　)
F.H. Gr. 38 Stg　　　　　(Dopp.Z.S/60 Fl　) T. and P.
F.H. Gr. 38 Stg FES　　　(Dopp.Z.S./60 v　)

The ballistic performance of these six shells, all of which weigh 14.81 kg. (32 lbs 11 ozs), is identical and is the same in all respects as when fired by the old model of le.F.H.18.
(N.B. Although the same range tables are used for these six shells, it is pointed out in the range tables that shells marked F E S (Iron driving band) should not be used on the same fire tasks as the other types, as this would result in a large and haphazard zone of dispersion. Further, they should not be used for predicted shooting with charge 1 to 3).

F.H.Gr. 39　　　　　　　fuzed kl. A.Z.23 (0.15)
10.5 cm Sprgr 43 Pg　　 fuzed A.Z. 23v (0.15) or Dopp.Z.S/60 v

The F.H.Gr. 39 weighs 13.48 kg (29 lbs 10 ozs) and has a maximum range of 10,500 m (11,483 yds) and an M.V. of 1597 fs with charge 6.

The 10.5 cm Sprgr 43 Pg. is a new type of cast steel H.E. shell with the steel in the pearlite condition (pg = perlitguss). Detailed ballistic information is not yet available.

F.H.Gr. 38 Kh.　　　　　fuzed kl. A.Z.23 (0.15)

This shell consists of the body of the FHGr.38 Nb filled H.E. instead of smoke. It retains the central burster tube of the original smoke shell, but has no smoke producing composition, and is therefore difficult to observe. It weighs 14.64 kg (32 lbs 3 ozs) and has a maximum range of 10,450 m (11428 yds) and M.V. of 1551 fs with charge 6.

(ii) The long range shell

This shell, the F.H.Gr.F., is fired with a special charge, the "Fern Ladung," and attains a maximum range of 13,480 yds. The shell weighs 14.81 kg (32 lbs 11 ozs), the same as the other H.E. shell, and is fuzed with A.Z. 23 v (0.15), Dopp.Z.S/60 Fl^x, Dopp Z.S/60 v. The muzzle velocity is 1772 fs.

(iii) Smoke shell

Six types of smoke shell are fired:-
F.H.Gr.Nb.　　　　fuzed kl.A.Z.23 Nb or kl.A.Z.40 Nb (Pr)
F.H.Gr.38 Nb　　　　"　　"　　　　"　　　"　　　"
F.H.Gr.39 Nb　　　　"　　"
F.H.Gr.40 Nb　　　　" Dopp.Z.S/60 Fl^x or Dopp.Z.S/60 v.
F.H.Gr.40 Deut.　　 " Dopp.Z.S/60 Fl^x
F.H.Gr.41 Nb　　　　" kl.A.Z.23 (0.15)

The characteristics of these shells are as follows:-

	Weight	Muzzle Velocity (fs)					
		1	2	3	4	5	6
F.H.Gr.Nb	14 kg. (30 lbs 23 ozs)	682	787	892	1070	1315	1575
F.H.Gr.38 Nb	14.71 kg. (32 lbs 5 ozs)	663	768	879	1060	1309	1568
F.H.Gr.40 Nb	15.25 kg. (33 lbs 9 ozs)	653	754	856	1024	1260	?
F.H.Gr.40 Deut	14.63 kg. (32 lbs 3 ozs)	656	761	866	1040	1283	1542

The F.H.Gr.38 Nb produces a larger cloud than the F.H.Gr.Nb.

The F.H.Gr.40 Nb is of the base ejection type and is fired with a time fuze to give an air-burst, with an ejection height varying between 80 and 250 metres (90 to 270 yds) depending on the charge and elevation. It is manufactured either with a bi-metallic or sintered iron driving band. The F.H.Gr.40 Deut or Indicator shell, is used primarily to guide aircraft on to enemy positions. It emits a blue cloud lasting from 1 to 2 minutes and functions similarly to the F.H.Gr.40 Nb.

(iv) **Incendiary shell**

There are tow types of incendiary shell:-

F.H.Gr.Spr.-Br. fuzed A.Z.23v (0.15)
F.H.Gr. Br. fuzed A.Z.23v (0.15), A.Z.23(Pr), A.Z.1. A.Z.23 Zn, or A.Z. 23/42.

The characteristics of these shells are as follows:-

		Muzzle Velocity (fs)					
		1	2	3	4	5	6
F.H.Gr.Spr.Br.	15.75 kg. (34 lb 13 ozs)	640	741	843	1013	1246	1502
F.H.Gr.Br.	15.24 kg (33 lb 9 ozs.)	623	728	833	1010	1265	1516

(v) **Star shell (10.5 cm Lt.Gs.)**

This shell is fuzed with either Dopp.Z.S/60 Fl^x or Dopp. Z.S/60 v. It weighs 14.00 kg. (30 lb 12 ozs) and is fired only with charge 6 at an M.V. of 1575 fs. It has a maximum range of 780 m (853 yds). The range tables are so calculated that, at a range determined by the fuze setting, the star element attached to a parachute is blown out of the shell at a height of about 500 m (1600 ft.) above the level of the gun position. The time of burning of the star element is approximately 25 seconds.

(vi) **Propaganda shell**

This shell, the 10.5 cm Weiss-Rot Geschoss, is designed to drop leaflets over the enemy lines. The shell consists of the body of the F.H.Gr.40 filled with a roll of leaflets. It may be fuzed with either the Dopp.Z.S/60 Fl or a Czech fuze the M23(t). Only charges 4 and 5 are used and the shell is not fired at long ranges or great elevations. Characteristics are as follows:-

	M.V.(f.s.)	Range (yds)	T.E.(mils)	Weight of shell
Charge 4	1083	6015	458	30 lbs.
Charge 5	1575	7440	378	

The range table height of burst is 200 m (656 feet) and under ideal conditions one round will distribute leaflets over an area of 150 m. (164 yds) square).

(vii) **A.P. projectiles**

Four types of hollow charge shell are fired and one A.P. shell:

10 cm Gr.39 rot Hl	fuzed A.Z.38	Weight	11.76 kg (24 lbs 9 ozs)
10 cm Gr.39 rot Hl/A	"	"	12.30 kg (27 lbs 1 oz)
10 cm Gr.39 rot Hl/B	"	"	12.10 kg (26 lbs 9 ozs)
10 cm Gr.39 rot Hl/C	"	"	12.35 kg (27 lbs 2 ozs)
10 cm Pzgr.			

The first type, the 10 cm Gr.39 rot is obsolescent; the rounded nose renders it ballistically inferior to the more modern types. It is fired with charge 5; the metre graduations on the sight drum can be used, 50 m. (55 yds) being added to the ground range. The remaining three types are fired with either charge 5 (M.V.1360 f.s.), or charge 6. (M.V.1625 f.s.). The maximum range for anti-tank purposes is 1500 m. (1640 yds).

If no hollow charge ammunition is available, then according to the range tables the 10 cm Pzgr or the H.E. shell may be used against armour, fired with charge 5 and the fuze set at instantaneous. In exceptional cases, charge 6 may be used with the same metre graduations as for charge 5. $\frac{3}{4}$ of

/ the

the ground range should be set on the range drum.

Thus:

Range		Range Set	
m	yds.	m.	yds.
1600	1750	1200	1312
1000	1094	750	820
600	656	450	492

At ranges less than 600 m (656 yds) the range set on the drum should be 450 m (492 yds), since the vertex of the trajectory of the shell at this elevation is lower than the height of a tank.

(viii) "Sabot" type shell

There are two "sabot" shell, an H.E. and an A.P.

10.5 cm. Sprgr. 42 TS   H.E. fuzed A.Z.23
10.5 cm Pzgr. 39 TS   A.P.

Type	Initial calibre	Emergent Calibre	Weight complete	Weight of emergent projectile	Muzzle Velocity. f.s.
H.E.	10.5 cm.	8.8 cm	23 lb 1 oz.	20lb. 9½oz.	-
A.P.	10.5 cm.	7.5 cm	-	17 lbs	2520

The Germans claim the following penetration for the 10.5 cm Pzgr 39 TS:-

at normal, 180 mm at 100 m, 91 at 500, 80 mm at 1000 m and 71 mm at 1500 m.

(ix) There is one further projectile which is in process of evolution known as the 10.5 cm Minen Granate. It is un-rotated and is stabilised in flight by fins.

Weight (approx)   28 kg   62 lbs
M.V.   (")   270 ms   890 fs
Max Range (approx) 5200 m 5700 yds

N.B. Neither the "Sabot" type shell nor the 10.5 cm Minen Granate can be fired by the 10.5 cm le F.H. 18/40 with the present muzzle brake. A new cage muzzle brake is reported to be in process of development.

(b) Propellant

(i) Charges 1 - 6

It is stated in the Range Tables that in future charge bags 2 and 3 will be combined into one to be called charge bag 3. Consequently only charges 1,3,4,5,6 and long Range can be fired. There are three forms of propellant composed as follows:-

Flake Gudel

	Increment (gms)				
	1	2 & 3	4	5	6
Nz Man NP (1.5,1.5)	20				20
Digl.Bl.P.-10.5- (10,10,0.2)	190				
Gu.Bl.P.-A0- (4,4,0.6)		152	137	216	
Gu.Str.P.-A0.5- (175,7,0.7)					Approx 1045

/The

The individual charges are composed thus:-

Charge	Nz Man NP (1.5,1.5)	Digl.Bl.P-10.5- (10,10,0.2)	Weight in gms Gu.Bl.P - AO - (4,4,0.6)	Gu.Str.P -AO.5- (175,7,0.7)
1	20	190		
3	20	190	152	
4	20	190	289	
5	20	190	505	
6	20			about 1045

Notrocellulose

Type	1	2 & 3	Increment (gms) 4	5	6
Nz.Man.NP (1.5,1.5)	20				20
Digl.Bl.P.-10.5 - (10,10,0.2)	190				
Nz.Bl.P (6,6,1)		150	145	215	
Nz.R P (175,5.5/2)					about 1060

The individual charges are composed thus:-

Charge	Nz.Man.NP (1.5,1.5)	Digl.Bl.P - 10.5- (10,10.0.2)	Weight in gms. Nz Bl.P (6,6,1)	Nz. R P (175, 5.5/2)
1	20	190		
3	20	190	about 150	
4	20	190	about 295	
5	20	190	about 510	
6	20			about 1060

Flake Diglycol

Type	1	2 & 3	Increment (grms) 4	5	6
Nz.Man.NP (1.5,1.5)	20				
Digl.Bl.P - 10.5- (3,3,0.8)	245	133	123	195	222
Digl.Bl.P - 10.5 - (4,4,1.2)					800

/The individual

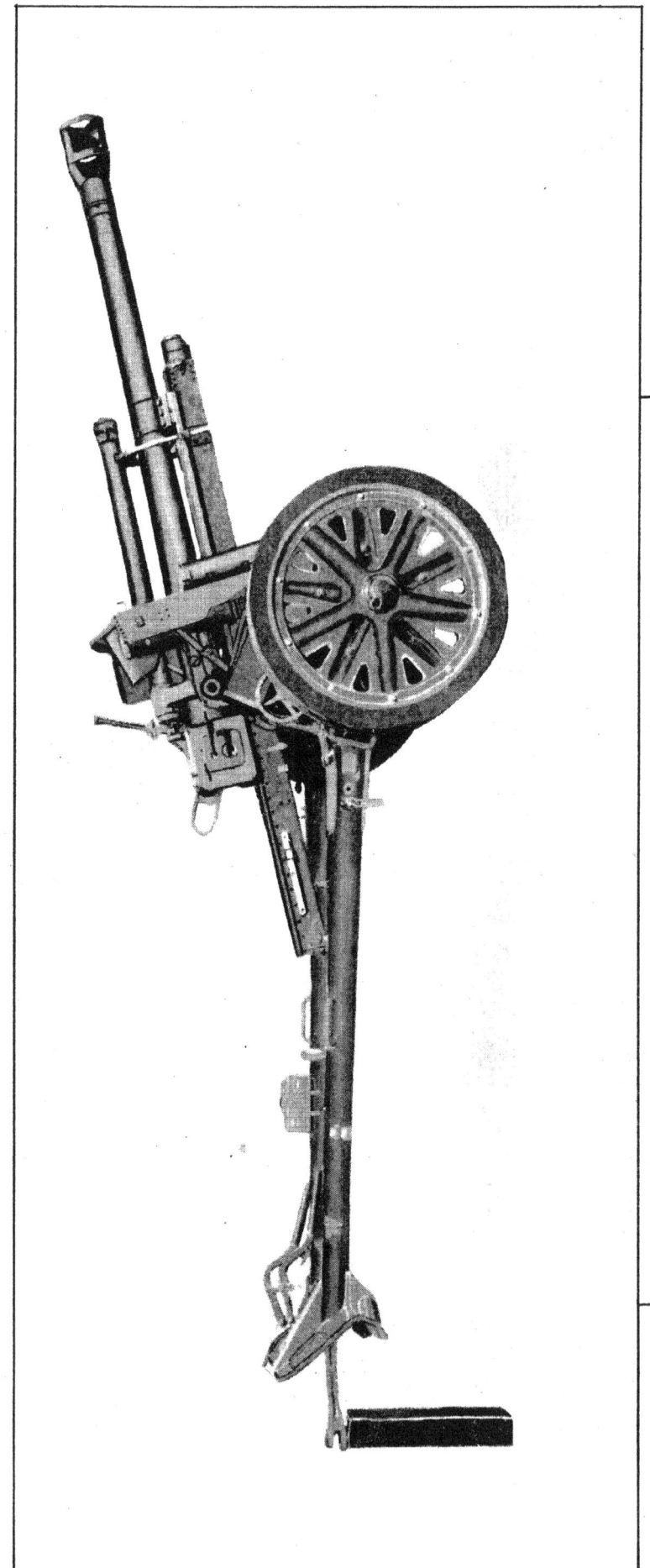

FIG. 78. 10·5 cm. le F.H. 18/40.
(4·13 in. LIGHT FIELD HOWITZER MODEL 18/40.)

The individual charges are composed thus:-

Charge	Weight in grms		
	Nz.Man NP (1.5,1.5)	Digl.Bl.P - 10.5 - (3,3,0.8)	Digl.Bl.P - 10.5 - (4,4,1.2)
1	20	245	
3	20	378	
4	20	501	
5	20	696	
6	-	222	800

(ii) Long range charge (Fern Ladung)

The propellant for the long range charge may take the form of diglycol or gudol, but in tubular form. The compositions are:-

Tubular Diglycol

20 gm. Nz.Man. NP (1.5,1.5)
1810 gm. Digl.R.P.-G 0.5 -(200,2.6/1)

Tubular Gudol

20 gm Nz.Man.NP.(1.5,1.5)
1530 gm.Gu.R.P.- A 0.75 - (200,3.6/1.2)

N.B. The long range charge must be used only with the long range shell, and conversely. Neither may be used if the muzzle brake is for any reason removed.

L. 10.5 cm le Feldhaubitze 18/42 (le.F.H.18/42)   (4.13 in Light Field Howitzer Model 18/42)

(See fig. 79)

1. This equipment is a modified version by Krupp of the le.F.H.18/40 but was never introduced into service. The barrel length was increased and the performance stepped up slightly.

2. Data : le F.H.18/42.

	Metric	British
Calibre	105 mm	4.13 ins
Length of piece (31 Cals)	3255 mm	128.15 ins
Rifling - Increasing Right Hand Twist Angle of pitch 6° to 9°.		
Traverse	60°	
Elevation	- 5° + 45°	
Weight in action	2035 kg	2 Tons
Weight of standard HE projectile	14.81 kg	32.6 lbs
Maximum muzzle velocity	585 m/sec	1920 f.s.
Maximum range	12700 metres	13,900 yds
Chamber pressure	2500 atmospheres	16.4 Tons sq ins
No. of charges	7	

M. 10.5 cm le F.H.42 (4.13 in Light Field Howitzer Model 42) See fig:- 80

1. This equipment was intended to replace the 10.5 cm le F.H.18 and the le F.H. 18/40. It is of orthodox design but considerably lighter in weight than the earlier models, and has increased track width and a lower silhouette in action. The carriage incorporates torsion bar suspension and allowance is made for stability of the equipment in action on uneven terrain. The weight in action has been reduced by some 350 kg (about 7 cwts) on earlier models and ballistically the le F.H.42 is not inferior to these and uses the standard projectiles of the le F.H. series.

/ The

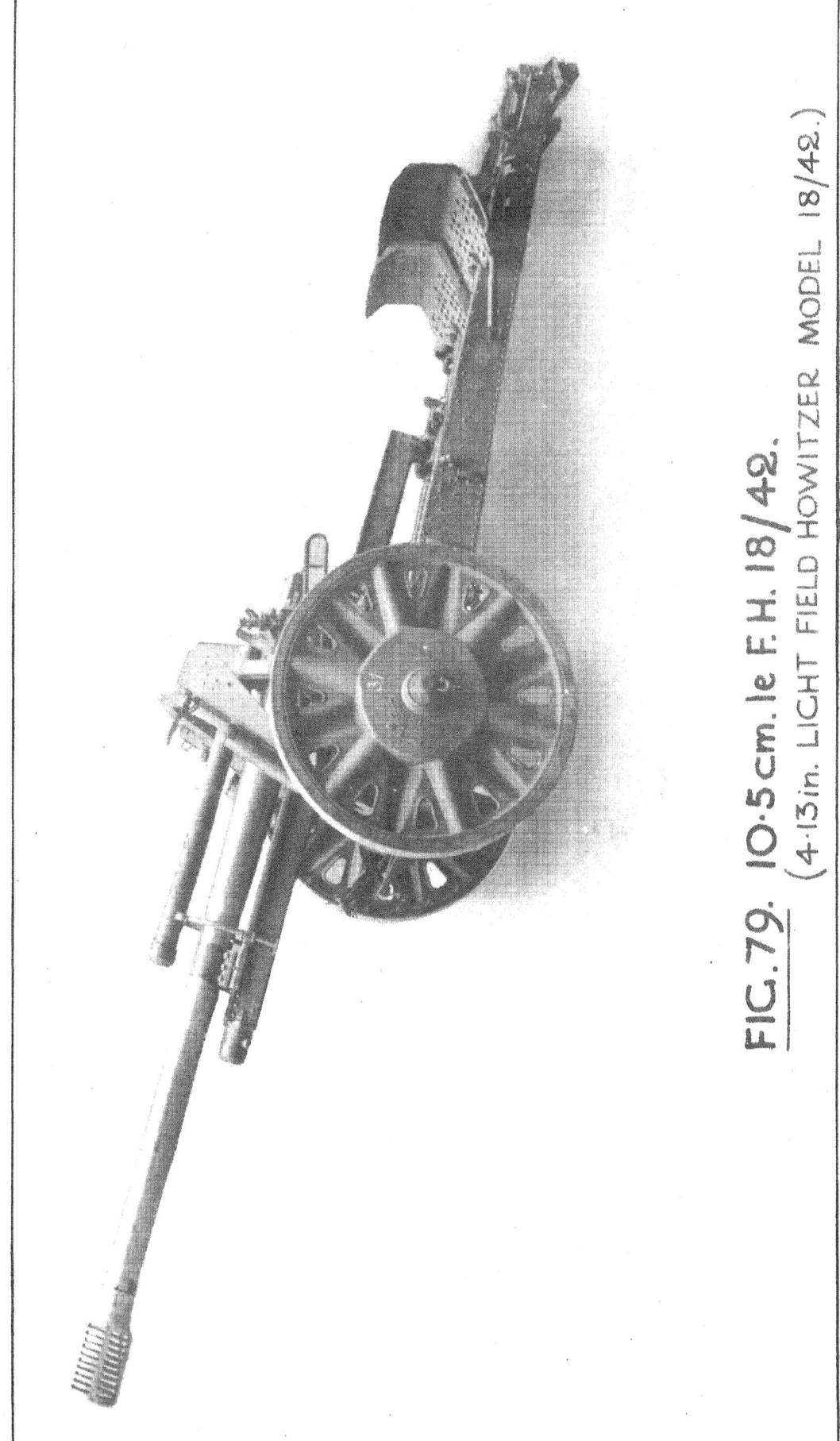

FIG. 79. 10·5 cm. le F.H. 18/42.
(4·13 in. LIGHT FIELD HOWITZER MODEL 18/42.)

The le F.H. 42 was not accepted for production because, by the time it was ready, the requirements of the Army had again been modified. Wartime experience had shown, especially in the Russian campaign, that artillery emplaced in forward zones of operation found it necessary to engage tanks at close range, also, in well wooded country, ability to fire in the upper registery was indispensible. The German designers therefore pressed forward with designs for the le F.H. 43 which had to satisfy these further requirements.

The equipment under review has a monobloc barrel with detachable breech ring and muzzle brake.

The orthodox type recoil system is located in the trough type cradle below the gun barrel and the one equilibrator is of the hydro-pneumatic kind.

The carriage is of the split trail type, the trails being of tubular construction. The Standard German sighting gear is fitted, having a telescope with a power of 3X8.

The gun is fired by the electric method.

2. Data : le F.H. 42.

	Metric	British
Calibre	105 mm	4.13 ins
Length of piece (28 Cals)	2940 mm	115.75 ins
Traverse	70°	
Elevation	− 5° + 45°	
Weight in action	1630 kg	1.6 Tons
Weight of standard HE projectile	14.81 kg	32.6 lbs
Maximum muzzle velocity	595 m/sec	1950 fs
Maximum range	13000 metres	14,200 yds
No. of charges	7	

N. **10.5 cm le Feldhaubitze 43 (le.F.H.43)** (4.13 in Light Field Howitzer Model 43)

(See Figs :- 81, 82 and 83)

1. This equipment, which did not reach the operational stage, was developed to satisfy the requirement for an improved light field howitzer which -
    (a) Would fire in the upper register.
    (b) Have a maximum range of 13000 metres with the standard ammunition.
    (c) Possess all round traverse.
    (d) Not be heavier than the le F.H.18/40.

Three exeperimental solutions were produced one by Skoda and the other two by Krupp.

2. SKODA MODEL

    (a) The barrel is fitted with a muzzle brake similar to the le F.H.18/40, but the ordnance is longer and the chamber capacity increased.

    The recoil system is of H.P. variable type with 3 stage variation and is located immediately below the barrel.

    The carriage is unorthodox and, in addition to normal carriage, consists of a firing pedestal with an extra pair of trail legs which extend forward and in the travelling position are clamped to the piece. In the firing position the pedestal is pivotted downwards where it is locked. Both front and rear trails spread to provide outriggers equally spaced around the pedestal, and securing pickets are driven into the ground.

    Two spring equilibrators are fitted.

    The carriage has disc wheels with pneumatic tyres and independent suspension with leaf springs.

    The following data is taken from documentary sources and by insepction of a complete model.

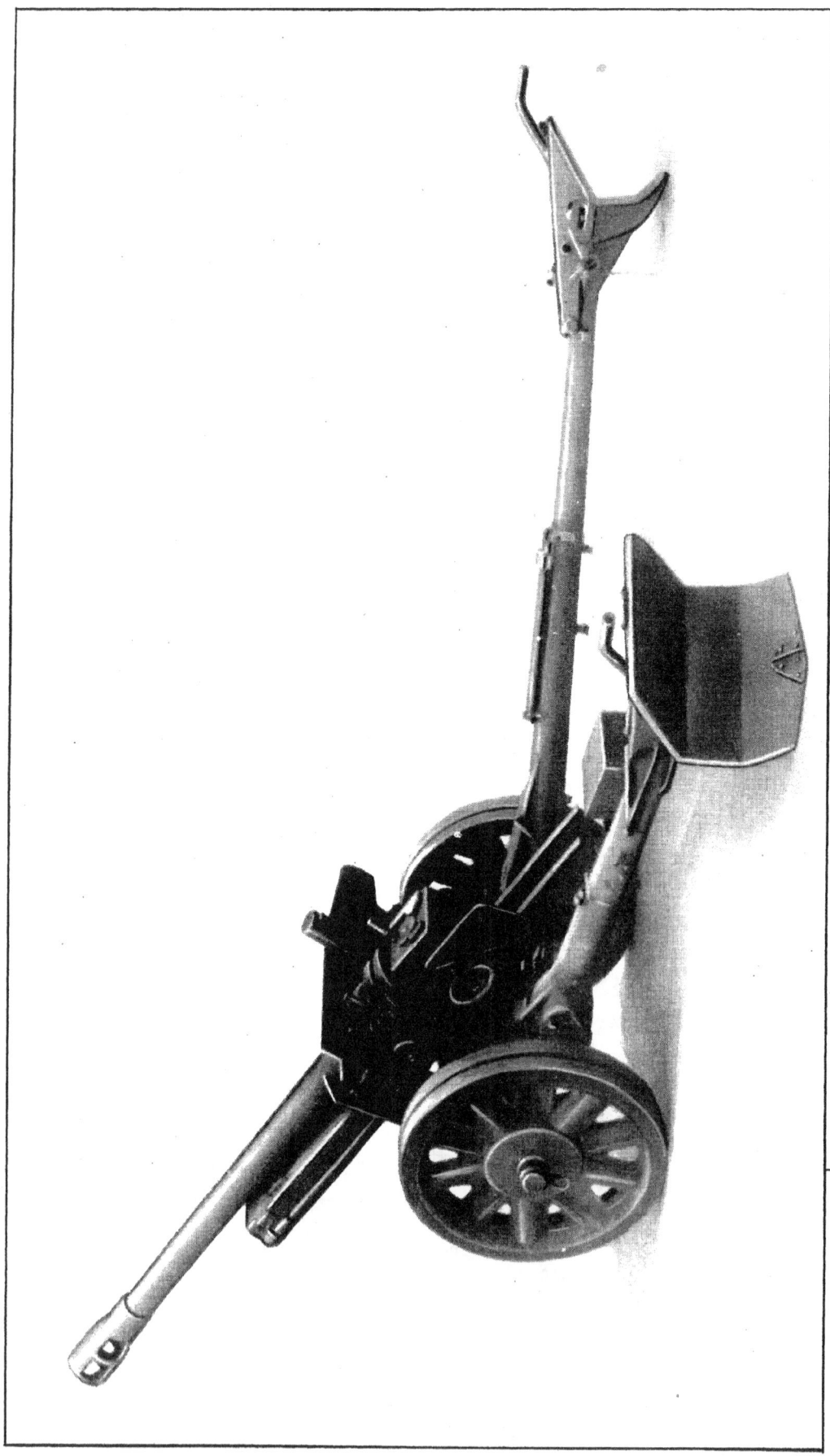

FIG. 80. 10·5 cm. le F.H. 42.
(4·13 in. LIGHT FIELD HOWITZER MODEL 42.)

FIG. 81. 10.5 cm. le F.H.43.
(4.13 in. LIGHT FIELD HOWITZER MODEL 43. — SKODA PROTOTYPE.)

FIG. 82. 10.5cm. le F.H.43.
(4.13 in. LIGHT FIELD HOWITZER MODEL 43.
—SKODA PROTOTYPE.)

FIG. 83. 10.5 cm. le F.H. 43.
(4.13in. LIGHT FIELD HOWITZER MODEL 43 – KRUPP PROTOTYPE.)

(b)

Data	Metric	British
Calibre	105 mm	4.13 ins
Length of piece	3456 ins	136 ins
Traverse	6400 mils	360°
Elevation	$-5° + 75°$	
Length of recoil (variable three stages)	1550/1150/850 mm	61 ins/45 ins/33 ins.
Weight in firing position	2200 kg	2.12 Tons
Weight of projectile (Standard HE)	14.81 kg	32.6 lbs
Maximum Muzzle Velocity	610 m/sec	2000 fs
Chamber Pressure	2600 Atmospheres	17 Tons sq ins
Maximum Range	13000	14,210 yds

3. KRUPP MODELS

(a) One equipment incorporated a carriage which is based on the cruciform platform design of the successful 88 mm Pak 43, the other was of somewhat similar design to the Skoda model with 4 trails.

(b) Cruciform Platform Model - Data :-

	Metric	British
Calibre	105 mm	4.13 ins
Length of piece (35 Cals)	3675 mm	144.7 ins
Traverse	360°	
Elevation	$-10° + 70°$	
Electric Firing		
Angle of pitch of rifling	9°	
Weight of Standard HE Projectile	14.81 kg	32.6 lbs
No. of charges	7	
Maximum Muzzle Velocity	655 m/sec	2150 fs
Chamber Pressure	2500 Atmospheres	16.4 Tons sq ins
Maximum Range	14200 metres	15,525 yds

(c) Four Trail Model. - Data:-

	Metric	British
Calibre	105 mm	4.13 ins
Length of piece (28 Cals)	2941 mm	115.8 ins
Traverse	360°	
Elevation	$-4° + 70°$	
Weight of Standard HE Projectile	14.81 kg	32.6 lbs
Maximum Muzzle Velocity	595 m/sec	1950 fs
Maximum Range	13000 metres	14,210 yds

O. 10 cm K 17 or K 17/04 (4.13 ins Gun Model 17 or Model 17/04) See fig: 84

1. This weapon, a development of the 10 cm K 14, was produced to satisfy the requirement for increased performance during the third year of World War I. In order to avoid the disruption of the production lines producing the model 14, as many components as possible of this model were used in the new weapon.

The 35 calibres length barrel of the model 14 was discarded and a barrel of 45 calibres was used.

The equipment follows the typical design of the 1914-18 war and was mounted on a box trail type of carriage. Orthodox wooden artillery wheels were fitted and the barrel could be pulled back on to the box trail in the travelling position.

It was intended that the old type spring recuperator should be replaced by a more modern air recuperator but, owing to reproduction difficulties, it was decided to fit a spring recuperator, made of improved material and design.

/ The

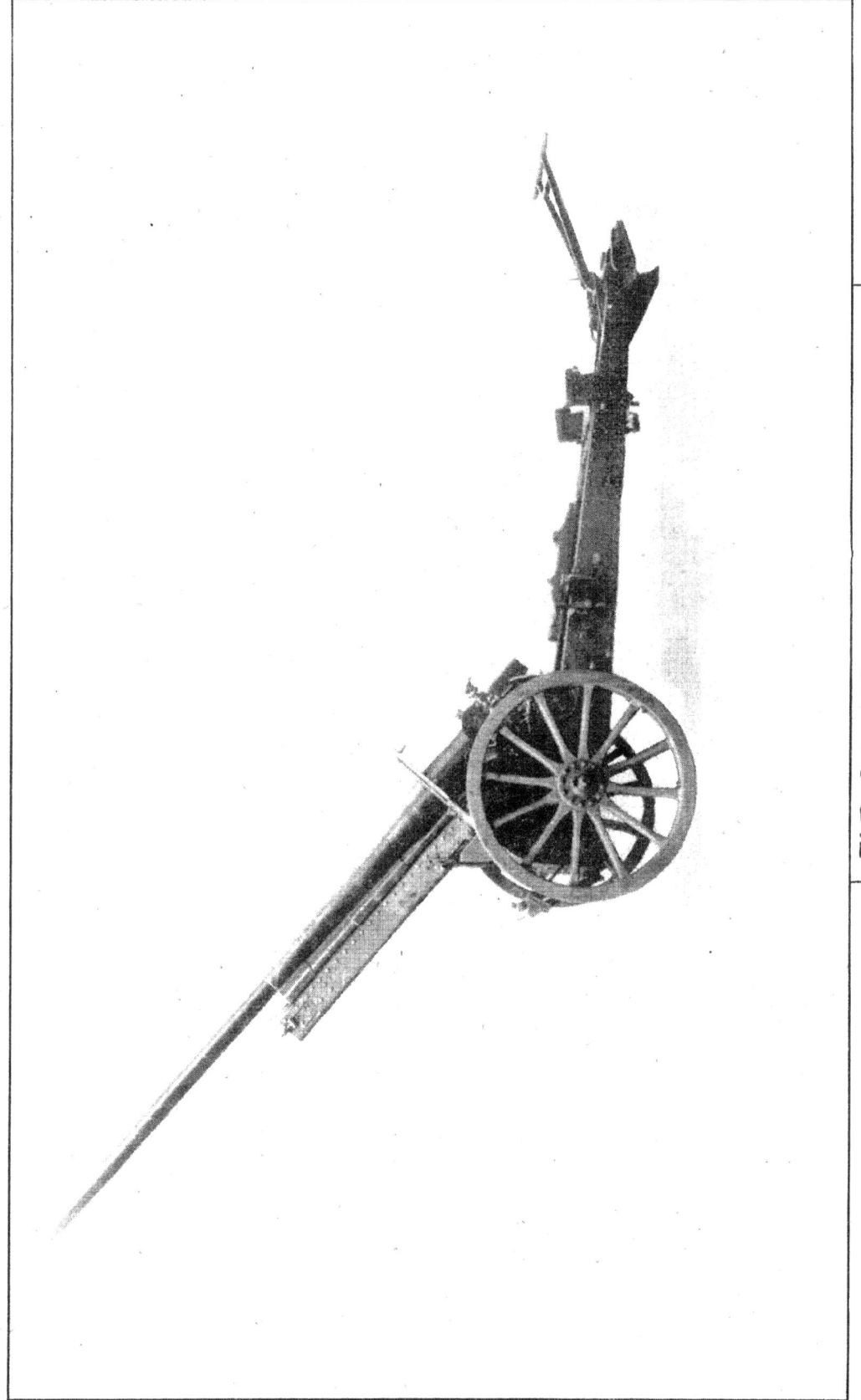

FIG. 84. 10 cm. K.17.
(4.14 in. LIGHT GUN MODEL 17)

The recoil system is fitted within the trough type cradle.

The weapon was fitted with simplified and more modern sighting gear.

2. Data: K.17.

	Metric	British
Calibre	105 mm	4.13 ins
Length of piece (45 calibres)	4725 mm	186 ins
Muzzle Velocity	650 m/s	2130 f.s.
Maximum Range (Projectile Gr 15 Hb)	14100 metres	15400 yds
Maximum Range (Projectile Gr 18 Hb)	16500 metres	18050 yds
Rifling - No. of grooves	32	
Elevation	$-2° + 45°$	
Traverse	6°	
Weight in action	3300 kg	3.2 tons
Weight of projectile 10 cm Gr 15	18.5 kg	40.7 lbs

P. 10 cm le Kanone 41 (4.14 ins light Gun Model 41). See fig: 85

1. Prototype models of this gun were produced to meet the requirement for a light field gun having greater range than the le FH 18 (light Field Howitzer 18) without sacrificing mobility. Although generally speaking these conditions were fulfilled, development ceased in 1941. The equipment combines many of the features found in the previous weapons, which it was to replace.

The piece consists of a monobloc barrel secured in a removeable breech ring by a screwed collar. A double baffle type muzzle brake is fitted. The horizontal sliding breech block, which opens to the right, is similar to the standard type used for other 10.5 cm weapons.

The trough type riveted construction cradle houses the hydraulic buffer below the gun barrel. The orthodox hydro-pneumatic recuperator is located above the barrel.

The single elevating arc is secured to the right side of the cradle.

Two equilibrators or balancing springs are used being of the hydro-pneumatic type and fitted between cradle and saddle.

Both elevating and traversing gears are of normal German design.

There is nothing unusual about the carriage body except that it is of lighter weight that that associated with equipments of this size. Following modern German practice twin torsion rod carriage suspension is used in the axle assembly. The cranks of the stub axles appear to be longer than is normally the case. The carriage suspension is locked in the firing position, the action being effected by the opening out of the split trails.

The wheels are of the pressed spoke metal type, fitted with solid rubber tyres.

2. The following data details are extracted from the Rheinmetall Borsig specification :-

	Metric	British
Calibre	105 mm	4.14 ins
Length of piece (40 calibres)	4200 mm	165.35 ins
Elevation	$-5° + 45°$	
Traverse	60°	
Weight of standard projectiles	15 kg	33 lbs
Muzzle Velocity	665 m/secs	2182 f.s.
Maximum range	15000 metres	16,400 yds
Weight in action	2640 kg	2.6 tons

CHAPTER VII

THE DEVELOPEMENT OF GERMAN MEDIUM ARTILLERY

General.

1. The schwere 10 cm Kanone 18 (actual calibre 105 mm) (Medium 4.1 inch Gun Model 18) and the 15 cm schwere Feldhaubitze (s.FH 18) (5.9 inch Medium Field Howitzer Model 18) form the backbone of the German Medium Artillery. They were developed by Krupp and Rheinmetall during the period 1926 to 1930 and finally introduced into service about 1933 to 1934 the production model, generally speaking, of the s.FH.18 incorporating the Rheinmetall gun and the Krupp carriage.

The same carriage is used by the 10 cm Gun and the 15 cm Howitzer.

The equipments are designed for motorised or horse drawn transport, the former as a single load with the piece extracted, or in two horse drawn loads.

In addition to its normal role as a medium gun, the s.10 cm.K. was also used as a mobile Coast Defence gun and was provided with a special sea ranging shell which produces a bright green splash on burst. There is some evidence that the German Army considered that this equipment was unsatisfactory on account of the comparatively light shell for a medium gun. At an early date a Rocket Assisted Shell weight 41 kg (90.2 lbs), was introduced for the s.FH. 18. This ranged up to 19000 metres (20,800 yds) and it was hoped would make production of the s.10 cm.K unnecessary, but difficulties of manufacture and fuze design coupled with erratic dispersions at extreme ranges were encountered for the rocket assisted shell. The further development and modifications during the war follow a rather similar course to that already outlined for the 10.5 cm le FH equipments. As early as 1938 the German High Command asked for increased ballistic performance of the s.FH and ability to fire in the upper register; both Krupp and Rheinmetall produced prototype models in 1941, but the model 40 was not introduced as it was found impracticable to change production at a moment when increased production of le.FH and s.FH was the first consideration.

2. The piece of the s.FH 40 is 32.5 calibres long and is fitted with a muzzle brake, chamber capacity is increased from 7.22 litres to 9.85 litres to enable heavier charges to be fired and maximum range thus stepped up to 15400 metres (16,850 yards).

Modifications to the carriage include pneumatic equilibrators, variable recoil and torsion bar suspension.

A small number of equipments known, as the s.10 cm. K 18/40 and s.FH 18/40, were produced and later given the model number 42.

3. In the s.10 cm.K 18/40 (42) (Medium 4.1 inch Gun Model 18/40 (42)), a barrel 60 calibres long replaces the 52 calibres barrel of the model 18 and chamber capacity is increased from 8.23 litres to 10.15 litres. The carriage is modified to the extent of replacing spring equilibrators by those of pneumatic type, reinforcing the axle springing and spades and certain alterations to the recoil system. Maximum range is 21000 metres (23,000 yards).

4. The s.FH 18/40 (42) (4.1 inch Medium Field Howitzer Model 18/40 (42)) comprises the ordnance of the s.FH 40 with modified rifling mounted on the carriage of the s.FH 18. Maximum range is 15100 metres (16,500 yards). A total of 46 equipments in all were produced. At short and medium ranges accuracy was not as consistent as with the s.FH 18.

/ 5.

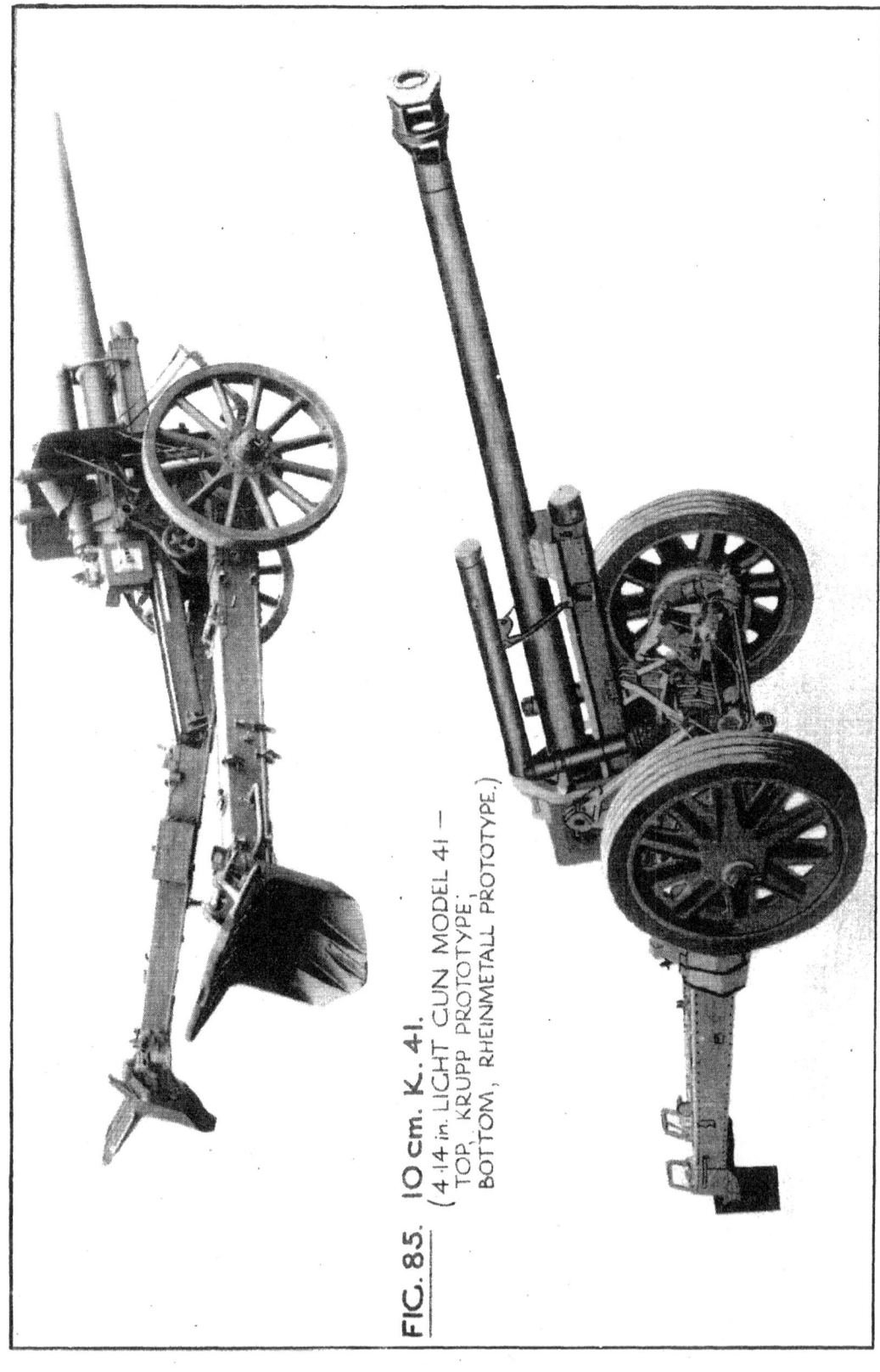

FIG. 85. 10 cm. K. 41.
(4.14 in. LIGHT GUN MODEL 41 —
TOP, KRUPP PROTOTYPE;
BOTTOM, RHEINMETALL PROTOTYPE.)

5. The s.FH 43 (4.1 inch Medium Field Howitzer). As a result of experience in the Russian campaign, it was decided to produce a medium howitzer with 360° traverse, capable of firing in the upper register and with a maximum range of 18 km (19,700 yds) - this in view of the 17.3 km (19,000 yds) range of the standard Russian medium howitzer Model 37.

Krupp produced designs for a carriage with extra trails on similar lines to the le FH 43 but later decided to use a cruciform carriage standardised to take the s.FH ordnance or the 12.8 cm (5 inch) duel purpose Medium Anti-Tank Gun.

One interesting feature is that owing to shortage of steel for cartridge case manufacture, it was decided to use a screw type breech or ring obturation in the new designs for the s.FH 43. The barrel was to be 31.5 calibres long with a muzzle brake.

6. The 15 cm s.FH 36 (5.9 inch Medium Howitzer) was intended to meet the General Staff requirement for a medium howitzer of lighter construction than the s.FH 18, being sutiable for horse drawn transport in one load. Development took place during 1936 to 1939 and both Krupp and Rheinmetall produced prototype models. Production ceased altogether in 1942. The equipment is of orthodox German design and has no outstanding features. The barrel is a monobloc and is shorter than that of the s.FH 18; a muzzle brake is fitted. The ammunition listed for this equipment is similar to that for the model 18 but only 7 charges are fired. Total weight in action is 3280 kg (3.2 Tons and maximum range with the standard 43.5 kg (95.7 lbs) HE shell is 12300 metres (13500 yds).

7. The lange schwere Feldhaubitze 13 (Long Medium Field Howitzer Model 13) is a Krupp production of the 1914/1918 war and was introduced early in 1917. The 15 cm piece is 17 calibres long and is mounted on a box trail carriage designed for horse drawn transport in one load. Maximum range is 8600 metres with a 40.8 kg shell.

8. The 12.8 cm (5 inch) Dual Purpose High Velocity Medium A/Tk Gun was introduced for service in the later stages of the war and is an extremely important equipment.

The ordnance comprises a barrel of orthodox design 55 calibres long fitted with a muzzle brake. This gun was also intended as the main armament of the Tiger Tank. For the field carriage mounting a cruciform platform with front and rear travelling bogies was adopted as the result of the satisfactory performance of the 8.8 cm Pak 43 in action. Both Krupp and Rheinmetall prototypes were produced and the final decision of the Ordnance Directorate is not recorded. The first Krupp prototype restricted maximum elevation and appears to have considered almost exclusively the A/Tk role. The later model allowed elevation from -5° to + 45° and could also be used to mount a standard s.FH Medium Howitzer.

The equipment weighs just over 9 tons in action and fires the standard 26 kg (57.2 lbs) HE shell to a maximum range of 21000 metres (23,000 yds). A special long range shell ranges up to 24400 metres (26,700 yds). An APCBC/HE shell is fired at an MV of 920 met/secs (3020 fs) against AFVs and a penetration of 202 mm (7.95 inches) against homogeneous plate at 1000 metres (1094 yards) range at 30° is claimed.

The ammunition is of separate QF type and medium and full charges are provided.

Experimental work was in progress with AP sub-calibre projectiles for this gun.

Nomenclature is extremely confusing in the various documents recovered from the files of the designers and the official German ordnance publications. The 12.8 gun on the cruciform carriage was known as the 12.8 K 43, 12.8 cm K 44 and 12.8 cm K 81 at various stages of development, apart from the large variety of nomenclatures for the tank and A/Tk SP versions.

At one stage of development, in order to gain experience in the field the gun was mounted on improvised carriages using the carriage of captured foreign equipment, the French 155 mm GPF-T and the Russian 152 mm Howitzer M 1937, these hybrid equipments being known as 12.8 cm K 81/1 and K 81/2 respectively.

9. **15 cm s.FH 18/43 (5.9 inch Medium Howitzer Model 18/43).** This is a development of the stantard 15 cm s.FH 18. The outstanding feature is the incorporation of "ring obturation", thus retaining the horizontal sliding breech block at the same time obviating the need for a cartridge case.

The piece with minor exceptions is the same as the s.FH 18. The lip at the rear end of the barrel has been removed and there are no recesses for extractors. A continuous pull firing mechanism is contained within a block, which slides in a horizontal plane on the right side of the breech block - a percussion tube leads through the breech block diagonally to the front face.

The obturator assembly fits into a recess in the front of the breech block and consists of 3 parts - an outer ring, an inner ring and a spacer ring.

The outer ring has an "L" shaped section - the inner ring also - radial holes are bored through the inner ring - the spacer ring is flat and chamfered to seat in the bottom of the recess in the breech block and several spare rings of varying thickness are supplied for each obturator.

When the breech block is closed the outer ring is brought into contact with the rear face of the barrel. On firing, the propellant gases pass through the holes of the inner ring into the annular chamber between outer and inner rings and the pressure thus exerted forces the outer ring against the rear face of the piece and thus achieves obturation.

B. **10.5 cm s K 18.** (4.1 inch Medium Gun Model 18). See Fig: 86 and 87
and
15cm s FH 18 (5.9 inch Medium Field howitzer Model 18). See Fig: 88 and 89

1. The piece is of a jacket and tune construction with detachable breech ring and hand operated horizontal sliding breech block designed for percussion firing. The hydraulic buffer with cooling jacket is in the cradle below the barrel and a hydro-pneumatic recuperator above the barrel.

The split trail field carriage has rivetted trail legs and detachable spades. The axle has tranverse leaf type springing which is locked when the equipment is in the firing position. Perforated disc wheels of light metal are fitted with either solid rubber tyres, or iron for motorised or horse drawn transport respectively.

In addition to its normal role as a medium field gun, the 10.5 cm s K 18 was also used as a mobile Coast Defence gun and was provided with a special sea ranging shell. The filling of this shell produced a bright green splash on burst. There is some evidence that the German Army considered that this equipment was unsatisfactory on account of the comparatively light shell for a medium gun.

A winch operated bollard drum, the surface of which was grooved to take a wire hawser was fitted to the carriage to facilitate the movement of the gun barrel form the travelling to the firing position and vice versa.

2. Data: **10.5 cm s K.18** (4.13 inch Medium Gun Model 18)

	Metric	British
(a) Calibre	105 mm	4.13 ins
Length of gun	5460 mm	214.95 ins
Chamber capacity	8.23 litres	476 cu. ins
Length of rifling	4252 mm	167.3 ins
Rifling -		
Number of grooves	36	
Type of rifling. Increasing Right Hand Twist $4\frac{1}{2}°$ to $6°$		
Percussion or electric firing		Percussion

/

(a) contd.

	Metric	British
Maximum recoil	970 mm	38.2 ins
Normal recoil	920 mm	36.2 ins
Type of Sights.	Z E 34 (with Rbl F 16,32,36 or 37)	
Traverse	1066 mils	64°
Rate of traverse. One turn of handwheel	= 30 minutes	
Elevation	0-800 mils	0° - 48°
Rate of elevation, One turn of handwheel	= 1° 30'	
Rate of fire	6	
Traverse position -		
Overall length		26.83 ft
Overall width		7.4 ft
Overall height		5.6 ft
Travelling position weight (one load)	6434 kg	6.3 tons
Weight in action	5642 kg	5.55 tons
Maximum Muzzle Velocity	835 m/s	2739 f s
Chamber pressure	2650 atmospheres	17.4 tons sq. ins.
Muzzle energy	538 m/tons	
Maximum range	19,075 metres	20,860 yds.

(b) **Ammunition**

3 charges are used, viz: Small, Medium and Full Charge.

Projectile	Projectile Weight	Muzzle Velocity	Max Range
HE 10 cm Gr 19	15.14 kg (33.3 lbs)	S = 550 m/s (1800 fs)	12725 m (13900 yds)
		M = 690 m/s (2263 fs)	15750 m (17230 yds)
		Full Charge = 835 m/s (2740 fs)	19075 m (20,860 yds)
HE 10 cm Gr 19 F E S	(Same ballistics as for Gr 19 - shown above for 3 charges)		
Smoke 10 cm Gr 38 Nb	14.71 kg (32.36 lbs)	827 m/s (2710 fs)	18300 m (20000 yds)
APCBC HE/Tracer 10 cm Pzgr Rot	15.56 kg (34.2 lbs)	Medium Charge (682 m/s (2230 fs))	13850 m (15146 yds)
AP/HE 10 cm Pzgr Rot	15.56 kg (34.2 lbs)	Full Charge (822 m/s (2695 fs))	16000 m (17500 yds)

(c) **Fuzes**

Nose Percussion - A Z 23 v, A Z 23/28 and A Z 23/42 used with the HE and Smoke shell.

Time and Percussion - Dopp Z S/60 (lM) and Dopp Z S/60 s are used with HE shell.

Nose Fuzes - Kl A Z 23 (Pr) and Kl A Z 23 with Smoke shell

Base Fuze - Bd Z f. with APCBC HE/Tracer

Nose Percussion - AZ 38 used with a Sea Ranging shell

(d) **Extract from Range Table**

Charge	M V (fs)	Max Range (yds)	Time of Flight (secs)	50% Zone (yards)		
				Length	Breadth	Height
Small	1800	13,920	54.2	137	17.5	561
Medium	2260	17,200	62.2	136	19.5	627
Large	2718	20,860	71.2	236	22	1230

/ 12.8 cm

3. **Data:** 15 cm s F H 18 (5.9 inch Medium Field Howitzer Model 18)

(a)
	Metric	British
Calibre	150 mm	5.9 ins
Length of Gun	4440 mm	174.8 ins
Length of barrel	3985 mm	156.88 ins
Length of rifling	3623 mm	142.63 ins
Rifling –		
Number of grooves	40	
Type of rifling. Increasing Right Hand Twist	5° to 10°	
Chamber capacity	722 litres	
Percussion electric firing	Percussion	
Maximum recoil	1170 mm	46 ins
Normal recoil	1120 mm	44 ins
Type of Sights. Z E 34 (with Rbl F 16, 32, 36 or 37)		
Traverse	1062 mils	64°
Rate of Traverse. 1 turn of handwheel = 30 minutes		
Elevation	0-800 mils	-3° to 45°
Rate of Elevation. 1 turn of handwheel = 1°30'		
Rate of fire	5 rpm	
Travelling position		
Overall length		25.75 ft
Overall width		7.4 ft
Overall height		5.6 ft
Travelling position	6304 kg	6.65 tons
Weight in action	5512 kg	5.4 tons
Maximum Velocity (HE)	520 m/sec	1710 f s
Chamber pressure	2500 atm	16.4 tons sq in.
Muzzle Energy	599.5 m/tons	
Maximum Range	13325 metres	14600 yds

(b) **Ballistic Characteristics – HE**

(i) Condensed Range Table

Charge	Muzzle Velocity (f s)	Max Range (yds)	Time of Flight (secs)	50% Zone yds Length	50% Zone yds Breadth	Drift (Mils)	Fuze Length	Remaining Velocity	Angle of strike
I	690	4375	27.2	42.3	7.6	30	165	617	46°14'
II	755	5140	29.3	42.7	7.6	30	177	666	44°39'
III	820	6015	33.7	53.4	8.7	34	201	709	41°31'
IV	915	7220	34.3	45.2	8.7	30	205	771	43°46'
V	1050	8970	39.5	50.7	9.8	28	234	843	42°24'
VI	1230	10610	43.3	53.4	10.9	25	255	909	40°44'
VII	1425	12250	47.9	61.2	13.1	28	282	965	38° –
VIII	1710	14550	54.0	70	14.2	33	317	1024	36°49'

(ii) **Use of Charges VII and VIII – before introduction of muzzle brake**

Normal charges for s F H 18 were I – VI inclusive. Charges VII VIII could be used with the s F H 18 only in exceptional cases, the need for which had to be substantiated by the troop commander. Not more than ten rounds were permitted to be fired consecutively with either Charge VII or VIII, as otherwise the brakes and the recuperator were liable to overstrain. Rounds fired with Charges VII and VIII, were entered in the barrel history sheet (Rohrbuch) of the s F H 18, and the entries had to be initialled by the troop commander.

Owing to severe pitting having been caused in the chamber of the 15 cm s F H 18 after frequent use of the special charges VII and VIII it became impossible to obtain a gas-tight seal round the cartridge case in the smooth end of the bore. At the beginning of 1942, therefore, a renewable chamber liner was introduced. Up to

/that

that time comparatively little use had been made of Charges VII and VIII owing to the strain they caused on the mounting and the brakes, but this strain was largely obviated by the incorporation of a muzzle brake. About the same time the "R" Granate, with a charge rather larger than VIII, was dveloped.

(c) Ammunition

The following types are used:-

(i) HE Shell with percussion fuze (15 cm Granate 19)

Weight: 95.7 lbs
Fuze: A Z 23 with optional delay (0.15 secs)

(ii) HE Shell with time and percussion fuze (15 cm Granate 19)

Weight: 95.7 lbs
Fuze: Dopp Z S/60

(iii) Anti-concrete (15 cm Granate 19 Beton)

Weight: 83.25 lbs
Colour: painted dark green overall

(iv) Armour Piercing (15 cm Gr 39 FES - H1/A - Hollow Charge

Weight: 54.16 lbs
Colour: field grey
Single soft iron driving band
Markings: H1/A in black. FES in white
Charge used: No. VI
M V 1510 f s
Fuze: kl A Z 40 Nb Pr
Also two new types of HE projectile

(v) HE Shell (15 cm Granate 19 FES)

Identical in shape and dimensions with 15 cm Gr 19 but fitted with single soft iron driving band instead of the usual two bimetallic driving bands.

(vi) HE Shell (15 cm Granate 36 FES)

Longer than 15 cm Gr 19. Streamlined below single soft iron driving band.

(vii) Smoke Shell (15 cm Gr 19 Nb)

Weight: 85.7 lb
Fuze: A Z 23 Nb

(viii) Smoke Shell (15 cm Gr 38 Nb)

Fuze: kl A Z 40 Nb

(ix) Reaction assisted Shell (15 cm R Gr 19) = (Rückstossgranate or Reaction Propulsion Shell)

Weight: 99.5 lb
Fuze: El A Z
El A Z mR
Dopp Z S/90   Range = 19000 metres (21000 yds)

Fired only by 15 cm s F H (M) i.e. fitted with muzzle brake, owing to strain on recuperating system. The R Gr is propelled initially by a charge larger than Charge VIII. May not be in general service.

(x) HE sub-calibre shell with disintegrating bands

Weight: 65 lb, may not be in general service.

/(d)

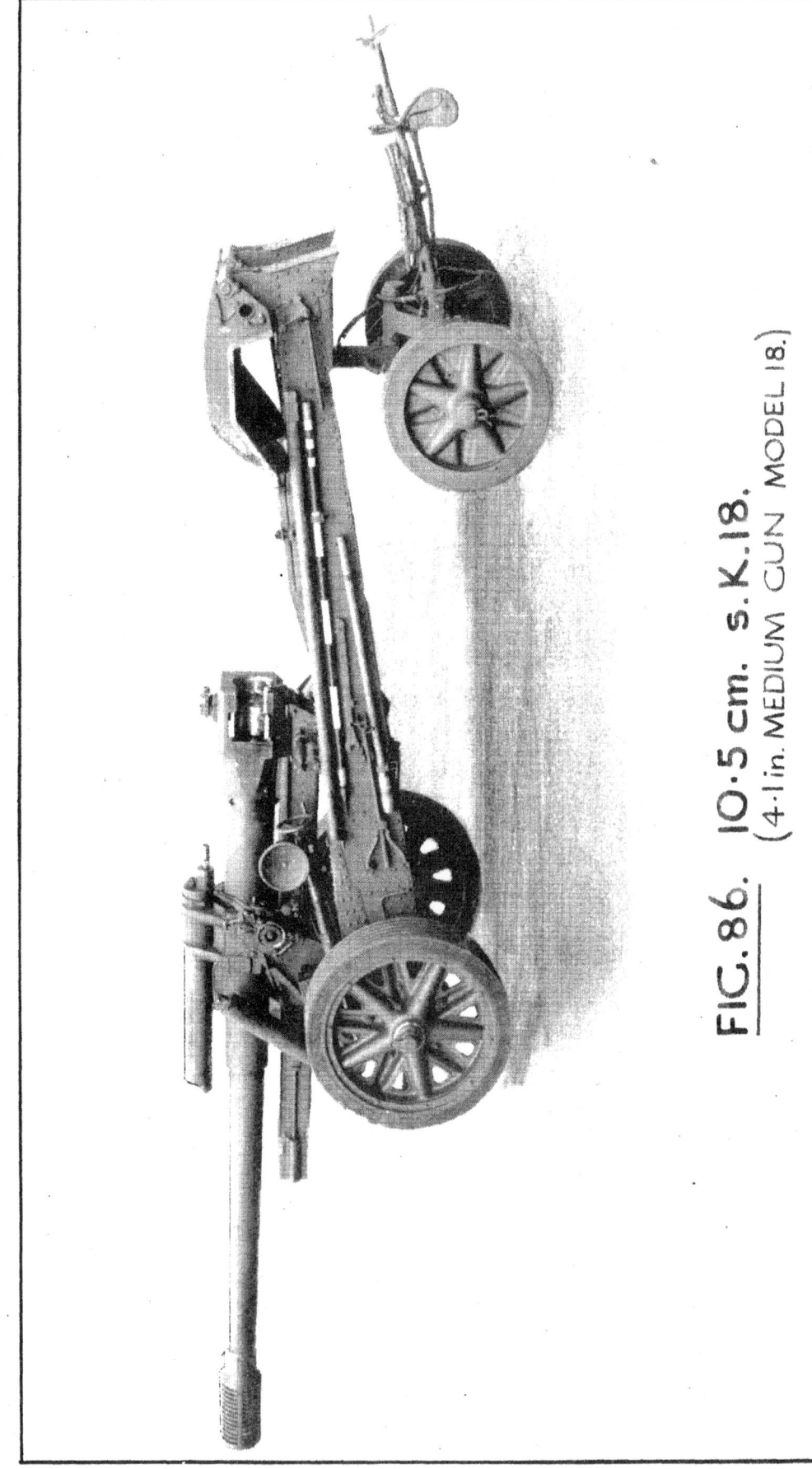

FIG. 86. 10·5 cm. s.K.18.
(4·1 in. MEDIUM GUN MODEL 18.)

FIG. 87. 10·5 cm. s.K.18.
(4·1 in. MEDIUM GUN MODEL 18.)

FIG. 88. 15 cm. s. F.H.18.
(5·9 in. MEDIUM FIELD HOWITZER MODEL 18.)

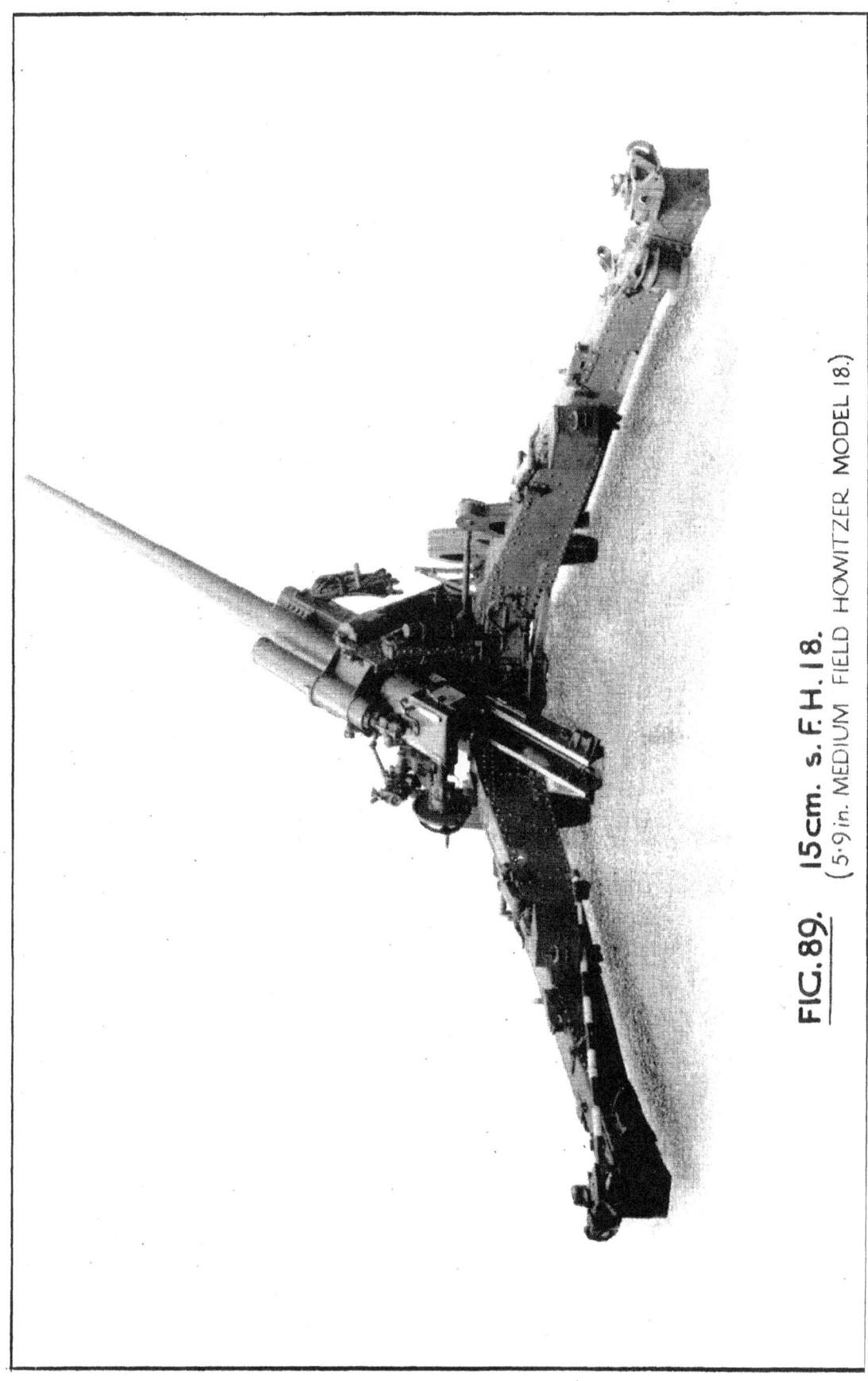

FIG. 89. 15 cm. s.F.H.18.
(5·9 in. MEDIUM FIELD HOWITZER MODEL 18.)

(d) The Primer

The primer C/12 nA is permanently fixed in the base of the cartridge case

(e) **The Shells**

H E Shell is painted grey-green and has **two** driving bands.

The two types of fuze AZ 23 (direct action graze) and Dopp Z S/60 (Time and percussion) are fixed in advance.

Smoke shell is painted grey-green with the letters "Nb or 38 Nb" in white on the body of the shell.

A P C B C. There is none for the 15 cm Howitzer.

The 10 cm Gun A P C B C shell is painted black. It has a base fuze and tracer.

Anti-concrete Shell. Exists only for the 15 cm Howitzer. It is effective against concrete, and has been used against tanks.

(f) **Fuzes.** All shells are issued fuzed.

AZ 23 umg (0.15) (direct action and graze) is adjustable to O/V (i.e. no delay) or M/V (i.e. delay 0.15 secs) by turning the slit of the setting bolt on the side of the fuze.

AZ 23 (0.8) umg and AZ 23 umg m 2 V. Both these fuzes are superseded by AZ 23 umg 0.15. The second has two optional delays.

Base fuze in 15 cm anti-concrete shell can be set to Kl/V, Gr/V or O/V, viz: short, long or no delay, respectively.

Dopp Z S/60. This can be set only by a special handfuze setter to divisions of the setter taken from the Range Tables.

C. 10.5 cm s K 18/40 (42) and 15 cm s F H 18/40 (42). See Figs: 90
(4.1 inch Medium Field Gun Model 18/40(42) and
5.9 inch Medium Field Howitzer Model 18/40(42))

1. As early as 1938 the German High Command asked for increased performance of the 10.5 s K 18 and the 15 cm s F H 18 weapons and further development and modification during the war followed a rather similar course to that already outlined for the 10.5 cm light field howitzer equipment. In addition to increased ballistic performance the ability to fire in the upper register was considered essential.

Both Krupp and Rheinmetall produced prototype models in 1941 and these were known as models 40. These models were not introduced into service as it was found impracticable to change production at a moment when increased production of light and medium field howitzers was the first consideration.

A small number of equipments known as the 10.5 cm s K 18/40 and 15 cm s F H 18/40 were produced and later given the model number 42.

Modifications included pneumatic equilibrators, variable recoil and torsion bar suspension; in addition the spades were strengthened.

Basically the equipments consist of the Model 40 Gun piece and a modified Model 40 Howitzer piece mounted on a modified s F H 18 carriage.

2. The 10.5 cm s K 18/40(42) barrel is 60 calibres long compared with the 52 calibres of the model 18 and the chamber capacity increased from 8.23 litres to 10.15 litres. The maximum range is 21000 metres (23000 yds).

3. The 15 cm s FH 18/40(42) barrel is the s F H 40 barrel with modified rifling. Compared with the s F H 18 barrel the length had been increased to 32.5 calibres and the chamber capacity increased from 7.22 litres to 9.85 litres to enable heavier charges to be fired and maximum range thus stepped

/ up

up to 15100 metres (16500 yds). A total of 46 equipments in all were produced. At short and medium ranges accuracy was not as consistent as with the s F H 18.

The barrel is fitted with a muzzle brake.

The same projectiles are fired by the s F H 18 and 18/40. Charges 1 to 8 are adjusted for the 18/40 to give the same velocities and ranges as for the s F H 18. An additional charge 9 is fired by the 18/40.

4. Data. 10.5 cm s K 18/40. (4.1 in Medium Gun Model 18/40.

	Metric	British
(a) Calibre	105 mm	4.1 ins
Length of Gun	6300 mm	248.03 ins
Length of Chamber	1034 mm	40.71 ins
Length of rifling	4849 mm	190.91 ins
Chamber capacity	10.15 litres	619.4 cu ins
Rifling -		
Number of grooves	36	
Depth of grooves	1.3 mm	0.051 ins
Width of grooves	5.0 mm	0.197 ins
Width of lands	4.16 mm	0.164 ins

Typ of rifling: Increasing Right Hand Twist
1 in 40 to 1 in 30 cals.

Percussion or electric firing		Percussion
Maximum recoil	800 mm	31.5 ins
Normal recoil	750 mm	29.35 ins

Type of Sights. Z E 34 (Rbl F 32, 36 or 37)

Traverse		56°
Rate of traverse. 1 Turn of handwheel	=	30 minutes
Elevation		0° to 45°
Rate of elevation 1 Turn of handwheel	=	40 minutes
Overall width in Firing Position	5600 mm	220.47 ins
Travelling Position Weight	6480 kg	6 tons 7.5 cwts
Weight in action	5680 kg	5 tons 11.75 cwts
Maximum Muzzle Velocity	910 m/sec	2900 f s
Maximum Range	21000 metres	23000 yds

(b) Ammunition

3 Charges are used viz: Small, Medium and Full Charge.

Projectile	Projectile Weight	Muzzle Velocity	Max Range
HE. 10 cm Gr 19	15.14 kg (33.3 lbs)	S = 550 m/s (1800 f s)	12725 m (13900 yds)
		M = 690 m/s (2263 f s)	15750 m (17230 yds)
		Full Charge = 835 m/s (2740 f s)	19075 m (20860 yds)
HE. 10 cm Gr 19 F E S	(Same ballistics as for Gr 19 - shown above for 3 charges)		
Smoke. 10 cm Gr 38 Nb	14.71 kg (32.36 lbs)	827 m/s (2710 f s)	18300 m (20000 yds)
A P C B C.HE/Tracer 10 cm Pzgr Rot	15.56 kg (34.2 lbs)	Medium Charge (682 m/s (2230 f s)	13850 m (15146 yds
A P H E 10 cm Pzgr Rot	15.56 kg (34.2 lbs)	Full Charge 822 m/s (2695 f s)	16000 m (17500 yds

(c) Fuzes

Nose Percussion - A Z 23 v, A Z 23/28 and A Z 23/42 used with the HE and Smoke Shell.

/ Time

(c) contd.

  Time and Percussion - Dopp Z S/60(LM) and Dopp Z S/60 are used with HE Shell

  Nose Fuzes   - Kl A Z 23 (Pr) and Kl A Z 23 with Smoke shell

  Base Fuze   - Bd Z f with APCBC HE/Tracer

  Nose Percussion - A Z 38 used with a Sea Ranging shell

(d) <u>Extract from Range Table</u>

Charge	M V (fs)	Max Range (yards)	Time of Flight (secs)	50% Zone yards		
				Length	Breadth	Height
Small	1800	13920	54.2	137	17.5	561
Medium	2260	17200	62.2	136	19.5	627
Large	2718	20860	71.2	236	22	1230

5. <u>Data 15 cm s. F H 18/40 (42) (5.9 inch Medium Field Howitzer Model 18/40(42))</u>

		Metric	British
(a)	Calibre	150 mm	5.9 ins
	Length of Gun	4875 mm	191.93 ins
	Length of chamber	506 mm	19.92 ins
	Length of rifling	3927 ins	154.61 ins
	Chamber capacity	9.85 litres	601 cu.ins.

Rifling -
 Number of grooves   40
 Depth of grooves   1.15 mm   0.059 ins
 Width of grooves   6.71 mm   0.264 ins
 Width of lands   5.0 mm   0.197 ins
Type of rifling. Increasing Right Hand Twist
  1 in 30 to 1 in 20 cals.

Percussion or electric firing   Percussion
Maximum recoil   920 mm   36.22 ins
Normal recoil   880 mm   34.65 ins
Type of Sights. ZE 34 (with Rbl F 32, 36 or 37)
Traverse   56°
Rate of traverse. 1 Turn of handwheel = 30 minutes
Elevation   45°
Rate of elevation. 1 Turn of handwheel = 40 minutes
Overall width in Firing Position 5600 mm   220.47 ins
Travelling Position Weight   6520 mm   6 Tons 18.25 cwts.
Weight in action   5720 kg   5 Tons 12.5 cwts.
Maximum Muzzle Velocity (Charge 9) 595 m/sec 1952 f s
Chamber Pressure   2410 atmospheres 16 tons sq in
Muzzle Energy   785 m.t.
Maximum Range (Charge 9) 15,100 metres 16514 yds

(b) <u>Ammunition.</u> (As for s.F.H. 18 and Charge 9).

Composition of Charge 9:-

 Tubular diglycol base powder.

  (Digl. R.P. - Gi - (470 x 4.1/1.8 mm)
    6.805 kg (15 lbs)

/Igniter powder

Igniter powder.

(NZ, Man. NP. (1.5 x 1.5 mm) 40 gms. (1.4 ozs)

Total weight of Charge 9 = 6.845 kg (15 lbs 1.4 ozs).

The following types of shell are used:-

(i) HE Shell with percussion fuze (15 cm Granate 19)

    Weight: 95.7 lbs
    Fuze: A Z 23 with optional delay (0.15 secs)

(ii) HE Shell with time and percussion fuze (15 cm Granate 19)

    Weight: 95.7 lbs
    Fuze: Dopp Z S/60

(iii) Anti-concrete (15 cm Granate 19 Beton)

    Weight: 83.25 lbs
    Colour: painted dark green overall

(iv) Armour Piercing (15 cm Gr 39 FES - Hl/A - Hollow Charge

    Weight: 54.16 lbs
    Colour: field grey
    Single soft iron driving band
    Markings: Hl/A in black. FES in white
    Charge used: No. VI
    M V 1510 f s
    Fuze: Kl A Z 40 Nb Pr
    Also two new types of HE projectile

(v) HE Shell (15 cm Granate 19 FES)

    Identical in shape and dimensions with 15 cm Gr 19 but fitted with single soft iron driving band instead of the usual two bimetallic driving bands.

(vi) HE Shell (15 cm Granate 36 FES)

    Longer than 15 cm Gr 19. Streamlined below single soft iron driving band.

(vii) Smoke Shell (15 cm Gr 19 Nb)

    Weight: 85.7 lb
    Fuze: A Z 23 Nb

(viii) Smoke Shell (15 cm Gr 38 Nb)

    Fuze: kl A Z 40 Nb

(ix) Reaction assisted Shell (15 cm R Gr 19) = (Rückstossgranate or Reaction Propulsion Shell)

    Weight: 99.5 lb
    Fuze: E1 A Z
          E1 A Z mR
          Dopp Z S/90 Range = 19000 metres (21000 yds)

    Fired only by 15 cm s F H (M) i.e. fitted with muzzle brake, owing to strain on recuperating system. The R Gr is propelled initially by a charge larger than Charge VIII. May not be in general service.

(x) HE sub-calibre shell with disintegrating bands.

    Weight: 65 lb, may not be in general service.

/ (c)

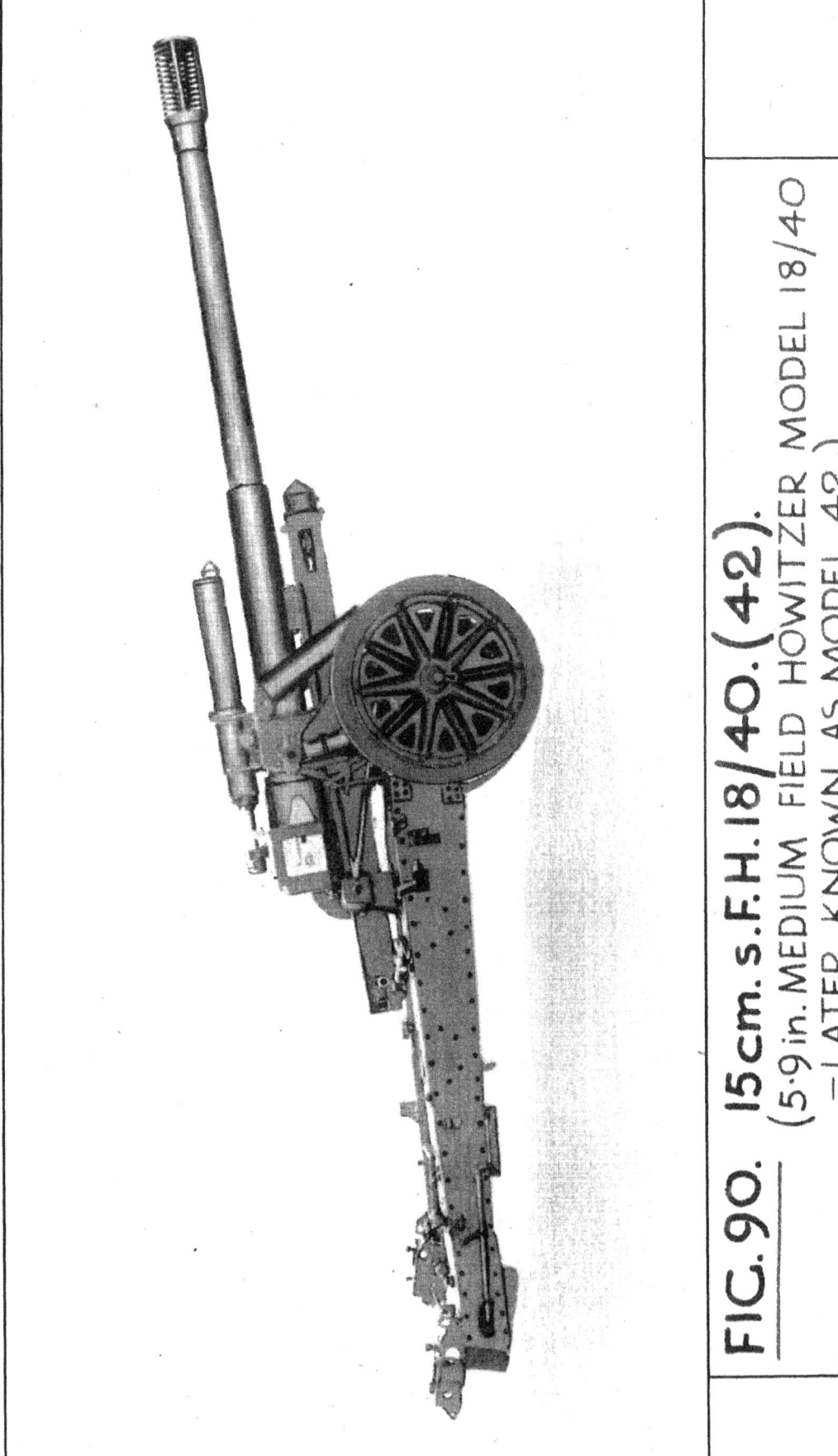

FIG. 90. 15 cm. s.F.H.18/40.(42).
(5·9 in. MEDIUM FIELD HOWITZER MODEL 18/40
— LATER KNOWN AS MODEL 42.)

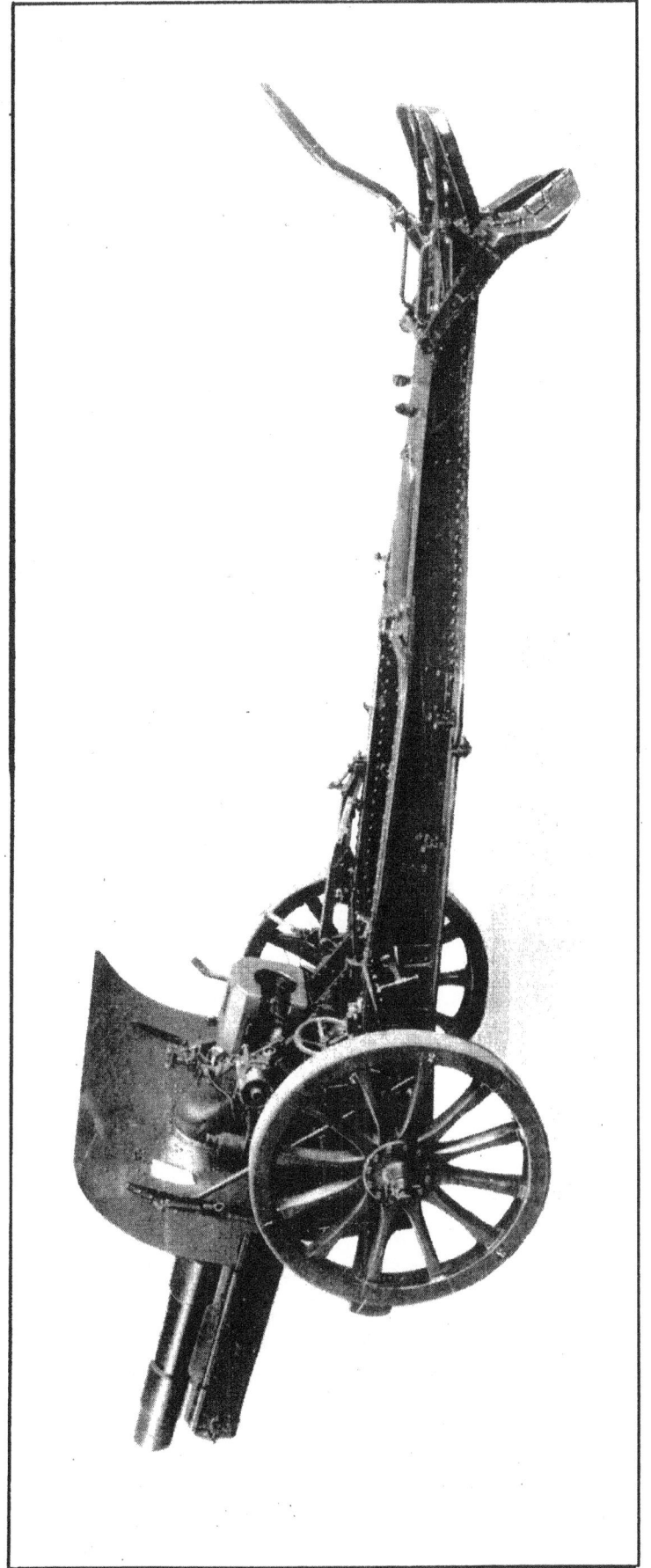

FIG. 91. 15 cm. s. F.H. 13.
(5·9 in. MEDIUM FIELD HOWITZER MODEL 13.)

(c) The Primer

The primer C/12 nA is permanently fixed in the base of the cartridge case.

(d) The Shells

HE Shell is painted grey-green and has two driving bands. The two types of fuze AZ 23 (direct action graze) and Dopp Z S/60 (Time and percussion) are fixed in advance.

Smoke shell is painted grey-green with the letters "Nb or 38 Nb" in white on the body of the shell

A P C B C. There is none for the 15 cm Howitzer.

The 10 cm Gun A P C B C shell is painted black. It has a base fuze and tracer.

Anti-concrete Shell. Exists only for the 15 cm Howitzer. It is effective against concrete, and has been used against tanks.

(e) Fuzes. All shells are issued fuzed.

AZ 23 umg (0.15) (direct action and graze) is adjustable to O/V (i.e. no delay) or M/V (i.e. delay 0.15 secs) by turning the slit of the setting bolt on the side of the fuze.

AZ 23 (0.8) umg and AZ 23 umg m 2 V. Both these fuzes are superseded by AZ 23 umg 0.15. The second has two optional delays.

Base Fuze in 15 cm anti-concrete shell can be set to Kl/v, Gr/V or O/V, viz: short, long or no delay, respectively.

Dopp Z S/60. This can be set only by a special handfuze setter to divisions of the setter taken from the Range Tables.

D. 15 cm s F H 13 (5.9 inch Medium Field Howitzer Model 13). See Fig: 91

1. This Krupp production of the 1914/1918 war was introduced into the service early in 1917. The 15 cm piece is 17 calibres (about 8 feet 4 inches) long and is mounted on a box trail carriage designed for horse drawn transport in a single load. The maximum range is 8600 metres (9500 yards) using a 40.8 kg (90 lbs) projectile. A projectile of 42 kg (92.6 lbs) is also used having a maximum range of 8500 metres (9296 yds).

2. Data

Muzzle Velocity : 381 m/s (1250 fs)   Rate of Fire: 4 rds per minute
No. of charges: = 7   Maximum Charge Wt: 1.35 kg (3 lbs)
Elevation: $-5° + 45°$ Weight in action: 2250 kg (2¼ tons)
Traverse: $-4\frac{1}{2}°$ Lt - $4\frac{1}{2}°$ Rt   Weight in Draught: 3000 kg (2.95 tons)

E. 15 cm s F H 36 (5.9 inch Medium Field Howitzer Model 36). See Fig: 92

1. This equipment was intended to meet the General Staff requirement for a medium howitzer of lighter construction than the s F H 18, being suitable for horse drawn transport in one load.

Development took place during 1936 to 1939 and both Krupp and Rheinmetall produced prototype models. The equipment is of orthodox German design and has no real outstanding features. The barrel is a monobloc and is shorter than that of the s F H 18; a muzzle brake is fitted. A plain axle without carriage suspension is used.

An interesting feature of the limber or trailer is that the weight of the draught pole is taken by two spring assemblies. The trailer is of the pintle attachment type and has spring controlled articulation.

The ammunition listed for this equipment is similar to that for the model 18 but only 7 charges are fired. Total weight in action is 3280 kg (3.225 tons) and maximum range with the standard 43.5 kg (95.7 lbs) HE Shell 12300 metres (13500 yds).

/Development

Development of this equipment was abandoned in 1942 owing to the shortage of light alloy metals required for its construction and also owing to the intention of the German High Command to motorise their Field and Medium equipment.

2. Data 15 cm s F H 36 (5.9 ins Medium Field Howitzer Model 36)

(a)
	Metric	British
Calibre	150 mm	5.9 ins
Length of Gun	3555 mm	139.95 ins
Length of barrel	2965 mm	116.7 ins
Length of rifling	2475 mm	97.4 ins
Length of chamber	490 mm	19.3 ins

Rifling -

Number of grooves		40	
Depth of grooves	2.75 mm	0.1 ins
Width of grooves	7 mm	0.27 ins
Width of lands	5.25 mm	0.2 ins

Type of rifling. Increasing Right Hand Twist

$6°$ to $10°$

Percussion or electric firing		Percussion
Maximum recoil	1160 mm	45.6 ins
Minimum recoil	980 mm	38.6 ins

Type of Sights. ZE 38 with Rbl F 32, 36, 37 or 38 used.
Traverse $56°$
Elevation $-1° + 43°$
Rate of fire 5 rpm

Travelling position -

Overall length	10,425 mm	34 ft 2 ins
Overall width	1752 mm	5 ft 9 ins
Overall height	1880 mm	6 ft 2 ins

Firing position -

Overall length	6300 mm	20 ft 8 ins
Overall width	4775 mm	15 ft 7 ins
Overall height	1780 mm	5 ft 10 ins

Travelling position weight	3500 kg	3.44 tons
Weight in action	3280 kg	3.2 tons
Maximum Muzzle Velocity	485 m/s	1590 f s
Chamber Pressure	2600 atmospheres	17 tons
Muzzle Energy	521 m/t	
Maximum range	12300 metres	13450 yds
No. of charges		7

(b) Ammunition (same as for 15 cm s F.H.18.)
The following types are used :-
(i) HE Shell with percussion fuze (15 cm Granate 19)
Weight: 95.7 lbs
Fuze A Z 23 with optional delay (0.15 secs)

(ii) HE Shell with time and percussion fuze (15 cm Granate 19)
Weight 95.7 lbs
Fuze: Dopp Z S/60

(iii) Anti-concrete (15 cm Granate 19 Beton)
Weight: 83.25 lbs
Colour: painted dark green overall

/ (iv)

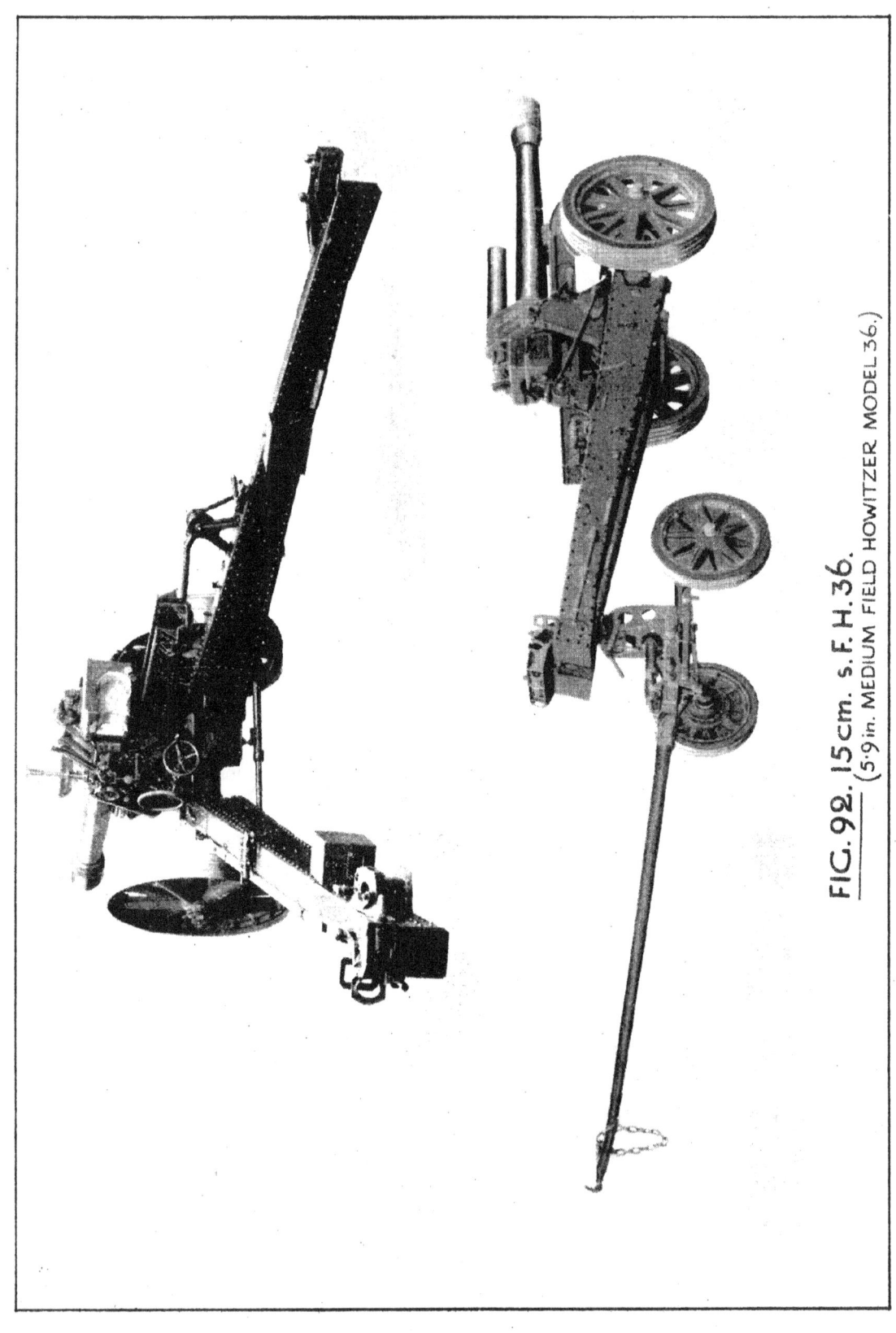

FIG. 92. 15 cm. s.F.H. 36.
(5·9 in. MEDIUM FIELD HOWITZER MODEL 36.)

(iv) Armour piercing (15 cm Gr 39 F E S - HL/A-Hollow Charge)
Weight: 54.16 lbs
Colour: Field Grey
Single soft iron driving band
Markings: HL/A in black, F E S in white
Charge used: No. VI
M V: 1510 f s
Fuze: Kl A Z 40 Nb. Pr.
Also new types of HE projectiles:-

(v) HE Shell 15 cm Granate 19 F E S
Identical in shape and dimensions of 15 cm Granate 19, but fitted with soft iron driving band instead of the usual two bimetallic driving bands.

(vi) HE Shell (15 cm Granate 36 F E S)
longer than the 15 cm Gr 19. Streamlined below single soft iron driving band.

(vii) Smoke Shell (15 cm Gr 19 Nb)
Weight: 85.7 lbs
Fuze: A Z 23 Nb

(viii) Smoke Shell (15cm Gr 38 Nb)
Fuze: Kl A Z 40 Nb

(ix) HE Sub-calibre, or discarding sabot projectile.
Weight: 65 lbs.

(c) The Primer
The percussion Primer C/12 nA is used.

(d) Charges
7 charges are used :

Charges	I	II	III	IV	V	VI	VII
	210 m/s	230 m/s	250 m/s	280 m/s	320 m/s	400 m/s	485 m/s
	688 f s	750 f s	820 f s	920 f s	1050 f s	1312 f s	1590 f s

F. 15 cm s F H 40 (5.9 inch Medium Field Howitzer Model 1940). See Fig:- 93

1. The development of this equipment began in 1938 to meet a O K H requirement for a field howitzer generally similar to the s F H 18, but with increased performance and capable of firing in the upper register.

Prototype Models were produced by Krupp and Rheinmetall Borsig in 1941.

The piece is 32.5 calibres long and generally similar in design to the s F H 18, but a muzzle brake is fitted.

The carriage incorporates torsion bar suspension and hydro-pneumatic equilibrators.

The equipment was not introduced into service, but certain design features of it were incorporated in later weapons.

2. Data: s F H 40

	Metric	British
Calibre	149.1 mm	5.9 ins
Length of piece (32.5 cals)	4875 mm	192 ins
Length of rifling	3927 mm	154.6 ins
Twist of rifling - Increasing right hand		
No. of grooves		40
Chamber capacity	9.85 litres	
Traverse		60°
Elevation		0° to 70°

/ Weight

FIG. 93. 15 cm. s.F.H. 40.
(5·9 in. MEDIUM FIELD HOWITZER MODEL 40.)

FIG. 94. 15 cm. s. F.H. 43.
(5·9 in. MEDIUM FIELD HOWITZER MODEL 43.)

	Metric	British
Weight in action	5400 kg	5.3 tons
Weight travelling position	6200 kg	6.1 tons
Weight of standard HE Projectile	43.5 kg	95.7 lbs.
No of charges	9	
Maximum range	15400 metres	16850 yds
Maximum Muzzle Velocity	595 m/s	1952 f s
Chamber Pressure	2600 atmospheres	17 tons sq in.
Muzzle Energy	784 m. t.	
Ranges of muzzle velocities for Charges I to IX =	210 to 595 m/s	690 to 1952 f.s.

G. 15 cm s F H 43 (5.9 inch Medium Field Howitzer Model 43) See Fig: 94

1. As a result of experience in the Russian campaign it was decided to produce a medium howitzer with 360° traverse, capable of firing in the upper register and with a maximum range 18 km (19700 yds) - this in view of the 17.3 km (19000 yds) - range of the standard Russian medium gun howitzer model 37.

Krupp produced designs for a carriage with extra trails on similar lines to the 10.5 cm le F H 43 but later decided to use a cruciform carriage standardised to take the 15 cm ordnance or the 12.8 cm dual purpose medium anti-tank gun.

An interesting feature is that owing to shortage of steel for cartridge case manufacture it was decided to use a screw type breech or ring obturation in the new designs for the s F H 43. The barrel was to be 35.5 calibres long with a muzzle brake.

It is unlikely that many equipments were produced.

The principle new features of design were the fitting of two additional trail legs at the front of the equipment and an arrangement whereby the equipment is supported on a drop pedestal type of central support, in addition to the trails, when in action. The wheels are raised from the ground by leverage action of the trail legs in conjunction with the central support.

2. Data: s F H 43

	Metric	British
Calibre	150 mm	5.9 ins
Length of barrel	6158 mm	242.44 ins
No. of charges	8	
Percussion or Electric Firing	Percussion	
Weight if standard projectile	43.5 kg	95.7 lbs
Maximum range	18000 metres	19700 yds
Range of muzzle velocities for Charges I to VIII	250 to 660 m/s	820 to 2165 f s
Traverse	360°	
Elevation	-5° +70°	
Weight in action	7400 - 7900 kg	7.27 to 7.77 tons
Weight travelling	8400 - 8975 kg	8.26 to 8.75 tons

Projectiles used were of the same types as used with the 15 cm s F H 18.

H. 15 cm s F H 18/43 (5.9 inch Medium Field Howitzer Model 18/43).

This equipment is a development of the standard 15 cm s F H 18, the principal difference being the incorporation of "ring obturation" with a horizontal sliding breech block, eliminating the use of cartridge cases.

/This

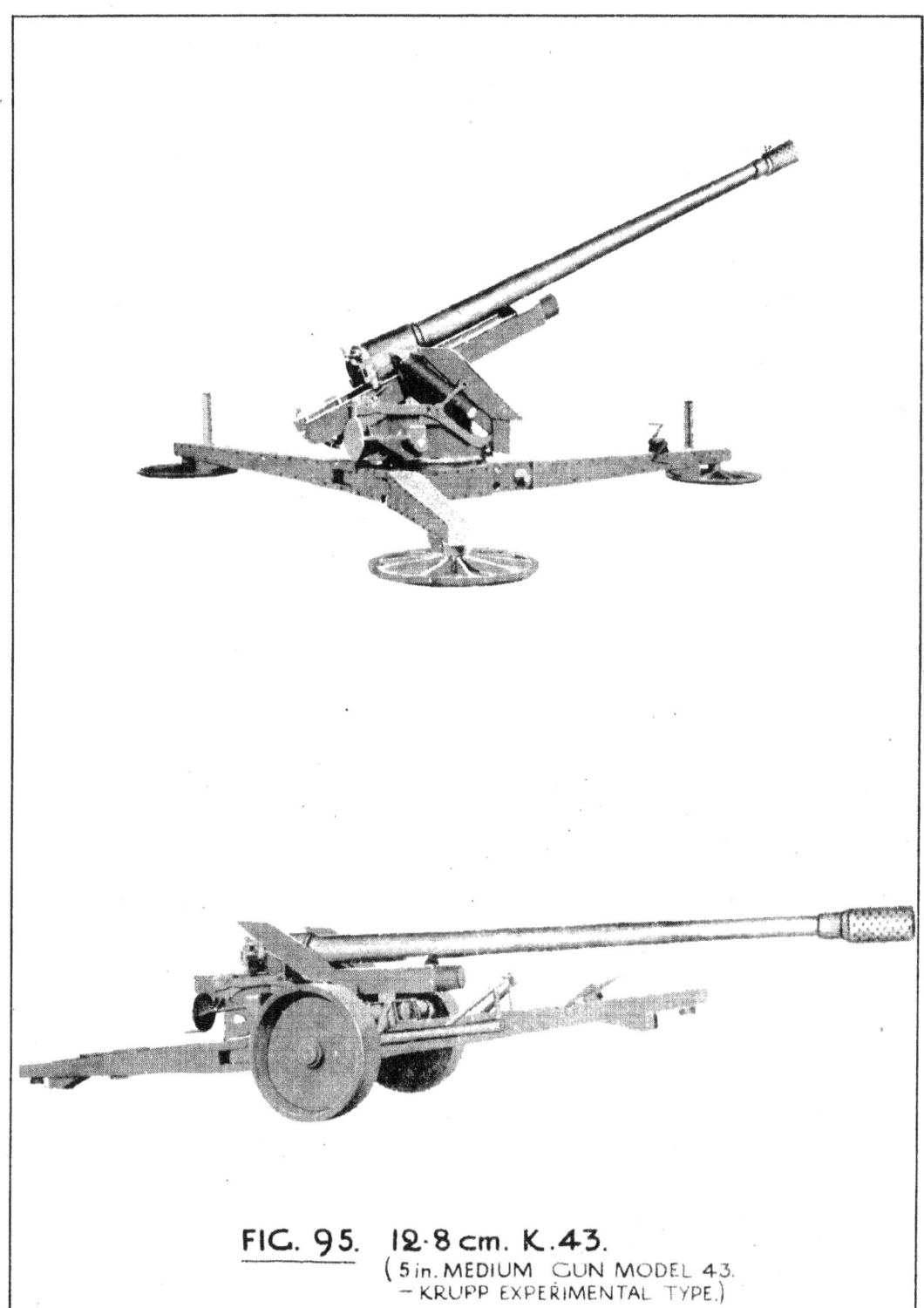

FIG. 95. 12·8 cm. K.43.
(5 in. MEDIUM GUN MODEL 43.
— KRUPP EXPERIMENTAL TYPE.)

This development of "ring obturation" was made necessary by the shortage of brass and steel for the manufacture of cartridge cases.

The details of the arrangements of ring obturation are as follows :-

The barrel with minor exceptions is the same as the standard s F H 18. The lip at the rear end of the barrel has been removed and there are no recesses for the "not now required" cartridge case extractors.

A trip percussion firing mechanism is contained within a "slide box" which slides in a horizontal plane in the right face of the breech block. The tube chamber is in the inner face of the slot for the slide box. A flash vent or channel in the shape of a "bent arm" passes diagonally from the back end of the tube chamber to the front face of the breech block. To fire the gun the tube is placed in the tube chamber and the "slide box" moved along to "stops" where the firing pin is opposite to and masks the tube.

The obturator ring assembly fits into a ring recess in the front face of the breech block, and consists of three parts - an outer "L" ring, an inner "I" ring and one, or more flat space adjusting rings. The inner "I" ring has radial holes bored through it. The space adjusting rings fit into the bottom of the ring recess, and, as their name implies are used to adjust the obturation so that it is not too loose, or too tight, to close the breech block with reasonable effort.

When the breech is closed, the outer ring is brought into bearing contact with the rear face of the barrel. On firing, the propellant gases pass through the holes of the inner ring into an annular chamber between the outer and inner rings and the pressure thus exerted forces the outer ring against the rear face of the barrel and thus achieves obturation, i.e. seals the escape of gas to the rear from the chamber.

Further development is required before this system can be accepted as a complete success and safe.

J.   **12.8 cm Krupp Kanone Model 43.** (5inch Krupp Gun Model 43) See Figs: 95

This extremely light experimental equipment was produced by Krupp, in order to satisfy a requirement put forward by the German High Command for a medium gun having a superior performance to that of the 10.5 cm series. About this period, 1943, experience in Russia had shown the need for all round traverse and this was provided by producing a carriage with three trail legs thus giving three point carriage support in action.

Owing to the shortage of brass and steel for providing cartridge cases the normal horizontal sliding breech block was discarded in favour of a breech screw mechanism.

Complete details of the construction and performance of this weapon are not known, but is is believed that the gun was ballistically similar to the barrel of the later model K.44

It is not thought that this equipment progressed further than the prototype stage. It is believed that it was discarded in favour of the very efficient and well designed model K.44, which, by the way, reverted to the normal type sliding breech block.

K.   **12.8 cm K 44** (5.04 ins. Dual Purpose Medium/Anti-Tank Gun Model 44)
See Figs :- 96 and 97.

1. This weapon, considered by many to be of outstanding design, was introduced towards the end of the war. It was not a large scale production, but a number of equipments using various carriages, in some cases makeshifts, were issued for trails in the field.

The ordnance comprises a high velocity gun, the barrel of which is 55 calibres long fitted with a muzzle brake. The breech mechanism has electrical firing gear. The gun is mounted on a cruciform platform carriage with front and rear bogies. The design is a development of the successful 88 mm Pak 43 (anti-tank Gun Model 43).

/Both

Both Krupp and Rheinmetall Borsig produced prototypes, the carriages differing in design.

The Rheinmetall model has a two-wheeled front transporter and a four-wheeled rear bogie. The bogie remains on the equipment when in action, the wheels of course raised from the ground, and is traversed with the superstructure. This increased the stability in action.

The Krupp effort consisted of two prototypes, one the K 44, which we are primarily concerned with here, and also a universal carriage which would take both the K 44 gun and also a 15 s F H barrel believed known as the 15 cm s F H 44.

The Krupp K 44 equipment was conisdered to be a better equipment than the Rheinmetall version and had two-wheeled transporters both of which remained on the equipment in action. The wheels were raised from the ground during the lowering of the equipment to the ground by an ingenious pinion gear and twin arc rack arrangement. This enabled the equipment to be brought into action very quickly for a weapon of this size. The raising and lowering gear was not as robust as it should have been and rather indicated that the design had been hurried.

The principle weakness in the Krupp equipment was the design of the traversing arrangement. This consisted of quite a short pivot of the plain spigot type, which is to the centre of the plate, to which is fitted the all round traverse rack, the whole being bolted and welded to the upper surface of the cruciform platform. On the traverse plate is a narrow circular roller pathway, over which travel the four rollers on the underface of the superstructure. The design is faulty, in that the pivot is too small and there is too much play between the basic and superstructures. The roller pathway was badly indented due to the hammering of the rollers during firing and travelling, especially the latter. If a roller race, like that used with the Rheinmetall Borsig equipment had been used, the Krupp equipment would indeed have been a good equipment.

An interesting new feature with the Krupp K 44 is the use of vertical spades on the cruciform platform to assist in preventing ground recoil during firing.

Both HE and Armour Piercing projectiles are fired with medium and full charge. The ammunition is of the QF separate type

2. Other equipments using the K 44 - 12.8 cm Barrel L/55

The gun was intended for the main armament for the Tiger Tank, and for such role was known as the 12.8 cm K W K 82.

(a) 12.8 cm K 81

This is believed to be the original nomenclature given to the 12.8 cm Field/Anti-Tank Project.

(b) 12.8 cm K 81/1

The gun is mounted on the French 155 mm GPF-T gun carriage. This carriage is of the split trail type (See Fig: No. 32).

(c) 12.8 cm K 81/2

The carriage of this equipment is of the Russian 15.2 cm Gun-How Model 1937 (See Fig: No. 33).

Certain modifications to the carriage were made viz:
(a) German cylindrical cradle used.
(b) German recoil system - located above the gun.
   The attachment of the recoil system was very frail and crude.
(c) No equilibrators. Elevating handwheel efforts very small.
(d) No shield fitted.
(e) Traverse limited to 40 degrees.

3. **Data 12.8 cm K44 (5.04 ins Gun Model 44) (Krupp Model)**

(a)
	Metric	British
Calibre	12.8 cm	5.047 ins
Length of Gun	7023 mm	276.5 ins
Length of barrel	6625 mm	260.7 ins
Length of rifling	5550 mm	217.95 ins

Rifling -
- Number of grooves — 40
- Depth of grooves — 1.55 mm — .06 ins
- Width of grooves — 6.37 mm — .25 ins
- Width of lands — 3.8 mm — .15 ins

Type of rifling. P P S. Increasing R H Twist
  1 in 27 to 1 in 24.76

Percussion or electric firing — Electric
Maximum recoil — 1300 mm — 51.5 ins
Minimum recoil — 700 mm — 27.5 ins
Type of Sights. Z E 34 Graduated 0-800 mils
Traverse — 360°
Rate of traverse. 1 turn of handwheel High 1° 36' Low 48'
  + 45° 27'
  - 7° 51'
Rate of elevation 1 turn of handwheel High 1°07' Low 20'
Rate of fire — 5 rpm

Travelling position -
- Overall length — 10900 mm — 35' 9 ins
- Overall width — 2476 mm — 8' 1½ ins
- Overall height — 2160 mm — 7' 1 ins
- Ground clearance — 254 mm — 10 ins

Firing Position -
- Overall length — 10900 mm — 35' 9 ins
- Overall width — 6126 mm — 20' 1 ins
- Overall height — 1830 mm — 6' 0 ins

Travelling Position weight — 10160 kg — 10 tons 26½ lbs
Weight in action — 10160 kg — 10 tons 26½ lbs

(b) **Ballistic Details**

H E (L/5.0)
- Maximum Muzzle Velocity — 920 m/s — 3018 f s
- Chamber pressure — 3100 atmospheres — 20.35 tons sq in.
- Muzzle energy — 1208 t/m — —
- Maximum Range — 24414 metres — 26700 yds

Ammunition	Charge	Range yds	M V	Muzzle Energy ft/tons	Chamber Pressure tons/sq in.
H E 12.8 cm Sprgr Flak 40 m R 9	Medium	—	2460	2408	11.1
	Full	23000	3018	3623	19.1
H E 12.8 cm Sprgr 5151(L/5.0)	Medium	—	2460	2593	12
	Full	23700	3018	3902	20.6
A P 12.8 cm Pzgr 43	Medium	—	2460	2621	—
	Full	—	3018	3943	20.6

Armour penetration claimed = 200 mm armour at 1000 metres at 30 degrees.

(c) **Ammunition**

Nomenclature	Fuzes	Range Table Weight
HE 12.8 cm Sprgr Flak 40 M R9	A Z 23/38 (0.10) A Z 23/28 (Pr 0.10)	26 kg (57 lbs)
HE 12.8 cm Sprgr 5151 L/5.0)	Dopp Z S/90 St (Nose Fuzes)	28 kg (62.26 lbs)
AP 12.8 cm Pzgr 43	Bd Z 5121 (Base Fuze)	28.3 kg (62.26 lbs)

/ The

The Dopp Z S/90 St is not safe against dropping and unlike the Dopp Z S/90 has no safty pin, therefore this fuze should be inserted in the projectile at the gun position.

The QF cartridges have primers C/22 or C/22 St and are loaded with medium and full charge as follows :-

Medium Charge: 12 kg (26.4 lbs) G u RP-G05-(820.5, 8/2.5)
  + 65 gr (2 oz 5 drs) Man NP (1.5, 1.5)
Full Charge: 15 kg (33 lbs) G R P-G0 5 - (820.5, 8/2.5)
  + 65 gr (2 oz 4 drs) Man NP (1.5, 1.5)

The cartridges are fitted with a cap which must be removed before loading.

The HE round 12.8 cm Sprgr Flak 40(L/4.5) is also fired by this equipment.

4. **12.8 cm (5 in) Guns**

(a) 12.8 cm K 81 — Cruciform Platform
     12.8 cm K 81/1 — Carriage that of French 155 mm GPT-T
     12.8 cm K 81/2 — Carriage is modified Russian 152 mm Gun How M 1937.

(b) **Data**

	K 81	K 81/1	K 81/2
Length of barrel including breech ring	7040 mm (277.13 in)	7020 mm (276.37 in)	7020 mm (276.37 in)
Rifling: Length	5533 mm	5533 mm	5533 mm
Twist	1 in 27 to	1 in 24.76	
nature	Increasing Right Hand		
Length of chamber	977.6 mm (38.46 in)		
Chamber capacity	20.6 litres		
Recoil length : Minimum	740 mm (29.13 in)	870 mm (34.25 in)	870 mm (34.25 in)
Maximum	1050 mm (41.34 in)	930 mm (36.61 in)	930 mm (36.61 in)
Elevation	-5° to + 45°	-4° to + 45°	-4° to + 45°
Traverse	360°	60°	58°
Weight in action	9.15 tons	11.9 tons	8.1 tons
Sights	Z E 34 graduated 0-800 mils		

(c) **Ballistics**

Ammunition	Charge	Range yds	M V f s	Muzzle Energy ft/tons	Chamber pressure tons/sq in
12.8 cm Sprgr Flak 40 m R 9	Medium	-	2460	2408	11.1
	Full	23000	3018	3623	19.1
12.8 Sprgr 5151 L/5.0)	Medium	-	2460	2593	12
	Full	26700	3018	3902	20.6
12.8 cm Pzgr 43	Medium	-	2460	2621	-
	Full	-	3018	3943	20.6

(d) **Ammunition**

Nomenclature	Fuses	Range Table Weight
HE 12.8 cm Sprgr Flak 40 m R 9	A Z 23/38(0.10) A Z 23/28(Pr) (0.10)	26 kg (57 lbs)
HE 12.8 cm Sprgr 5151 L/5.0)	Dopp Z S/90 St	28 kg (62 lbs)
AP 12.8 cm Pzgr 43	Bd Z 5121	28.3 kg (62.26 lbs)

/The

The Dopp Z S/90 St is not safe against dropping and unlike the Dopp Z S/90 has no safety pin, therefore this fuze should be inserted in the projectile only at the gun position.

The JF cartridges have primer C/22 or C/22 St and are loaded with medium or full charge as follows :-

Medium charge: 12 kg (26.4 lbs) Gu R P - G O 5 - (820.5, 8/2.5)
+ 65 gr (2 oz 5 dr) Man NP (1.5,1.5)

Full charge: 15 kg (33 lbs) G R P - GO 5 - (820.5, 8/2.5)
+ 65 gr (2 oz 5 dr) Man NP (1.5,1.5)

The cartridges are delivered fitted with a cap - this must be removed before loading.

The 12.8 cm Sprgr Flak 40 (L/4.5) is also fired by these equipments.

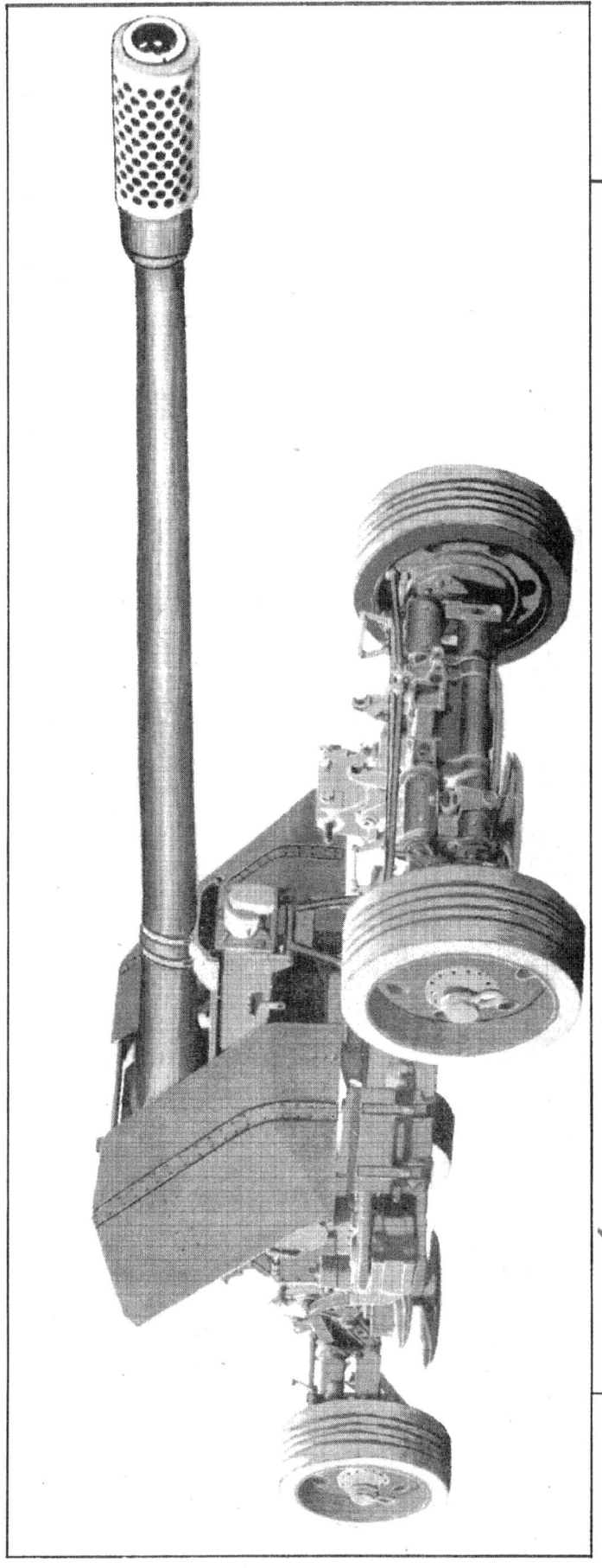

FIG. 96. 12·8 cm. K. 44.
(5in DUAL PURPOSE MEDIUM/A.TK GUN MODEL 44 – KRUPP TYPE.)

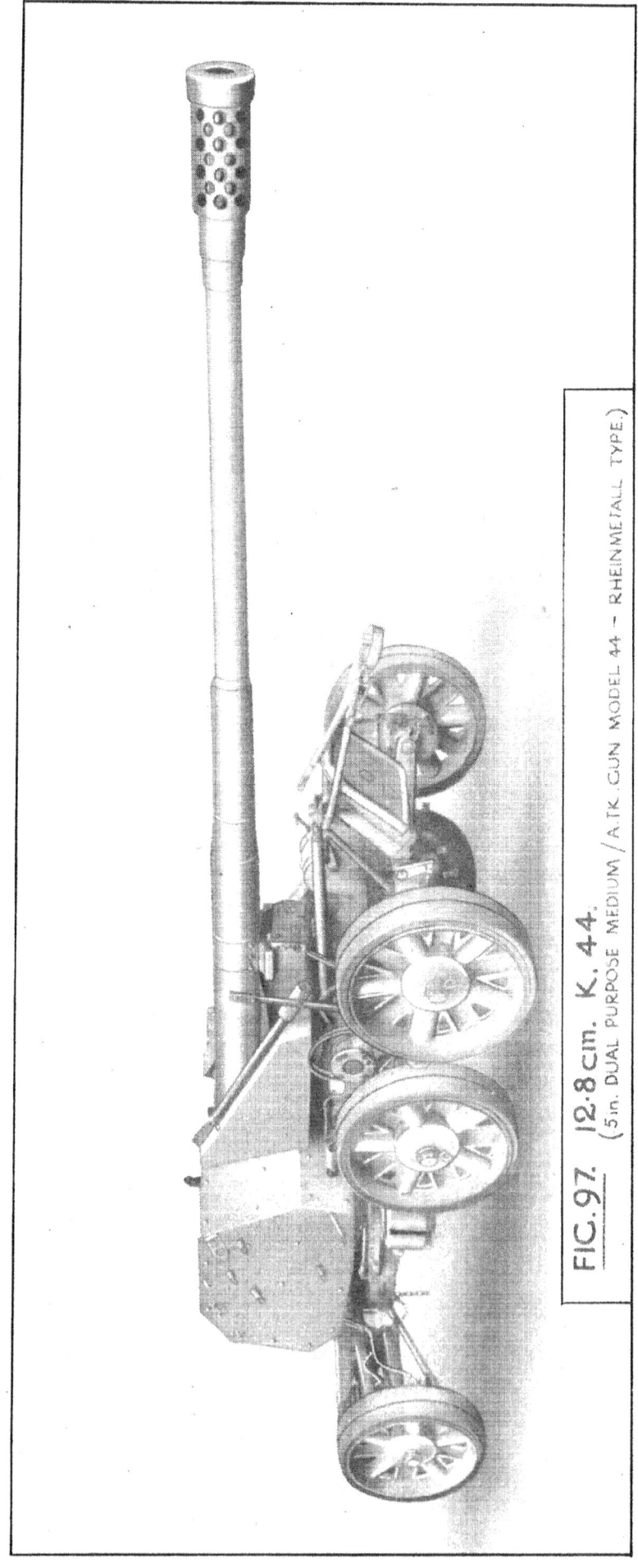

FIG. 97. 12.8 cm. K. 44.
(5in. DUAL PURPOSE MEDIUM/A.TK. GUN MODEL 44 - RHEINMETALL TYPE.)

CHAPTER VIII

THE DEVELOPMENT OF GERMAN HEAVY AND SUPER-HEAVY ARTILLERY

A. General

1. The backbone of the German "Heavies" was made up by two equipments, the 21 cm Mörser 18 (8.3 inch Howitzer Model 18), a heavy howitzer introduced into service in 1939, and the 17 cm Kanone in Mörserlafette (6.8 inch Gun on Howitzer carriage) introduced in 1941, which used the same carriage as the 21 cm Mörser. Both equipments were designed by Krupp for motorized transport in two loads, although for short distances gun and carriage can be moved together as one load. The 21 cm Mrs 18 replaced an equipment of obsolescent design known as the langer 21 cm Morser which dates from 1916 and was originally intended for horse-drawn transport in two loads. The langer 21 cm Mörser weighed 6680 kg in action and was transported in two loads of 4160 kg and 4740 kg. A later model of this equipment was produced for motorised transport in one load weighing 11275 kg including the limber and gun stores.

2. The 17 cm K.18 in.Mrs Laf replaced a number of 15 cm equipments which did not prove equal to the ballistic requirements for a heavy gun.

3. The 15 cm K.16 (5.9 inch Gun Model 16) was developed by Krupp and originally introduced in 1917. This gun fired a 51.4 kg shell to a max range of 22000 metres. Weight in action was 10870 kg.

4. The 15 cm K.18 (5.9 inch Gun Model 18) was developed by Rheinmetall Borsig from 1933 onwards and introduced into service in 1938. The only improvement of note over the Model 16 was to provide a ground traversing platform, which was anchored by means of securing pickets in the firing position. This allowed 360° traverse.

The 43 kg HE shell ranges up to 24500 metres. Weight in action was 12760 kg.

5. The 15 cm K.39 (5.9 inch Gun Model 39) was developed by Krupp in 1937 for a Turkish order for a dual purpose Heavy Field/CD equipment. Two complete equipments are believed to have been delivered by 1939, while the remainder of the original order, some 40 old equipments, were taken into service by the German Army in 1940. For Coast Defence role a sectional platform is used.

The 15 cm K 39 was designed to fire the same projectiles as the 15 cm K 18 and is almost identical ballistically with the latter.

The 15 cm K 39 as a field equipment weighs 12200 kg in action and is transported in two loads of 9200 and 9100 kg respectively.

The firing platform is carried on a trail transporter, total weight 11300 kg.

Pending large scale production of the 17 cm gun, which it was proposed to mount on the 21 cm Howitzer carriage, a number of 15 cm Naval guns, the 15 cm SK (Schnellade Kanone) C/28 (QF Gun Model C/28) were mounted on this carriage and the equipment was given the official nomenclature 15 cm K in Mrs Laf (5.9 inch Gun on How.Carriage). The ordnance was modified to fire the standard projectiles of the 15 cm K.18 and 39.

Prior to and in the early stages of the war, the German Army continued the requirements for a heavy mobile gun of 21 cm calibre; finally in 1942, it was decided to abandon this calibre and concentrate on production of the 17 cm K and also to give high priority to the designs for the newer 24 cm equipments. Two 21 cm guns were used by the German Army, the 21 cm K.39 (and later models K 39/40, K39/41) and the 21 cm K.38.

6. The 21 cm K 39 (8.3 inch Gun Model 39) was originally designed by Skoda for a Turkish order and a number of equipments were taken over by the German Army under the above nomenclature. Weight in action is 33800 kg. The equipment breaks down into three loads, each of which is mounted on a two axled bogie with pneumatic tyres. The three travelling loads weigh approx. 15000 kg each. Maximum range of the 21 cm K.39 is 30000 metres with a 135 kg projectile.

7. The 21 cm K.38 (8.3 inch Gun Model 38) was designed by Krupp to a 1938 order of the German High Command, who required 15 equipments by 1940; by 1943 about 7 equipments had been delivered and one sent to Japan. Production was then discontinued.

The equipment represents a considerable advance in design on the Skoda model 21 cm K. 39, indeed the German designers considered it their outstanding design effort of the war.

The standard HE projectile, weighing 120 kg, has a max range of about 34,000 metres. Weight in action is 25300 kg and the equipment is designed for motorised transport in two loads of 18175 kg and 16650 kg respectively. The carriage is to some extent in the tradition of the 21 cm Mrs. 18 and 17 cm K in Mrs Laf, in that a firing platform integral with the gun carriage is provided and dual recoil systems are employed for barrel and carriage recoil.

8. **24 cm equipments**

The 24 cm Howitzer Model 39 and 39/40 are products of Skoda and were built to a Turkish order in 1938 for 12 equipments, two had been delivered by 1939 and the remainder were taken over by the German Army. The 24 cm H. 39 is really a companion piece to the 21 cm K. 39 and the design and method of tranpsort closely resemble the latter.

The equipment weighs 27000 kg in action and fires a 166 kg projectile to 18000 metres. It has 360° traverse and elevation from -4° to +70°.

9. The 24 cm K.3 was introduced for service in 1938, designs having been begun as early as 1935. The Rheinmetall Borsig design was finally accepted, but the majority of 24 cm K. 3 equipments were built up by Krupp to the Rheinmetall designs.

The whole equipment weighs 54000 kg in action and is transported in five loads, weighing from 14700 kg to 18200 kg.

The HE projectile, weighing 151 kg, ranges up to 37000 metres.

The K 3 was soon considered to be unsatisfactory owing to the changed tactical requirements for super-heavy equipments. The method of transport proved slow and cumbersome and considerably increased range was required for this calibre: an empermental gun was made with a muzzle attachment and emergent calibre of 21 cm; this fired an 82 kg projectile with a muzzle velocity of over 1100 met/secs and reached approx 50 km range, but it was decided to produce an entirely redesigned equipment, the K.4.

10. The requirements were for a range of 48/49000 metres with a 160 kg projectile and greatly increased mobility. Both Rheinmetall Borsig and Krupp produced designs but no final decision was reached and no models of the K 4 were actually produced. One experimental model was in course of construction at Essen but work was stopped owing to bombing.

Both design firms were working on similar lines since the Ordnance Dept specifications were for transport (a) in two loads, (b) as a single unit.

The latest project which appears to have found approval on all sides was to produce an equipment designed to mount the 24 cm gun or a 30.5 cm Howitzer as an alternative Ordnance. The mounting incorporated a platform allowing 360° traverse and the complete equipment was intended to be transported on two fully tracked vehicles, modified Tiger chassis, one at either end and fitted with hydraulic jacks, so that the equipment could be lowered to the ground in the firing position: time into action was estimated at approx 40 mins. This type of mounting was also capable of being transported in a single load by rail using two special bogies.

This method of transport for heavy and super-heavy guns and howitzers by using fully tracked vehicles found great favour with the German designers and Ordnance engineers and represents the latest phase in their development.

11. The 35 cm Heavy Howitzer M. 1 was designed by Rheinmetall Borsig and introduced into service in 1939 as the standard super-heavy siege howitzer.

The general construction resembles that of the 24 cm K.3. The 575 kg HE (SAP) shell has a maximum range of 20,000 metres. The equipment fires only in the upper register from 45° to 70°. Weight in action is 77500, and the equipment is transported in seven loads of approx 18000 kg each. For assembly it was necessary to use a crane. It is believed that only 9 models of the M.1 were produced.

12. The 42 cm Howitzer ("Gamma" Mörser) was a product of the 1914/1918 war; in fact designs were begun by Krupp in 1906. Altogether, according to the Krupp records 10 complete equipments with 18 barrels were produced. A number of components escaped destruction following the 1918 Armistice and it was found to be possible, in 1936/37, to reconstruct one equipment which was assembled at MEPPEN Firing Ranges and was used for experiments and trials in connection with the attack on concrete fortifications.

The standard anti-concrete SAP/HE shell weighs 1020 kg and has a maximum range of 14200 metres. Rate of fire is approx 8 rounds per hour. The whole equipment weighs 140 metric tons in action and was transported on ten railway "flat" cars.

B.   15 cm K.16 (15 cm Kanone 16) (5.9 in Gun Model 16) See fig:- 98

1. The weapon was developed by Krupp and introduced into service during 1917.

The gun is of jacket and tube construction with detachable breech ring fitted with a horizontal sliding breech block.

The carriage is of the box trail type with leaf spring axle fitted with steel wheels having solid rubber tyres. Two spring equilibrators are used. The recoil system comprises a hydraulic buffer located in the cradle below the piece and a hydro-pneumatic recuperator above the gun. Recoil is variable controlled. A four inch shield is fitted. The equipment is normally transported in two loads.

This equipment was the standard medium gun of the German artillery until replaced by the 15 cm K.18 which is dealt with in the following section.

2.   Data : 15 cm. K 16

	Metric	British
Calibre	150 mm	5.9 ins
Length of piece (43 calivres)	6410 mm	252.4 ins
Rifling - Uniform twist of 7° 9'.		
Traverse	8°	
Elevation	- 3° +43°	
Weight in action	10870 kg	10.7 tons
Travelling weight -		
Barrel and Transporter	8300 kg	8.2 tons
Carriage	6320 kg	6.2 tons
No. of charges	3	
Weight of standard HE projectile	51.4 kg	113 lbs
Maximum range	22000 metres	24,050 yds
Maximum muzzle velocity	757 m/sec	2485 fs
Chamber pressure	2950 Atmospheres	19.37 tons sq ins.
Muzzle energy	1501 mt	

3. Ammunition

	Fuzes	Weight of Projectile	M.V.
HE with ballistic cap-			
15 cm Hbgr 16	Hbgr Z.17/23	51.4 kg	555 m/s
	Hbgr Z.17/23	(113 lbs)	696 m/s
15 cm Hbgr 16 nmg	A.Z. Hbgr		757 m/s

C.   15 cm Kanone 18 (15 cm K.18) (5.9 inch Gun Model 18) See fig:- 99

1. Rheinmetall Borsig commenced the development of this equipment during 1933 and it was introduced into service in 1938.

The equipment is very cumbersome, judged by modern standards, and carries a two piece plate platform which is dropped to the ground and secured by pickets. Folding ramps are secured to the box type trail. These are used as runways for the barrel transporter during the mounting and dismounting of the gun barrel. The equipment is transported in two loads.

A double triangle supporting bracket, attached to the axle assembly and the platform, so pivots on the latter, that the carriage can be hauled into a

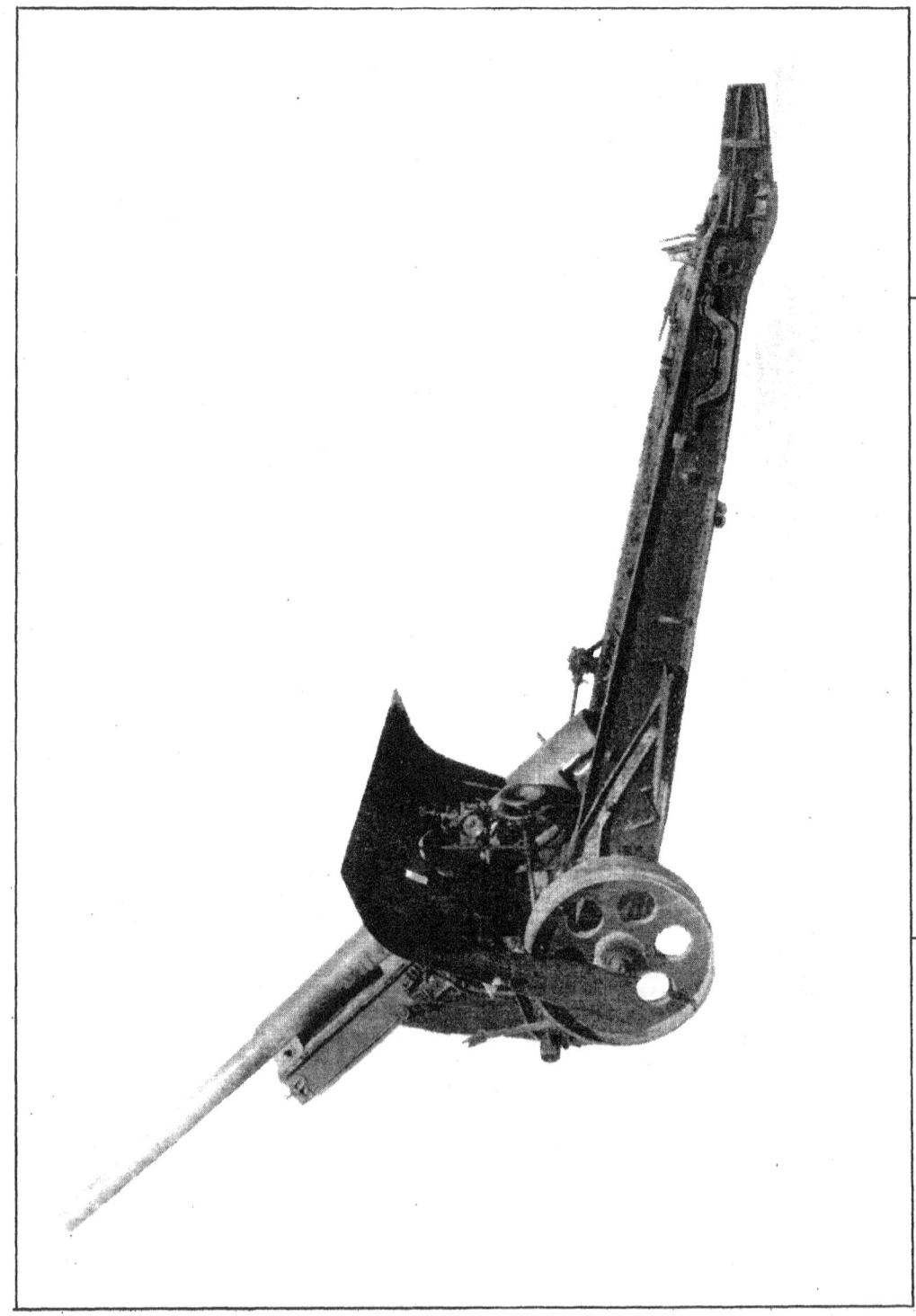

FIG. 98. 15 cm. K. 16 (5·9 in GUN. MODEL 16.)

The centre of the platform is in the form of a turntable which thus gives all round traverse to the carriage. A limited amount of top traverse can be obtained between sadle and carriage body.

The piece is of monobloc loose barrel construction with detachable breech ring fitted with an horizontal sliding breech block. The recoil system comprises a hydraulic buffer located in the cradle and the hydro-pneumatic recuperator above the piece. Two hydro-pneumatic equilibrators are fitted.

2. Data: 15 cm. K. 18.

	Metric	British
Calibre	150 mm	5.9 ins
Length of piece (55 Cals)	8200 mm	322.8 ins
Length of rifling	6432 mm	253.16 ins
Rifling - Constant right hand twist.	Angle 6°	
Capacity of chamber	24 litres	
Traverse - 10° Top traverse and, with platform - 360°		
Elevation		-2° + 45°
Weight in action	12760 kg	12.56 tons
Travelling Weight - Carriage	9060 kg	9 tons
Barrel and Transporter	9250 kg	9.1 tons
No. of charges	3	
Weight of standard HE projectile	43 kg	94.6 lbs
Maximum muzzle velocity	890 m/sec	2920 fs
Chamber pressure	2900 Atmospheres	19 tons sq in
Maximum range	24500 metres	26800 yds.

3.

Ammunition	Fuzes	Weight of Projectile
HE 15 cm K. Gr. 18	A.Z. 23.v (0.25) A.Z. 23 v (0.15) Dopp Z.S/90	43 kg (94.6 lbs)
Anti Concrete 15 cm Gr. 19. BE.Rot	Bd Z fur. 15 Gr. 19. Be.	43.5 kg (95.7 lbs)

D. 15 cm Kanone 39 (15 cm K.39) (5.9 in Gun Model 39) (See Fig. 100, 101 and 102)

1. This equipment was developed by Krupp for a Turkish order in 1939. The weapon was introduced into the German Army during 1940.

The weapon was used as a dual purpose Heavy Field and mobile Coast Defence gun.

Used in the normal field army role the equipment consists of an orthodox heavy Q.F. gun mounted on a split trail carriage, but the equipment can easily be converted to perform a Coast Artillery role by mounting it on a portable turntable platform.

Twelve outrigger arms can be attached radially to this platform and the outer ends of adjacent outriggers then connected by arc shaped sections to form a complete circle. When the equipment is mounted on the central turntable, the trail legs are left locked together in the normal travelling position and the spigot recesses, which usually house orthodox spades, receive the two spigots of a small trolley wheel assembly. All round traverse is then permitted by running the trolley wheels along the circular path formed by the twelve arc pieces, the turntable being able to rotate on internal rollers. The simple sprocket wheel drive of the trolley wheel assembly is hand operated. The final lay for line is effected by the normal carriage traverse gear, six degrees being the permissible top traverse with the trail legs locked together. The maximum elevation of 45 degrees is not restricted in any way.

Shallow pits for the turntable platform, outrigger arms and traverse rack sections, require to be dug before the equipment can be emplaced in this manner.

The leaf-spring suspension of the carriage is eliminated and the

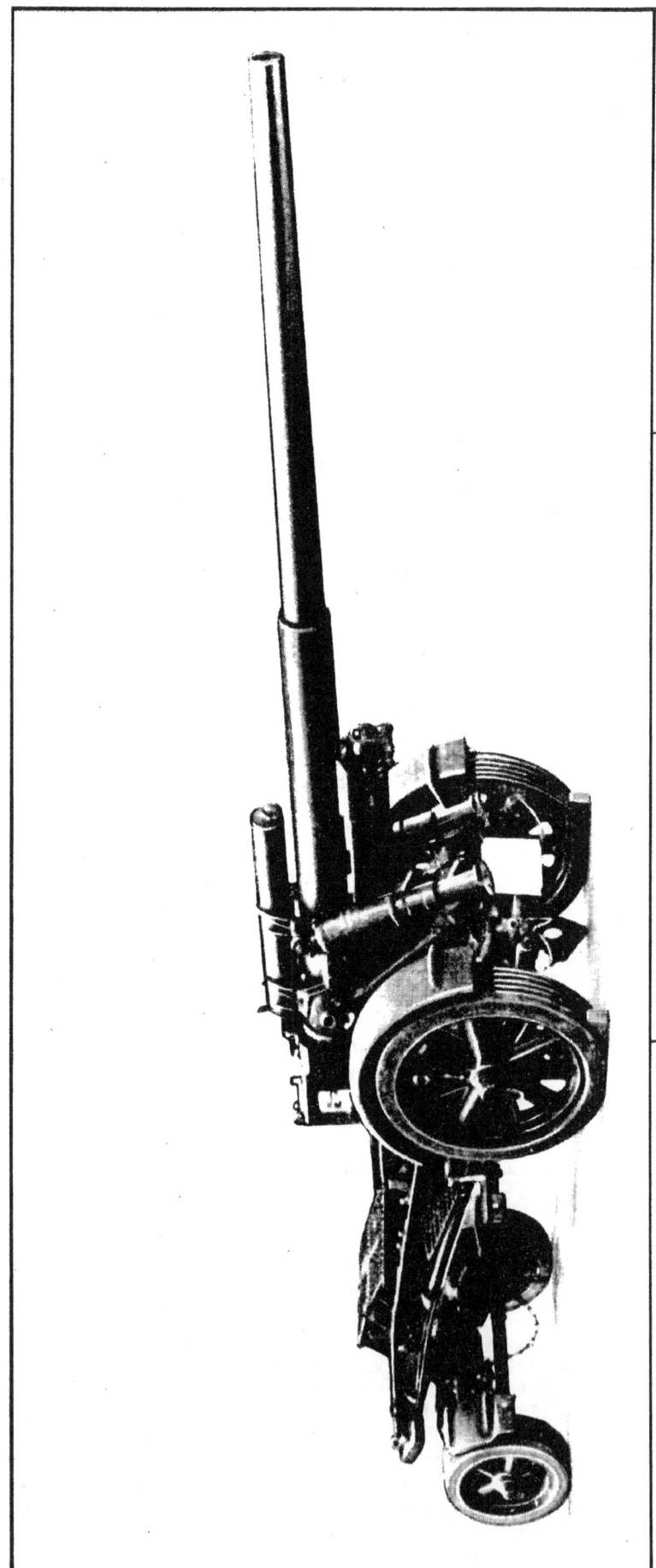

FIG. 99. 15cm. K.18.
(5·9in GUN. MODEL 18.)

of the position of the trail legs; the process is reversed for travelling.

A tipping ramp on the trailer has two trolley wheels on its dipping extremity which, when the gun is being unlimbered, make contact with the ground. This arrangement thus forms an inclined moving ramp down which the ends of the trails move. Two rollers beneath the latter engage two roller paths on the ramp to facilitate movement. Movement during unlimbering is controlled, and during limbering-up, effected by a hand operated winch and chain.

The complete equipment, including the platform, is transported in three loads, gun barrel and transporter, carriage, platform and transporter.

2. Data: 15 cm. K. 39.

	Metric	British
Calibre	149.1 mm	5.88 ins
Length of Gun	8255 mm	324.96 ins
Length of barrel	7868 mm	309.6 ins
Length of rifling	6505 mm	256.1 ins
Chamber capacity	24.9 litres	
No. of charges	3	
Weight of standard projectile (HE)	43 kg	94.6 lbs

Type of rifling. Increasing right hand twist. Angle of Twist 4° 20' - 6° 00'.

Percussion or electric firing — Percussion.

	Metric	British
Maximum recoil	1472 mm	4 ft. 10 ins
Minimum recoil	1250 mm	4 ft. 1 in

Type of Sights: Normal field role type.
Traverse: Split trail = 60°. Platform 6° and 360°.
Rate of traverse 1 Turn of handwheel = 15'. 1 Turn of trolley traverse handwheel = 5°.
Elevation — 3° + 46°
Rate of elevation 1 Turn of handwheel = 55 minutes.
Rate of fire 5 r.p.m.

Travelling Position (without gun barrel) -

	Metric	British
Overall length	8550 mm	28ft. 0 ins.
Overall width	2593 mm	8 ft. 6 ins.
Overall height	2750 mm	9 ft. 0 ins.

Turntable platform -

	Metric	British
Diameter overall	1620 mm	5 ft. 4 ins.
Height overall	866 mm	2 ft. 10 ins.

Outrigger arms (each) -

	Metric	British
Length overall	4750	15 ft 7 ins.
Width overall	230 mm	9 ins.
Height overall	356 mm	1 ft. 2 ins.

Travelling Position Weight -

	Metric	British
Barrel and transporter	9,200 kg	9.05 tons
Carriage	9,100 kg	9.0 tons
Platform and transporter	11,300 kg	11.1 tons
Weight in action (without platform)	12,200 kg	12.0 tons
Maximum Velocity	865 m/sec	2840 fs
Chamber Pressure	3000 atmospheres	19.7 tons sq in
Muzzle Energy	1642 m/t	
Maximum Range	24700 metres	27,000 yds

FIG. 100. 15 cm. K.39
(5·9 in GUN. MODEL 39.)

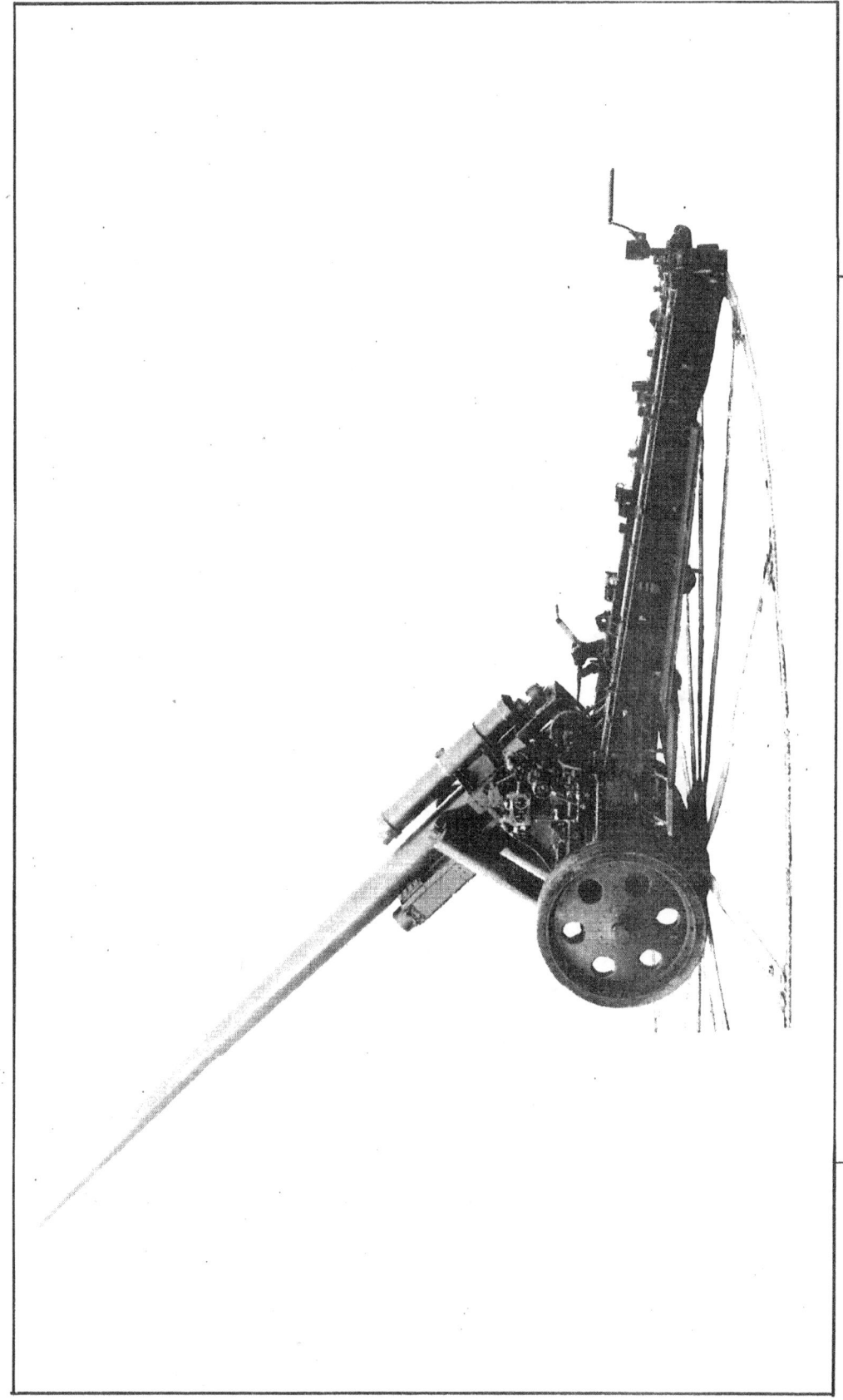

FIG. 101. 15cm. K.39
(5·9in GUN. MODEL 39 — COAST DEFENCE ROLE)

FIG. 102. 15 cm. K.39
(5·9 in GUN. MODEL 39.)

3. Ammunition

Projectile German Nomenclature British equivalent	Fuzes	Weight of Projectile	Muzzle Velocity /sec	Max. Range Metres
HE 15 cm K Gr 18	A.Z. 23 v (0.25)	43 kg (94.6 lbs)		
HE Anti-Concrete CP. 15 Gr 19 Rot Be	A.Z. 23 v (0.15)	43.5 kg (95.7 lbs)	3,865 (2840 fs)	24700 metres (27,000 yards)
	Dopp Z S/90		2,780 (2560 fs)	27,000
	Bd Z		1,620 (2050 fs)	
(HE 15 cm Sprgr L/4.6	Nose	45 kg (99 lbs)	890 (2920 fs)	
✱(HE CP 15 Halb pzgr	Base	"	720 (2360 fs)	25400 metres 28,000 yards
(APC BC HE 15 Pzgr	Base	"	550 (1800 fs)	

✱ Produced for the Turkish Order.

E. **15 cm SK. C/28 (5.87 in Mobile Coast Defence Gun C/28) (See Fig.103,104 and 105.).**

1. This mobile coast artillery equipment has the neat, compact appearance of a well-conceived efficient weapon, giving a very low silhouette in the firing position, considering the size of the gun which is mounted.

An interesting feature is the use of two four-wheeled transporters each fitted with longitudinal torsion-rod suspension as well as pneumatic tyres. These transporters can be detached from or attached to the mounting very quickly and simply with corresponding speed and ease in lowering and raising the mounting to and from the firing position.

The equipment may be towed from either end, since each transporter can be made capable of steering or following.

An ingenious use of torsion rods is made to assist the raising of the outrigger arms of the platform from the firing to the travelling position.

No means of levelling the superstructure relative to the platform is provided and maintenance of level depends completely upon the six levelling jacks.

The gun is an orthodox barrel fitted with a normal jacket, unusually large breech ring and a normal mechanism. Two alternative muzzle brakes are provided on the equipment under examination, a "Pepper-Pot" low efficiency type and an 'Open-Baffle' comparatively high efficiency type.

A considerable number of trials were carried out in an endeavour to find a suitable high efficiency muzzle brake, indeed one was so efficient that it caused casualties amongst the gun detachment.

The most unusual feature of the gun is the presence of a superfluous spring-loaded plunger which serves no useful purpose. The whole mechanism may have been slightly modified from its original form however because the Breech Ring is quite different from those shown on photographs previously seen of guns described as 15 cm. S.K. C/28 and referred to as being of the 'Gneisenau' Battleship class (U.S. Seacoast Evaluation Board Report on German Seacoast Defences).

/An additional

An additional interesting feature is the use of two loading trays. These are secured to the rear extremity of the cradle and below the breech ring. The arms are so hinged, one at the left rear and the other at the right rear of the cradle, that the trays are swung clear of the breech opening during the firing of the gun into a convenient and lower position suitable for placing the next shell and cartridge on the trays.

2. Data: S.K. C/28.

	Metric	British
Calibre	149.1 mm	5.87 ins
Length of Gun	8291 mm	364.4 ins
Length of barrel	7815 mm	307.7 ins
Length of rifling	6584 mm	259.2 ins

Rifling - System Polygroove Plain Section increasing right hand twist
   Twist - 1 in 50 to 1 in 30.

	Metric	British
Number of grooves	44	
Depth of grooves	1.63 mm	.063 ins
Width of grooves	6.1 mm	.24 ins
Width of lands	5 mm	.197 ins
Firing mechanism protrusion		.106 ins
Percussion or electric firing	Percussion	
Maximum recoil	640 mm	25 ins
Minimum recoil	300 mm	12 ins

Type of Sights: Range and Bearing Receiving Dials with follow the pointer operation. Displacement corrector cams incorporated.

Traverse	360°	
Rate of traverse: 1 Turn of handwheel =	2½°	
Elevation	- 7° 30' + 47° 30'.	
Rate of elevation: 1 Turn of handwheel =	2°	
Wheel track	2693 mm	ft. 10 ins
Travelling Position -		
Overall length	12853 mm	42 ft. 2 ins.
Overall width	2769 mm	9 ft. 1 in.
Overall height	2950 mm	9 ft. 8 ins.
Firing Position -		
Overall length	10,668 mm	35 ft. 0 ins.
Overall width	6287 mm	20 ft. 7½ ins.
Overall height	2515 mm	8 ft. 3 ins.
Travelling Position Weight	26163 kg	25.75 tons
Weight in action	19761 kg	19.45 tons.
Maximum Muzzle Velocity	875 m/sec	2870 fs
Maximum Range	23,500 metres	25700 yds
Weight of Standard HE Projectile	45.3 kg	99.7 lbs

3. Ammunition

The ammunition used in this weapon is a mixed bag of Naval and Army types.

The principle types are as follows:-

Projectile	Fuzes	Wt. of Projectile	Muzzel Velocity
HE Anti-Concrete Common Pointed 15 cm. Gr. 19 Rot.Be (Army)	Bd Z. f. 15 cm. Gr. 19 Be.	43.5 kg (95.7 lbs)	875 m/sec (2870 fs)
HE (Naval) with Ballistic Cap 15 cm Sprgr. L/4.6 Kg.m Haube	K2. C/27 St O.Tm. M. Dopp Z. S/90 st.	43.5 kg (95.7 lbs)	875 m/sec (2870 fs)
HE Base Fuzed w/Cap 15 cm Sprgr L/4.5 Bdz m Hb	Bd Z. C/38	45.3 kg (99.7 lbs)	875 m/sec (2870 fs)
APCBC/HE 15 cm Pz Sprgr L/3.8 m Hb	Bd Z. C/38	45.3 kg (99.7 lbs)	875 m/sec (2870 fs)

/DEVELOPMENT OF A

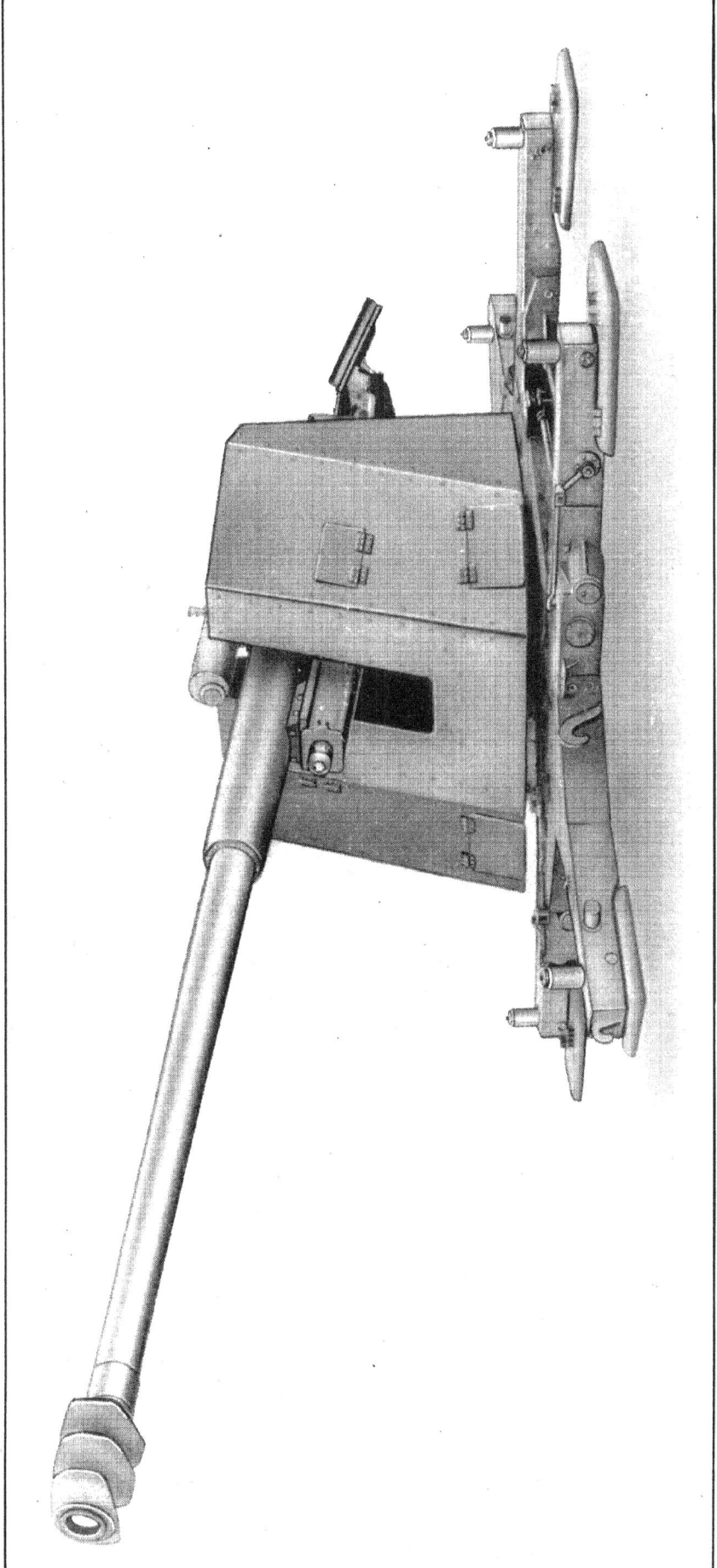

FIG. 103. 15 cm. S.K. c/28.
(5·9 in MOBILE COAST DEFENCE GUN. MODEL C/28.)

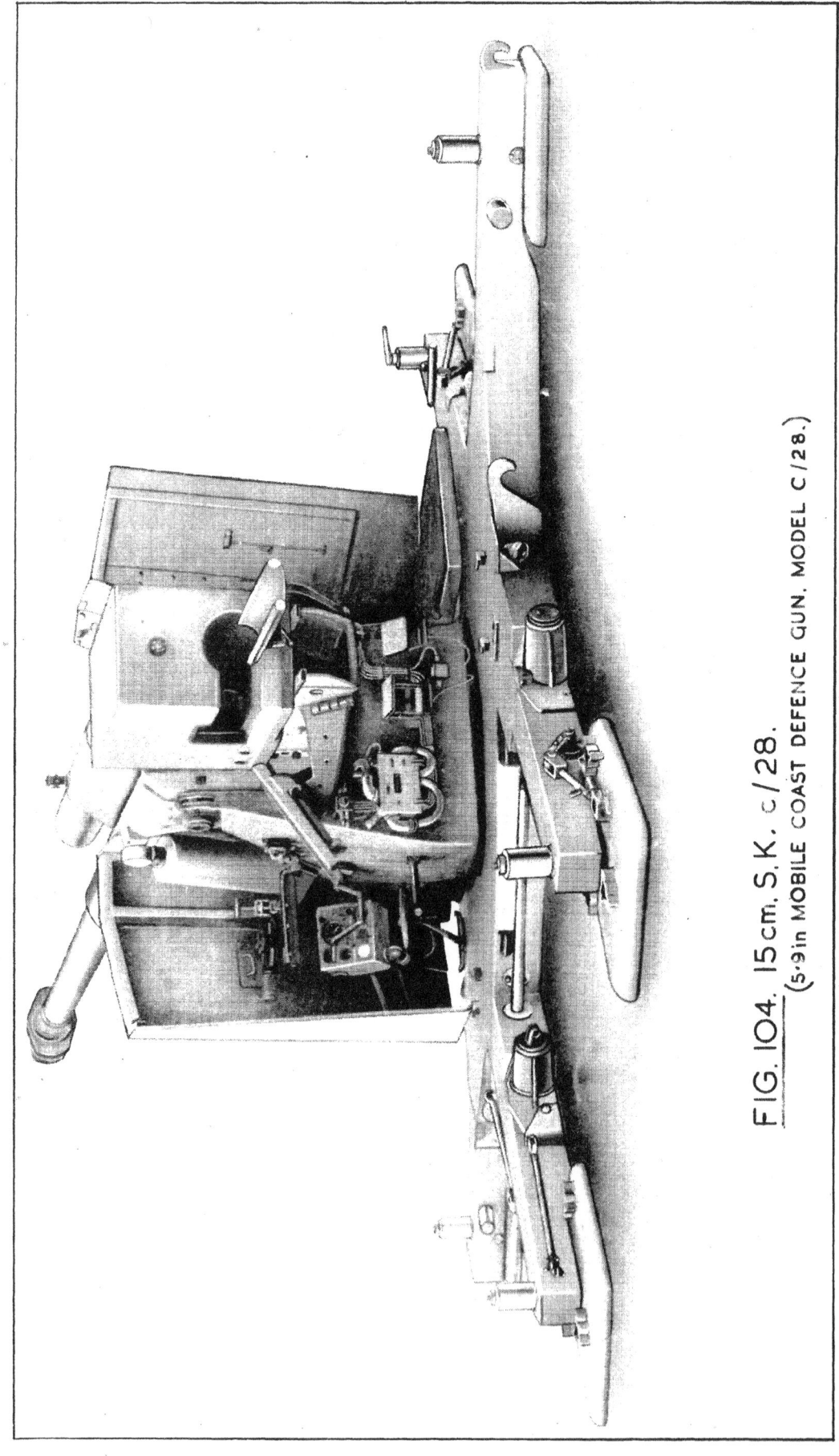

FIG. 104. 15 cm. S.K. c/28.
(5·9in MOBILE COAST DEFENCE GUN. MODEL C/28.)

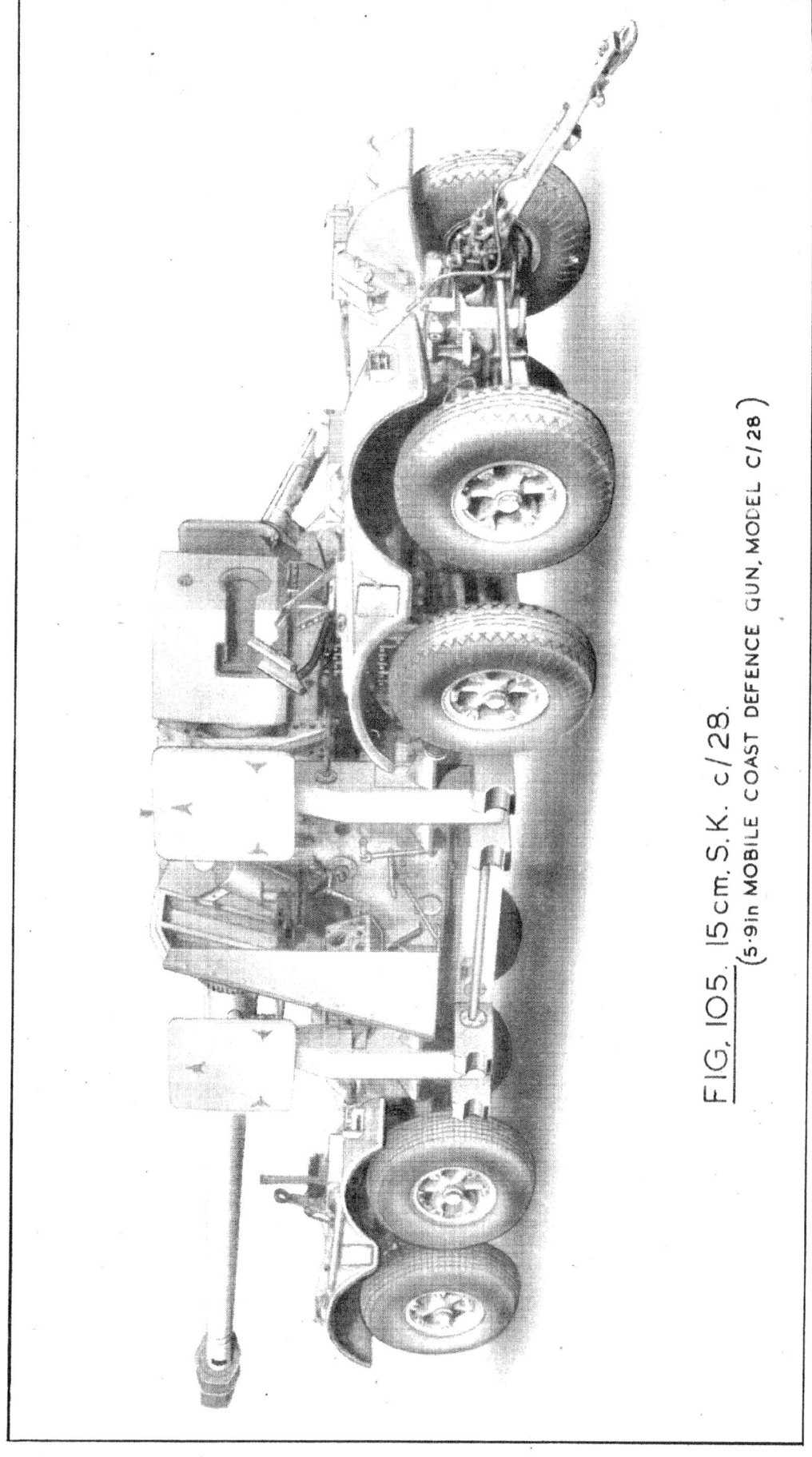

FIG. 105. 15 cm. S.K. c/28.
(5·9in MOBILE COAST DEFENCE GUN, MODEL C/28)

Development of a Mobile Heavy Coastal Gun (Translated from a German document.) by a German designer.

Each new design is more or less a further development of an existing gun, as a result of detailed examination, or a combination of different and already existing types of gun. It is the task of the designer during development of a gun, to take note of the tactical problems of the gun, and to solve them by the simplest means.

The gun is an apparatus on which the highest demands are made, and which is subjected to the roughest treatment. The soldier is not a careful tender of machinery.

A design does not take shape at the first attempt, but is developed, rejected and re-developed. Often during the final development, other solutions to one or another series of problems are recognised as more advantageous and subsequently incorporated in the design.

Below, I give a short description of how the 15 cm SK C/28 M mit LC/38 was designed.

The Naval Command ordered a mobile 15 cm coastal gun with the performance of the 15 cm SK C/28M. The Army Command recommended the use of the 15 cm R1S either unaltered, or with very slight alteration for this purpose. The Naval and Army Commands and I, as designer of the 15 cm R1S took part in a trial with the troops of this gun, and realised that the demands made by the Navy were not practicable, as far as the 15 cm R1S was concerned. The Navy therefore commissioned the firm Rhein-Metall Borsig A.G. to deliver a design for a mobile 15 cm coastal gun (ballistic performance the same as the 15 cm SK C/28 M), suitable for use in the tropics and Polar regions. The gun had to be able to engage sea and land targets. The barrel length, L/55 was stipulated as well as the ballistic performance. The demand for stability, at small elevation and if possible even when depressed, made it essential to use a high efficiency muzzle brake.

The barrel department had the task of designing such a barrel, given details of the weight of the barrel, the position of the centre of gravity and the efficiency of the muzzle brake.

From existing designs, conclusions were drawn. Thus the measurements of the cradle guides for the barrel of the 15 cm SK C/28 M mit LC/38 were the same as those of the 15 cm K.8 etc. The first barrel design was unsuitable as the centre of gravity lay too near the muzzle, but after a second or third barrel design, a draft of the gun was made. The approximate trunnion height was stipulated on the assumption that good loading is possible. There remained the problem of using constant recoil. Mounting recoil seemed unsuitable because of the rate of fire. The length of recoil at maximum elevation was decided and as the ballistic details, the weight of the barrel and the efficiency of the muzzle brake were already stipulated, the brake pressure was calculated. The weights of the individual parts, cradle, barrel brake, air-recuperator, revolving mounting, elevating and traversing mechanism were then estimated; comparable values were available, or calculated from previous designs. The shape of the cruciform platform was decided and its weight calculated, and the length of the legs calculated, so that the gun would be stable even in an unfavourable firing position.

The folding and unfolding of the side legs was very difficult. Calculations showed that 5 or 6 men were necessary. The people involved did not play their parts simultaneously, so casualties could easily occur when under fire. Folding with a winch is complicated. Folding the legs sideways, as in heavy A.A. guns seriously affected the manoeuvring angle of the vehicle. Thus arose the well known method of compensating the legs by means of torsion bar springs, so that one or two men can fold and unfold the legs.

The gun was dismantled into three parts for transporting:-

1. The barrel on the barrel vehicle
2. The mounting on the mounting vehicle
3. The cruciform platform was transportable on two special trailers like A.A. guns.

The gun could be erected and dismantled without hoisting gear. Each part had a weight of 10000 Kg (i.e. Vehicle plus part of gun borne = 10000 Kg.) The wheels for the barrel chute and the mounting vehicle were the same as those of the 15 cm. K.S. The wheels for 3 special trailers taken from A.A. have pneumatic tyres.

After the basi principles for the design had been thus established, the design was completely drawn, put before the Naval Command and approved.

The Firm sent to the Naval Command, without instructions, a new design as it was known that the Army had developed a new heavy transporter, and we, as a firm had found a way of building four-axled vehicles, with which manoeuvres in a relatively small space were possible. The new design was pronounced very good by the Navy, as the following advantages were obtained:-

(a) Quicker erection and dismantling of the gun

(b) The dismantling of the gun into three parts needs coupling parts, the failure of which means the failure of the gun.

(c) All wheels for the gun are the same.

(d) Instead of 3 medium transporters, only one heavy one is required.

(e) Instead of 3 x 2 = 6 drivers, each transporter has one driver and one co-driver, therefore only 2 drivers are necessary.

(f) The time taken in moving is substantially shorter.

A calculation of the cruciform mounting showed that the longitudinal legs had to be strengthened, as they were now subjected to the greatest strain in travelling and not in firing.

A wooden model, scale 1: 1 was built to test clearances, serviceability, etc.

Each individual part of the gun was designed, the connecting parts were established and the calculations for them were made. After that a final design was worked out with all details, taking into consideration economic production, and maintenance and spare parts. After the gun was already in the process of manufacture, the Naval Command asked for a 13 mm. thick armoured shield to be built on. The experimental one was built, and tested with the constant cooperation of the manufacturing department, to get to known all production difficulties and if possible to eradicate them, and to make known the results of the tests on firing and travelling.

The gun was completely stable at about - 6° as calculated. The muzzle brake however broke after a few shots, as it could not be forged in advance sufficiently because of the lack of the requisite dies and the necessary raw materials were lacking. The loading pressures were worked out by the "Reich Chemical-Technical Establishment" and were too high.

The Navy did away with stability of the gun on depression, proposed a new muzzle brake with lower efficiency and carried out a thorough trial with troops after the barrel buffer had been adjusted for the finally introduced muzzle brake. I was present at the conclusion of the trials, and at the discussion thereon. The gun ass pronounced good. The Coastal Artillery ordered mobile, heavy coastal guns. The gun was laid out in series, but as a result of bomb damage, no more were delivered.

Further investigation went on to build in a 17 cm. barrel instead of the 15 cm. With the 17 cm. a reduction of recoil from 900/600 mm. (i.e. 900 mm. horizontal or depressed, 600 mm. maximum elevation) would have to be considered, to achieve satisfactory stability.

G. **15 cm SK C/28 in Morserlafette** (5.87 ins SK C/28 on Howitzer Carriage)

1. This equipment consists of the Naval gun SK C/28 modified and mounted in the carriage of the 21 cm Howitzer Model 18. This was a temporary expedient pending the introduction of the 17 cm K.18 for mounting in the same type mounting.

   The equipment was transported in two loads, the barrel transporter of the 21 cm Howitzer being used for this purpose.

   Only eight equipments were produced, the year of production being 1941.

2. Data : S.K. C/28 in Mrs Laf.

	Metric	British
Calibre	149.1 mm	5.87 ins
Length of piece	8291 mm	326.4 ins
Length of barrel	7815 mm	307.7 ins
Length of rifling	6584 mm	259.2 ins
Rifling - System PPS increasing right hand twist		
Twist 1 in 50 to 1 in 30.		
Number of grooves	44	
Depth of grooves	1.6 mm	.063 ins
Width of grooves	6.1 mm	.24 ins
Width of bands	5 mm	.197 ins
Traverse Top traverse 16°	All round 360°	
Elevation	0° to 50°	
Standard HE Projectile Weight	43 kg	94.6 lbs
Maximum Range	23700 metres	25,920 yds
Weight in action	16870 kg	16.6 Tons
Weight Travelling - Barrel and Transporter	10735 kg	10.5 tons
Carriage	12000 kg	11.85 tons
Maximum Muzzle Velocity	890 m/sec	2920 fs
Chamber Pressure	2800 Atmospheres	18.38 tons sq in
Muzzle Energy	1736 tm	

3. Ammunition

Projectile	Fuzes	Weight of Projectile	Muzzle Velocity	Max Range
HE (Army) 15 cm K Gr 18	AZ 23 v (0.15)			
	AZ 23 v (0.25)	43 kg (94.6 lbs)	890 m/sec	23700 metres
	Dopp Z S/90			
HE Anti-Concrete CP (Army) 15 cm Gr 19 Rot Bc.	Bd Zf 15 cm Gr 19 Be.	43.5 kg (95.7 lbs)	890 m/sec	23700 metres
HE (Naval) w/Ballistic Cap 15 cm Sprgr L/4.6 Kz m. Haube	K2 C/27 St O.In M Dopp Z S/90 st.	45.3 kg (99.7 lbs)	875 m/s (2870 fs)	
HE Base fuzed w/Cap 15 cm Sprgr L/4.5 Bdz m.Hb.	Bd Z C/38	45.3 kg (99.7 lbs)		23500 metres (25700 yds)
APC BC HE 15 cm Pz Sprgr L/3.8 m.Hb.	Bd Z C/38	45.3 kg (99.7 lbs)		

/H. 17 cm

17 cm Kanone 18 in. Mörserlafette (17 cm K. 18 in Mrs Laf) (See Fig. 106 and 107)

(6.8 ins Gun Model 18 on Howitzer Carriage)

1. This equipment introduced in 1941, formed the backbone (with the 21 cm Mörser 18) of the German Heavy Field Artillery weapons. Both equipments were designed by Krupp for motorised transport in two loads, although for short distances gun and carriage can be moved together as one load. The same type carriage is used by both equipments.

The 17 cm K. in Mrs Laf replaced a number of 15 cm equipments, which did not prove equal to the ballistic requirements for a heavy gun. Pending large scale production of the 17 cm gun, a number of 15 cm Naval guns were mounted in the carriage intended for it.

The gun is of orthodox German design of monobloc loose barrel construction with a detachable breech ring fitted with a horizontal sliding breech block. The cradle which encloses the gun buffer is provided with a bridge type arrangement which supports the gun recuperator above the barrel. The equipment has what is known as dual recoil, i.e. in addition to the orthodox gun recoil the saddle which supports the gun and cradle is also allowed to recoil. The saddle recoil system is of similar design to that used with the gun and is secured between the lower carriage and saddle. Both recoil systems consist of a hydraulic buffer and a hydro-pneumatic recuperator.

The elevating gear has two speed ratios, one high for quick movement and the other a low gear for fine laying by the layer. Two hydro-pneumatic equilibrators or elevation balancing springs are used.

The lower carriage with box trial is provided with an integral platform, which is lowered to the ground by gearing, the weight of the equipment being transferred to it by three jacks with castor wheels which run around the pathway near the edge of the circular platform. A central pivot is also provided. The wheels are thus lifted clear of the ground during action. Limited traverse of 8 degrees right and left is provided by an arc mounted on the spade plate. To obtain larger amounts of traverse the rear of the three platform jacks is operated to lift the trail and spade plate clear of the ground. In this position the all round traverse is effected by turning the equipment on the three platform castor wheeled jacks. The carriage suspension during travelling is obtained by a two wheeled spring limber at the front on which the trail end pivots with articulation and the two wheeled sprung suspension of the carriage itself.

The wheels are of light alloy metal with solid rubber tyres. For transporting, the barrel is normally carried on a barrel transporter. The latter is provided with an endless chain and manual winch gear for moving the barrel on to and off the transporter.

2. Data : K. 18 in Mrs Laf.

	Metric	British
Calibre	172.5 mm	6.8 ins
Length of Gun (50 calibres)	8529.5 mm	28 ft 0 ins
Length of barrel	8103 mm	26 ft. 7 ins
Length of rifling	6464 mm	21 ft. 2.5 ins
Chamber capacity	41.6 litres	
Rifling -		
Number of grooves	48	
Depth of grooves	1.65 mm	0.065 ins
Width of grooves	6.8 mm	0.268 ins
Type of rifling: P.P. Increasing Rt Hand Twist.		
Percussion or electric firing		Percussion
Maximum recoil of gun	950 mm	37.4 ins
" " " saddle	1480 mm	58. 2 ins
Normal recoil of gun	860 mm	33.8 ins
" " " saddle	1250 mm	49.2 ins
Traverse: Top Traverse 16° and also all round - 360°		
Elevation		0° to 50°
Rate of fire		1 r.p.m.

/Travelling

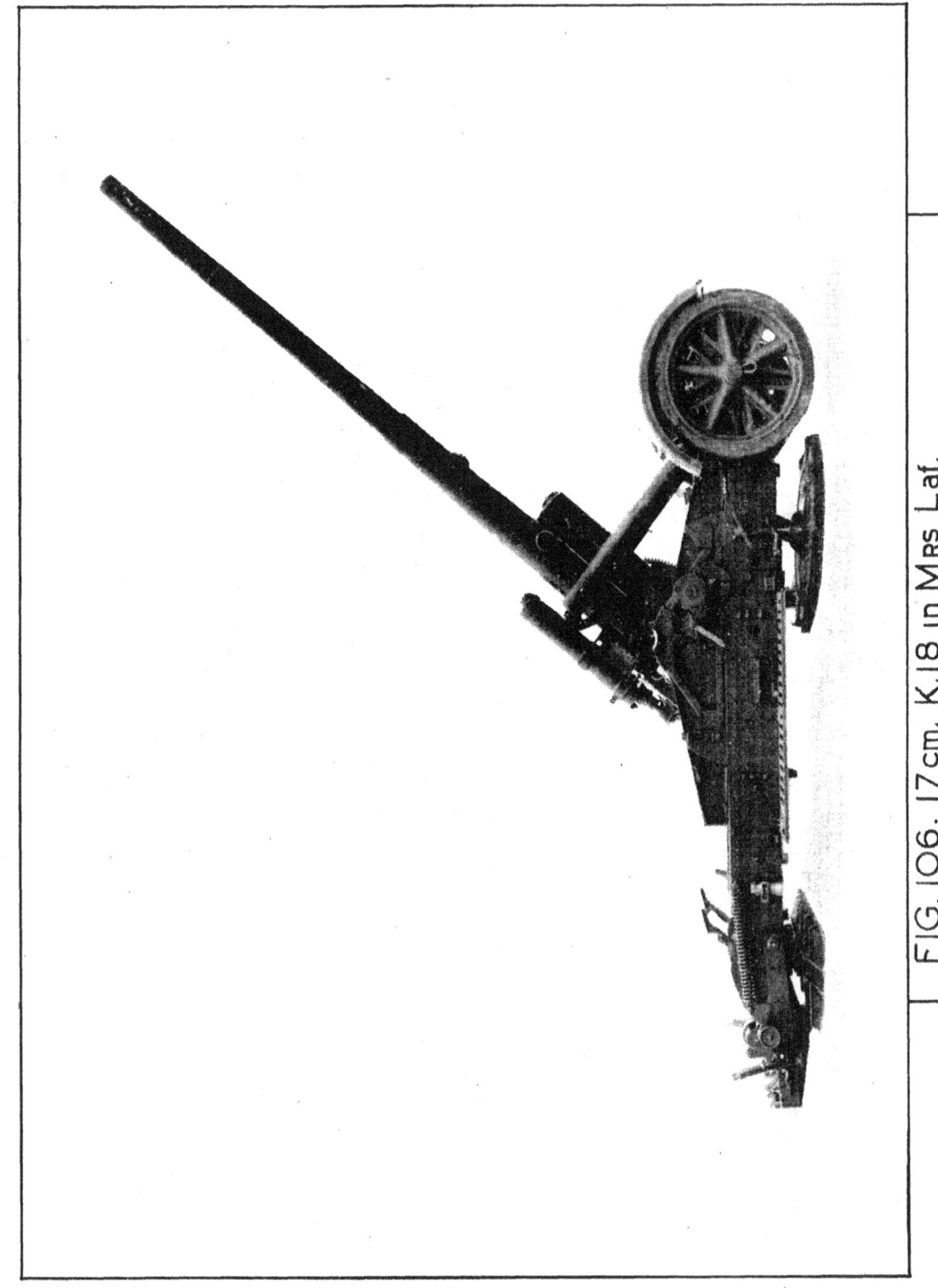

FIG. 106. 17cm. K.18 in Mrs Laf.
(6·8 in GUN MODEL 18 ON HOWITZER CARRIAGE)

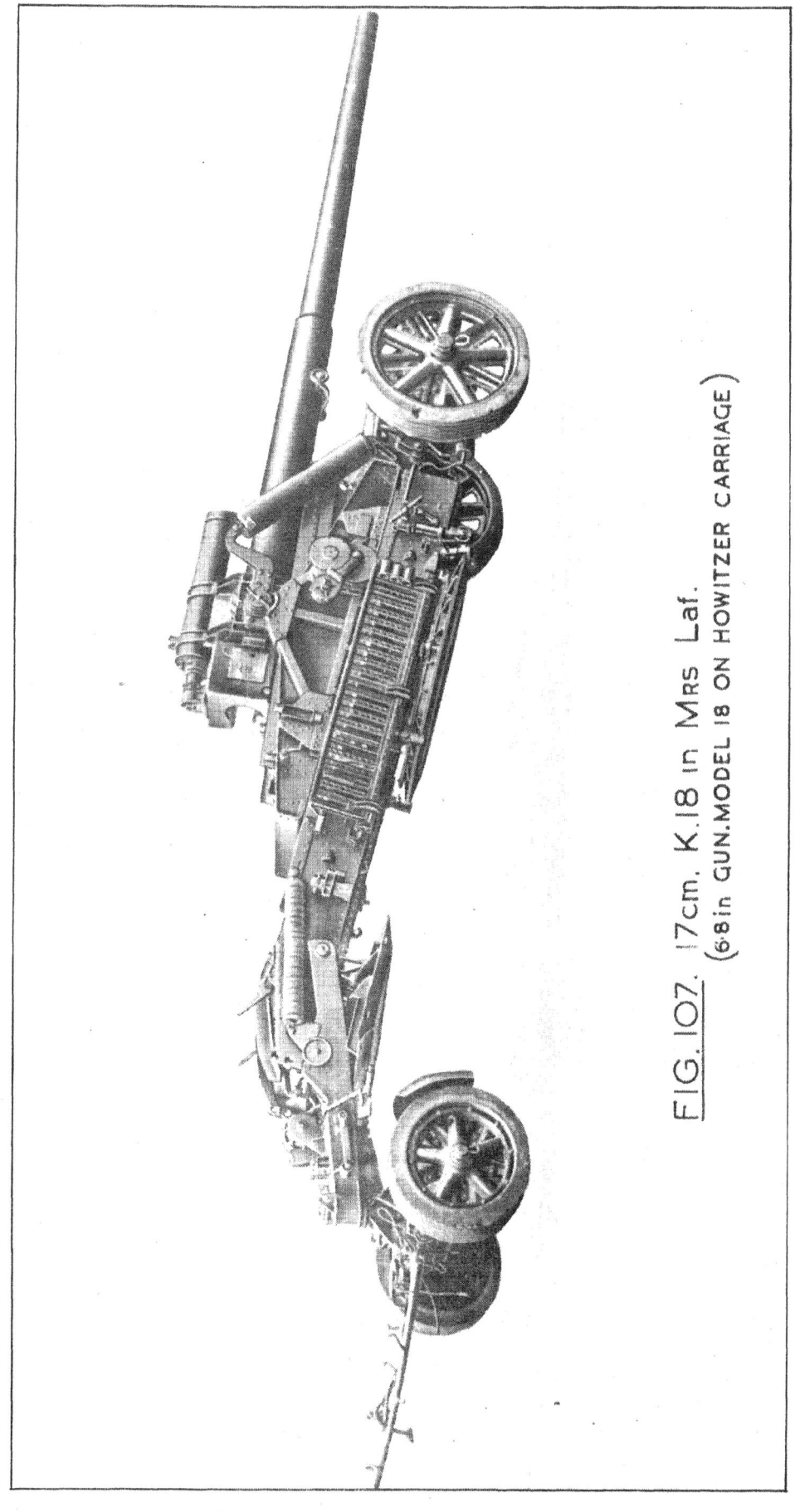

FIG. 107. 17cm. K.18 in Mrs Laf. (6·8in GUN. MODEL 18 ON HOWITZER CARRIAGE)

	Metric	British
Travelling Position -		
Wheel tread	304 mm	1 ft. 0 ins
Track	2670 mm	8 ft. 9 ins
Wheel base	7250 mm	23 ft. 9.5 ins
Ground clearance	406 mm	1 ft. 4 ins
Overall length	12810 mm	42 ft. 0 ins
Overall width	2830 mm	9 ft. 3.5 ins
Overall height	3110 mm	10 ft. 2.5 ins
Travelling Position Weight Barrel	11375 kg	11.2 tons
Carriage	12000 kg	11.8 tons
Weight in action	17520 kg	17.2 tons
Maximum Muzzle Velocity	925 m/s	3035 fs
Chamber Pressure	3200 Atmospheres	21 tons sq in
Muzzle Energy	2739 tm	
Maximum Range	29600 metres	32,375 yds

(With special long range HE round)

3. Ammunition

Projectile	Fuzes	Weight of Projectile	Muzzle Velocity	Max Range.
17 cm K Gr 39 Standard He	AZ 35 K Dopp Z S/90 K	68 kg (149.6 lbs)	I. 620 m/s (2035 fs)	18300 metres (20,000 yds)
17 cm K Gr 38 hb Long range He with ballistic cap	Hbgr Z 35 K Dopp Z S/90 K	62.8 kg (138.16 lbs)	II. 740 m/s (2430 fs)	22700 metres (24,825 yds)
			III. 860 m/s (2820 fs)	28,000 metres (30,625 yds)
			IV. 925 m/s (3035 fs) with Charge IV only.	29600 metres (32,375 yds)

Four charges fired viz:- Charge I, II, III and IV.

J. **Langer 21 cm Morser (lg 21 cm Mrs). 8.3 ins long-barrelled Howitzer**
(See Fig. 108.)

1. This equipment was introduced into service in 1916. It was designed by Krupp to increase the performance of the then standard 21 cm Howitzer by increasing the barrel length.

The barrel is of jacket and tube construction with a horizontal sliding breech block. One spring equilibrator is fitted. The recoil mechanism consists of a twin hydraulic buffer enclosed within the cradle and a hydro-pneumatic recuperator located above the barrel.

The gun is mounted on a box trail carriage with steel spoke wheels and removable skid belts.

The equipment is intended for horsedrawn transport in two loads.

A later model of the lg 21 cm Mrs was produced for motorised transport in one load. The weight in action of this equipment is 9220 kg (9.8 tons) and in the travelling position including limber and gun stores is 11257 kg (11 tons approx).

2. Data: lg 21 cm Mrs. Two load 1916 Model

	Metric	British
Calibre	211 mm	8.3 ins
Length of piece (14.5 calibres)	3063 mm	120.6 ins
Length of rifling	2296 mm	90.4 ins
Chamber capacity	11.6 litres	

/Traverse

	Metric	British
Traverse	4°	
Elevation	- 6° + 70°	
Weight of standard HE Projectile	113 kg	248.6 lbs
No. of charges	7	
Maximum Range	11,100 metres	12,140 yds
Weight in Action	6680 kg	6.1 tons
Weight travelling - barrel and transporter	4160 kg	4.1 tons
Carriage	4740 kg	4.63 tons
Maximum Muzzle Velocity	393 m/sec	1290 fs
Chamber Pressure	2400 Atmospheres	15.75 tons sq in.
Muzzle Energy	890 mt	

3.

Ammunition	Fuzes	Wt of Projectile	Muzzle Velocity
HE - 21 cm Gr 18 (or 18 Stg)	A.Z.23 (0.15) A.Z.23 2V Dopp Z. S/90	113 kg (248.6 lbs)	I. 247 m/s. 810 fs. II. 269 m/s. 880 fs.
HE - Anti-Concrete CP 21 cm Gr 18 Be.	Bd Z. f. 21 cm Gr Be.	121.4 kg (267.1 lbs)	III. 290 m/s 920 fs. IV. 310 m/s 1020 fs. V. 335 m/s 1100 fs. VI. 359 m/s 1175 fs. VII. 393 m/s 1290 fs.

Charges 1 to VII used for both types.

K. 21 cm Mörser. 18 (21 cm Mrs 18). (8.27 ins Howitzer Model 18)(See Fig. 109, 110 & 111.)

1. This heavy howitzer, designed by Krupp, was introduced into service in 1939. The Mrs 18 replaced an equipment of obsolescent design known as the langer 21 cm Mörser, which dated from 1916 and was originally intended for horsedrawn transport in two loads. This old equipment weighed 6680 kg (6.58 Tons) in action and was transported in two loads of 4160 kg and 4740 kg (4.1 Tons and 4.63 Tons). The piece was 14.5 calibres long and ranged up to 11,000 metres (12,030 yds) with a 113 kg (248.6 lbs). A later model of the langer 21 cm Mörser was produced for motorised transport in one load, weighing 11275 kg (11 tons approx) including the limber and stores.

The carriage of the 21 cm Mörser 18 is the same as that used with the 17 cm K in Mrs Laf described in a previous section except that whereas the elevation of the 17 cm gun is limited to 50 degrees by limiting stops on the elevating arc, the maximum elevation of the 21 cm Mrs 18 is approximately 70 degrees.

Prior to and in the early stages of World War II the German Army continued the requirement for a heavy mobile gun of 21 cm calibre, finally in 1942 it was decided to abandon this calibre and concentrate on the production of 17 cm K and also to give high priority to the design of the newer 24 cm equipments.

2. Ballistic Performance

The howitzer fires in both upper and lower register. Minimum range in the lower register is 3000 m. (3280 yds).

/Gas Pressure

FIG. 108. lg 21cm Mrs.
(8.3in LONG BARRELLED HOWITZER)

	Gas Pressure Atmos	Tons sq.in.	MV m/s	MV f/s	Max Range m	Max Range yds
HE Projectile						
With Gr 18 or 18 Stg						
Charge I	570	3.6	225	737	4650	5090
II	650	4.1	225	836	5850	6400
III	800	5.05	290	952	7325	8010
IV	1100	6.95	355	1165	9800	10720
V	1700	10.8	440	1440	12500	13670
VI	2450	15.5	565	1850	16700	18260
Anti-Concrete Proj:						
With Gr 18 Be						
Charge I	570	3.6	218	715	4350	4760
II	650	4.1	247	810	5500	6015
III	800	5.05	281	922	7000	7655
IV	1100	6.95	344	1130	9600	10500
V	1700	10.8	426	1395	12400	13560
VI	2450	15.5	550	1805	16725	18285

3. Data : 21 cm Mrs 18.

	Metric	British
Calibre	210.9	8.3 ins
Length of Gun (31 calibres)	6510 mm	256.3 ins
Length of barrel	6070 mm	239.3 ins
Length of rifling	5274 mm	207.6 ins
Chamber capacity	24.5 litres	
Rifling -		
Number of grooves		64
Depth of grooves	2.4 mm	0.094 ins
Width of grooves	5.6 mm	0.219 ins
Width of lands	3.9 mm	0.156 ins
Type of rifling: P.P.S. Increasing Rt Hand Twist.		
Percussion or electric firing		Percussion
Maximum recoil of gun	850 mm	33.5 ins
" " " saddle	1200 mm	47.2 ins
Minimum recoil of gun	500 mm	19.7 ins
" " " saddle	1000 mm	39.4 ins
Traverse Limited 16° and all round - 360°		
Elevation		0° to 70°
Rate of fire		1 r.p.m.
Travelling Position -		
Wheel Tread	304 mm	1 ft. 0 ins
Track	2670 mm	8 ft. 9 ins
Wheel base	7250 mm	23 ft. 9.5 ins
Ground clearance	406 mm	1 ft. 4 ins
Overall length	12810 mm	42 ft. 0 ins
Overall width	2830 mm	9 ft. 3.5 ins
Overall height	3110 mm	10 ft. 2.5 ins
Travelling Position Weight -		
Gun	10700 kg	10.5 tons
Carriage	12000 kg	11.8 tons
Weight in action	16700 kg	16.4 tons
Maximum Muzzle Velocity	565 m/s	1855 fs
Chamber Pressure	2450 atmospheres	16 tons sq in
Muzzle Energy	1839 tm	
Weight of Standard Projectile (HE)	113 kg	248.6 lbs
Maximum Range	16700 metres	18,250 yds

/4. Ammunition

4. Ammunition

(a) Shell:-

Nomenclature	Type of Shell	Weight	Fuzes used
21 cm Gr 18	HE Streamline, Nose Fuzed	113 kg (249 lbs)	A.Z.23 umg (0.15) or A.Z.23 umg M.2V. or Dopp Z. S/90
21 cm Gr 18 Stg	HE Streamline, Nose Fuzed (Cast Steel)	113 kg (249 lbs)	A.Z.23 umg (0.15) or A.Z.23 umg M.2V. or Dopp.Z. S/90
21 cm Gr 18 Be	Anti-Concrete, Streamline with ballistic cap. Base fuzed.	121.4 kg (249 lbs)	Bd Z f 21 cm Gr 18 Be
21 cm Gr 37			
21 cm Rö Gr 42	Sub-calibre anti-concrete shell, believed rocket assisted.		
21 cm Rö Gr 44	Sub-calibre anti-concrete shell, believed rocket assisted.		

Recognition:- Gr 18, 18 Stg and 18 Be all have two bimetallic driving bands and are painted olive green. The Gr 18 Stg has "Stg" stencilled on it in black.

(b) Fuzes:-

A.Z.23 umg (0.15) is a D.A. and Graze action percussion fuze with an optional delay of 0.15 secs. The fuzes are issued set to non-delay. To set for delay, the upper part of the fuze head is turned by means of two slots so that the line on the lower part of the fuze head comes in line with the marking "0/15".

A.Z.23 umg m.2V. is a D.A. and Graze action percussion fuze with two alternative optional delays of 0.2 secs and 0.8 secs. The fuzes are issued set to non-delay. The construction of the fuze and the method of setting for delay are the same as for the A.Z.23 umg (0.15), the two delay marks being "0/2" and "0"/8".

Dopp. Z. S/90 is a mechanical time and percussion fuze with a maximum time of running of 90 secs. The fuze is set by means of a special graduated key.

(c) Cartridge Case:-

Solid drawn, either of brass, design No. 6351; or of steel brass plated design No. 6351 St.

Length	410 mm	15.14 ins.
Diameter at mouth	222 mm	8.74 ins
" of base	242 mm	9.53 ins.

(d) Primer:-

Either a brass C/12 n.A or steel C/12 n.A St.

(e) Igniter:-

509 (772 grains) Nz.Man.N.P. (1.5 x 1.5).

/(f) Decoppering

FIG. 109. 21 cm. Mrs 18.
(8·27 in. HOWITZER. MODEL 18.)

FIG. 110. 21cm. Mrs 18.
(8·27in HOWITZER. MODEL 18.)

FIG. III. 21 cm. Mrs. 18.
(8·27 in. HOWITZER MODEL 18.)

(f) **Decoppering agent:-** 80 g (1235 grains) of lead wire (not with Gudol Charge).

(g) **Propelling Charge:-**

Charge	Kg (lbs)					
	I	II	III	IV	V	VI
Gudol Make up.						
Gu. Bl.P.-A.O-(4x4x0.6)	1.000 (2.2)	1.000 (2.2)	1.000 (2.2)	1.000 (2.2)	1.000 (2.2)	
Gu.Rg.P.-AL 2-(1.8x15/4)	1.620 (3.57)	2.240 (4.94)	2.980 (6.57)	4.570 (10.08)	6.780 (14.95)	
Digl.Make up						
Digl.Bl.P - 10.5 - (3 x 3 x 0.8)	1.000 (2.2)	1.000 (2.2)	1.000 (2.2)	1.000 (2.2)	1.000 (2.2)	(With 100 g 1544 grains of igniter)
Digl.Rg.P-10.5 - (1.9 x 15/4)	1.430 (3.15)	1.960 (4.32)	2.670 (5.89)	4.160 (9.17)	6.300 (13.89)	
Digl R.P. - Gl - (500 x 5.6/3)						15.700 (34.6)
Ngl Make up						
Ngl.Bl.P - 12.5 - (4 x 4 x 1)	.895 (1.97)	.895 (1.97)	.895 (1.97)	.895 (1.97)	.895 (1.97)	(With 100 g 1544 grains) of igniter)
Ngl.Rg.P - 11.5 - (2.4 x 15/4)	1.250 (2.75)	1.750 (3.86)	2.400 (5.29)	3.780 (8.33)	5.800 (12.79)	
Ngl.R.P. - 8.2 - (360 x 6.5/3)						13.950 (30.8)

(h) **Make up of Charges:-**

Charges I to V consist of the part charge of the same number and all the preceding parts. Charge VI is delivered complete as part charge 6.

(j) **Packing of Ammunition:-**

Shell are packed singly with a grummet and nose protector in a basket.

Weight 21 cm Gr 18 or (Stg) 121 kg (267 lbs)
21 cm Gr 18 Be 129.4 kg (285 lbs)

Cartridges together with part charges 1 - 5 are packed singly in a metal box.
Weight 22 kg (48.5 lbs)
Part Charge 6 (Charge VI) are packed singly in a metal box.
Weight 20.9 kg (46.1 lbs)

L. **21 cm Krupp L/50 Gun (8.3 in. Krupp Model L/50 Gun)**

1. This equipment is a product of Krupp of Essen, which was offered by them for export before World War II. Little was seen of it during the course of the war and it is improbable that many exist.

This heavy field gun is mounted on a box trail type carriage. It was normally used with a radially rigged platform of somewhat similar type to that used with the K.39. A toothed traverse rack around the periphery of the platform provided all round traverse. Quick rough traverse was obtained by operating a sprocket type gear at the rack but the final exact traverse was obtained by operating the traverse handwheel on the carriage.

/When used as

When used as a coast defence gun, electric transmission dials were fitted to the carriage to provide the training and elevation data. In the field role normal type field sights were used.

The gun consists of a jacket, removable liner and a screwed on breech ring. A horizontal sliding breech block opening to the right is fitted.

Two equilibrators are provided to counteract the muzzle preponderance. The hydraulic buffer is located within the cradle whilst the hydro-pneumatic recuperator is supported above the barrel.

The box trail carriage is provided with sprung suspension and the wheels have solid rubber tyres.

The time taken to excavate the ground and lay the platform is about three to four hours. About one and a half hours is required to mount the equipment on the platform.

The equipment is transported in three loads, the gun on a barrel transporter, the carriage on its own wheels, and the platform on a special type transporter.

2. Data : L/50 Gun.

	Metric	British
Muzzle Velocity	875 m/s	2870 fs
Maximum Range	34,000 metres	37,185 yds
Muzzle Energy	4736 t/m	
Calibre	209.3 mm	8.25 ins
Length of Piece (50 Calibres)	10500 mm	34.9 ft.
Weight of Standard Projectile (HE)	120 kg	264 lbs
Traverse	360°	
Elevation	-4° +45°	
Recoil (Variable)	1800 to 1200 mm	71" to 47"
Height of trunnions	2250 mm	7 ft. 5 ins.
Track width	2400 mm	7 ft. 10 ins
Diameter of rear wheels	1600 mm	5 ft. 3 ins
Diameter of front wheels	1050 mm	3 ft. 5 ins
Weight in Action without platform	24600 kg	24 tons
Weight of platform	10500 kg	10 tons
No. of loads	3	
Weight of each load (approx)	15000 kg	14.8 tons
Time into action (less platform)	30 minutes	
Time to emplace platform	3.4 hours	
Time to mount on platform	1.5 hours	

3. Ammunition

HE shells with percussion fuze, and AP and Semi-AP projectiles with delay action base fuze are used.

The filling in each case is TNT.

The cartridge case is separate and there are three charges.

Weight of the projectile HE 21 cm Gr 38	120 kg	264 lbs
Weight of filling HE Shell	9 kg	19.8 lbs
Weight of AP/HE Shell	3 kg	6.6 lbs
Weight of Semi AP Shell	6 kg	13.2 lbs
Weight of cartridge case with maximum charge	62 kg	136.4 lbs

ii. 21 cm Kanone 38 (21 cm K.38) (8.3 in. Gun Model 38) (See Fig. 112, 113 and 114.)

1. Two 21 cm guns were used by the German Army; the 21 cm K.39, designed by Skoda for a Turkish order, and the 21 cm K.38. The latter was a much better equipment and was designed by Krupp to an order of the German High Command in 1938, who required 15 equipments by 1940. About 7 equipments had been produced by 1943 and one sent to Japan. Production was then discontinued.

/The equipment

The equipment is of dual recoil design being a further development of the carriage used with the 21 cm Mörser 18 and the 17 cm K. The same team of Krupp designers produced the designs.

The equipment can really be termed as of unique design, in that by making use of sloped surfaces on the under surface fore and rear of the mounting and moving the front and rear transporter towards each other under the mounting, the latter was raised from the ground on to the transporters without the aid of a crane. Conversely with the equipment in the travelling position, the mounting is lowered to the ground by moving the transporters away from each other. The movements of the transporters could be effected manually with the aid of winch handles and rack gear on the mounting or by means of hawsers and the motive power of the towing vehicle.

The dual recoil arrangement is most interesting, in that in addition to the normal gun recoil, the whole of the mounting recoils with the exception of a circular firing platform and crosshead mounting support and the spade plate and its crosshead trail supporting bracket. Ground recoil of the firing platform is prevented by four ground picket plate hold-fasts, which are connected to the periphery of the firing platform by wire ropes laid out radially from the latter.

The firing platform crosshead mounting supporting bracket is supported on the platform by a centre pivot and three jacks with castor wheels. The latter travel around the circular pathway on the platform in a manner similar to those of the 21 cm Mörser 18 and 17 cm K. Limited top traverse of 17 degrees is obtained by a traverse arc rack on the spade. If a larger traverse is required the rear jack is operated to raise the rear of the equipment clear of the ground. The whole of the superstructure is then traversed on the three jack castor wheels. If a big traverse is made the ground picket holdfasts must be adjusted accordingly. The Krupp designers were very proud of this mounting and it is considered that they had every reason to be.

The equipment travels in two loads plus a stores vehicle.

2. Data : 21 cm. K.38.

	Metric	British
Calibre	210.9 mm	8.3 ins
Length of Gun (55.5 Calibres)	11620 mm	457.5 ins
Length of barrel	11075 mm	436 ins
Length of rifling	8717 mm	343.2 ins
Chamber capacity	90.5 litres	
Rifling -		
Number of grooves		56
Depth of grooves	2.4 mm	.094 ins
Width of grooves	7.24 mm	.3 ins
Width of lands	4.6 mm	.18 ins
Type of rifling: Increasing Rt Hand Twist - 4° 29' 27" to 5° 30'		
Percussion or electric firing		Percussion
Maximum recoil - gun	900 mm	35 ins
" " - carriage	1850 mm	72.8 ins
Minimum recoil - gun	500 mm	19.7 ins
" " - carriage	1350 mm	53 ins
Traverse		17° or 360°
Rate of traverse: 1 Turn of handwheel -		3½'
Elevation		0° to 50°
Rate of elevation: 1 Turn of handwheel.		High = 30' Low 9'
Weight of Standard Projectile (HE)	120 kg	264 lbs
Firing Position Dimensions		
Overall length	14987 mm	49 ft. 2 ins
Overall width	3277 mm	10 ft. 9 ins
Overall height	2769 mm	9 ft. 1 in
Travelling Position Weight -		
Carriage and Transporters	18175 kg	18 Tons
Barrel and Transporters	16650 kg	16.4 Tons
Weight in action	25300 kg	24.9 Tons
Maximum Muzzle Velocity	905 m/s	2970 fs
Chamber Pressure	2900 Atmospheres	19 Tons sq in
Muzzle Energy	5280 m/t	
Maximum Range	33,900 metres	37,075 yds

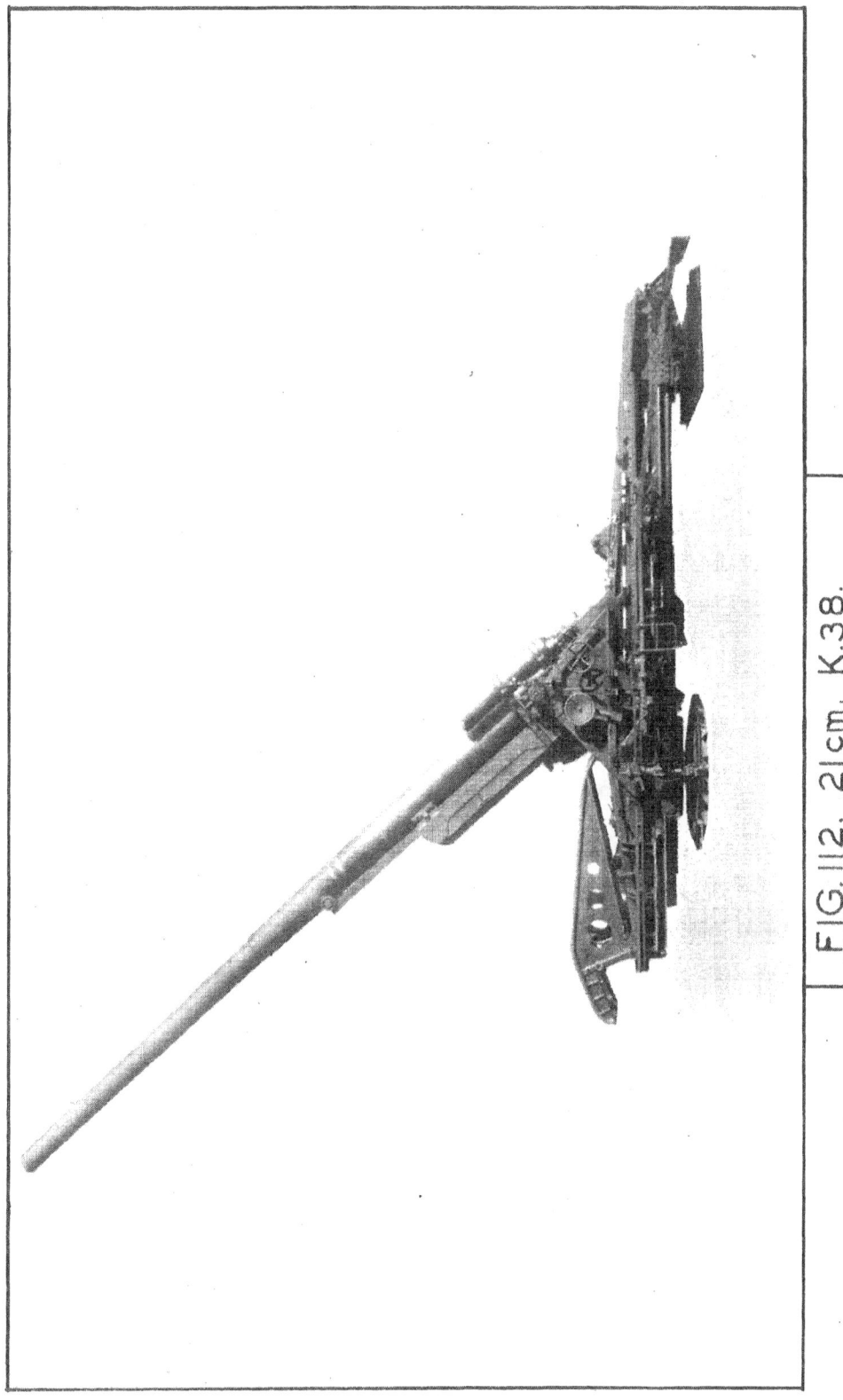

FIG. 112. 21cm. K.38.
(8·3in GUN. MODEL 38)

FIG. 113. 21cm. K.38.
(8·3in GUN. MODEL 38.)

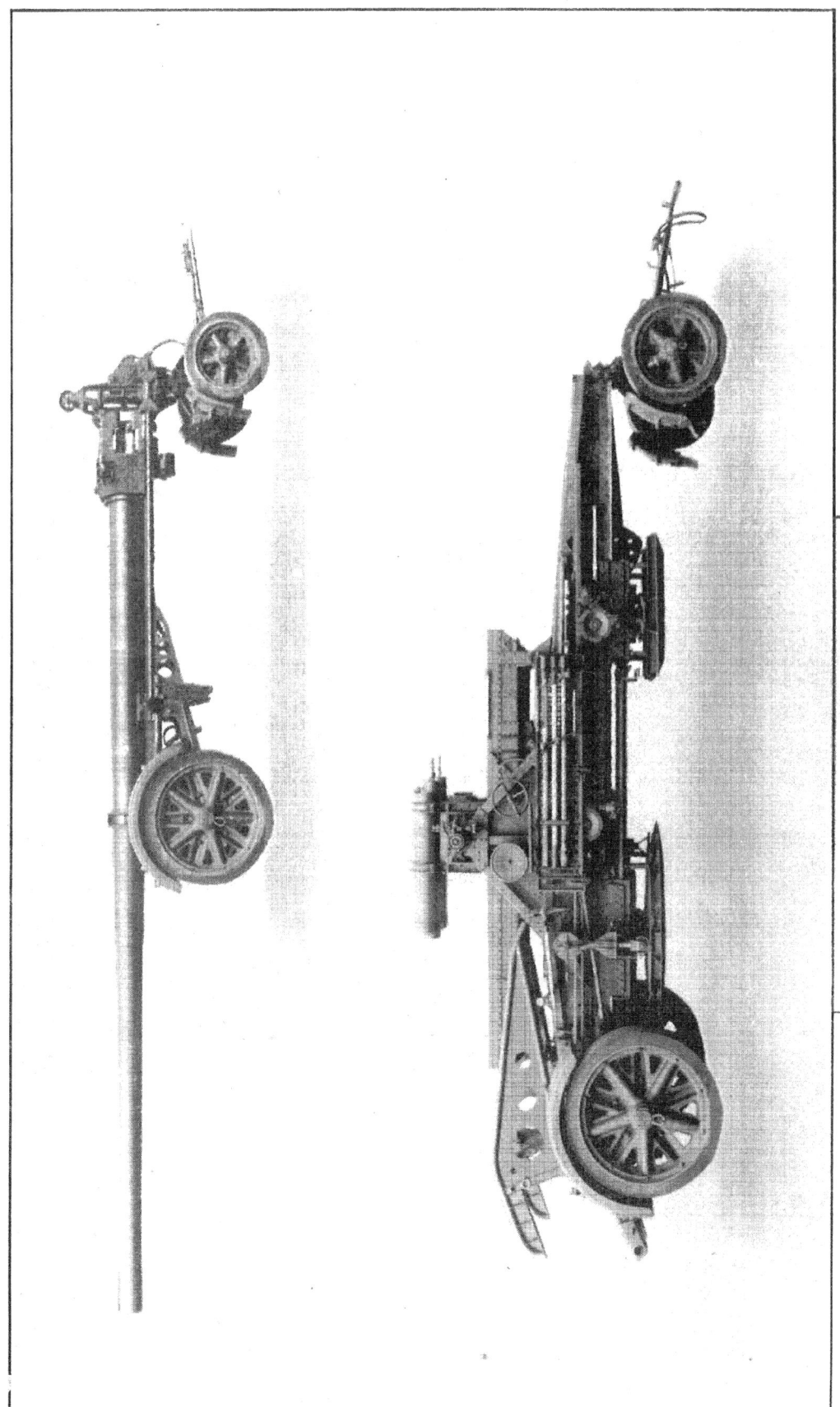

FIG. 114. 21cm. K.38.
(8·3in GUN. MODEL 38.)

3. Ammunition

   3 Charges of Digl R.P. Weights 34, 42.2 and 60.2 kg.
   Projectile - HE with Ballistic Cap - 21 cm K.Gr.38.
   Fuzes - Hbgr Z.35/3 and Dopp Z.28.K.
   Muzzle Velocity: Charge I = 680 m/s (2230 fs), Charge II = 790 m/s
   (2590 fs) Charge III = 905 m/s

N. 21 cm Kanone 39 (K.39) (8.3 inch Gun Model 39) (See Fig. 115)

1. This equipment was originally designed by Skoda for a Turkish order and a number of weapons were taken over by the German Army under the above nomenclature. Most of these equipments were used on the Russian Front early in the war.

The gun comprises an autofrettaged monobloc barrel with jacket and breech ring. The breech mechanism consists of an interrupted screw thread breech screw, obturator pad, vent axial and percussion lock. The piece recoils through a cylindrical sleeve cradle. An orthodox hydraulic buffer is located below the piece whilst the hydro-pneumatic recuperator is fitted above.

The saddle is secured to a turntable, which is supported on a ball race mounted on the firing platform. The latter consists of a rectangular box structure which is dug into the ground at the gun position. At the corners of the platform there are 4 movable arms, the ends of which bear on the ground by means of special feet. For transport these arms are lowered and serve to support the platform on its bogies. Both elevating and traversing gears have high and low speed ratio handwheels.

The gun is loaded at 8 degrees of elevation by means of a special two wheeled shell trolley.

The equipments break down into three loads for travelling viz:- Barrel, Superstructure, and lastly the platform basic structure. Each of these three are transported on a two axled bogie, the wheels of which are fitted with pneumatic tyres.

The K.39/40 is an improved model of the K.39 though the main performance details are unaltered. It is believed that twenty of these models were produced.

The K.39/41 is a further improvement over the K.39/40 but again the performance is unaltered. Experiments were carried out with this model in order to develop a muzzle brake for heavy guns. It is believed that some of these models were indeed fitted with a muzzle brake; if this is so, this is the largest German weapon to be fitted with a muzzle brake.

All three models used the same breech loading ammunition.

2. Data : 21 cm. K.39

	Metric	British
Calibre	210 mm	8.3 inch
Length of Gun (45 Calibres)	9530 mm	31.3 ft.
Rifling - Constant twist. Angle - 7°		
Elevation	$-4° + 45°$	
Traverse	360°	
Trunnion heights	2070 mm	81.5 ins
Weight of piece	10670 kg	
Weight in action	33800 kg	33.5 Tons
Weight of standard projectile	135 kg	298 lbs
No. of charges	3	
Maximum range	30,000 metres	32,800 yds
Maximum Muzzle Velocity	800 m/sec	2625 fs
Muzzle energy	4404 mt	
Time into action		6-8 hours
Weight travelling Position -		
Piece	15200 kg	
Carriage	15000 kg	
Platform	14850 kg	

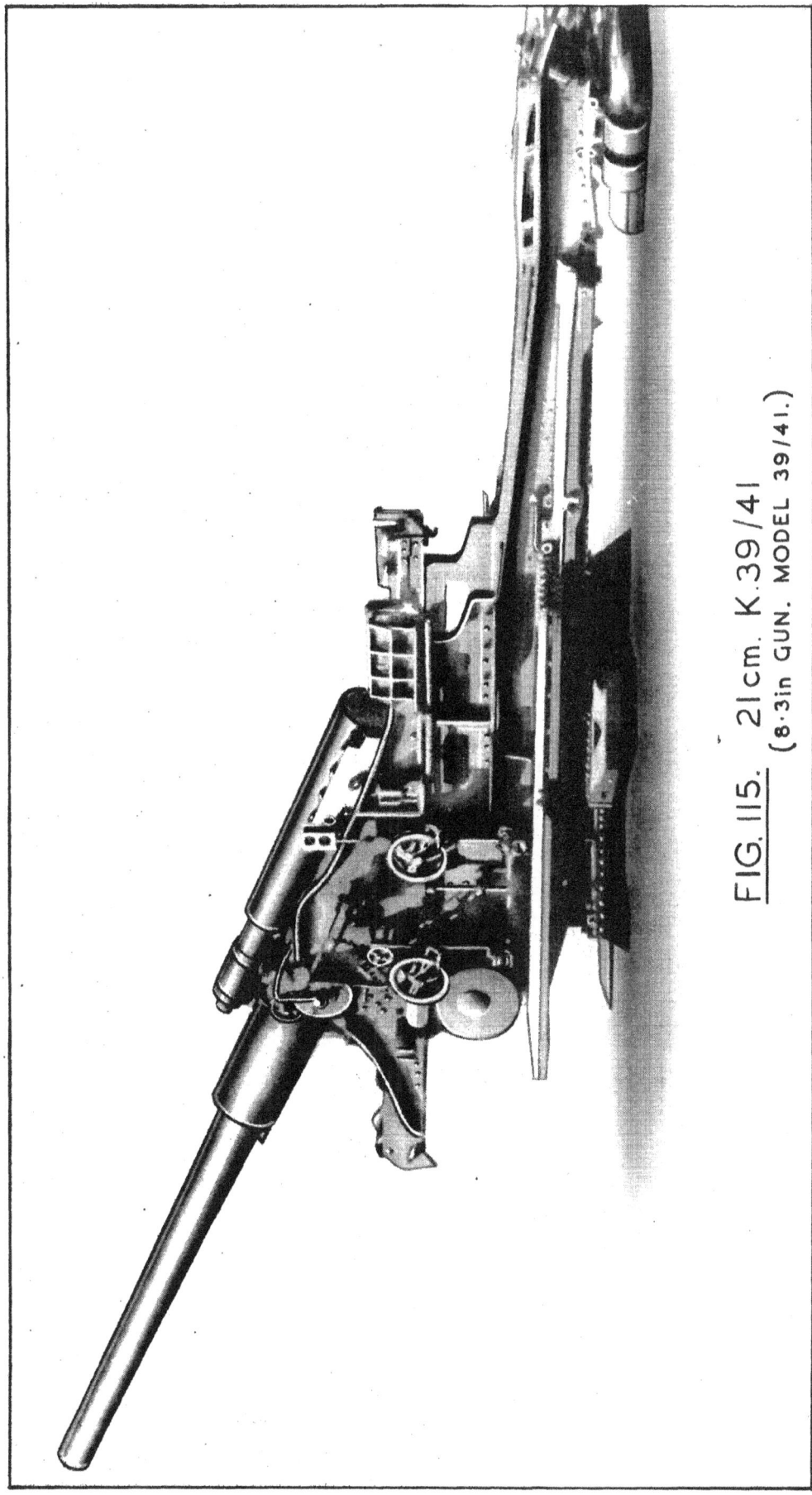

FIG. 115. 21 cm. K.39/41
(8·3in GUN. MODEL 39/41.)

	Metric	British
Wheel base of piece transporter	3600 mm	11 ft. 9¾ ins
" " " carriage transporter	4100 mm	13 ft. 5½ ins
" " " platform transporter	5100 mm	16 ft. 9 ins

3. Ammunition

(a) Shell :-

Nomenclature	Type	Weight Shell	H.E. Filling	Fuses Fitted
21 cm A.Z.Gr.39	Original Czech HE Shell	135 kg (298 lb)	18.8 kg (41.4 lb)	A.Z. SKHZR & Bd.Z.DZR.
21 cm Gr.40	German version of the Gr. 39. The base fuze is omitted.	135 kg (298 lb)	21.77 kg (48 lb)	A.Z. 35 k or Dopp.Z.S/90
21 cm Gr.39 BE (Formerly Halbpzgr)	Anti-concrete shell with ballistic cap and base fuze.	135 kg (298 lbs)	8.1 kg (17.9 lb)	Bd.Z.DVER
21 cm Pzgr 39	A.P. Shell with base fuze	135 kg (298 lb)	2.8 kg (62 lb)	

(b) Fuzes :-

A.Z. SKHZR is a Skoda D.A. and graze action nose fuze with an optional delay.
A.Z. 35k is a German D.A. and graze action nose fuze with an optional delay of (0.15) sec.
Bd.Z.DZR. is a Skoda base fuze incorporating a delay
Bd.Z.DVZR is a Skoda base fuze with optional delay.
Dopp Z.S./90 is a German mechanical time and graze action nose fuze with a maximum running time of 90 secs.

(c) Propelling Charges :-

There are three charges which are made up as follows :-

Charge I = kl.Ladung = 21.65 kg (47.6 lbs)
" II = " " + Teilkartusch 2 = 21.65 kg (60.83 lbs)
" III = " " + " 2 & 3 = 37.65 kg (82.83 lbs)

All three part charges are enclosed in art. silk bags, the kl.Ladung having a gunpowder igniter, sewn to the base.

Teilkartusch 2 = 6 kg (13 lb) Ngl.Str.P - M.38 - (3.9 x 39 x 650)
Teilkartusch 3 = 10 kg (22 lb) Ngl.Str.P - M.38 - (3.9 x 39 x 650)

The propellant is cordite in the form of strips, the dimensions in mm being given in brackets.

(d) Tube Percussion :-

A Czech percussion tube M40 or M40 St. is used.

Dimensions :-

Length	50 mm.	1.97 in.
Diameter	11 mm.	0.43 in.
Diameter over rim	14 mm.	0.55 in.

24 cm Haubitze 39 (24 cm H39) (9.45 inch Howitser Model 39) (See Fig. 116, 117, 118 and 119.).

1. In December 1938, 12 howitzers of this calibre were ordered by Turkey from Skoda.

/By July

By July 1939, only two had been delivered and a later report (November 1939) stated that the remainder had been taken over by the German Army.

The 24 cm H.39 is really a companion piece to the 21 cm Gun K.39 and the design and method of transport closely resembles the latter. The equipment is transported in three loads and comprises the gun on its transporter, the carriage or superstructure with its transporter, and finally the basic structure or box shaped platform on its transporter.

The Skoda nomenclature was Model 166/600, which is derived from the fact that the weight of projectile is 166 kg and the muzzle velocity 600 metres/sec.

It has been reported that Skoda considered this weapon to be the best heavy type equipment that they have produced.

A later model, H.39/40, had a performance similar to the H.39.

2. Data : 24 cm H.39.

	Metric	British
Calibre	240 mm	9.45 ins
Length of piece (28 calibres)	6765 mm	266.34 ins
Weight of Standard Projectile (HE)	166 kg	365 lbs
Maximum range	18000 metres	19,685 yds
Maximum muzzle velocity	600 m/sec	1670 fs
Traverse	360°	
Elevation	$-4° + 70°$	
Muzzle energy	3046 mt	
Weight in action	27000 kg	26.58 Tons
Weight in travelling position - 3 loads each approx.	13000 kg	12.8 Tons

3. Ammunition

Projectile	Fuzes	Wt of Projectile	Wt of filling
(a) HE Czech 24 cm A.Z. Gr.39	AZ.SKH.ZR or Bd.Z.DZR	166 kg (365 lbs)	23.66 kg (52.05 lbs)
(b) HE 24 cm Gr.39 ung. Service 1 modified for German fuzes.	A.Z23 ung (0.15) or Dopp. Z. S/90	166 kg (365 lbs)	22.9 kg (50.38 lbs)
(c) HE Anti-Concrete C.P. 24 cm Gr.39.Be.		166 kg (365 lbs)	10.4 kg (22.88 lbs)
(d) HE French 16 FAM.		162.3 kg (357 lbs)	81 kg (39.6 lbs)

No. of Charges = 5 - Nitroglycerine Strip Powder.

Weights -	Charge I	Charge II	Charge III	Charge IV	Charge V
	8.75 kg (19.25 lbs)	19.45 kg (42.79 lbs)	30.75 kg (67.65 kg)	41.75 kg (91.85 lbs)	52.75 kg (116 lbs)

P. 24 cm Kanone L/46 (K.L/46) (9.45 ins Gun Model L/46)

1. This equipment was introduced by Krupp in 1937, but it is believed that only a very limited number was introduced into service. In action the weapon is mounted on a radially rigged platform of similar design to that used with the 15 cm K.39.

The weapon is transported in three loads, namely - the gun and transporter, the mounting and transporter and finally the dismantled platform and transporter, and sometimes even in four loads. In the latter case the breech ring is unscrewed from the barrel and transported on a fourth transporter.

/The gun

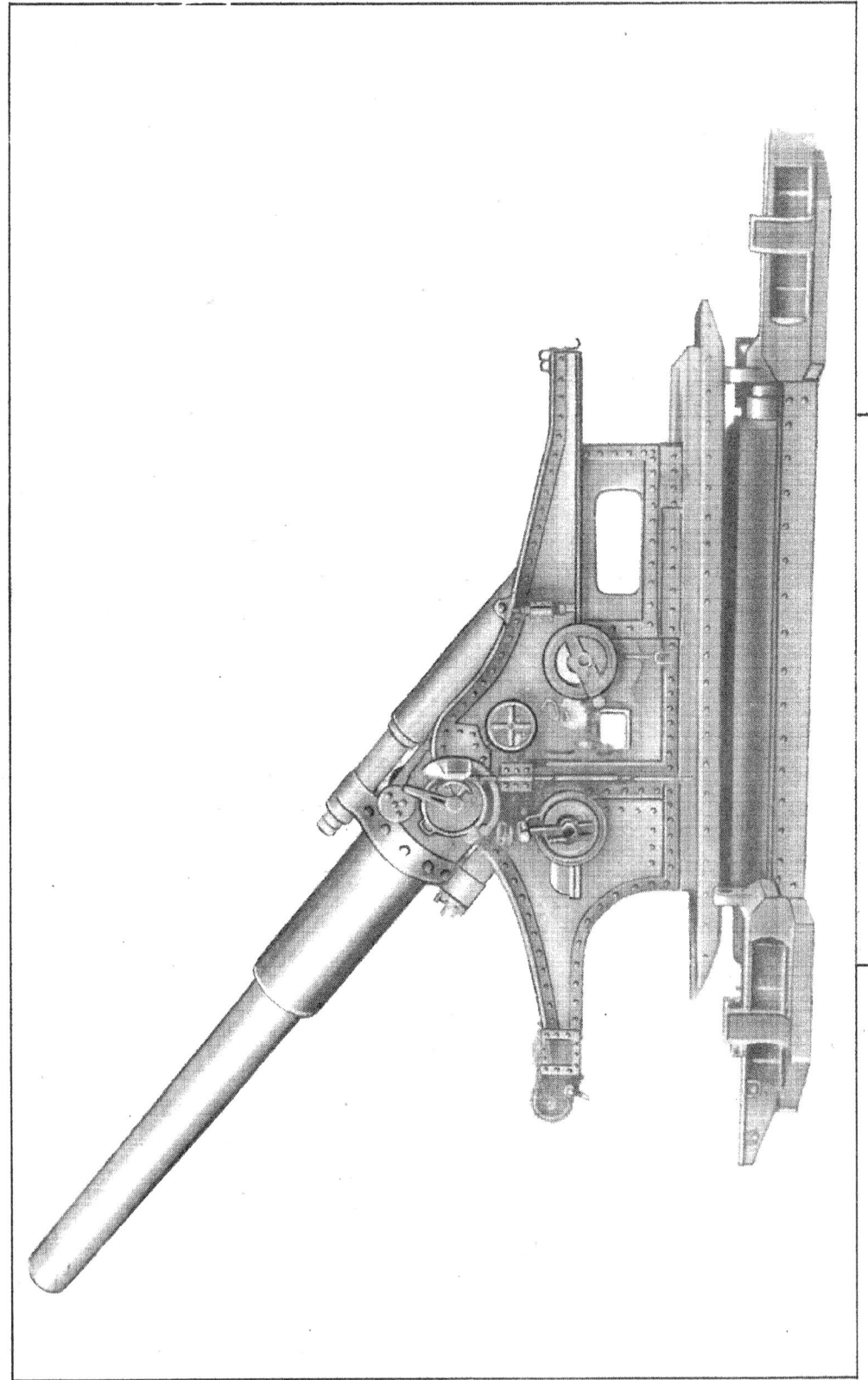

FIG. 116. 24 cm. H. 39.
(9·45 in HOWITZER. MODEL 39.)

FIG. 117. 24 cm. H.39.
(9·45 in HOWITZER. MODEL 39.)

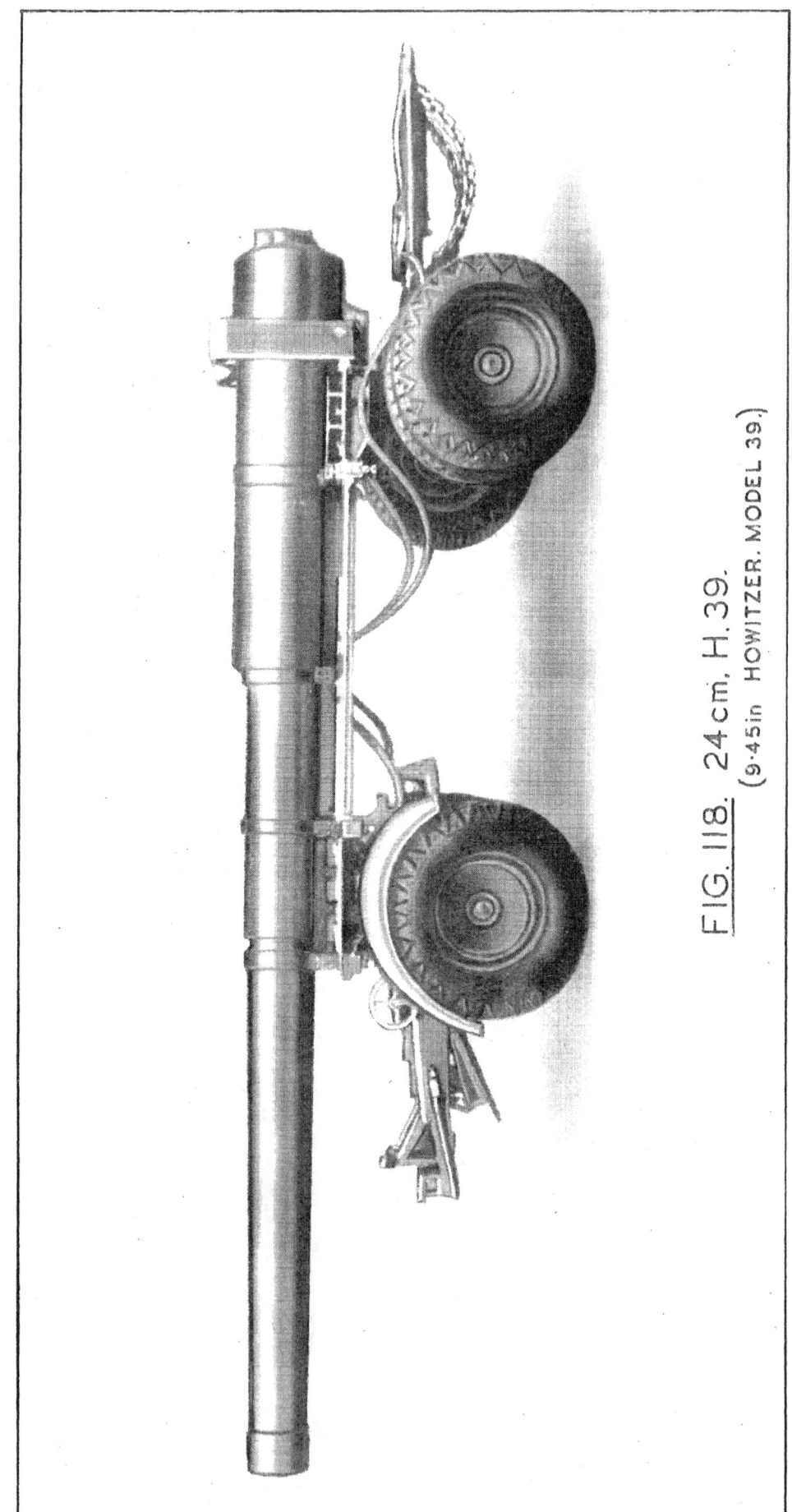

FIG. 118. 24 cm. H.39.
(9·45in HOWITZER. MODEL 39.)

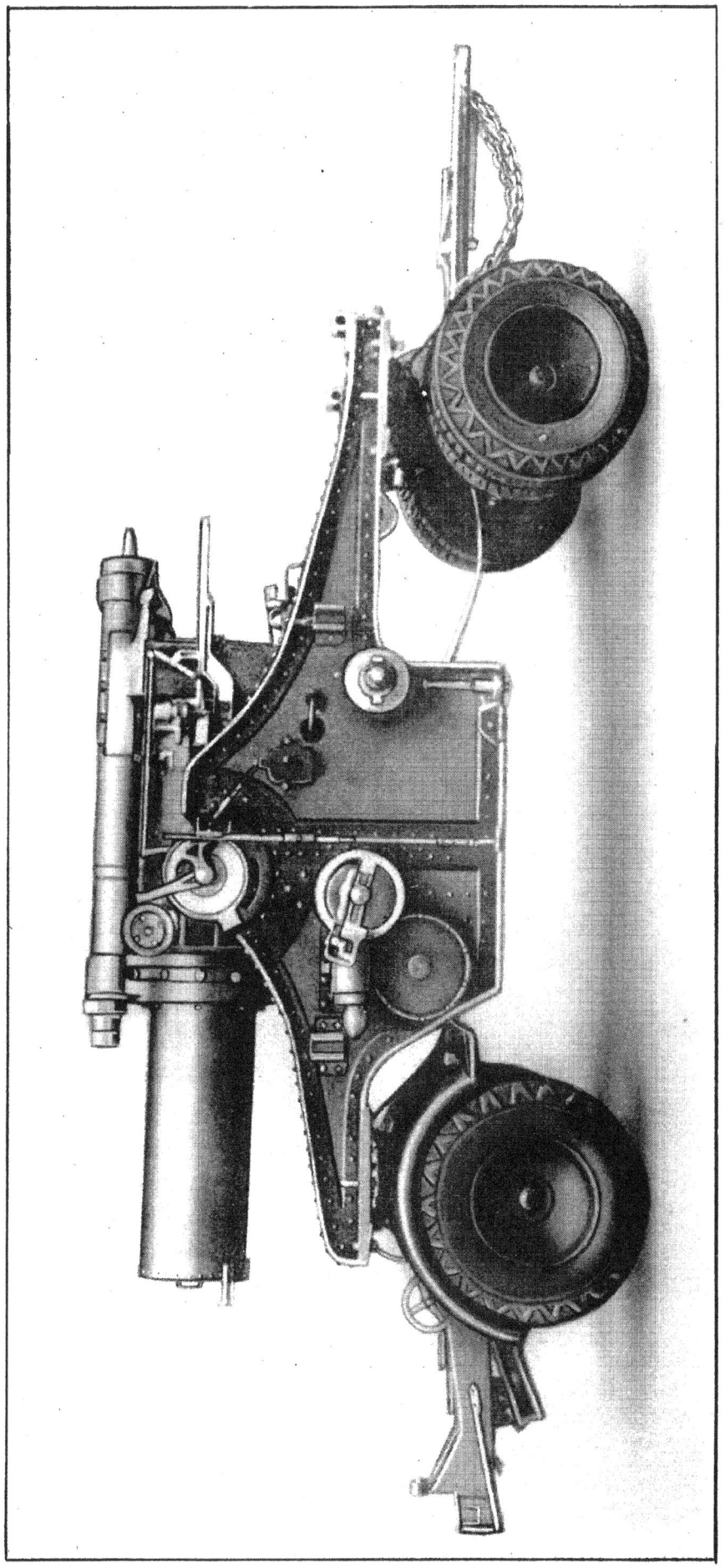

FIG. 119. 24cm. H.39/40 (9·45in HOWITZER. MODEL 39/40.)

The gun consists of a loose barrel, a jacket and a removable breech ring in which is fitted a horizontal sliding breech block opening to the right.

The mounting consists of a box type trail carriage, the suspension of which is cut out when in action. The road brakes are of the internal expanding type of usual construction.

The hydraulic buffer is located within the cradle below the barrel, whilst the hydro-pneumatic recuperator is located above. The muzzle preponderance of the weapon is compensated by means of two equilibrators.

In principle, laying is always done indirectly by means of a synchronised dial system. The firing data is passed electrically from the central fire predictor to the indicator "follow the pointer" dials on the equipment. If the system fails normal field sights are used. In order to lay the gun parallel to the zero line of the predictor the external edge of the platform is provided with a training arc.

The platform consists of a circular base plate which is put first in place. The ends of twelve outriggers placed like the spokes of a wheel, are connected with the base plate. The outer ends of these outriggers are fixed to 12 segments which together form a closed circle. The outriggers are connected with the pivot plate. The latter bears two lateral trunnions on which the carriage mounting reposes. The trail end of the carriage rests on a sprung roller, the teeth of which engage the rack recesses of the traversing circle. In order to traverse quickly the trail end is provided with a crank gear. The platform allows a total traverse of 360 degrees.

2. Data: 24 cm. L/46.

	Metric	British
Calibre (Exact 238 mm)	240 mm	9.45 ins
Length of piece (46 calibres)	10948 mm	431 ins
Muzzle Velocity - Maximum charge	850 m/s	2790 fs
Medium charge	700 m/s	2295 fs
Minimum charge	550 m/s	1805 fs
Weight of standard projectile (HE)	180 kg	396 lbs
Range at 45 Degrees - Maximum charge	32000 m	35000 yds
Medium charge	23500 m	25700 yds
Low charge	17,000 m	18,600 yds
Traverse	360°	
Elevation	-4° +45°	
Muzzle energy	6225 mt	
Trunnion height	2250 mm	88.6 ins
Length of recoil	1450 mm	57 ins
Rate of Fire	2 r.p.m.	
Time into action	2 hours	
Weight in action (without platform)	29600 kg	29.1 Tons
Platform	15600 kg	15.3 Tons
Weight in travelling position -		
Barrel and Transporter	20700 kg	20.4 Tons
Carriage Mtg and Transporter	18200 kg	18 Tons
Platform and Transporter	18300 kg	18 Tons
Lengths in travelling position -		
Barrel and Transporter	13200 mm	43 ft. 3.6 ins
Carriage Mtg and Transporter	9100 mm	29 ft. 6.3 ins
Platform and Transporter	8800 mm	28 ft. 10.4 ins
Wheel Base in travelling position -		
Barrel Transporter	4700 mm	15 ft. 5 ins
Carriage Mtg Transporter	6100 mm	20 ft. 0 ins
Platform Transporter	4700 mm	15 ft. 5 ins
Track	2400 mm	7 ft. 10.5 ins

3. Ammunition

Weight of projectile	180 kg	396 lbs
" " maximum charge	50 kg	110 lbs
" " cartridge case	76 kg	167.2 lbs

Q. **24 cm Kanone 3 (K.3). (9.45 inch Gun Model 3) (See Fig.120)**

(a) **Preface**

Development of this equipment commenced in 1935 but it was not until 1938 that it was introduced into service. The Rheinmetall Borsig design was finally accepted, but the majority of the 24 cm K.3 equipments were built up by Krupp to the Rheinmetall design. The equipment is of the dual recoil type, i.e. in addition to the orthodox gun recoil, the upper portion of the carriage mounting is allowed to recoil. In effect it is a further example of the dual recoil design as used with the 21 cm Mrs 18 and 21 cm K.38 dealt with in previous pages.

This fully mobile equipment is transported in five loads, viz:-
(1) Firing Platform, (2) Carriage and Saddle, (3) Cradle, (4) Gun, (5) Breech ring and mechanism. An electric generator set accompanies the equipment and makes a sixth load.

The weight of the equipment in draught is approx. 83 Tons and in the firing position approx. 54 Tons, the weight is fairly evenly distributed over the transporting vehicles, which are all equipped with pneumatic tyred wheels. The heaviest load is approx. 17.1/2 Tons and the lightest approx. 15 Tons.

The gun is capable of being elevated between 0° and 56° either by hand or power operation at fast or slow rates.

Traverse is by hand operation only and although this is limited to 6° (3° R. and 3° L.) on the carriage, the equipment can be readily traversed through 360° if required. This operation can be done in approx. one minute.

The main features of the equipment are :-

(i) The ratio of the weight of the recoiling mass to that of the static mass, 46 Tons and 8 Tons respectively. This is mainly achieved by the introduction of a dual recoil system, the arrangement of which is somewhat unusual.

The lower recoil system is on the firing platform on which the carriage recoils and the upper system is in the cradle in which the gun recoils. The action of the two systems is entirely reversed.

The lower system comprises one buffer and two recuperator cylinders whilst the upper system has two buffer and one recuperator cylinders. In the lower system the cylinders are withdrawn from their stationary piston rods whilst in the upper system the piston rods are withdrawn from the stationary cylinders.

(ii) The comparatively easy manner in which the gun can be elevated or depressed by hand is indicative of some special feature.

Balance is obtained by hydro-pneumatic equilibrators, the design of which is orthodox except for the introduction of a perforated steel cylinder, which, when assembled in the outer cylinder forms an annulus. This annulus is paced with a large quantity of small brass foil cylinders (approx. 18,000 and weighing 15-lbs). The action of these brass foil cylinders is obscure and without scientific investigation could not be determined, but it would appear that their primary object is an effort to obtain the desirable feature of compression and expansion of the air (or Nitrogen) content adiabatically (i.e. without loss or gain of heat).

(iii) The method of securing the breech ring to the jacket is novel. This is accomplished by means of a revolving interrupted collar inside the breech ring.

When the mating faces of the Breech ring and jacket adjoin each other the interrupted collar is revolved by means of a spindle and gear in the upper portion of the breech ring. By this means the breech ring and jacket are locked without any rotary movement of the ring in relation to the jacket.

/The top

The top front of the breech ring also contains the locking device for the buffer piston rods in the cradle. This device is automatic in as much as it unlocks the buffer piston rods from their travelling position in the cradle before locking them in their firing position in the breech ring. This action is reversed on dismantling, i.e. they are unlocked from the breech ring and then locked in their travelling position in the cradle before the breech ring can be withdrawn.

Until such time as the revolving interrupted collar and the buffer and recuperator locking nuts are secured in the fully locked position the breech block cannot be opened for loading, this is achieved by means of a stop which can only be withdrawn after correct assembly.

(iv.) The width of the saddle and carriage for an equipment of this nature is reasonably narrow. This, in some ways, is due to the construction of the breech ring which has no lugs or mechanism parts protruding from either side as every item is accommodated in recesses, so that when the breech block is closed and ready for firing they are flush with the sides of the breech ring. The width of the breech ring is thus kept to a minimum, this in turn correspondingly reduces the width of the saddle and carriage through which it recoils.

(v) The method of mounting and dismounting the equipment in its selected firing position is ingenious. Cranes are not provided and the various loads are assembled in their respective positions by means of trolleys on inclined ramps after their transporting vehicles have been got into position behind the carriage with runways, bridging rails etc.

The necessary power for these operations is provided by :-

(a) Towing vehicles when sufficient space is available.

(b) Power or hand operated winch gear when sufficient space is not available for the towing vehicles.

The means to assemble or dismount the equipment in its firing position in the shortest possible time and with the least physical effort by the gun detachment must have received particular attention from its designers and in this respect they have succeeded very well. Safety devices are provided to prevent any of the loads accidentally running back on the ramps in the event of a failure of the towing or winching cables.

The equipment was erected and dismounted without difficulty in a very limited space in this country, by personnel who had no previous experience with the equipment.

The work of mounting and dismounting was not continuous, therefore the time taken has no relationship to the time a trained detachment under favourable conditions would take to do the job.

Two telescopic hydraulic jacks on the platform and a traversing lock with a limited amount of movement play an important part in the erection of the equipment.

The extent to which the designers have gone to simplify and make things as easy as possible for the gun detachment might be emphasised by a short reference to the holding down pickets for the firing platform. The design of the picket is such as to render it readily adaptable to a picket driver in the form of a falling weight. In addition to the picket driver a means of withdrawing the pickets is also provided. This picket extractor has telescopic legs for easy adjustment, and although hand operated it is capable of exerting a pull of 15 Tons to withdraw the picket with very little effort by the operator.

(b) General

The QF gun comprises a barrel, jacket with sealing collar and a breech ring with a horizontal sliding block opening to the right and designed for percussion firing.

/The complete

The complete absence of any projection from any side of the breech ring is a noteworthy feature.

The cradle is of the sleeve type with recoil system block. The latter is bored out to take the various cylinders of the buffer and recuperator, which control the gun recoil. Towards the rear of the block, and on the right and left sides, are connected the trunnions. The twin elevating arc segments of the elevating gear are connected to the lower face of the block.

There are no outstanding features of design in the saddle. A well on the underface of the saddle receives the upper portion of the centre pivot assembly.

The carriage is of the box short trail type in the centre of the forward portion of which is located the centre pivot assembly. The latter, in connection with stops, permits of limited top traverse between saddle and carriage.

The firing platform consists of a rectangular base plate, at the centre of which is a circular ball race and centre pivot, together with a lower non recoiling framework, which can traverse on the ball race, and an upper framework containing the carriage recoil system. The upper framework, with the carriage, recoils over the slides on the upper surface of the lower frame work. The base plate is secured to the ground by means of ground pickets.

The rear of the carriage is supported on a wheeled trolley which, during recoil travels over the rear spade plate. The latter is secured to the lower framework of the firing platform by means of two longitudinal tie rods.

In addition to the weapon described here, a barrel having 8 grooved rifling and using pre-rifled projectiles was also in service in very limited numbers. The ballistic performance of this equipment was very similar to that of the weapon of 64 grooved rifling, the data sheet of which follows :-

2. Data: 24 cm. K.3.

	Metric	British
Calibre	240 mm	9.386 ins
Length of Gun (55 Cals)	13102 mm	515.85 ins
Length of barrel	12480 mm	491.3 ins
Length of rifling	10177 mm	400.6 ins
Rifling -		
Number of grooves	64	
Depth of grooves	2.05 mm	.080 ins
Width of grooves	6.5 mm	.250 ins
Width of lands	5.45 mm	.214 ins
Type of rifling : P.S.S. Constant twist 1 in 30.		
Percussion or electric firing		Percussion
Maximum recoil - Gun	1000 mm	3 ft. 3¾ ins
" " - Carriage	1240 mm	4 ft. 0¾ ins
Weight of Recoiling Mass - Gun	22515 kg	22.16 Tons
" " " " - Carriage	46951 kg	46.21 Tons
Traverse : Limited Top Traverse = 6°		360°
Rate of traverse : 10 Turns of handwheel		1°
Elevation		0° to 56°
Elevation of gun for loading		4.5°
Rate of elevation : 5 Turns of handwheel		1°
Rate of Fire		1 r. per 4 minutes.
Time into action with detachment of 25 men.		1 to 1½ hours
Travelling Position - 5 Transporters.		
Overall lengths	7774 to 13600 mm	25 ft.6 ins to 44 ft.7 ins.
Overall widths	2846 mm	9 ft. 4 ins
Overall heights	1830 to 3050 mm	6 ft. to 10 ft.
Ground clearance	280 to 420 mm	11 ins to 16.5 ins.

/Firing

	Metric	British
Firing Position –		
Overall length	17200 mm	56 ft. 5 ins
Overall width	2874 mm	9 ft. 5 ins
Overall height	3175 mm	12 ft. 5 ins
Travelling Position Weight Total for 6 loads	84636 kg	83 Tons 6 cwts 2 qrs.
Weight in action	54866 kg	54 Tons
Maximum Muzzle Velocity	970 m3S	3182 fs
Maximum Range	37,500 m	41,000 yds
Weight of Standard Projectile (HE)	151.4 kg	333.1 lbs
Standard Projectile HE – 24 Cm Gr.35	Fuze Percussion A.Z.35.K.	
No. of charges	2	

2. TRANSPORTING VEHICLES – WEIGHTS AND DIMENSIONS

(a) **Breech ring**

	TONS	CWTS	QRS.	LBS.
Breech ring	10	4	2	10
Lifting beam tackle		1	0	19
Transporter with trolley	5	12	2	27
Weight in draft	15	18	2	0

Length over towing bar	25' – 6"
Width overall	9' – 4"
Height overall	7' – 3"
Ground clearance	1' – 4"

(b) **Barrel**

	TONS	CWTS	QRS.	LBS.
Barrel	11	12	3	11
Breech end clamp		4	2	2
Muzzle end clamp		3	3	21
Transporter	4	14	9	10
Weight in draft	16	15	1	16

Length over towing bar	44' – 7"
Width overall	9' – 4"
Height overall	6' – 0"
Ground clearance	1' – 4½"

(c) **Cradle**

	TONS	CWTS	QRS.	LBS.
Cradle	6	18	0	0
Transporter with trolley	6	10	0	22
Ramp equipment etc		16	3	24
Weight in draft	14	5	0	18

Length over towing bar	29' – 9"
Width overall	9' – 4"
Height overall	9' – 9½"
Ground clearance	1' – 1"

(d) **Carriage and Saddle**

	TONS	CWTS	QRS.	LBS.
Carriage	9	19	1	10
Saddle	6	15	0	21
Forward limber	1	5	1	3
Weight in draft	17	19	3	6

Length over towing bar	30' – 8"
Width overall	9' – 4"
Height overall	10' – 0"
Ground clearance	11"

		TONS	CWTS	QRS.	LBS.
(e)	Firing Platform				
	Platform	8	7	3	13
	Ramps, pickets etc	2	4	2	16
	Transporter	5	17	3	19
	Weight in draft	16	10	1	20

Length over towing bar ...... 31' – 0"
Width overall ...... 9' – 4"
Height overall ...... 7' – 8"
Ground clearance ...... 1' – 2½"

		TONS	CWTS	QRS.	LBS.
(f)	The Generator Set				
	Weight in draft	1	17	1	12

Length over towing bar ...... 12' – 4"
Width overall ...... 6' – 3"
Height overall ...... 5' – 9½"
Ground clearance ...... – 11"

4. **TOTAL WEIGHT IN DRAFT**

		TONS	CWTS	QRS.	LBS.
a.	Breech Ring	15	18	2	0
b.	Barrel	16	15	1	16
c.	Cradle	14	5	0	18
d.	Carriage & saddle	17	19	3	6
e.	Firing platform	16	10	1	20
f.	Generator Set	1	17	1	12
	TOTAL	83	6	2	16

5. **EQUIPMENT WEIGHTS**

	Tons	Cwts	Qrs.	Lbs.
Breech Ring	10	4	2	10
Barrel	11	12	3	11
Complete gun	21	17	1	21
Cradle	6	18	0	0
Saddle	6	16	1	10
Carriage	10	0	1	26
Firing platform	8	7	3	13
Equipment complete.	54	0	0	14

	TONS	CWTS	QRS.	LBS.
Gun recoiling mass	22	3	1	0
Carriage recoiling mass	46	4	1	3
Carriage stationary mass	7	15	3	11
Recoiling weight on firing platform	41	14	0	0
Recoiling weight on back plate	4	10	1	3
Ground load – firing platform	47	2	3	14
Ground load – Back plate	6	17	1	0
Weight for Top 6° limit traverse	35	11	3	3
Weight for bottom 360° traverse	49	1	3	1

/R. 24 cm

FIG. 120. 24 cm. K.3
(9·45 in GUN. MODEL 3.)

R. **24 cm Kanone 4 (24 cm K4) (9.45 inch Gun Model 4)**

1. The K3 equipment was soon considered to be unsatisfactory owing to the changed tactical requirements for super-heavy equipments. The method of transport was slow and cumbersome and considerably more range was required for this calibre: an experimental gun was then made with muzzle squeeze attachment and an emergent calibre of 21 cm. This gun fired an 82 kg (180.4 lbs) projectile with a muzzle velocity of over 1100 m/sec (3608 fs) and reached approximately 50 km (54,700 yards) range, but it was decided to produce an entirely redesigned equipment, the K4.

The requirements were for a range of 48/49 km (52,500/53,600 yards) with a 160 kg (352 lbs) projectile and greatly increased mobility. Both Rheinmetall Borsig and Krupp produced designs and worked on the same lines since the Ordnance Dept. specifications were for transport (a) in two loads, (b) as a single unit. No final decision was reached as to which was the better equipment, but one experimental model was in course of construction at Krupp (Essen), but work was stopped owing to bombing.

The Krupp Model K4, into which design Krupp put much thought because they wished it to rival the Rheinmetall K3, was produced as a two load equipment. It was also proposed to put this weapon on a tracked chassis for one load transport.

2. Data : 24 cm. K.4.

	Metric	British
Calibre	240 mm	9.45 ins
Length of gun (72 calibres)	17280 mm	680.3 ins
Traverse	16° and 360°	
Elevation	0° to 55°	
Muzzle Velocity	1100 m/s	3608 fs
Maximum Range	49000 metres	53600 yds
Wt. of Standard Projectile	160 kg	352 lbs
Wt. in action	55000 kg	54.13 tons
Weight in Travelling Position -		
Gun and Transporter	24,500 kg	24.11 Tons
Carriage	41,000 kg	40.13 Tons

S. **28 cm Haubitze L/12 (11.02 inch Howitzer L/12) (See Fig.121)**

1. This howitzer which used breech loading charge ammunition is of old design and believed obsolete. A few equipments were still being used during the recent war, but they were normally used in a static position owing to the length of time required to emplace the equipment.

2. Data : 28 cm. H. L/12.

	Metric	British
Calibre	283 mm	11.14 ins
Length of Piece (12 Calibres)	3396 mm	133.7 ins
No. of charges	7	
Weight of Standard Projectile	350 kg	770 lbs
Weight of full charge	16.9 or 17.3 kg. Depending upon powder. (37.2 or 38 lbs.)	
Muzzle Velocity	350 m/s	1148 fs
Maximum Range	10400 metres	11370 yds
Weight in action	50,300 kg	49.5 Tons
Time in action	3 to 4 days	
HE Projectile used	28 cm Sprgr L/3.5 m Bdz. Fuze Bd.Zf.Sprgr mk (f 28 cm H).	

T. **28 cm Küsten Haubitze (11.02 inch Coastal Defence Howitzer). (See fig. 122).**

1. This equipment is somewhat similar to the L/12 equipment but of lighter construction. The same type projectile is used, but a QF cartridge case is used with the Küsten Haubitze.

/2. Data

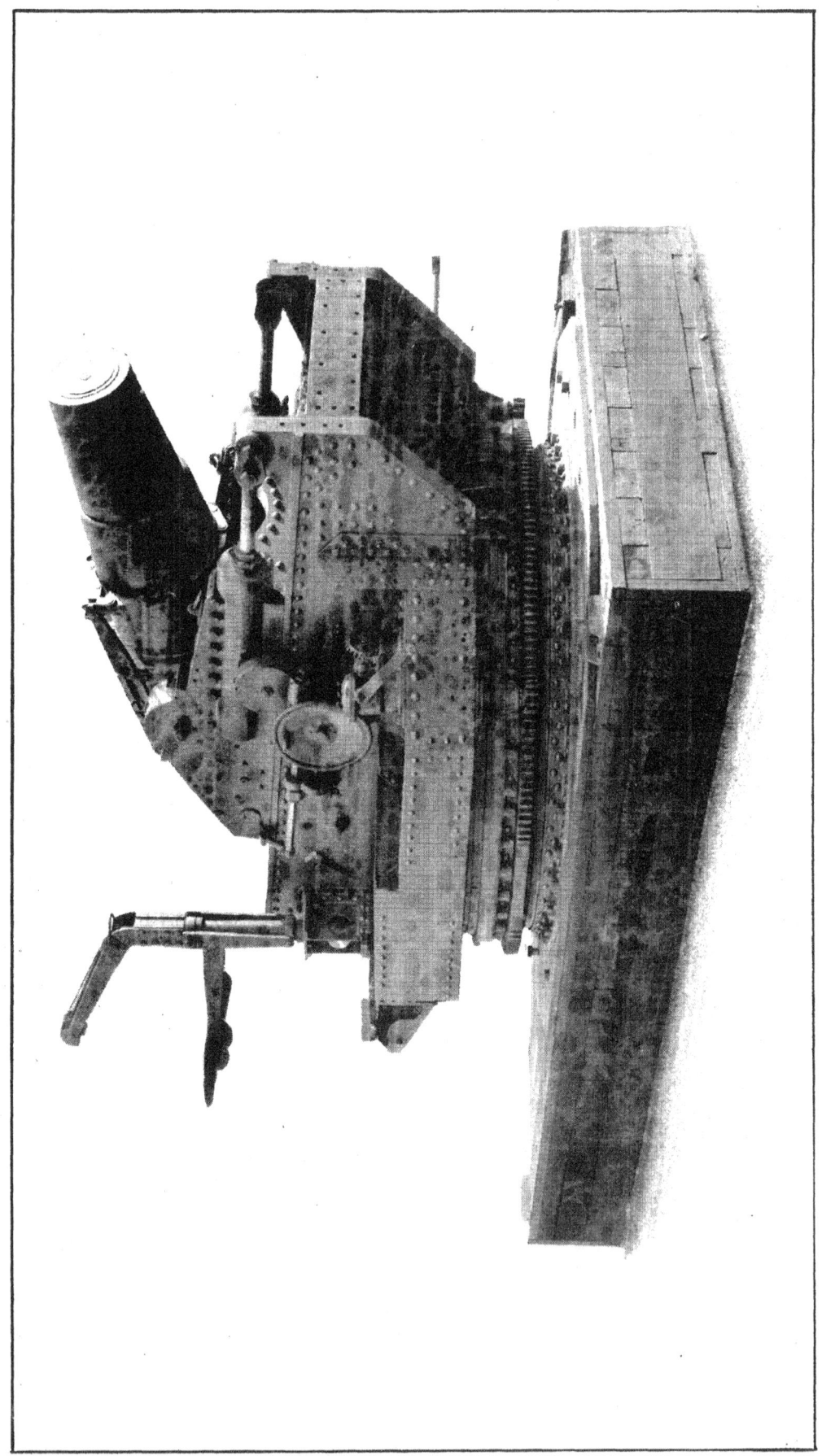

FIG. 121. 28 cm. H. L/12 (11 in HOWITZER. MODEL L/12.)

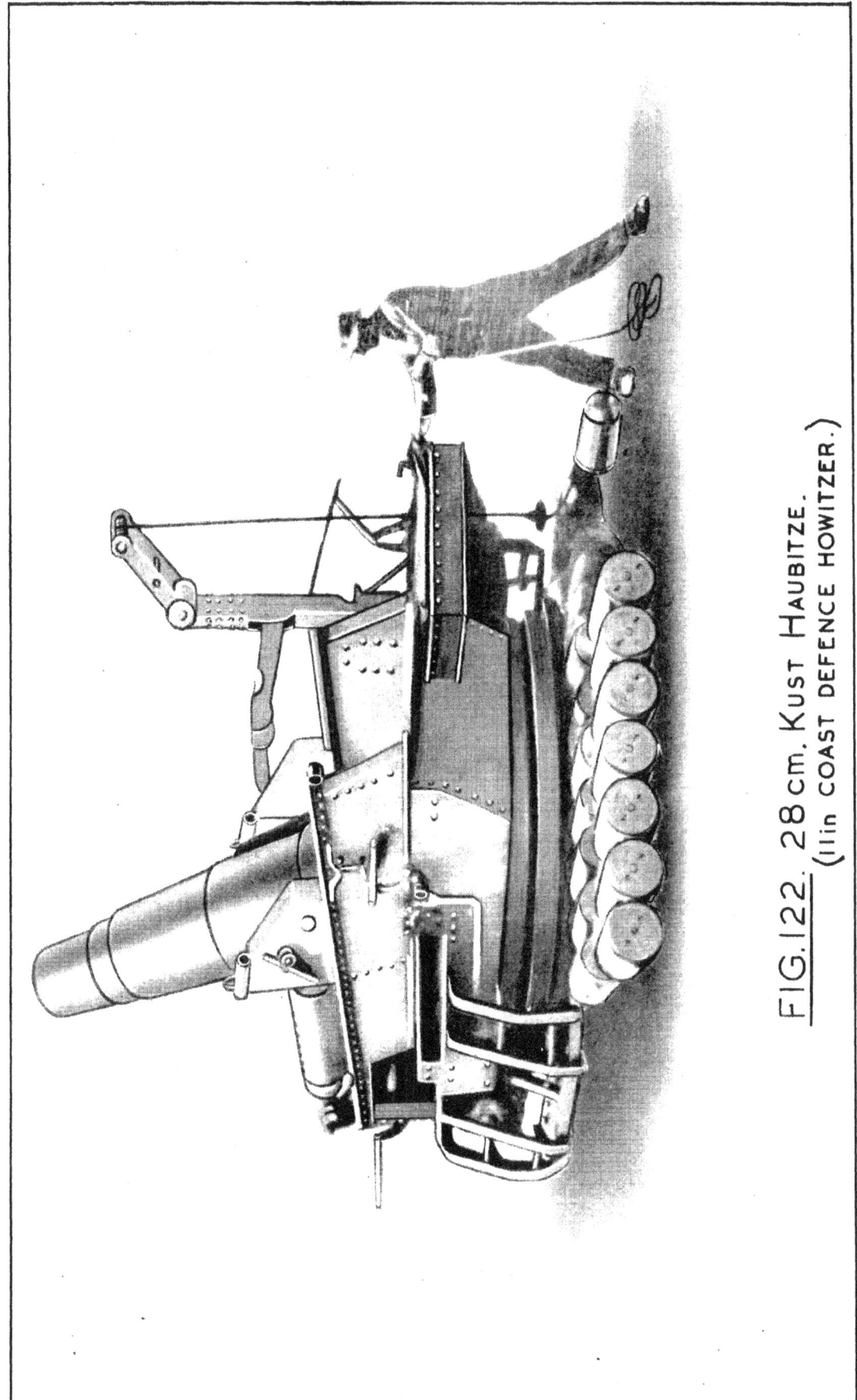

FIG. 122. 28 cm. KUST HAUBITZE.
(11in COAST DEFENCE HOWITZER.)

2. Data : 28 cm. Kst.H.   Metric   British

    Calibre   283 mm   11.14 ins
    No. of charges   6
    Weight of standard projectile   350 kg   770 lbs
    Weight of full charge   17.0 or 20.8 kg   37.4 or 45.76 lbs.
    Muzzle Velocity   379 m/s   1243 fs
    Maximum Range   11,400 metres   12,470 yds
    Weight in Action   37,000 kg   36.5 Tons
    Time in Action   3 to 4 days
    HE Projectile used   28 cm Sprgr L/3.5 n Bdz.
                                             Fuze Bd.Z.f.Sprgr mk (f 28 cm H)

35.5 cm Haubitze M.1 (14 inch Howitzer Model M.1.)

1. This heavy howitzer, first developed by Rheinmetall Borsig in 1936 for the German High Command, was introduced into service in 1939. The design of the howitzer conforms to modern German practice, the carriage being based on a double recoil system. A two point mounting is used with provision for lifting the rear platform so that the equipment can be traversed through 360 degrees. In general it can be said that the howitzer embodies the same principle, transferred to the super-heavy class, as were first observed in the 21 cm Mrs. 18 and further developed in the 21 cm K.38 and the 24 cm K.3.

The weapon is transported in 6 parts, each of which is carried on a 6 wheeled trailer fitted with pneumatic tyres. The gantry makes up a seventh load and all seven loads are towed by 18 ton semi-tracked tractors.

The six loads are as follows:-

    The Piece.   Cradle.   Upper Carriage.
    Lower Carriage.   Front base plate.   Rear base plate.

To assemble the weapon, the travelling gantry carried on the seventh trailer is erected and used to unload the parts from the tractors and assemble them. The gantry is electrically operated.

The barrel consists of the barrel and a short shrunk-on jacket. The outside of the jacket at its lowest face forms the recoil slide. The removable breech ring is of rectangular shape and is fitted with a horizontal sliding breech block opening to the right.

The cradle is of the sleeve type formed in a block which also houses the recoil system. To this block is secured the rear trunnions and to its under face the single elevating arc.

The upper and lower carriages are each construced in the form of a rectangular steel box without top or bottom. The two are held together by clamps at the four corners.

The front base plate has a traverse turntable recessed into its centre. The turntable is supported on a spring loaded roller race. Fixed to the top of the turntable is the crosshead supporting bracket with recoil slides. The base plate is secured to the ground by ground pickets. A second recoil slideway is mounted on the rear base plate. When in action the two base plates are connected together by longitudinal tie rods.

The carriage recoils on the two slideways mounted on the base plates controlled by two buffers and one recuperator. The three cylinders of the carriage recoil system are housed in the carriage slider above the front main base plate, their piston rods being secured to a block fixed to the front of the slideway. Clip plates prevent the recoiling carriage lifting away from the slideways during firing. Limited top traverse is applied by traversing gear which moves the rear of the carriage over the rear base plate. To obtain larger traverse up to 360°, the rear of the equipment is raised clear of the ground by a power operated jack.

The elevating gear has both high and low ratio gear for manual operation and also provision for power operation. Two hydro-pneumatic equilibrators are provided to compensate for muzzle preponderance.

/The upper

The upper carriage is platformed for the gun detachment and ammunition trolley and power hoists are provided.

2. Data : 35.5 cm. H.M.I.

	Metric	British
Calibre	356 mm	14.02 ins
Length of piece (27 calibres)	9585 mm	377.3 ins
Length of rifling	8050 mm	316.9 ins
Rifling - No. of grooves	96	
Width of lands	4.5 mm	0.16 ins
Traverse	6° or 360°	
Elevation	45° to 75°	
Weight of standard projectile	575 kg	1267½ lbs
Weight in action	75000 kg	73.8 Tons
Maximum range	20000 metres	21,875 yds
Maximum muzzle velocity	570 m/sec	1870 fs
No. of charges (QF ammunition)	4	
Type of projectile - 35.5 cm Gr.Be.(Forged steel)		
35.5 cm Gr.Be.Stg.(Cast steel).		
Time in action	2 hours	
Travelling position weight - 7 sections each approximately	17000 kg	16.75 Tons

V. **42 cm Gamma Mörser** (16.5 inch Howitzer "Gamma") (See Fig. 123).

1. This weapon was a product of the 1914/1918 war, in fact designs were begun by Krupp in 1906. Altogether, according to the Krupp records, 10 complete equipments with 18 barrels were produced. A number of components escaped destruction following the 1918 Armistice and it was found to be possible in 1936/37 to reconstruct one equipment which was assembled at Meppen Firing Ranges and was used for experiments and trials in connection with the attack on concrete fortifications.

The howitzer has a **barrel** 16 calibres long of jacket and tube built up construction. The trunnions are at the centre of gravity of the piece.

The recoil system consists of two hydraulic buffers above the piece and a hydro-pneumatic recuperator below.

The whole equipment weighs 140 metric tons (137.8 tons) in action and was transported on ten railway "flat" wagons.

2. Data: 42 cm. Mrs.

	Metric	British
Calibre	420 mm	16.535 ins
Length of piece (16 calibres)	6720 mm	
Traverse	46°	
Elevation	+ 43° to 75°	
Weight of projectile	1020 kg	2249 lbs
Muzzle velocity	452 m/s	1483 fs
Maximum range	14,200 metres	15,530 yds
Rate of fire	Approx. 8 rounds per hour.	
Weight in action	140,000 kg	137.8 Tons
Time into action	1½ to 2½ days.	
Type of standard projectile -		

Anti-Concrete SAP/HE - 42 cm S Gr. Be.

FIG. 123. 42 cm. GAMMA MÖRSER. (16·5 in "GAMMA" HOWITZER.)

Appendix A.

DATA FOR GERMAN ARTILLERY EQUIPMENTS

Standard A.Tk Guns

	Calibre in ins.	Length of ordnance in ins.	Length of rifling in ins.	No. of grooves	Recoil in ins.	Traverse	Elevation	Overall dimensions in draught - Length	Overall dimensions in draught - Width	Overall dimensions in draught - Height	Weight complete in lbs in draught	Wt. of proj.	M.V. in f/s	Penetration performance - Range x/ penetration in mm at 30°
2.8 cm S Pz B 41	1.1/.787	67.5	50	12	normal 9.49 max 11.02	60° at 0°-90° at 45°-30°	-5° to 45°	8 ft 10 in	3 ft 2 in	2 ft 9 in	505	4¼ ozs	4599	100x/69 300x/50 600x/48 800x/41
3.7 cm Pak	1.46	65.5	51.19	16	22.05	60°	25°	11 ft 2 in	5 ft 5 in	3 ft10 in	952	12¼ ozs	3378	100x/66 200x/61 300x/55 400x/49
4.2 cm le Pak 41	1.65/1.18	88.6	66.93	12		41°	15°	13 ft	5 ft 5¼ in	3 ft11½ in	992	11¾ ozs	4149	250x/83 500x/72 750x/62 1000x/53
5 cm Pak 38	1.97	124.96	93.75	20	normal 27.56 max 28.74	65°	-8° to 27°	15ft 7 in	6 ft 0¼ in	3 ft 7¼ in	2174	2 lb 2¼ oz	3930	250x/109 500x/86 750x/69 1000x/55
7.5 cm Pak 40	2.95	145.67	96.85	32	normal 34.06 max 35.43	65°	-5° to 22°	20 ft 3¼ in	6 ft 10 in	4 ft 1 in	3306	7 lbs	3060	500x/115 1000x/96 1500x/80 2000x/66
7.5 cm Pak 41	1.95/2.17	170.08	94.88	28	normal 26.61 max 32.99	60°	16° 45'	24 ft 7 in	6 ft 3 in	5 ft 11in	2988	5 lb. 7¼ oz	3969	500x/171 1000x/145 1500x/122 2000x/102

Appendix A (contd.). -254-

	Calibre in ins	Length of ordnance in ins	Length of rifling in ins.	No. of grooves	Recoil in ins	Traverse	Elevation	Length	Width	Height	Weight complete in lbs in draught	Wt. of proj.	M.V. in f/s	Range x/penetration in mm at 30°
7.62 cm Pak 36	3	164.56	115.32	32	normal 35.43 max 39.37	60°	-6° to 25°	24 ft	6 ft 6½in	4 ft 7 in	3770	8 lb. 14½ozs.	3249	500x/113 1000x/92 1500x/71 2000x/55
8.8 cm Pak 43/41	3.46	260.23	201.75	32	normal 26.77 max 28.35	56°	-5° to 38°	30 ft 1in	8 ft 3½in	5 ft 8 in	9656	16 lb. 1½ oz.	3708	500x/226 1000x/192 1500x/162 2000x/136
12.8 cm Pak K 44	5.047	260.7	217.95	40	normal 35 max 51.5	360°	-8° to 45°	35 ft 9in	8 ft 1½in	7 ft 1 in	22400	62.4 lbs.	3018	1094x/202
8.8 cm Pak 43	3.46	260.23	201.75	32	normal 29.5 max 47.25	360°	-8° to 40°	30 ft 2ins	7 ft 2½in	6 ft 9 in	11025	16 lbs 1½ozs	3708	500x/226 1000x/192 1500x/162 2000x/136

Appendix B.

DATA FOR GERMAN ARTILLERY EQUIPMENTS

INFANTRY GUNS

SERIAL	NOMENCLATURE	LENGTH OF BARREL	WEIGHT IN ACTION	WEIGHT OF STANDARD PROJECTILE	MAX. HORIZONTAL RANGE	MAX. MUZZLE VELOCITY	NO. OF CHARGES	ELEVATION	TRAVERSE (total)	REMARKS
1	7.5 cm (2.95 ins.) leichtes Infanterie Geschutz 18 (le I.G. 18)	900 m.m. 35.4 ins.	400 kgs. 881 lbs.	5.45 kgs. 12 lbs. ¼ oz.	3550 m. 3880 yds	221 m/s. 724 fps.	5	− 10° + 75°	12°	Box trail carriage. Developed by Rheinmetal in 1927. A hollow charge fixed round is fired for anti-tank work. (Wt. 3.0 Kg − max MV 330 m/s.)
2	7.5 cm (2.95 ins.) Infanterie Geschutz 37 (7.5 cm I.G.37)	1575 m.m. 62 ins.	510 kgs. 1124 lbs.	5.45 kgs. 12 lbs. ¼ oz.	5150 m. 5630 yds	280 m/s. 919 fps.	6	− 10° + 22½°	58°	Introduced in 1944. An emergency equipment using the obsolete 3.7 cm PAK carriage. Max elevation increased to 40° by digging in the trails.
3	7.5 cm (2.95 ins.) Infanterie Geschutz 42 Alter Art (7.5 cm I.G. 42 a.A.)	1500 m.m. 59 ins.	445 kgs. 981 lbs.	5.45 kgs. 12 lbs. ¼ oz.	5150 m. 5630 yds	350 m/s. 1148 fps.	6	− 6° + 24°	60°	Early prototype model by Krupp in 1940. NOT introduced for service.

-255-

/4 7.5 cm

Appendix B. (Contd.)

SERIAL	NOMENCLATURE	LENGTH OF BARREL	WEIGHT IN ACTION	WEIGHT OF STANDARD PROJECTILE	MAX. HORIZONTAL RANGE	MAX. MUZZLE VELOCITY	NO. OF CHARGES	ELEVATION	TRAVERSE (total)	REMARKS
4	7.5 cm (2.95 ins.) Infanterie Geschutz 42 (7.5 cm I.G.42)	1575 m.m. 62 ins.	?	5.45 kgs. 12 lbs. ¼ oz.	5150 m 5630 yds	280 m/s. 919 fps	6	$-6°$ $+32°$	$60°$	Standard production model. Ballistically identical with the I.G.37, but having the carriage designed also for the light smooth bore a/tk. gun 8 cm P.A.W 600.
5	15 cm (5.9 ins.) schwere Infanterie Geschutz 33 (s. I.G. 33)	1725 m.m. 67.9 ins.	1550/ 1700 kgs. 3417/ 3747 lbs.	38 kgs. 83.6 lbs.	4700 m. 5140 yds	240 m/s. 790 fps.	6	$0°$ $75°$	$12°$	Standard heavy Infantry howitzer (actual calibre is 149.1 m.m.). Also fires a muzzle stick bomb, wt 89.5 kg. to a range of 1025 m.

DATA FOR GERMAN ARTILLERY EQUIPMENTS

MOUNTAIN GUNS

SERIAL	NOMENCLATURE	LENGTH OF BARREL	WEIGHT IN ACTION	WEIGHT OF STANDARD PROJECTILE	MAX. HORIZONTAL RANGE	MAX. MUZZLE VELOCITY	NO. OF CHARGES	ELEVATION	TRAVERSE (total)	REMARKS
1	7.5 cm (2.95 ins.) leichtes Gebirgs Infantorie Geschütz 18 (le Geb. I.G. 18)	900 m.m. 35.4 ins.	435 kg. 959 lbs.	5.45 kg. 12 lbs. ¼ oz.	3550 m. 3880 yds	221 m/s 724 fps	5	-10° +73½°	35°	Introduced in 1937. Has the same piece as the standard le I.G. 18, but is fitted with a tubular split trail carriage. Breaks down into six packs or 10 man loads.
2	7.5 cm (2.95 ins.) Gebirgskanone 15 (Geb. K. 15)	800 m.m. 31.5 ins.	630 kg. 1389 lbs.	5.47 kg. 12 lbs. 1 oz.	6650 m. 7270 yds	386 m/s 1266 fps	4	-9° +50°	7°	A skoda gun. Used pending large scale production of the Geb. G.36. Breaks down into 7 pack loads - (78 - 156 kg.)
3	7.5 cm (2.95 ins.) Gebirgsgeschütz 36 (Geb. G. 36)	1500 m.m. 59 ins.	750 kg. 1653 lbs.	5.74 kg. 12 lbs. 10½ oz.	9250 m. 10115 yds	475 m/s 1558 fps	5	-2° +70°	40°	Introduced in 1938. Breaks down into 6 pack loads.
4	7.5 cm (2.95 ins.) Gebirgsgeschütz 43 (Geb. G.43)	1388 m.m. 54.6 ins.	650 kg. 1433 lbs.	5.74 kg. 12 lbs. 10½ oz.	9250 m. 10115 yds	475 m/s 1558 fps	5	-5° +70°	40°	Designed by Bohler and replaced the Model 36. It has better stability and improved break-down into 7 pack loads.
5	10.5 cm (4.13 ins.) Gebirgshaubitze 40 (Geb. H. 40)	3150 m.m. 124 ins.	1660 kg. 3659 lbs.	14.81 kg. 32 lbs. 10½ oz.	12625 m. 13800 yds	570 m/s 1870 fps	7	-85 +1244 mils	900 mils	Not designed for pack loads - but for 4 separate wheeled loads 680 to 720 kg.

Appendix C.

Appendix D.

DATA FOR GERMAN ARTILLERY EQUIPMENTS

RECOILLESS GUNS

SERIAL	NOMENCLATURE	LENGTH OF BARREL	WEIGHT IN ACTION	WEIGHT OF STANDARD PROJECTILE	MAX. HORIZONTAL RANGE	MAX. MUZZLE VELOCITY	ELEVATION	TRAVERSE (total)	REMARKS
1	7.5 cm (2.95 ins.) Leichtes Geschütz 40 (7.5 cm L.G.40)	750 m.m. 29.5 ins.	145 kg. 321 lbs.	5.83 kg. 12 lbs. 13 oz.	6800 m. 7435 yds	350 m/s 1148 fps	-15° +42°	360°	At max. elevation, traverse is limited to about 60°.
2	10.5 cm (4.13 ins.) Leichtes Geschütz 40 (10.5 cm L.G.40)	1380 m.m. 54.33 ins	388 kg. 855 lbs.	14.81 kg. 32 lbs. 10 oz.	7950 m. 8694 yds	335 m/s 1099 fps	-15° +40°	80°	
3	10.5 cm (4.13 ins.) Leichtes Geschutz 42 (10.5 cm L.G.42)	1374 m.m. 54.1 ins.	552 kg. 1217 lbs	14.81 kg. 32 lbs. 10 oz.	7950 m. 8694 yds	335 m/s 1099 fps	-12° +42°	360°	At max elevation, traverse is limited to about 70°.
4	10.5 cm (4.13 ins.) Leichtes Geschütz 43 (10.5 cm L.G.43)	1377 m.m. 54.2 ins.	524 kg. 1155 lbs	14.81 kg. 32 lbs. 10 oz.	7950 m. 8694 yds	335 m/s 1099 fps	-25° +40°	360° up to 13° elevation, 70° at max. elevation.	Generally similar to the L.G. 42, except for carriage design. For use as a special purpose infantry gun. Suitable for airborne and mountain units.

Appendix "E".

DATA FOR GERMAN ARTILLERY EQUIPMENTS

FIELD GUNS

SERIAL	NOMENCLATURE	LENGTH of BARREL	WEIGHT IN ACTION	WEIGHT OF STANDARD PROJECTILE	MAX. HORIZONTAL RANGE	MAX. MUZZLE VELOCITY	NO. OF CHARGES	ELEVATION	TRAVERSE (total)	REMARKS
1	7.5 cm (2.95 in.) Feldkanone 16 (neuer Art) (FK 16.n.A.)	2700 m.m. 106 ins.	1524 kg. 3360 lbs.	6.62 kg. 14 lbs. 9½ ozs.	12875 m. 14078 yds	650 m/s 2132 fps.	4	-160 mils +782	72 mils	Replaced the 77 m.m. gun of World War 1. Box trail carriage. Horse drawn.
2	7.5 cm (2.95 in.) leichte Feldkanone 18 (le F.K.18)	1950 m.m. 76.8 ins.	1120 kg. 2469 lbs.	5.83 kg. 12 lbs. 13½ ozs.	9425 m. 10307 yds	485 m/s 1590 fps.	3	-5° +45°	60°	Lighter than Serial 1. Split trail. Horse drawn.
3	7.5 cm (2.95 in.) Feldkanone 38 (F.K.38)	2550 m.m. 100 ins.	1366 kg. 3011 lbs.	5.83 kg. 12 lbs. 13½ ozs.	11500 m. 12576 yds.	605 m/s 1985 fps.	Fixed	-5° +45°	50°	Designed by Krupp for a Brazilian order; balance of order delivered to the O.K.H. in 1942. Split trail. Muzzle brake. SA horizontal sliding breech block.
4	7.5 cm (2.95 in.) Feldkanone 7 M.85 (F.K. 7 M.85)	3450 m.m. 136 ins.	1788 kg. 3919 lbs.	5.74 kg 12 lbs. 10¼ oz.	10275 m. 11236 yds	550 m/s 1804 fps.	3	-5° +42°	30° 30'	Late emergency production incorporating the 7.5 cm PAK 40 piece with a modified 10.5 cm le FH 18/40 carriage. Semi-fixed ammunition.
5	10.5 cm (4.13 in.) leichte Feldhaubitze 16 (le F.H.16)	2310 m.m. 91 ins.	1525 kg. 3361 lbs.	14.81 kg. 32 lbs. 10¼ ozs.	9225 m. 10088 yds	-395 m/s 1295 fps.	5	-160 mils +711	72 mils	Box trail carriage. Superceded by le F.H. 18.
6	10.5 cm (4.13 in.) leichte Feldhaubitze 18 (le F.H.18)	2730 m.m. 107.5 ins.	1985 kg. 4376 lbs.	14.81 kg. 32 lbs. 10¼ oz.	10675 m. 11673 fps.	470 m/s. 1542 fps.	6	-89 mils +747	996 mils	Introduced 1935. Split trail carriage. Standard field gun of Div Arty, later replaced by le F.H. 18 M and 18/40.
7	10.5 cm (4.13 in.) leichte Feldhaubitze 18 (Mit Mündungsbremse) (le F.H.18 M)	2730 m.m. 107.5 ins	1986 kg. 4378 lbs.	14.81 kg. 32 lbs. 10¼ ozs.	12325 m. 13478 yds	540 m/s 1770 fps.	6 and long range	-89 mils +747	996 mils	Same as serial 6 with a muzzle brake added, and the recoil gear modified to take a heavier charge and a special long range shell.
8	10.5 cm (4.13 in.) leichte Feldhaubitze 18/39 (le F.H. 18/39)	2730 m.m. 107.5 ins	1950 kg. 4308 lbs.	14.81 kg. 32 lbs. 10¼ ozs.	12325 m. 13478 yds.	540 m/s 1770 fps.	6 and long range	-89 mils +747	996 mils	Ballistically identical to the le F.H. 18 M and 18/40. The ordnance is mounted on a KP carriage - for export to Holland.
9	10.5 cm (4.13 in.) leichte Feldhaubitze 18/40 (le F.H. 18/40)	2730 m.m. 107.5 ins.	1955 kg. 1.9 tons	14.81 kg. 32 lbs. 10¼ ozs.	12325 m. 13478 yds	540 m/s 1770 fps.	6 and long range	-6° +40°	56°	Uses the 7.5 cm PAK 40 carriage modified.
10	10.5 cm (4.13 ins.) leichte Feldhaubitze 18/42 (le F.H. 18/42)	3255 m.m. 128 ins.	2033 kg. 4486 lbs.	14.81 kg. 32 lbs. 10¼ ozs.	12700 m. 13888 yds.	585 m/s 1920 fps.	7	-5° +45°	60°	Not introduced for service. Modified version by Krupp.
11	10.5 cm (4.13 ins.) leichte Feldhaubitze 42 (le F.H.42)	2940 m.m. 115.7 ins	1630 kg. 3593 lbs.	14.81 kg. 32 lbs. 10½ oz.	13000 m. 14217 yds	595 m/s 1952 fps.	7	-5° +45°	70°	Not introduced for service. Further new design by Krupp.
12	10.5 cm (4.13 ins.) leichte Feldhaubitze 43 (le F.H. 43)	2940 m.m. 115.7 ins. or 3675 m.m. 145 ins.	2200 kg. 2.12 tons	14.81 kg. 32 lbs. 10¼ ozs.	13000 m. 14217 yds and 14000 m. 15310 yds	595 m/s 1952 fps and 655 m/s 2150 fps.	7	-5° +70°/75°	360°	Latest design to give 360° traverse and upper register firing. Krupp made two experimental models. Skoda one prototype model.
13	10 cm (3.94 ins.) leichte Kanone 41 (le 10 cm K 41)	4200 m.m. 165.3 ins.	2640 kg. 2.6 tons	15 kg. 33 lbs.	15000 m. 16400 yds.	655 m/s 2182 yds	Fixed	-5° +45°	60°	Development ceased in 1941.

Appendix "F".

DATA FOR GERMAN ARTILLERY EQUIPMENTS

MEDIUM GUNS

SERIAL	NOMENCLATURE	LENGTH OF BARREL	WEIGHT IN ACTION	WEIGHT OF STANDARD PROJECTILE	MAX. HORIZONTAL RANGE	MAX. MUZZLE VELOCITY	NO OF CHARGES	ELEVATION	TRAVERSE (total)	REMARKS
1	10 cm (3.94 ins.) schwere Kanone 18 (s.10 cm K.18)	5200 m.m. 205 ins.	5642 kg. 12438 lbs.	15.14 kg. 33 lbs. 6 ozs.	19075 m. 20860 yds	835 m/s 2740 fps.	3	0/800 mils	1066 mils	Actually 105 m.m. calibre. Standard medium gun with the same carriage as a s.F.H.18. (Horsedrawn 2 loads - Motorised one load). Also used as a mobile C.D. gun.
2	10 cm (3.94 ins.) schwere Kanone 18/40 (42) (s.10 cm K.18/40 (42)	6000 m.m. 236 ins.	5680 kg. 12522 lbs.	15.14 kg. 33 lbs. 6 ozs.	21000 m. 22965 yds	910 m/s 2985 fps.	3	0° 45°	56°	Model 40 Gun piece on a modified s.F.H. 18 carriage
3	12.8 cm (5.04 ins.) Kanone 44 (12.8 cm K.44)	7040 m.m. 277 ins.	10160 kg. 10 ton 26 lbs.	26/28 kg. 57¼/61¾ lbs.	21000 m. 22965 yds and 24400 m. 26685 yds.	920 m/s 3018 fps.	2	-5° +45°	360°	Outstanding design. Electrical firing gear. Main armament for the Tiger Tank.
4	12.8 cm (5.04 ins.) Kanone 81/1 12.8 cm (5.04 ins.) Kanone 81/2	7020 m.m. 276.4 ins.	11.9 tons) 8.1 tons)	Same as for serial 3 above				-4° +45°	60° 58°	Mounted on the French 155 m.m. GPF-T gun carriage (split trail type). The K 81/2 was mounted on the Russian 152 m.m. gun-how model 37 carriage. Both also used in the A/Tk. role.
5	15 cm (5.9 ins.) schwere Feldhaubitze 13 (15 cm s.F.H. 13)	2550 m.m. 100 ins.	2250 kg. 2¼ tons	40.8 kg. 90 lbs.	8600 m. 9500 yds	381 m/s 1250 fps.	7	-5° +45°	9°	Introduced into service 1917. Now obsolescent.
6	15 cm (5.9 ins.) schwere Feldhaubitze 18 (s.F.H. 18)	4425 m.m. 174 ins.	5512 kg. 12151 lbs.	43.5 kg. 95 lbs. 14 ozs.	13325 m. 14572	520 m/s 1705 fps.	8	0° 45°	60°	Actual calibre 149 m.m. Standard medium gun-howitzer introduced in 1933/4.
7	15 cm (5.9 ins) schwere Feldhaubitze 36 (s. F.H. 36)	3600 m.m. 142 ins.	3280 kg. 7230 lbs.	43.5 kg. 95 lbs. 14 oz.	12300 m. 13450 yds	485 m/s 1590 fps.	7	-1° +43°	56°	Designed for horse drawn transport in one load. Discontinued in 1942 owing to shortage of light alloy metals and intention to motorise.
8	15 cm (5.9 ins.) schwere Feldhaubitze 40 (s.F.H. 40)	4875 m.m. 192 ins.	5620 kg. 12390 lbs.	43.5 kg. 95 lbs. 14 oz.	15400 m. 16841 yds	595 m/s 1952 fps.	9	0° 65°	60°	Development began in 1938 to achieve increased performance over s.F.H.18. Prototypes produced in 1941. Not introduced for service.
9	15 cm (5.9 ins.) schwere Feldhaubitze 18/40 (42) (s.F.H. 18/40 (42))	4875 m.m. 192 ins.	5650 12456 lbs.	43.5 kg. 95 lbs. 14 ozs.	15100 m. 16513 yds	595 m/s 1952 fps.	9	0° 45°	56°	Basically the piece of the s.F.H.40 on the s.F.H. 18 carriage.
10	15 cm (5.9 ins.) schwere Feldhaubitze 43 (s.F.H. 43)	6300 m.m. 248 ins.	7400/7900 kg. 16314/17416 lbs.	43.5 kg. 95 lbs. 14 oz.	18000 m. 19685 yds	660 m/s 2165 fps.	8	-5° +70°	360°	All round traverse and upper register firing. Design only by Krupp incorporating two extra trail legs. Ring obturation, owing to shortage of steel for cartridge cases.
11	15 cm (5.9 ins.) schwere Feldhaubitze 18/43 (s.F.H. 18/43)	4425 m.m. 174 ins.	?	43.5 kg. 95 lbs. 14 oz.	?	?	?	?	?	A development of the standard 15 cm s.F.H. 18 - but with ring obturation.

Appendix "G".

DATA FOR GERMAN ARTILLERY EQUIPMENTS

HEAVY and SUPER HEAVY GUNS

SERIAL	NOMENCLATURE	LENGTH OF BARREL	WEIGHT IN ACTION	NO. OF TRAVELLING LOADS AND WEIGHTS	WEIGHT OF STANDARD SHELL	MAX. HORIZONTAL RANGE	MAX. MUZZLE VELOCITY	NO. OF CHARGES	ELEVATION	TRAVERSE (total)	REMARKS
1	15 cm (5.9 ins.) Kanone 16 (15 cm K. 16)	6450 m.m. 254 ins.	10870 kg. 214 cwt.	2 loads 8300/5320 kg. 163/124 cwts	51.4 kg. 113 lbs. 5 ozs.	22000 m. 24060 yds.	757 m/s 2483 fps	3	-3° +43°	8°	Developed by Krupp. Introduced into service in 1917.
2	15 cm (5.9 ins.) Kanone 18 (15 cm K. 18)	8250 m.m. 325 ins.	12760 kg. 251 cwt.	2 loads 9060/9250 kg. 178/182 cwts.	43 kg. 94 lbs. 12 oz.	24500 m. 26800 yds.	890 m/s 2920 fps	3	-2° +45°	10° (360° with platform)	Developed by Rheinmetall. Introduced into service 1938.
3	15 cm (5.9 ins.) Kanone 39 (15 cm K. 39)	8250 m.m. 325 ins.	12200 kg. 240 cwt.	3 loads 9200/9100/11300 kg. 181/179/222 cwts.	43 kg. 94 lbs. 12 oz.	24700 m. 27000 yds	865 m/s 2838 fps	3	-3° +46°	60° or 360°	Dual purpose Heavy Field/C.D. gun developed by Krupp for a Turkish order in 1939. Last load shown is the platform and transporter.
4	15 cm (5.9 ins.) SK. C/28 Mobile C.D. gun and Field weapon	8250 m.m. 325 ins.	19760 kg. 19½ tons	1 load 26163 kg. 25¾ tons	45.3 kg. 99.7 lbs.	23500 m. 25700 yds	875 m/s 2870 fps	1	-7° 30' +47° 30'	360°	Developed primarily as a mobile Coast Defence gun. Two loading trays.
5	15 cm (5.9-ins.) Schnellade Kanone C/28 in Mörserlafette (15 cm SK.C/28 in Mrs Laf.)	8250 m.m. 325 ins.	16870 kg. 332 cwts.	2 loads 10735/12000 kg. 211/236 cwts.	43 kg. 94 lbs. 12 oz.	23700 m. 25920 yds	890 m/s 2920 fps	1	0° +50°	16° or 360°	A temporary expedient pending introduction of the 17 cm K. in Mrs Laf. Uses a naval piece on the 21 cm Mrs 18 carriage. Only eight equipments produced in 1941.
6	17 cm (6.69 ins.) Kanone in Mörserlafette (17 cm K. in Mrs Laf.)	8500 m.m. 335 ins.	17520 kg. 345 cwts.	2 loads 11375/12000 mg. 224/236 cwts.	68 kg. 150 lbs. and 62.8 kg. 138½ lbs.	28000 m. 30620 yds and 29600 m. 32370 yds	860 m/s 2820 fps and 925 m/s 3035 fps	3 and 4	0° +50°	16° or 360°	Introduced in 1941 as the standard heavy gun of the Field Army - superceding the 15 cm models. Carriage is interchangeable with that of 21 cm Mrs 18.
7	21 cm (8.27 ins.) langer Mörser (lg 21 cm Mrs.)	3045 m.m. 120 ins.	6680 kg. 131½ cwts	2 loads if horse drawn 4160/4740 kg. 82/93 cwts.	113 kg. 249 lbs.	11100 m. 12140 yds	393 m/s 1290 fps	7	-6° +70°	4°	Introduced in 1916 - now obsolescent. A later model was introduced for MT in one load - wt. in action then 9220 kg.
8	21 cm (8.27 ins.) Mörser 18 (21 cm Mrs. 18)	6510 m.m. 256 ins.	16700 kg. 329 cwts	2 loads 10700/12000 kg. 210/236 cwts	113 kg. 249 lbs.	16700 m. 18260 yds	565 m/s 1853 fps	6	0° +70°	17° or 360°	Standard heavy howitzer - carriage interchangeable with the 17 cm K. Upper and lower register firing. Introduced in 1939.
9	21 cm (8.27 ins.) L/50 Kanone (Krupp model)	10500 m.m. 413 ins.	35100 kg. 34 tons	3 loads 15000 kg. 14.8 tons each	120 kg. 264 lbs.	34000 m. 37185 yds	875 m/s 2870 fps	3	-4° +45°	360°	Krupp export model pre World War II.
10	21 cm (8.27 ins.) Kanone 38 (21 cm K. 38)	11655 m.m. 459 ins.	25300 kg. 498 cwts.	2 loads 18175/16650 kg. 358/328 cwts.	120 kg. 264 lbs.	33900 m. 37075 yds	905 m/s 2970 fps	3	0° +50°	16° 360°	Designed by Krupp to order of the OKH in 1940 - 15 equipments ordered. Not introduced into service to any great extent.
11	21 cm (8.27 ins.) Kanone 39 (21 cm K. 39)	9450 m.m. 372 ins.	33800 kg. 665 cwt	3 loads 15200/15000/14850 kg. 299/295/292 cwts.	135 kg. 297½ lbs	30000 m. 32800 yds	800 m/s 2625 fps	3	-4° +45°	360°	Originally designed by Skoda for a Turkish order; later models were given the nomenclature 21 cm K. 39/40, K. 39/41 and K. 52.

/12. 24 cm (9.45 ins.)

Appendix "G" (contd.).

DATA FOR GERMAN ARTILLERY EQUIPMENTS
HEAVY and SUPER HEAVY GUNS

SERIAL	NOMENCLATURE	LENGTH OF BARREL	WEIGHT IN ACTION	NO. OF TRAVELLING LOADS AND WEIGHTS	WEIGHT OF STANDARD SHELL	MAX. HORIZONTAL RANGE	MAX. MUZZLE VELOCITY	NO. OF CHARGES	ELEVATION	TRAVERSE (total)	REMARKS
12	24 cm (9.45 ins.) Haubitze 39 and 39/40 (24 cm H. 39)	6720 m.m. 264 ins.	27000 kg. 532 cwts.	3 loads 13000 kg. 256 cwts each	166 kg. 366 lbs.	18000 m. 19685 yds	600 m/s. 1970 fps	5	- 4° + 70°	360°	Designed by Skoda for a Turkish Order for 12 in 1938. Ten were taken over by the OKH in 1939. Design closely resembles the 21 cm K.39.
13	24 cm (9.45 ins.) Kanone L/46 Krupp model	11040 m.m. 435 ins.	45200 kg. 44½ tons	3 loads 20700/18200/ 18300 kg. 20½/18/ 18 tons	180 kg. 396 lbs.	32000 m. 35000 yds	850 m/s 2790 fps	3	- 4° + 45°	360°	Introduced by Krupp in 1937. Only a very limited number introduced into service.
14	24 cm (9.45 ins.) Kanone 3 (24 cm K.3)	13104 m.m. 516 ins.	54000 kg. 1063 cwt	5 loads 14700 to 18200 kg. 290 to 358 cwts	151½ kg. 333¾ lbs.	37000 m. 40460 yds.	970 m/s 3182 fps	2	- 5° + 56°	360°	Developed by Rheinmetall from 1935 and introduced in 1938. No crane required for assembly.
15	24 cm (9.45 ins.) Kanone 4 (24 cm K. 4)	17280 m.m. 680 ins.	55 tonnes 54 tons	2 loads 24½/41 tonnes 24/40 tons	160 kg. 353 lbs.	49000 m. 53600 yds	1100 m/s 3610 fps	1	0° + 55°	16° 360°	Developed by Krupp as a rival to the K.3. It was also proposed to mount this gun on a tracked chassis for one load transport.
16	28 cm (11 ins.) Haubitze L/12	3360 m.m. 132 ins.	50300 kg. 990 cwts.	mostly static	350 kg. 771½ lbs	10400 m. 11370 yds	350 m/s 1150 fps	7	-	-	Obsolescent - practically obsolete.
17	35.6 cm (14 ins.) Haubitze M.1	9585 m.m. 377 ins.	77500 kg. 1525 cwt.	Seven loads of approx. 17000 kg. 16¾ tons	575 kg. 1267½ lbs.	20000 m. 21875 yds	570 m/s 1870 fps	4	+ 45° + 75°	6° or 360°	Development for the OKH began in 1936 - introduced into service 1939.
18	42 cm (16.5 ins.) "Gamma" Mörser	6720 m.m. 264 ins.	140 tonnes 137 tons	10 railway flats	1020 kg. 1 ton	14200 m. 15530 yds	452 m/s 1480 fps	?	+ 43° + 75°	46°	Development by Krupp began in 1906. In 1935, one was reconstructed for trials against concrete fortifications.

www.ingramcontent.com/pod-product-compliance
Lightning Source LLC
Chambersburg PA
CBHW080908230426
43664CB00017B/2760